Concurrent Programming in Java™

Design Principles and Patterns

Second Edition

The Java™ Series

Lisa Friendly, Series Editor
Tim Lindholm, Technical Editor
Please see our web site (http://www.awl.com /cseng/javaseries) for more information on these titles.

Ken Arnold and James Gosling, *The Java™ Programming Language, Second Edition*
ISBN 0-201-31006-6

Mary Campione and Kathy Walrath, *The Java™ Tutorial, Second Edition: Object-Oriented Programming for the Internet* (Book/CD)
ISBN 0-201-31007-4

Mary Campione, Kathy Walrath, Alison Huml, and the Tutorial Team, *The Java™ Tutorial Continued: The Rest of the JDK™* (Book/CD)
ISBN 0-201-48558-3

Patrick Chan, *The Java™ Developers Almanac 1999*
ISBN 0-201-43298-6

Patrick Chan and Rosanna Lee, *The Java™ Class Libraries, Second Edition, Volume 2: java.applet, java.awt, java.beans*
ISBN 0-201-31003-1

Patrick Chan, Rosanna Lee, and Doug Kramer, *The Java™ Class Libraries, Second Edition, Volume 1: java.io, java.lang, java.math, java.net, java.text, java.util*
ISBN 0-201-31002-3

Patrick Chan, Rosanna Lee, and Doug Kramer, *The Java™ Class Libraries, Second Edition, Volume 1: Supplement for the Java™ 2 Platform, Standard Edition, v1.2*
ISBN 0-201-48552-4

Li Gong, *Inside Java™ 2 Platform Security: Architecture, API Design, and Implementation*
ISBN 0-201-31000-7

James Gosling, Bill Joy, and Guy Steele, *The Java™ Language Specification*
ISBN 0-201-63451-1

James Gosling, Frank Yellin, and The Java Team, *The Java™ Application Programming Interface, Volume 1: Core Packages*
ISBN 0-201-63453-8

James Gosling, Frank Yellin, and The Java Team, *The Java™ Application Programming Interface, Volume 2: Window Toolkit and Applets*
ISBN 0-201-63459-7

Jonni Kanerva, *The Java™ FAQ*
ISBN 0-201-63456-2

Doug Lea, *Concurrent Programming in Java™, Second Edition: Design Principles and Patterns*
ISBN 0-201-31009-0

Sheng Liang, *The Java™ Native Interface: Programmer's Guide and Specification*
ISBN 0-201-32577-2

Tim Lindholm and Frank Yellin, *The Java™ Virtual Machine Specification, Second Edition*
ISBN 0-201-43294-3

Bill Shannon, Mark Hapner, Vlada Matena, Eduardo Pelegri-Llopart, Larry Cable, and James Davidson, *Java™ 2 Enterprise Edition Specifications*
ISBN 0-201-70456-0

Henry Sowizral, Kevin Rushforth, and Michael Deering, *The Java™ 3D API Specification*
ISBN 0-201-32576-4

Kathy Walrath and Mary Campione, *The JFC Swing Tutorial: A Guide to Constructing GUIs*
ISBN 0-201-43321-4

Seth White, Maydene Fisher, Rick Cattell, Graham Hamilton, and Mark Hapner, *JDBC™ API Tutorial and Reference, Second Edition: Universal Data Access for the Java™ 2 Platform*
ISBN 0-201-43328-1

Concurrent Programming in Java™

Design Principles and Patterns
Second Edition

Doug Lea

ADDISON-WESLEY
An imprint of Addison Wesley Longman, Inc.

Reading, Massachusetts • Harlow, England • Menlo Park, California
Berkeley, California • Don Mills, Ontario • Sydney
Bonn • Amsterdam • Tokyo • Mexico City

Library of Congress Card Number 99-066823
ISBN 0-201-31009-0

Text printed on recycled and acid-free paper.

ISBN 0201310090

3 4 5 6 7 8   MA   03 02 01 00

3rd Printing   February 2000

Acknowledgments

This book began as a small set of Web pages that I put together in spring 1995, while trying to make sense of my own early attempts to use Java concurrency features in experimental development efforts. Then it grew; first on the World Wide Web, where I extended, expanded, and removed patterns to reflect my and other people's increasing experience with Java concurrency; and now into this book, which places patterns within the broader perspective of concurrent software development. The web pages also live on, but they now serve as a supplement to the conceptual presentations best suited to book form.

There have been many changes along the way, in a process that has benefited from commentary, suggestions, errata reports, and exchanges with many kind and knowledgeable people. These include Ole Agesen, Tatsuya Aoyagi, Taranov Alexander, Moti Ben-Ari, Peter Buhr, Bruce Chapman, Il-Hyung Cho, Colin Cooper, Kelly Davis, Bruce Eckel, Yacov Eckel, Saleh Elmohamed, Ed Falis, Randy Farmer, Glenn Goldstein, David Hanson, Jyrki Heikkinen, Alain Hsiung, Jerry James, Johannes Johannsen, Istvan Kiss, Ross Knippel, Bil Lewis, Sheng Liang, Jonathan Locke, Steve MacDonald, Hidehiko Masuhara, Arnulf Mester, Mike Mills, Trevor Morris, Bill Pugh, Andrew Purshottam, Simon Roberts, John Rose, Rodney Ryan, Joel Rosi-Schwartz, Miles Sabin, Aamod Sane, Beverly Sanders, Doug Schmidt, Kevin Shank, Yukari Shirota, David Spitz, David Stoutamire, Henry Story, Sumana Srinivasan, Satish Subramanian, Jeff Swartz, Patrick Thompson, Volker Turau, Dennis Ulrich, Cees Vissar, Bruce Wallace, Greg Wilson, Grant Woodside, Steve Yen, and Dave Yost, as well as people who submitted anonymous electronic mail commentary.

The members of Ralph Johnson's patterns seminar (especially Brian Foote and Ian Chai) read through early forms of some patterns and suggested many improvements. Raj Datta, Sterling Barrett, and Philip Eskelin of the New York City Patterns Group, and Russ Rufer, Ming Kwok, Mustafa Ozgen, Edward Anderson, and Don Chin of the Silicon Valley Patterns Group performed similar valuable service for preliminary versions of the second edition.

Official and unofficial reviewers of the first- and second-edition manuscripts made helpful comments and suggestions on tight schedules. They include Ken Arnold, Josh Bloch, Joseph Bowbeer, Patrick Chan, Gary Craig, Desmond D'Souza, Bill Foote, Tim Harrison, David Henderson, Tim Lindholm, Tom May, Oscar Nierstrasz, James Robins, Greg Travis, Mark Wales, Peter Welch, and Deborra Zukowski. Very special thanks go to Tom Cargill for his many insights and corrections, as well as for permission to include a description of his Specific Notification pattern. Very special thanks also go to David Holmes for, among many contributions, helping to develop and extend material for tutorials that in turn became included in the second edition.

Rosemary Simpson contributed numerous improvements in the course of creating the index. Ken Arnold patiently helped me deal with FrameMaker. Mike Hendrickson and the editorial crew at Addison-Wesley have been continually supportive.

This book would not have been possible without the generous support of Sun Labs. Thanks especially to Jos Marlowe and Steve Heller for providing opportunities to work collaboratively on fun and exciting research and development projects.

Thanks above all to Kathy, Keith, and Colin for tolerating all this.

Doug Lea, September, 1999

Table of Contents

1   Concurrent Object-Oriented Programming **1**

1.1   Using Concurrency Constructs 5
    1.1.1   A Particle Applet 5
    1.1.2   Thread Mechanics 13
    1.1.3   Further Readings 18
1.2   Objects and Concurrency 19
    1.2.1   Concurrency 19
    1.2.2   Concurrent Execution Constructs 21
    1.2.3   Concurrency and OO Programming 24
    1.2.4   Object Models and Mappings 26
    1.2.5   Further Readings 33
1.3   Design Forces 37
    1.3.1   Safety 39
    1.3.2   Liveness 44
    1.3.3   Performance 46
    1.3.4   Reusability 48
    1.3.5   Further Readings 54
1.4   Before/After Patterns 57
    1.4.1   Layering 57
    1.4.2   Adapters 59
    1.4.3   Subclassing 61
    1.4.4   Method Adapters 64
    1.4.5   Further Readings 66

2   Exclusion **69**

2.1   Immutability 71
    2.1.1   Applications 71
    2.1.2   Construction 74
2.2   Synchronization 75
    2.2.1   Mechanics 76
    2.2.2   Fully Synchronized Objects 78
    2.2.3   Traversal 80
    2.2.4   Statics and Singletons 85
    2.2.5   Deadlock 87
    2.2.6   Resource Ordering 88
    2.2.7   The Java Memory Model 90
    2.2.8   Further Readings 98

2.3   Confinement. 99
    2.3.1   Confinement Across Methods 100
    2.3.2   Confinement Within Threads 103
    2.3.3   Confinement Within Objects. 107
    2.3.4   Confinement Within Groups 111
    2.3.5   Further Readings 115
2.4   Structuring and Refactoring Classes 117
    2.4.1   Reducing Synchronization 118
    2.4.2   Splitting Synchronization 124
    2.4.3   Read-Only Adapters 132
    2.4.4   Copy-on-Write. 136
    2.4.5   Open Containers 142
    2.4.6   Further Readings 145
2.5   Using Lock Utilities. 147
    2.5.1   Mutexes 148
    2.5.2   Read-Write Locks 157
    2.5.3   Further Readings 158

3   State Dependence. 159
3.1   Dealing with Failure 161
    3.1.1   Exceptions 162
    3.1.2   Cancellation. 169
    3.1.3   Further Readings 177
3.2   Guarded Methods. 179
    3.2.1   Guarded Suspension 180
    3.2.2   Monitor Mechanics 184
    3.2.3   Guarded Waits. 187
    3.2.4   Notifications 189
    3.2.5   Timed Waits. 194
    3.2.6   Busy Waits. 196
3.3   Structuring and Refactoring Classes 199
    3.3.1   Tracking State 199
    3.3.2   Conflict Sets 203
    3.3.3   Subclassing 207
    3.3.4   Confinement and Nested Monitors 215
    3.3.5   Further Readings 217
3.4   Using Concurrency Control Utilities. 219
    3.4.1   Semaphores 220
    3.4.2   Latches 229
    3.4.3   Exchangers 231
    3.4.4   Condition Variables. 233
    3.4.5   Further Readings 235
3.5   Joint Actions 237
    3.5.1   General Solutions 238
    3.5.2   Decoupling Observers. 245
    3.5.3   Further Readings 248
3.6   Transactions. 249
    3.6.1   Transaction Protocols 251

	3.6.2	Transaction Participants	252
	3.6.3	Creating Transactions	258
	3.6.4	Vetoable Changes	261
	3.6.5	Further Readings	264
3.7		Implementing Utilities	265
	3.7.1	Acquire-Release Protocols	265
	3.7.2	Delegated Actions	268
	3.7.3	Specific Notifications	275
	3.7.4	Further Readings	280

4 Creating Threads **281**

4.1		Oneway Messages	285
	4.1.1	Message Formats	286
	4.1.2	Open Calls	287
	4.1.3	Thread-Per-Message	288
	4.1.4	Worker Threads	290
	4.1.5	Polling and Event-Driven IO	299
	4.1.6	Further Readings	304
4.2		Composing Oneway Messages	305
	4.2.1	Composition	307
	4.2.2	Assembly Line	311
	4.2.3	Further Readings	324
4.3		Services in Threads	325
	4.3.1	Completion Callbacks	325
	4.3.2	Joining Threads	329
	4.3.3	Futures	332
	4.3.4	Scheduling Services	337
	4.3.5	Further Readings	341
4.4		Parallel Decomposition	343
	4.4.1	Fork/Join	344
	4.4.2	Computation Trees	358
	4.4.3	Barriers	362
	4.4.4	Further Readings	366
4.5		Active Objects	367
	4.5.1	CSP	369
	4.5.2	Further Readings	376

Index **377**

CHAPTER 1

Concurrent Object-Oriented Programming

THIS book discusses some ways of thinking about, designing, and implementing concurrent programs in the Java™ programming language. Most presentations in this book assume that you are an experienced developer familiar with object-oriented (OO) programming, but have little exposure to concurrency. Readers with the opposite background — experience with concurrency in other languages — may also find this book useful.

The book is organized into four coarse-grained chapters. (Perhaps *parts* would be a better term.) This first chapter begins with a brief tour of some frequently used constructs and then backs up to establish a conceptual basis for concurrent object-oriented programming: how concurrency and objects fit together, how the resulting design forces impact construction of classes and components, and how some common design patterns can be used to structure solutions.

The three subsequent chapters are centered around use (and evasion) of the three kinds of concurrency constructs found in the Java programming language:

Exclusion. Maintaining consistent states of objects by preventing unwanted interference among concurrent activities, often using `synchronized` methods.

State dependence. Triggering, preventing, postponing, or recovering from actions depending on whether objects are in states in which these actions could or did succeed, sometimes using *monitor* methods `Object.wait`, `Object.notify`, and `Object.notifyAll`.

Creating threads. Establishing and managing concurrency, using `Thread` objects.

Each chapter contains a sequence of major sections, each on an independent topic. They present high-level design principles and strategies, technical details surrounding constructs, utilities that encapsulate common usages, and associated design patterns that address particular concurrency problems. Most sections conclude with an annotated set of further readings providing more information on selected topics. The online supplement to this book contains links to additional online resources, as well as updates, errata, and code examples. It is accessible via links from:

```
http://java.sun.com/Series or
http://gee.cs.oswego.edu/dl/cpj
```

If you are already familiar with the basics, you can read this book in the presented order to explore each topic in more depth. But most readers will want to read this book in various different orders. Because most concurrency concepts and techniques interact with most others, it is not always possible to understand each section or chapter in complete isolation from all the others. However, you can still take a breadth-first approach, briefly scanning each chapter (including this one) before proceeding with more detailed coverage of interest. Many presentations later in the book can be approached after selectively reading through earlier material indicated by extensive cross-references.

You can practice this now by skimming through the following preliminaries.

Terminology. This book uses standard OO terminological conventions: programs define *methods* (implementing *operations*) and *fields* (representing *attributes*) that hold for all *instances* (objects) of specified *classes*.

Interactions in OO programs normally revolve around the responsibilities placed upon a *client* object needing an action to be performed, and a *server* object containing the code to perform the action. The terms *client* and *server* are used here in their generic senses, not in the specialized sense of distributed client/server architectures. A client is just any object that sends a request to another object, and a server is just any object receiving such a request. Most objects play the roles of both clients and servers. In the usual case where it doesn't matter whether an object under discussion acts as a client or server or both, it is usually called a *host*; others that it may in turn interact with are often called *helpers* or *peers*. Also, when discussing invocations of the form `obj.msg(arg)`, the recipient (that is, the object bound to variable `obj`) is called the *target* object.

This book generally avoids dealing with transient facts about particular classes and packages not directly related to concurrency. And it does *not* cover details about concurrency control in specialized frameworks such as Enterprise JavaBeans™ and Servlets. But it does sometimes refer to branded software and trademarked products associated with the Java™ Platform. The copyright page of this book provides more information.

Code listings. Most techniques and patterns in this book are illustrated by variants of an annoyingly small set of toy running examples. This is not an effort to be boring, but to be clear. Concurrency constructs are often subtle enough to get lost in otherwise meaningful examples. Reuse of running examples makes small but critical differences more obvious by highlighting the main design and implementation issues. Also, the presentations include code sketches and fragments of classes that illustrate implementation techniques, but are not intended to be complete or even compilable. These classes are indicated by leading comments in the listings.

Import statements, access qualifiers, and even methods and fields are sometimes omitted from listings when they can be inferred from context or do not impact relevant functionality. The `protected` qualifier is used as a default for non-public features whenever there is no particular reason to restrict subclass access. This emphasizes opportunities for extensibility in concurrent class design (see §1.3.4 and §3.3.3). Classes by default have no access qualifier. Sample listings are sometimes formatted in nonstandard ways to keep them together on pages or to emphasize the main constructions of interest.

The code for all example classes in this book is available from the online supplement. Most techniques and patterns in this book are illustrated by a single code example showing their most typical forms. The supplement includes additional examples that demonstrate minor variations, as well as some links to other known usages. It also includes some larger examples that are more useful to browse and experiment with online than to read as listings.

The supplement provides links to a package, `util.concurrent`, that contains production-quality versions of utility classes discussed in this book. This code runs on the Java 2 Platform and has been tested with 1.2.x releases. Occasional discussions, asides, and footnotes briefly mention changes from previous releases, potential future changes known at the time of this writing, and a few implementation quirks to watch out for. Check the online supplement for additional updates.

Diagrams. Standard UML notation is used for interaction and class diagrams (see the Further Readings in §1.1.3). The accompanying diagrams (courtesy of Martin Fowler) illustrate the only forms used in this book. Other aspects of UML notation, methodology, and terminology are not specifically relied on.

Most other diagrams show *timethreads* in which free-form gray curves trace threads traversing through collections of objects. Flattened arrowheads represent blocking. Objects are depicted as ovals that sometimes show selected internal features such as locks, fields, and bits of code. Thin (usually labeled) lines between objects rep-

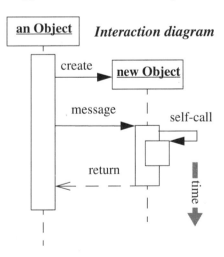

Interaction diagram

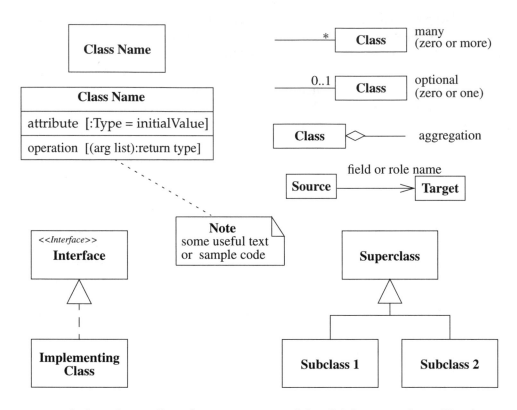

resent relations (normally references or potential calls) between them. Here's an otherwise meaningless example showing that thread A has acquired the lock for object X, and is proceeding through some method in object Y that serves as a helper to X. Thread B is meanwhile somehow blocked while entering some method in object X:

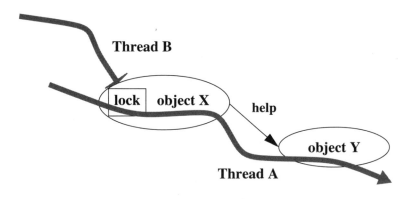

1.1 Using Concurrency Constructs

This section introduces basic concurrency support constructs by example and then proceeds with a walk-through of the principal methods of class Thread. Other concurrency constructs are briefly described as they are introduced, but full technical details are postponed to later chapters (mainly §2.2.1 and §3.2.2). Also, concurrent programs often make use of a few ordinary Java programming language features that are not as widely used elsewhere. These are briefly reviewed as they arise.

1.1.1 A Particle Applet

ParticleApplet is an Applet that displays randomly moving particles. In addition to concurrency constructs, this example illustrates a few of the issues encountered when using threads with any GUI-based program. The version described here needs a lot of embellishment to be visually attractive or realistic. You might enjoy experimenting with additions and variations as an exercise.

As is typical of GUI-based programs, ParticleApplet uses several auxiliary classes that do most of the work. We'll step through construction of the Particle and ParticleCanvas classes before discussing ParticleApplet.

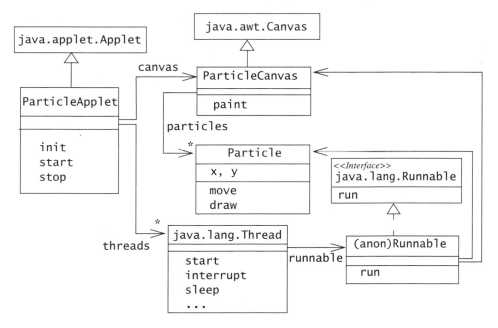

1.1.1.1 Particle

The `Particle` class defines a completely unrealistic model of movable bodies. Each particle is represented only by its (x, y) location. Each particle also supports a method to randomly change its location and a method to draw itself (as a small square) given a supplied `java.awt.Graphics` object.

While `Particle` objects do not themselves exhibit any intrinsic concurrency, their methods may be invoked across multiple concurrent activities. When one activity is performing a `move` and another is invoking `draw` at about the same time, we'd like to make sure that the `draw` paints an accurate representation of where the `Particle` is. Here, we require that `draw` uses the location values current either *before* or *after* the move. For example, it would be conceptually wrong for a `draw` operation to display using the y-value current before a given move, but the x-value current after the move. If we were to allow this, then the `draw` method would sometimes display the particle at a location that it never actually occupied.

This protection can be obtained using the `synchronized` keyword, which can modify either a method or a block of code. *Every instance* of class `Object` (and its subclasses) possesses a lock that is obtained on entry to a `synchronized` method and automatically released upon exit. The code-block version works in the same way except that it takes an argument stating which object to lock. The most common argument is `this`, meaning to lock the object whose method is executing. When a lock is held by one thread, other threads must block waiting for the holding thread to release the lock. Locking has no effect on non-synchronized methods, which can execute even if the lock is being held by another thread.

Locking provides protection against both high-level and low-level conflicts by enforcing *atomicity* among methods and code-blocks `synchronized` on the same object. Atomic actions are performed as units, without any interleaving of the actions of other threads. But, as discussed in §1.3.2 and in Chapter 2, too much locking can also produce liveness problems that cause programs to freeze up. Rather than exploring these issues in detail now, we'll rely on some simple default rules for writing methods that preclude interference problems:

- **Always lock during updates to object fields.**
- **Always lock during access of possibly updated object fields.**
- **Never lock when invoking methods on other objects.**

These rules have many exceptions and refinements, but they provide enough guidance to write class `Particle`:

```
import java.util.Random;

class Particle {
  protected int x;
  protected int y;
  protected final Random rng = new Random();

  public Particle(int initialX, int initialY) {
    x = initialX;
    y = initialY;
  }

  public synchronized void move() {
    x += rng.nextInt(10) - 5;
    y += rng.nextInt(20) - 10;
  }

  public void draw(Graphics g) {
    int lx, ly;
    synchronized (this) { lx = x; ly = y; }
    g.drawRect(lx, ly, 10, 10);
  }
}
```

Notes:

- The use of `final` in the declaration of the random number generator `rng` reflects our decision that this reference field cannot be changed, so it is not impacted by our locking rules. Many concurrent programs use `final` extensively, in part as helpful, automatically enforced documentation of design decisions that reduce the need for synchronization (see §2.1).

- The `draw` method needs to obtain a consistent snapshot of both the x and y values. Since a single method can return only one value at a time, and we need both the x and y values here, we cannot easily encapsulate the field accesses as a `synchronized` method. We instead use a `synchronized` block. (See §2.4 for some alternatives.)

- The draw method conforms to our rule of thumb to release locks during method invocations on other objects (here g.drawRect). The move method appears to break this rule by calling `rng.nextInt`. However, this is a reasonable choice here because each `Particle` *confines* its own `rng` — conceptually, the `rng` is just a part of the `Particle` itself, so it doesn't count as an "other" object in the rule. Section §2.3 describes more general conditions under which this sort of reasoning applies and discusses factors that should be taken into account to be sure that this decision is warranted.

1.1.1.2 ParticleCanvas

ParticleCanvas is a simple subclass of java.awt.Canvas that provides a drawing area for all of the Particles. Its main responsibility is to invoke draw for all existing particles whenever its paint method is called.

However, the ParticleCanvas itself does not create or manage the particles. It needs either to be told about them or to ask about them. Here, we choose the former.

The instance variable particles holds the array of existing Particle objects. This field is set when necessary by the applet, but is used in the paint method. We can again apply our default rules, which in this case lead to the creation of little synchronized get and set methods (also known as *accessor* and *assignment* methods) for particles, otherwise avoiding direct access of the particles variable itself. To simplify and to enforce proper usage, the particles field is never allowed to be null. It is instead initialized to an empty array:

```
class ParticleCanvas extends Canvas {

  private Particle[] particles = new Particle[0];

  ParticleCanvas(int size) {
    setSize(new Dimension(size, size));
  }

  // intended to be called by applet
  protected synchronized void setParticles(Particle[] ps) {
    if (ps == null)
      throw new IllegalArgumentException("Cannot set null");

    particles = ps;
  }

  protected synchronized Particle[] getParticles() {
    return particles;
  }

  public void paint(Graphics g) { // override Canvas.paint
    Particle[] ps = getParticles();

    for (int i = 0; i < ps.length; ++i)
      ps[i].draw(g);

  }
}
```

1.1.1.3 ParticleApplet

The `Particle` and `ParticleCanvas` classes could be used as the basis of several different programs. But in `ParticleApplet` all we want to do is set each of a collection of particles in autonomous "continuous" motion and update the display accordingly to show where they are. To comply with standard applet conventions, these activities should begin when `Applet.start` is externally invoked (normally from within a web browser), and should end when `Applet.stop` is invoked. (We could also add buttons allowing users to start and stop the particle animation themselves.)

There are several ways to implement all this. Among the simplest is to associate an independent loop with each particle and to run each looping action in a different thread.

Actions to be performed within new threads must be defined in classes implementing `java.lang.Runnable`. This interface lists only the single method `run`, taking no arguments, returning no results, and throwing no checked exceptions:

```
public interface java.lang.Runnable {
  void run();
}
```

An `interface` encapsulates a coherent set of services and attributes (broadly, a *role*) without assigning this functionality to any particular object or code. Interfaces are more abstract than classes since they say nothing at all about representations or code. All they do is describe the *signatures* (names, arguments, result types, and exceptions) of public operations, without even pinning down the classes of the objects that can perform them. The classes that can support `Runnable` typically have nothing in common except that they contain a `run` method.

Each instance of the `Thread` class maintains the control state necessary to execute and manage the call sequence comprising its action. The most commonly used constructor in class `Thread` accepts a `Runnable` object as an argument, which arranges to invoke the `Runnable`'s `run` method when the thread is started. While any class can implement `Runnable`, it often turns out to be both convenient and helpful to define a `Runnable` as an anonymous inner class.

The `ParticleApplet` class uses threads in this way to put particles into motion, and cancels them when the applet is finished. This is done by overriding the standard `Applet` methods `start` and `stop` (which have the same names as, but are unrelated to, methods `Thread.start` and `Thread.stop`).

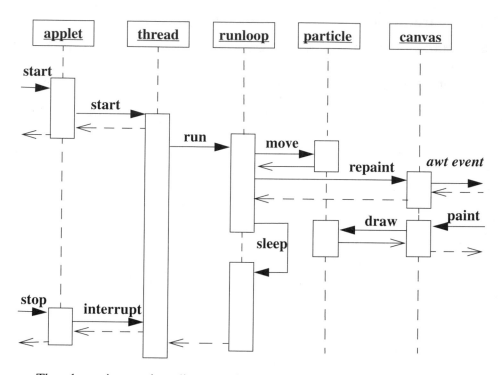

The above interaction diagram shows the main message sequences during execution of the applet. In addition to the threads explicitly created, this applet interacts with the AWT event thread, described in more detail in §4.1.4. The producer-consumer relationship extending from the omitted right hand side of the interaction diagram takes the approximate form:

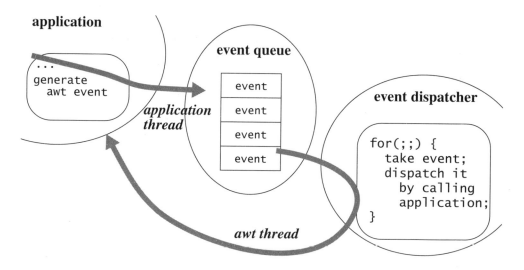

```
public class ParticleApplet extends Applet {

  protected Thread[] threads = null; // null when not running

  protected final ParticleCanvas canvas
                                       = new ParticleCanvas(100);

  public void init() { add(canvas); }

  protected Thread makeThread(final Particle p) { // utility
    Runnable runloop = new Runnable() {
      public void run() {
        try {
          for(;;) {
            p.move();
            canvas.repaint();
            Thread.sleep(100); // 100msec is arbitrary
          }
        }
        catch (InterruptedException e) { return; }
      }
    };
    return new Thread(runloop);
  }

  public synchronized void start() {
    int n = 10; // just for demo

    if (threads == null) { // bypass if already started
      Particle[] particles = new Particle[n];
      for (int i = 0; i < n; ++i)
        particles[i] = new Particle(50, 50);
      canvas.setParticles(particles);

      threads = new Thread[n];
      for (int i = 0; i < n; ++i) {
        threads[i] = makeThread(particles[i]);
        threads[i].start();
      }
    }
  }

  public synchronized void stop() {
    if (threads != null) { // bypass if already stopped
      for (int i = 0; i < threads.length; ++i)
        threads[i].interrupt();
      threads = null;
    }
  }
}
```

Notes:

- The action in `makeThread` defines a "forever" loop (which some people prefer to write equivalently as "`while (true)`") that is broken only when the current thread is interrupted. During each iteration, the particle moves, tells the canvas to repaint so the move will be displayed, and then does nothing for a while, to slow things down to a human-viewable rate. `Thread.sleep` pauses the current thread. It is later resumed by a system timer.

- One reason that inner classes are convenient and useful is that they *capture* all appropriate context variables — here `p` and `canvas` — without the need to create a separate class with fields that record these values. This convenience comes at the price of one minor awkwardness: All captured method arguments and local variables must be declared as `final`, as a guarantee that the values can indeed be captured unambiguously. Otherwise, for example, if `p` were reassigned after constructing the `Runnable` inside method `makeThread`, then it would be ambiguous whether to use the original or the assigned value when executing the `Runnable`.

- The call to `canvas.repaint` does not directly invoke `canvas.paint`. The `repaint` method instead places an `UpdateEvent` on a `java.awt.Event-Queue`. (This may be internally optimized and further manipulated to eliminate duplicate events.) A `java.awt.EventDispatchThread` asynchronously takes this event from the queue and dispatches it by (ultimately) invoking `canvas.paint`. This thread and possibly other system-created threads may exist even in nominally single-threaded programs.

- The activity represented by a constructed `Thread` object does not begin until invocation of the `Thread.start` method.

- As discussed in §3.1.2, there are several ways to cause a thread's activity to stop. The simplest is just to have the `run` method terminate normally. But in infinitely looping methods, the best option is to use `Thread.interrupt`. An interrupted thread will automatically abort (via an `InterruptedException`) from the methods `Object.wait`, `Thread.join`, and `Thread.sleep`. Callers can then catch this exception and take any appropriate action to shut down. Here, the `catch` in `runloop` just causes the `run` method to exit, which in turn causes the thread to terminate.

- The `start` and `stop` methods are `synchronized` to preclude concurrent starts or stops. Locking works out OK here even though these methods need to perform many operations (including calls to other objects) to achieve the required started-to-stopped or stopped-to-started state transitions. Nullness of variable `threads` is used as a convenient state indicator.

1.1.2 Thread Mechanics

A thread is a call sequence that executes independently of others, while at the same time possibly sharing underlying system resources such as files, as well as accessing other objects constructed within the same program (see §1.2.2). A java.lang.Thread *object* maintains bookkeeping and control for this activity.

Every program consists of at least one thread — the one that runs the main method of the class provided as a startup argument to the Java virtual machine ("JVM"). Other internal background threads may also be started during JVM initialization. The number and nature of such threads vary across JVM implementations. However, all user-level threads are explicitly constructed and started from the main thread, or from any other threads that they in turn create.

Here is a summary of the principal methods and properties of class Thread, as well as a few usage notes. They are further discussed and illustrated throughout this book. *The Java™ Language Specification* ("*JLS*") and the published API documentation should be consulted for more detailed and authoritative descriptions.

1.1.2.1 Construction

Different Thread constructors accept combinations of arguments supplying:

- A Runnable object, in which case a subsequent Thread.start invokes run of the supplied Runnable object. If no Runnable is supplied, the default implementation of Thread.run returns immediately.

- A String that serves as an identifier for the Thread. This can be useful for tracing and debugging, but plays no other role.

- The ThreadGroup in which the new Thread should be placed. If access to the ThreadGroup is not allowed, a SecurityException is thrown.

Class Thread itself implements Runnable. So, rather than supplying the code to be run in a Runnable and using it as an argument to a Thread constructor, you can create a subclass of Thread that overrides the run method to perform the desired actions. However, the best default strategy is to define a Runnable as a separate class and supply it in a Thread constructor. Isolating code within a distinct class relieves you of worrying about any potential interactions of synchronized methods or blocks used in the Runnable with any that may be used by methods of class Thread. More generally, this separation allows independent control over the nature of the action and the context in which it is run: The same Runnable can be supplied to threads that are otherwise initialized in different ways, as well as to other lightweight executors (see §4.1.4). Also note that subclassing Thread precludes a class from subclassing any other class.

Thread objects also possess a daemon status attribute that cannot be set via any Thread constructor, but may be set only before a Thread is started. The method setDaemon asserts that the JVM may exit, abruptly terminating the thread, so long as all other non-daemon threads in the program have terminated. The isDaemon method returns status. The utility of daemon status is very limited. Even background threads often need to do some cleanup upon program exit. (The spelling of *daemon*, often pronounced as "day-mon", is a relic of systems programming tradition. System daemons are continuous processes, for example print-queue managers, that are "always" present on a system.)

1.1.2.2 Starting threads

Invoking its start method causes an instance of class Thread to initiate its run method as an independent activity. None of the synchronization locks held by the caller thread are held by the new thread (see §2.2.1).

A Thread terminates when its run method completes by either returning normally or throwing an unchecked exception (i.e., RuntimeException, Error, or one of their subclasses). Threads are not restartable, even after they terminate. Invoking start more than once results in an InvalidThreadStateException.

The method isAlive returns true if a thread has been started but has not terminated. It will return true if the thread is merely blocked in some way. JVM implementations have been known to differ in the exact point at which isAlive returns false for threads that have been cancelled (see §3.1.2). There is no method that tells you whether a thread that is not isAlive has ever been started. Also, one thread cannot readily determine which other thread started it, although it may determine the identities of other threads in its ThreadGroup (see §1.1.2.6).

1.1.2.3 Priorities

To make it possible to implement the Java virtual machine across diverse hardware platforms and operating systems, the Java programming language makes no promises about scheduling or fairness, and does not even strictly guarantee that threads make forward progress (see §3.4.1.5). But threads do support priority methods that heuristically influence schedulers:

- Each Thread has a priority, ranging between Thread.MIN_PRIORITY and Thread.MAX_PRIORITY (defined as 1 and 10 respectively).

- By default, each new thread has the same priority as the thread that created it. The initial thread associated with a main by default has priority Thread.NORM_PRIORITY (5).

- The current priority of any thread can be accessed via method getPriority.

- The priority of any thread can be dynamically changed via method `setPriority`. The maximum allowed priority for a thread is bounded by its `ThreadGroup`.

When there are more *runnable* (see §1.3.2) threads than available CPUs, a scheduler is generally biased to prefer running those with higher priorities. The exact policy may and does vary across platforms. For example, some JVM implementations always select the thread with the highest current priority (with ties broken arbitrarily). Some JVM implementations map the ten `Thread` priorities into a smaller number of system-supported categories, so threads with different priorities may be treated equally. And some mix declared priorities with aging schemes or other scheduling policies to ensure that even low-priority threads eventually get a chance to run. Also, setting priorities may, but need not, affect scheduling with respect to other programs running on the same computer system.

Priorities have no other bearing on semantics or correctness (see §1.3). In particular, priority manipulations cannot be used as a substitute for locking. Priorities can be used only to express the relative importance or urgency of different threads, where these priority indications would be useful to take into account when there is heavy contention among threads trying to get a chance to execute. For example, setting the priorities of the particle animation threads in `ParticleApplet` below that of the applet thread constructing them might on some systems improve responsiveness to mouse clicks, and would at least not hurt responsiveness on others. But programs should be designed to run correctly (although perhaps not as responsively) even if `setPriority` is defined as a no-op. (Similar remarks hold for `yield`; see §1.1.2.5.)

The following table gives one set of general conventions for linking task categories to priority settings. In many concurrent applications, relatively few threads are actually runnable at any given time (others are all blocked in some way), in which case there is little reason to manipulate priorities. In other cases, minor tweaks in priority settings may play a small part in the final tuning of a concurrent system.

Range	Use
10	Crisis management
7-9	Interactive, event-driven
4-6	IO-bound
2-3	Background computation
1	Run only if nothing else can

1.1.2.4   Control methods

Only a few methods are available for communicating across threads:

- Each `Thread` has an associated boolean interruption status (see §3.1.2). Invoking `t.interrupt` for some `Thread t` sets `t`'s interruption status to `true`, unless `Thread t` is engaged in `Object.wait`, `Thread.sleep`, or `Thread.join`; in this case `interrupt` causes these actions (in `t`) to throw `InterruptedException`, but `t`'s interruption status is set to `false`.

- The interruption status of any `Thread` can be inspected using method `isInterrupted`. This method returns `true` if the thread has been interrupted via the `interrupt` method but the status has not since been reset either by the thread invoking `Thread.interrupted` (see §1.1.2.5) or in the course of `wait`, `sleep`, or `join` throwing `InterruptedException`.

- Invoking `t.join()` for `Thread t` suspends the *caller* until the target `Thread t` completes: the call to `t.join()` returns when `t.isAlive()` is `false` (see §4.3.2). A version with a (millisecond) time argument returns control even if the thread has not completed within the specified time limit. Because of how `isAlive` is defined, it makes no sense to invoke `join` on a thread that has not been started. For similar reasons, it is unwise to try to `join` a `Thread` that you did not create.

Originally, class `Thread` supported the additional control methods `suspend`, `resume`, `stop`, and `destroy`. Methods `suspend`, `resume`, and `stop` have since been *deprecated*; method `destroy` has never been implemented in any release and probably never will be. The effects of methods `suspend` and `resume` can be obtained more safely and reliably using the waiting and notification techniques discussed in §3.2. The problems surrounding `stop` are discussed in §3.1.2.3.

1.1.2.5   Static methods

Some `Thread` class methods can be applied only to the thread that is currently running (i.e., the thread making the call to the `Thread` method). To enforce this, these methods are declared as `static`.

- `Thread.currentThread` returns a reference to the current `Thread`. This reference may then be used to invoke other (non-static) methods. For example, `Thread.currentThread().getPriority()` returns the priority of the thread making the call.

- `Thread.interrupted` clears interruption status of the current `Thread` and returns previous status. (Thus, one `Thread`'s interruption status cannot be cleared from other threads.)

- `Thread.sleep(long msecs)` causes the current thread to suspend for at least `msecs` milliseconds (see §3.2.2).

- `Thread.yield` is a purely heuristic hint advising the JVM that if there are any other runnable but non-running threads, the scheduler should run one or more of these threads rather than the current thread. The JVM may interpret this hint in any way it likes.

Despite the lack of guarantees, `yield` can be pragmatically effective on some single-CPU JVM implementations that do not use time-sliced pre-emptive scheduling (see §1.2.2). In this case, threads are rescheduled only when one blocks (for example on IO, or via `sleep`). On these systems, threads that perform time-consuming non-blocking computations can tie up a CPU for extended periods, decreasing the responsiveness of an application. As a safeguard, methods performing non-blocking computations that might exceed acceptable response times for event handlers or other reactive threads can insert `yields` (or perhaps even `sleeps`) and, when desirable, also run at lower priority settings. To minimize unnecessary impact, you can arrange to invoke `yield` only occasionally; for example, a loop might contain:

```
if (Math.random() < 0.01) Thread.yield();
```

On JVM implementations that employ pre-emptive scheduling policies, especially those on multiprocessors, it is possible and even desirable that the scheduler will simply ignore this hint provided by `yield`.

1.1.2.6 `ThreadGroups`

Every `Thread` is constructed as a member of a `ThreadGroup`, by default the same group as that of the `Thread` issuing the constructor for it. `ThreadGroups` nest in a tree-like fashion. When an object constructs a `new` `ThreadGroup`, it is nested under its current group. The method `getThreadGroup` returns the group of any thread. The `ThreadGroup` class in turn supports methods such as `enumerate` that indicate which threads are currently in the group.

One purpose of class `ThreadGroup` is to support security policies that dynamically restrict access to `Thread` operations; for example, to make it illegal to `interrupt` a thread that is not in your group. This is one part of a set of protective measures against problems that could occur, for example, if an applet were to try to kill the main screen display update thread. `ThreadGroups` may also place a ceiling on the maximum priority that any member thread can possess.

`ThreadGroups` tend not to be used directly in thread-based programs. In most applications, normal collection classes (for example `java.util.Vector`) are better choices for tracking groups of `Thread` objects for application-dependent purposes.

Among the few `ThreadGroup` methods that commonly come into play in concurrent programs is method `uncaughtException`, which is invoked when a thread in a group terminates due to an uncaught unchecked exception (for example a `NullPointerException`). This method normally causes a stack trace to be printed.

1.1.3   Further Readings

This book is not a reference manual on the Java programming language. (It is also not exclusively a how-to tutorial guide, or an academic textbook on concurrency, or a report on experimental research, or a book on design methodology or design patterns or pattern languages, but includes discussions on each of these facets of concurrency.) Most sections conclude with lists of resources that provide more information on selected topics. If you do a lot of concurrent programming, you will want to read more about some of them.

The *JLS* should be consulted for more authoritative accounts of the properties of Java programming language constructs summarized in this book:

Gosling, James, Bill Joy, and Guy Steele. *The Java™ Language Specification*, Addison-Wesley, 1996. As of this writing, a second edition of *JLS* is projected to contain clarifications and updates for the Java 2 Platform.

Introductory accounts include:

Arnold, Ken, and James Gosling. *The Java™ Programming Language, Second Edition*, Addison-Wesley, 1998.

If you have never written a program using threads, you may find it useful to work through either the online or book version of the *Threads* section of:

Campione, Mary, and Kathy Walrath. *The Java™ Tutorial, Second Edition*, Addison-Wesley, 1998.

A concise guide to UML notation is:

Fowler, Martin, with Kendall Scott. *UML Distilled, Second Edition*, Addison-Wesley, 1999. The UML diagram keys on pages 3-4 of the present book are excerpted by permission.

A more extensive account of UML is:

Rumbaugh, James, Ivar Jacobson, and Grady Booch. *The Unified Modeling Language Reference Manual,* Addison-Wesley, 1999.

1.2   Objects and Concurrency

There are many ways to characterize objects, concurrency, and their relationships. This section discusses several different perspectives — definitional, system-based, stylistic, and modeling-based — that together help establish a conceptual basis for concurrent object-oriented programming.

1.2.1   Concurrency

Like most computing terms, "concurrency" is tricky to pin down. Informally, a concurrent program is one that does more than one thing at a time. For example, a web browser may be simultaneously performing an HTTP GET request to get an HTML page, playing an audio clip, displaying the number of bytes received of some image, and engaging in an advisory dialog with a user. However, this simultaneity is sometimes an illusion. On some computer systems these different activities might indeed be performed by different CPUs. But on other systems they are all performed by a single time-shared CPU that switches among different activities quickly enough that they appear to be simultaneous, or at least nondeterministically interleaved, to human observers.

A more precise, though not very interesting definition of concurrent programming can be phrased operationally: A Java virtual machine and its underlying operating system (OS) provide mappings from apparent simultaneity to physical parallelism (via multiple CPUs), or lack thereof, by allowing independent activities to proceed in parallel when possible and desirable, and otherwise by time-sharing. Concurrent programming consists of using programming constructs that are mapped in this way. Concurrent programming in the Java programming language entails using Java programming language constructs to this effect, as opposed to system-level constructs that are used to create new operating system processes. By convention, this notion is further restricted to constructs affecting a single JVM, as opposed to distributed programming, for example using remote method invocation (RMI), that involves multiple JVMs residing on multiple computer systems.

Concurrency and the reasons for employing it are better captured by considering the nature of a few common types of concurrent applications:

Web services. Most socket-based web services (for example, HTTP daemons, servlet engines, and application servers) are multithreaded. Usually, the main motivation for supporting multiple concurrent connections is to ensure that new incoming connections do not need to wait out completion of others. This generally minimizes service latencies and improves availability.

Number crunching. Many computation-intensive tasks can be parallelized, and thus execute more quickly if multiple CPUs are present. Here the goal is to maximize throughput by exploiting parallelism.

I/O processing. Even on a nominally sequential computer, devices that perform reads and writes on disks, wires, etc., operate independently of the CPU. Concurrent programs can use the time otherwise wasted waiting for slow I/O, and can thus make more efficient use of a computer's resources.

Simulation. Concurrent programs can simulate physical objects with independent autonomous behaviors that are hard to capture in purely sequential programs.

GUI-based applications. Even though most user interfaces are intentionally single-threaded, they often establish or communicate with multithreaded services. Concurrency enables user controls to stay responsive even during time-consuming actions.

Component-based software. Large-granularity software components (for example those providing design tools such as layout editors) may internally construct threads in order to assist in bookkeeping, provide multimedia support, achieve greater autonomy, or improve performance.

Mobile code. Frameworks such as the `java.applet` package execute downloaded code in separate threads as one part of a set of policies that help to isolate, monitor, and control the effects of unknown code.

Embedded systems. Most programs running on small dedicated devices perform real-time control. Multiple components each continuously *react* to external inputs from sensors or other devices, and produce external outputs in a timely manner. As defined in *The Java™ Language Specification*, the Java platform does not support *hard* real-time control in which system correctness depends on actions being performed by certain deadlines. Particular run-time systems may provide the stronger guarantees required in some safety-critical hard-real-time systems. But all JVM implementations support *soft* real-time control, in which timeliness and performance are considered quality-of-service issues rather than correctness issues (see §1.3.3). This reflects portability goals that enable the JVM to be implemented on modern opportunistic, multipurpose hardware and system software.

1.2.2 Concurrent Execution Constructs

Threads are only one of several constructs available for concurrently executing code. The idea of generating a new activity can be mapped to any of several abstractions along a granularity continuum reflecting trade-offs of autonomy versus overhead. Thread-based designs do not always provide the best solution to a given concurrency problem. Selection of one of the alternatives discussed below can provide either more or less security, protection, fault-tolerance, and administrative control, with either more or less associated overhead. Differences among these options (and their associated programming support constructs) impact design strategies more than do any of the details surrounding each one.

1.2.2.1 Computer systems

If you had a large supply of computer systems, you might map each logical unit of execution to a different computer. Each computer system may be a uniprocessor, a multiprocessor, or even a cluster of machines administered as a single unit and sharing a common operating system. This provides unbounded autonomy and independence. Each system can be administered and controlled separately from all the others.

However, constructing, locating, reclaiming, and passing messages among such entities can be expensive, opportunities for sharing local resources are eliminated, and solutions to problems surrounding naming, security, fault-tolerance, recovery, and reachability are all relatively heavy in comparison with those seen in concurrent programs. So this mapping choice is typically applied only for those aspects of a system that intrinsically require a distributed solution. And even here, all but the tiniest embedded computer devices host more than one process.

1.2.2.2 Processes

A process is an operating-system abstraction that allows one computer system to support many units of execution. Each process typically represents a separate running program; for example, an executing JVM. Like the notion of a "computer system", a "process" is a logical abstraction, not a physical one. So, for example, bindings from processes to CPUs may vary dynamically.

Operating systems guarantee some degree of independence, lack of interference, and security among concurrently executing processes. Processes are generally not allowed to access one another's storage locations (although there are usually some exceptions), and must instead communicate via interprocess communication facilities such as pipes. Most systems make at least best-effort promises about how processes will be created and scheduled. This nearly always entails *pre-emptive* time-slicing — suspending processes on a periodic basis to give other processes a chance to run.

The overhead for creating, managing, and communicating among processes can be a lot lower than in per-machine solutions. However, since processes share underlying computational resources (CPUs, memory, IO channels, and so on), they are less autonomous. For example, a machine crash caused by one process kills all processes.

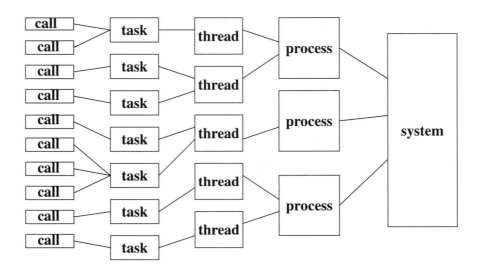

1.2.2.3 Threads

Thread constructs of various forms make further trade-offs in autonomy, in part for the sake of lower overhead. The main trade-offs are:

Sharing. Threads may share access to the memory, open files, and other resources associated with a single process. Threads in the Java programming language may share all such resources. Some operating systems also support intermediate constructions, for example "lightweight processes" and "kernel threads" that share only some resources, do so only upon explicit request, or impose other restrictions.

Scheduling. Independence guarantees may be weakened to support cheaper scheduling policies. At one extreme, all threads can be treated together as a single-threaded process, in which case they may *cooperatively* contend with each other so that only one thread is running at a time, without giving any other thread a chance to run until it blocks (see §1.3.2). At the other extreme, the underlying scheduler can allow all threads in a system to contend directly with each other via pre-emptive scheduling rules. Threads in the Java programming language may be scheduled using any policy lying at or anywhere between these extremes.

Communication. Systems interact via communication across wires or wireless channels, for example using sockets. Processes may also communicate in this fashion, but may also use lighter mechanisms such as pipes and interprocess signalling facilities. Threads can use all of these options, plus other cheaper strategies relying on access to memory locations accessible across multiple threads, and employing memory-based synchronization facilities such as locks and waiting and notification mechanisms. These constructs support more efficient communication, but sometimes incur the expense of greater complexity and consequently greater potential for programming error.

1.2.2.4 Tasks and lightweight executable frameworks

The trade-offs made in supporting threads cover a wide range of applications, but are not always perfectly matched to the needs of a given activity. While performance details differ across platforms, the overhead in creating a thread is still significantly greater than the cheapest (but least independent) way to invoke a block of code — calling it directly in the current thread.

When thread creation and management overhead become performance concerns, you may be able to make additional trade-offs in autonomy by creating your own lighter-weight execution frameworks that impose further restrictions on usage (for example by forbidding use of certain forms of blocking), or make fewer scheduling guarantees, or restrict synchronization and communication to a more limited set of choices. As discussed in §4.1.4, these tasks can then be mapped to threads in about the same way that threads are mapped to processes and computer systems.

The most familiar lightweight executable frameworks are event-based systems and subsystems (see §1.2.3, §3.6.4, and §4.1), in which calls triggering conceptually asynchronous activities are maintained as events that may be queued and processed by background threads. Several additional lightweight executable frameworks are described in Chapter 4. When they apply, construction and use of such frameworks can improve both the structure and performance of concurrent programs. Their use reduces concerns (see §1.3.3) that can otherwise inhibit the use of concurrent execution techniques for expressing logically asynchronous activities and logically autonomous objects (see §1.2.4).

1.2.3   Concurrency and OO Programming

Objects and concurrency have been linked since the earliest days of each. The first concurrent OO programming language (created circa 1966), *Simula*, was also the first OO language, and was among the first concurrent languages. Simula's initial OO and concurrency constructs were somewhat primitive and awkward. For example, concurrency was based around *coroutines* — thread-like constructs requiring that programmers explicitly hand off control from one task to another. Several other languages providing both concurrency and OO constructs followed — indeed, even some of the earliest prototype versions of C++ included a few concurrency-support library classes. And Ada (although, in its first versions, scarcely an OO language) helped bring concurrent programming out from the world of specialized, low-level languages and systems.

OO design played no practical role in the multithreaded systems programming practices emerging in the 1970s. And concurrency played no practical role in the wide-scale embrace of OO programming that began in the 1980s. But interest in OO concurrency stayed alive in research laboratories and advanced development groups, and has re-emerged as an essential aspect of programming in part due to the popularity and ubiquity of the Java platform.

Concurrent OO programming shares most features with programming of any kind. But it differs in critical ways from the kinds of programming you may be most familiar with, as discussed below.

1.2.3.1   Sequential OO programming

Concurrent OO programs are often structured using the same programming techniques and design patterns as sequential OO programs (see for example §1.4). But they are intrinsically more complex. When more than one activity can occur at a time, program execution is necessarily nondeterministic. Code may execute in surprising orders — any order that is not explicitly ruled out is allowed (see §2.2.7). So you cannot always understand concurrent programs by sequentially reading through their code. For example, without further precautions, a field set to one value in one line of code may have a different value (due to the actions of some other concurrent activity) by the time the next line of code is executed. Dealing with this and other forms of *interference* often introduces the need for a bit more rigor and a more conservative outlook on design.

1.2.3.2   Event-based programming

Some concurrent programming techniques have much in common with those in event frameworks employed in GUI toolkits supported by `java.awt` and `javax.swing`, and in other languages such as Tcl/Tk and Visual Basic. In GUI frameworks, events such as mouse clicks are encapsulated as Event objects that are placed in a single EventQueue. These events are then dispatched and processed one-by-one in a single *event loop*, which normally runs as a separate thread. As discussed in §4.1, this design can be extended to support additional concurrency by (among other tactics) creating multiple event loop threads, each concurrently processing events, or even dispatching each event in a separate thread. Again, this opens up new design possibilities, but also introduces new concerns about interference and coordination among concurrent activities.

1.2.3.3 Concurrent systems programming

Object-oriented concurrent programming differs from multithreaded systems programming in languages such as C mainly due to the encapsulation, modularity, extensibility, security, and safety features otherwise lacking in C. Additionally, concurrency support is built into the Java programming language, rather than supplied by libraries. This eliminates the possibility of some common errors, and also enables compilers to automatically and safely perform some optimizations that would need to be performed manually in C.

While concurrency support constructs in the Java programming language are generally similar to those in the standard POSIX pthreads library and related packages typically used in C, there are some important differences, especially in the details of waiting and notification (see §3.2.2). It is very possible to use utility classes that act almost just like POSIX routines (see §3.4.4). But it is often more productive instead to make minor adjustments to exploit the versions that the language directly supports.

1.2.3.4 Other concurrent programming languages

Essentially all concurrent programming languages are, at some level, equivalent, if only in the sense that all concurrent languages are widely believed not to have defined the right concurrency features. However, it is not all that hard to make programs in one language *look* almost equivalent to those in other languages or those using other constructs, by developing packages, classes, utilities, tools, and coding conventions that mimic features built into others. In the course of this book, constructions are introduced that provide the capabilities and programming styles of semaphore-based systems (§3.4.1), futures (§4.3.3), barrier-based parallelism (§4.4.3), CSP (§4.5.1) and others. It is a perfectly great idea to write programs using *only* one of these styles, if this suits your needs. However, many concurrent designs, patterns, frameworks, and systems have eclectic heritages and steal good ideas from anywhere they can.

1.2.4 Object Models and Mappings

Conceptions of objects often differ across sequential versus concurrent OO programming, and even across different styles of concurrent OO programming. Contemplation of the underlying object models and mappings can reveal the nature of differences among programming styles hinted at in the previous section.

Most people like to think of software objects as models of real objects, represented with some arbitrary degree of precision. The notion of "real" is of course in the eye of the beholder, and often includes artifices that make sense only within the realm of computation.

For a simple example, consider the skeletal UML class diagram and code sketch for class WaterTank:

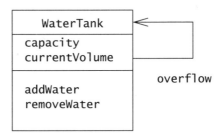

```
class WaterTank {                                    // Code sketch
    final float capacity;
    float currentVolume = 0.0f;
    WaterTank overflow;

    WaterTank(float cap) { capacity = cap; ... }

    void addWater(float amount) throws OverflowException;
    void removeWater(float amount) throws UnderflowException;
}
```

The intent here is to represent, or simulate, a water tank with:

- *Attributes*, such as capacity and currentVolume, that are represented as *fields* of WaterTank objects. We can choose only those attributes that we happen to care about in some set of usage contexts. For example, while all real

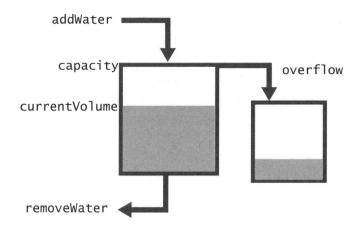

water tanks have locations, shapes, colors, and so on, this class only deals with volumes.

- *Invariant* state constraints, such as the facts that the currentVolume always remains between zero and capacity, and that capacity is nonnegative and never changes after construction.

- *Operations* describing behaviors such as those to addWater and removeWater. This choice of operations again reflects some implicit design decisions concerning accuracy, granularity and precision. For example, we could have chosen to model water tanks at the level of valves and switches, and could have modeled each water molecule as an object that changes location as the result of the associated operations.

- *Connections* (and *potential* connections) to other objects with which objects communicate, such as pipes or other tanks. For example, excess water encountered in an addWater operation could be shunted to an overflow tank that is known by each tank.

- *Preconditions and postconditions* on the effects of operations, such as rules stating that it is impossible to remove water from an empty tank, or to add water to a full tank that is not equipped with an available overflow tank.

- *Protocols* constraining when and how messages (operation requests) are processed. For example, we may impose a rule that at most one addWater or removeWater message is processed at any given time or, alternatively, a rule stating that removeWater messages are allowed in the midst of addWater operations.

27

1.2.4.1   Object models

The `WaterTank` class uses objects to model reality. Object models provide rules and frameworks for defining objects more generally, covering:

Statics. The structure of each object is described (normally via a class) in terms of internal attributes (state), connections to other objects, local (internal) methods, and methods or ports for accepting messages from other objects.

Encapsulation. Objects have membranes separating their insides and outsides. Internal state can be directly modified only by the object itself. (We ignore for now language features that allow this rule to be broken.)

Communication. Objects communicate only via message passing. Objects issue messages that trigger actions in other objects. The forms of these messages may range from simple procedural calls to those transported via arbitrary communication protocols.

Identity. New objects can be constructed at any time (subject to system resource constraints) by any object (subject to access control). Once constructed, each object maintains a unique identity that persists over its lifetime.

Connections. One object can send messages to others if it knows their identities. Some models rely on *channel* identities rather than or in addition to object identities. Abstractly, a channel is a vehicle for passing messages. Two objects that share a channel may pass messages through that channel without knowing each other's identities. Typical OO models and languages rely on object-based primitives for direct method invocations, channel-based abstractions for IO and communication across wires, and constructions such as event channels that may be viewed from either perspective.

Computation. Objects may perform four basic kinds of computation:

- ◆ Accept a message.
- ◆ Update internal state.
- ◆ Send a message.
- ◆ Create a new object.

This abstract characterization can be interpreted and refined in several ways. For example, one way to implement a `WaterTank` object is to build a tiny special-purpose hardware device that only maintains the indicated states, instructions, and connections. But since this is not a book on hardware design, we'll ignore such options and restrict attention to software-based alternatives.

1.2.4.2 Sequential mappings

Sequential JVM

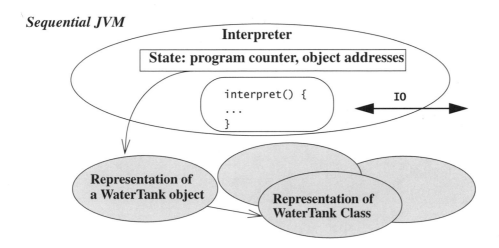

The features of an ordinary general-purpose computer (a CPU, a bus, some memory, and some IO ports) can be exploited so that this computer can pretend it is any object, for example a WaterTank. This can be arranged by loading a description of WaterTanks (via a .class file) into a JVM. The JVM can then construct a *passive* representation of an instance and then interpret the associated operations. This mapping strategy also applies at the level of the CPU when operations are compiled into native code rather than interpreted as bytecodes. It also extends to programs involving many objects of different classes, each loaded and instantiated as needed, by having the JVM at all times record the identity ("this") of the object it is currently simulating.

In other words, the JVM is itself an object, although a very special one that can pretend it is any other object. (More formally, it serves as a Universal Turing Machine.) While similar remarks hold for the mappings used in most other languages, Class objects and reflection make it simpler to characterize reflective objects that treat other objects as data.

In a purely sequential environment, this is the end of the story. But before moving on, consider the restrictions on the generic object model imposed by this mapping. On a sequential JVM, it would be impossible to directly simulate multiple concurrent interacting waterTank objects. And because all message-passing is performed via sequential procedural invocation, there is no need for rules about whether multiple messages may be processed concurrently — they never are anyway. Thus, sequential OO processing limits the kinds of high-level design concerns you are allowed to express.

1.2.4.3 Active objects

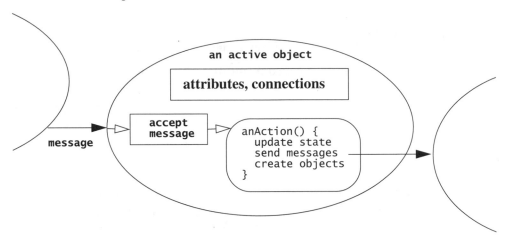

At the other end of the mapping spectrum are *active* object models (also known as *actor* models), in which *every* object is autonomous. Each may be as powerful as a sequential JVM. Internal class and object representations may take the same forms as those used in passive frameworks. For example here, each waterTank could be mapped to a separate active object by loading in a description to a separate JVM, and then forever allowing it to simulate the defined actions.

Active object models form a common high-level view of objects in distributed object-oriented systems: Different objects may reside on different machines, so the location and administrative domain of an object are often important programming issues. All message passing is arranged via remote communication (for example via sockets) that may obey any of a number of protocols, including one-way messaging (i.e., messages that do not intrinsically require replies), multicasts (simultaneously sending the same message to multiple recipients), and procedure-style request-reply exchanges.

This model also serves as an object-oriented view of most operating-system-level *processes*, each of which is as independent of, and shares as few resources with, other processes as possible (see §1.2.2).

1.2.4.4 Mixed models

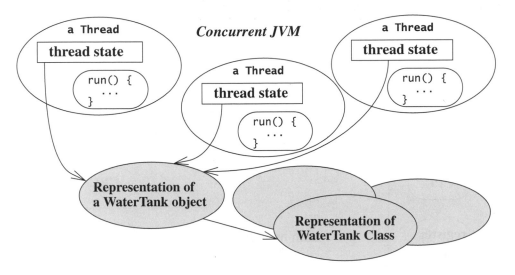

The models and mappings underlying concurrency support in the Java programming language fall between the two extremes of passive and active models. A full JVM may be composed of multiple threads, each of which acts in about the same way as a single sequential JVM. However, unlike pure active objects, all of these threads may share access to the same set of underlying passive representations.

This style of mapping can simulate each of the extremes. Purely passive sequential models can be programmed using only one thread. Purely active models can be programmed by creating as many threads as there are active objects, avoiding situations in which more than one thread can access a given passive representation (see §2.3), and using constructs that provide the same semantic effects as remote message passing (see §4.1). However, most concurrent programs occupy a middle ground.

Thread-based concurrent OO models conceptually separate "normal" passive objects from active objects (threads). But the passive objects typically display thread-awareness not seen in sequential programming, for example by protecting themselves via locks. And the active objects are simpler than those seen in actor models, supporting only a few operations (such as run). But the design of concurrent OO systems can be approached from either of these two directions — by smartening up passive objects to live in a multithreaded environment, or by dumbing down active objects so they can be expressed more easily using thread constructs.

One reason for supporting this kind of object model is that it maps in a straightforward and efficient way to stock uniprocessor and shared-memory multiprocessor (SMP) hardware and operating systems: Threads can be bound to CPUs when possible and desirable, and otherwise time-shared; local thread state maps to registers and CPUs; and shared object representations map to shared main memory.

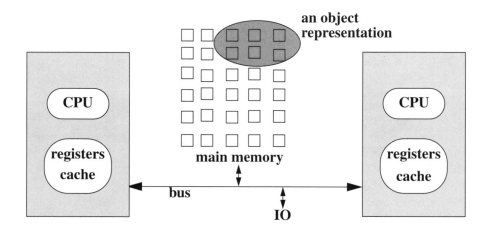

The degree of programmer control over these mappings is one distinction separating many forms of *parallel* programming from concurrent programming. Classic parallel programming involves explicit design steps to map threads, tasks, or processes, as well as data, to physical processors and their local stores. Concurrent programming leaves most mapping decisions to the JVM (and the underlying OS). This enhances portability, at the expense of needing to accommodate differences in the quality of implementation of these mappings.

Time-sharing is accomplished by applying the same kind of mapping strategy to threads themselves: Representations of Thread objects are maintained, and a scheduler arranges *context switches* in which the CPU state corresponding to one thread is saved in its associated storage representation and restored from another.

Several further refinements and extensions of such models and mappings are possible. For example, *persistent* object applications and systems typically rely on databases to maintain object representations rather than directly relying on main memory.

1.2.5 Further Readings

There is a substantial literature on concurrency, ranging from works on theoretical foundations to practical guides for using particular concurrent applications.

1.2.5.1 Concurrent programming

Textbooks presenting details on additional concurrent algorithms, programming strategies, and formal methods not covered in this book include:

Andrews, Gregory. *Foundations of Multithreaded, Parallel, and Distributed Programming*, Addison-Wesley, 1999. This is an expanded update of Andrews's *Concurrent Programming: Principles and Practice*, Benjamin Cummings, 1991.

Ben-Ari, M. *Principles of Concurrent and Distributed Programming*, Prentice Hall, 1990.

Bernstein, Arthur, and Philip Lewis. *Concurrency in Programming and Database Systems,* Jones and Bartlett, 1993.

Burns, Alan, and Geoff Davis. *Concurrent Programming*, Addison-Wesley, 1993.

Bustard, David, John Elder, and Jim Welsh. *Concurrent Program Structures*, Prentice Hall, 1988.

Schneider, Fred. *On Concurrent Programming*, Springer-Verlag, 1997.

The concurrency constructs found in the Java programming language have their roots in similar constructs first described by C. A. R. Hoare and Per Brinch Hansen. See papers by them and others in following collections:

Dahl, Ole-Johan, Edsger Dijkstra, and C. A. R. Hoare (eds.). *Structured Programming*, Academic Press, 1972.

Gehani, Narain, and Andrew McGettrick (eds.). *Concurrent Programming,* Addison-Wesley, 1988.

A comparative survey of how some of these constructs are defined and supported across different languages and systems may be found in:

Buhr, Peter, Michel Fortier, and Michael Coffin. "Monitor Classification", *ACM Computing Surveys*, 1995.

Concurrent object-oriented, object-based or module-based languages include Simula, Modula-3, Mesa, Ada, Orca, Sather, and Euclid. More information on these languages can be found in their manuals, as well as in:

Birtwistle, Graham, Ole-Johan Dahl, Bjorn Myhrtag, and Kristen Nygaard. *Simula Begin*, Auerbach Press, 1973.

Burns, Alan, and Andrew Wellings. *Concurrency in Ada*, Cambridge University Press, 1995.

Holt, R. C. *Concurrent Euclid, the Unix System, and Tunis*, Addison-Wesley, 1983.

Nelson, Greg (ed.). *Systems Programming with Modula-3*, Prentice Hall, 1991.

Stoutamire, David, and Stephen Omohundro. *The Sather/pSather 1.1 Specification*, Technical Report, University of California at Berkeley, 1996.

Books taking different approaches to concurrency in the Java programming language include:

Hartley, Stephen. *Concurrent Programming using Java*, Oxford University Press, 1998. This takes an operating systems approach to concurrency.

Holub, Allen. *Taming Java Threads,* Apress, 1999. This collects the author's columns on threads in the *JavaWorld* online magazine.

Lewis, Bil. *Multithreaded Programming in Java*, Prentice Hall, 1999. This presents a somewhat lighter treatment of several topics discussed in this book, and provides closer tie-ins with POSIX threads.

Magee, Jeff, and Jeff Kramer. *Concurrency: State Models and Java Programs*, Wiley, 1999. This provides a stronger emphasis on modeling and analysis.

Most books, articles, and manuals on systems programming using threads concentrate on the details of those on particular operating systems or thread packages. See:

Butenhof, David. *Programming with POSIX Threads*, Addison-Wesley, 1997. This provides the most complete discussions of the POSIX thread library and how to use it.

Lewis, Bil, and Daniel Berg. *Multithreaded Programming with Pthreads*, Prentice Hall, 1998.

Norton, Scott, and Mark Dipasquale. *Thread Time*, Prentice Hall, 1997.

Most texts on operating systems and systems programming describe the design and construction of underlying support mechanisms for language-level thread and synchronization constructs. See, for example:

Hanson, David. *C Interfaces and Implementations*, Addison-Wesley, 1996.

Silberschatz, Avi and Peter Galvin. *Operating Systems Concepts*, Addison-Wesley, 1994.

Tanenbaum, Andrew. *Modern Operating Systems*, Prentice Hall, 1992.

1.2.5.2 Models

Given the diverse forms of concurrency seen in software, it's not surprising that there have been a large number of approaches to the basic theory of concurrency. Theoretical accounts of process calculi, event structures, linear logic, Petri nets, and temporal logic have potential relevance to the understanding of concurrent OO systems. For overviews of most approaches to the theory of concurrency, see:

van Leeuwen, Jan (ed.). *Handbook of Theoretical Computer Science, Volume B,* MIT Press, 1990.

An eclectic (and still fresh-sounding) presentation of models, associated programming techniques, and design patterns, illustrated using diverse languages and systems, is:

Filman, Robert, and Daniel Friedman. *Coordinated Computing*. McGraw-Hill, 1984.

There are several experimental concurrent OO languages based on active objects, most notably the family of *Actor* languages. See:

Agha, Gul. *ACTORS: A Model of Concurrent Computation in Distributed Systems*, MIT Press, 1986.

A more extensive survey of object-oriented approaches to concurrency can be found in:

Briot, Jean-Pierre, Rachid Guerraoui, and Klaus-Peter Lohr. "Concurrency and Distribution in Object-Oriented Programming", *Computing Surveys*, 1998.

Research papers on object-oriented models, systems and languages can be found in proceedings of OO conferences including *ECOOP, OOPSLA, COOTS, TOOLS*, and *ISCOPE*, as well as concurrency conferences such as *CONCUR* and journals such as *IEEE Concurrency*. Also, the following collections contain chapters surveying many approaches and issues:

Agha, Gul, Peter Wegner, and Aki Yonezawa (eds.). *Research Directions in Concurrent Object-Oriented Programming,* MIT Press, 1993.

Briot, Jean-Pierre, Jean-Marc Geib and Akinori Yonezawa (eds.). *Object Based Parallel and Distributed Computing*, LNCS 1107, Springer Verlag, 1996.

Guerraoui, Rachid, Oscar Nierstrasz, and Michel Riveill (eds.). *Object-Based Distributed Processing,* LNCS 791, Springer-Verlag, 1993.

Nierstrasz, Oscar, and Dennis Tsichritzis (eds.). *Object-Oriented Software Composition*, Prentice Hall, 1995.

1.2.5.3 Distributed systems

Texts on distributed algorithms, protocols, and system design include:

Barbosa, Valmir. *An Introduction to Distributed Algorithms*. Morgan Kaufman, 1996.

Birman, Kenneth and Robbert von Renesse. *Reliable Distributed Computing with the Isis Toolkit*, IEEE Press, 1994.

Coulouris, George, Jean Dollimore, and Tim Kindberg. *Distributed Systems: Concepts and Design,* Addison-Wesley, 1994.

Lynch, Nancy. *Distributed Algorithms*, Morgan Kaufman, 1996.

Mullender, Sape (ed.), *Distributed Systems*, Addison-Wesley, 1993.

Raynal, Michel. *Distributed Algorithms and Protocols,* Wiley, 1988.

For details about distributed programming using RMI, see:

Arnold, Ken, Bryan O'Sullivan, Robert Scheifler, Jim Waldo, and Ann Wollrath. *The Jini™ Specification*, Addison-Wesley, 1999.

1.2.5.4   Real-time programming

Most texts on real-time programming focus on *hard real-time* systems in which, for the sake of correctness, certain activities must be performed within certain time constraints. The Java programming language does not supply primitives that provide such guarantees, so this book does not cover deadline scheduling, priority assignment algorithms, and related concerns. Sources on real-time design include:

Burns, Alan, and Andy Wellings. *Real-Time Systems and Programming Languages*, Addison-Wesley, 1997. This book illustrates real-time programming in Ada, occam, and C, and includes a recommended account of priority inversion problems and solutions.

Gomaa, Hassan. *Software Design Methods for Concurrent and Real-Time Systems,* Addison-Wesley, 1993.

Levi, Shem-Tov and Ashok Agrawala. *Real-Time System Design*, McGraw-Hill, 1990.

Selic, Bran, Garth Gullekson, and Paul Ward. *Real-Time Object-Oriented Modeling*, Wiley, 1995.

1.3 Design Forces

This section surveys design concerns that arise in concurrent software development, but play at best minor roles in sequential programming. Most presentations of constructions and design patterns later in this book include descriptions of how they resolve applicable forces discussed here (as well as others that are less directly tied to concurrency, such as accuracy, testability, and so on).

One can take two complementary views of any OO system, object-centric and activity-centric:

$$Systems = Objects + Activities$$

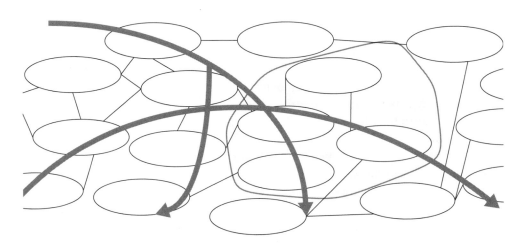

Under an object-centric view, a system is a collection of interconnected objects. But it is a structured collection, not a random object soup. Objects cluster together in groups, for example the group of objects comprising a `ParticleApplet`, thus forming larger components and subsystems.

Under an activity-centric view, a system is a collection of possibly concurrent activities. At the most fine-grained level, these are just individual message sends (normally, method invocations). They in turn organize themselves into sets of call-chains, event sequences, tasks, sessions, transactions, and threads. One logical activity (such as running the `ParticleApplet`) may involve many threads. At a higher level, some of these activities represent system-wide use cases.

Neither view alone provides a complete picture of a system, since a given object may be involved in multiple activities, and conversely a given activity may span multiple objects. However, these two views give rise to two complementary sets of *correctness* concerns, one object-centric and the other activity-centric:

Safety.

Nothing bad ever happens to an object.

Liveness.

Something eventually happens within an activity.

Safety failures lead to unintended behavior at run time — things just start going wrong. Liveness failures lead to no behavior — things just stop running. Sadly enough, some of the easiest things you can do to improve liveness properties can destroy safety properties, and vice versa. Getting them both right can be a challenge.

You have to balance the relative effects of different kinds of failure in your own programs. But it is a standard engineering (not just software engineering) practice to place primary design emphasis on safety. The more your code actually matters, the better it is to ensure that a program does nothing at all rather than something that leads to random, even dangerous behavior.

On the other hand, most of the time spent tuning concurrent designs in practice usually surrounds liveness and liveness-related efficiency issues. And there are sometimes good, conscientious reasons for selectively sacrificing safety for liveness. For example, it may be acceptable for visual displays to transiently show utter nonsense due to uncoordinated concurrent execution— drawing stray pixels, incorrect progress indicators, or images that bear no relation to their intended forms — if you are confident that this state of affairs will soon be corrected.

Safety and liveness issues may be further extended to encompass two categories of *quality* concerns, one mainly object-centric and the other mainly activity-centric, that are also sometimes in direct opposition:

Reusability.

The utility of objects and classes across multiple contexts.

Performance.

The extent to which activities execute soon and quickly.

The remainder of this section looks more closely at safety, liveness, performance, and reusability in concurrent programs. It presents basic terms and definitions, along with brief introductions to core issues and tactics that are revisited and amplified throughout the course of this book.

1.3.1 Safety

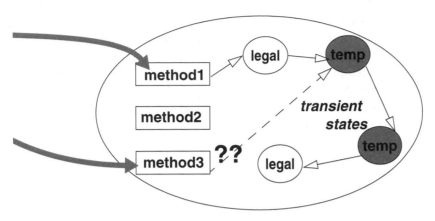

Safe concurrent programming practices are generalizations of safe and secure sequential programming practices. Safety in concurrent designs adds a temporal dimension to common notions of *type* safety. A type-checked program might not be correct, but at least it doesn't do dangerous things like misinterpret the bits representing a float as if they were an object reference. Similarly, a safe concurrent design might not have the intended effect, but at least it never encounters errors due to corruption of representations by contending threads.

One practical difference between type safety and multithreaded safety is that most type-safety matters can be checked automatically by compilers. A program that fails to pass compile-time checks cannot even be run. Most multithreaded safety matters, however, cannot be checked automatically, and so must rely on programmer discipline. Methods for *proving* designs to be safe fall outside the scope of this book (see the Further Readings). The techniques for ensuring safety described here rely on careful engineering practices (including several with roots in formalisms) rather than formal methods themselves.

Multithreaded safety also adds a temporal dimension to design and programming techniques surrounding *security*. Secure programming practices disable access to certain operations on objects and resources from certain callers, applications, or principals. Concurrency control introduces *transient* disabling of access based on consideration of the actions currently being performed by other threads.

The main goal in safety preservation is ensuring that all objects in a system maintain *consistent* states: states in which all fields, and all fields of other objects on which they depend, possess legal, meaningful values. It sometimes takes hard work to nail down exactly what "legal" and "meaningful" mean in a particular class. One path is first to establish conceptual-level *invariants*, for example the rule that water tank volumes must always be between zero and their capacities.

These can usually be recast in terms of relationships among field values in the associated concrete classes.

An object is *consistent* if all fields obey their invariants. Every public method in every class should lead an object from one consistent state to another. Safe objects may occasionally enter transiently inconsistent states in the midst of methods, but they never attempt to initiate new actions when they are in inconsistent states. If every object is designed to perform actions only when it is logically able to do so, and if all the mechanics are properly implemented, then you can be sure that an application using these objects will not encounter any errors due to object inconsistency.

One reason for being more careful about invariants in concurrent programs is that it is much easier to break them inadvertently than in most sequential programs. The need for protection against the effects of inconsistency arises even in sequential contexts, for example when processing exceptions and callbacks, and when making self-calls from one method in a class to another. However, these issues become much more central in concurrent programs. As discussed in §2.2, the most common ways of ensuring consistency employ exclusion techniques to guarantee the *atomicity* of public actions — that each action runs to completion without interference from others. Without such protection, inconsistencies in concurrent programs may stem from *race conditions* producing *storage conflicts* at the level of raw memory cells:

Read/Write conflicts. One thread reads a value of a field while another writes to it. The value seen by the reading thread is difficult to predict — it depends on which thread won the "race" to access the field first. As discussed in §2.2, the value read need not even be a value that was ever written by any thread.

Write/Write conflicts. Two threads both try to write to the same field. The value seen upon the next read is again difficult or impossible to predict.

It is equally impossible to predict the consequences of actions that are attempted when objects are in inconsistent states. Examples include:

• A graphical representation (for example of a `Particle`) is displayed at a location that the object never actually occupied.

• A bank account balance is incorrect after an attempt to withdraw money in the midst of an automatic transfer.

• Following the `next` pointer of a linked list leads to a node that is not even in the list.

• Two concurrent sensor updates cause a real-time controller to perform an incorrect effector action.

1.3.1.1 Attributes and constraints

Safe programming techniques rely on clear understanding of required properties and constraints surrounding object representations. Developers who are not aware of these properties rarely do a very good job at preserving them. Many formalisms are available for precisely stating predicates describing requirements (as discussed in most of the texts on concurrent design methods listed in the Further Readings). These can be very useful, but here we will maintain sufficient precision without introducing formalisms.

Consistency requirements sometimes stem from definitions of high-level conceptual attributes made during the initial design of classes. These constraints typically hold regardless of how the attributes are concretely represented and accessed via fields and methods. This was seen for example in the development of the WaterTank and Particle classes earlier in this chapter. Here are some other examples, most of which are revisited in more detail in the course of this book:

- A BankAccount has a *balance* that is equal to the sum of all deposits and interest minus withdrawals and service charges.

- A Packet has a *destination* that must be a legal IP address.

- A Counter has a nonnegative integral *count* value.

- An Invoice has a *paymentDue* that reflects the rules of a payment system.

- A Thermostat has a *temperature* equal to the most recent sensor reading.

- A Shape has a *location*, *dimension*, and *color* that all obey a set of stylistic guidelines for a given GUI toolkit.

- A BoundedBuffer has an *elementCount* that is always between zero and a *capacity*.

- A Stack has a *size* and, when not empty, a *top* element.

- A Window has a *propertySet* maintaining current mappings of fonts, background color, etc.

- An Interval has a *startDate* that is no later than its *endDate*.

While such attributes essentially always somehow map to object fields, the correspondences need not be direct. For example, the top of a Stack is typically not held in a variable, but instead in an array element or linked list node. Also, some attributes can be computed ("derived") via others; for example, the boolean attribute overdrawn of a BankAccount might be computed by comparing the balance to zero.

1.3.1.2   Representational constraints

Further constraints and invariants typically emerge as additional implementation decisions are made for a given class. Fields declared for the sake of maintaining a particular data structure, for improving performance, or for other internal book-keeping purposes often need to respect sets of invariants. Broad categories of fields and constraints include the following:

Direct value representations. Fields needed to implement concrete attributes. For example, a `Buffer` might have a `putIndex` field holding the array index position to use when inserting the next added element.

Cached value representations. Fields used to eliminate or minimize the need for computations or method invocations. For example, rather than computing the value of `overdrawn` every time it is needed, a `BankAccount` might maintain an `overdrawn` field that is true if and only if the current balance is less than zero.

Logical state representations. Reflections of logical control state. For example, a `BankCardReader` might have a `card` field representing the card currently being read, and a `validPIN` field recording whether the PIN access code was verified. The `CardReader` `validPIN` field may be used to track the point in a protocol in which the card has been successfully read in and validated. Some state representations take the form of *role variables*, controlling responses to all of a related set of methods (sometimes those declared in a single interface). For example, a game-playing object may alternate between active and passive roles depending on the value of a `whoseTurn` field.

Execution state variables. Fields recording the fine-grained dynamic state of an object, for example, the fact that a certain operation is in progress. Execution state variables can represent the fact that a given message has been received, that the corresponding action has been initiated, that the action has terminated, and that a reply to the message has been issued. An execution state variable is often an enumerated type with values having names ending in *-ing*; for example, `CONNECTING`, `UPDATING`, `WAITING`. Another common kind of execution state variable is a counter that records the number of entries or exits of some method. As discussed in §3.2, objects in concurrent programs tend to require more such variables than do those in sequential contexts, to help track and manage the progress of methods that proceed asynchronously.

History variables. Representations of the history or past states of an object. The most extensive representation is a *history log*, recording all messages ever received and sent, along with all corresponding internal actions and state changes that have been initiated and completed. Less extensive subsets are much more common. For example, a `BankAccount` class could maintain a `lastSavedBalance` field that holds the last checkpointed value and is used when reverting cancelled transactions.

Version tracking variables. An integer, time-stamp, object reference, signature code, or other representation indicating the time, ordering, or nature of the last state change made by an object. For example, a `Thermostat` may increment a `readingNumber` or record the `lastReadingTime` when updating its `temperature`.

References to acquaintances. Fields pointing to other objects that the host interacts with, but that do not themselves comprise the host's logical state: For example, a `callback` target of an `EventDispatcher`, or a `requestHandler` delegated to by a `WebServer`.

References to representation objects. Attributes that are conceptually held by a host object but are actually managed by other helper objects. Reference fields may point to other objects that assist in representing the state of the host object. So, the logical state of any object may include the states of objects that it holds references to. Additionally, the reference fields themselves form part of the concrete state of the host object (see §2.3.3). Any attempts to ensure safety must take these relationships into account. For example:

- A `Stack` might have a `headOfLinkedList` field recording the first node of a list representing the stack.

- A `Person` object might maintain a `homePageURL` field maintained as a `java.net.URL` object.

- The balance of a `BankAccount` might be maintained in a central repository, in which case the `BankAccount` would instead maintain a a field referring to the repository (in order to ask it about the current balance). In this case, some of the logical state of the `BankAccount` is actually managed by the repository.

- An object might know of its attributes only via access to property lists maintained by other objects.

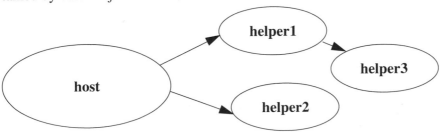

1.3.2   Liveness

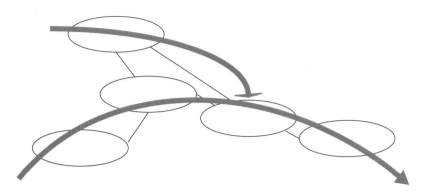

One way to build a guaranteed safe system is to arrange that no objects ever execute any methods, and thus can never encounter any conflicts. But this is not a very productive form of programming. Safety concerns must be balanced by liveness[1] concerns.

In live systems, every activity eventually progresses toward completion; every invoked method eventually executes. But an activity may (perhaps only transiently) fail to make progress for any of several interrelated reasons:

Locking. A `synchronized` method blocks one thread because another thread holds the lock.

Waiting. A method blocks (via `Object.wait` or its derivatives) waiting for an event, message, or condition that has yet to be produced within another thread.

Input. An IO-based method waits for input that has not yet arrived from another process or device.

CPU contention. A thread fails to run even though it is in a runnable state because other threads, or even completely separate programs running on the same computer, are occupying CPU or other computational resources.

Failure. A method running in a thread encounters a premature exception, error, or fault.

Momentary blockages in thread progress are usually acceptable. In fact, frequent short-lived blocking is intrinsic to many styles of concurrent programming.

---

[1] Some "liveness" properties may be construed as safety properties of sets of thread objects. For example, deadlock-freedom may be defined as avoiding the bad state in which a set of threads endlessly wait for each other.

The lifecycle of a typical thread may include a number of transient blockages and reschedulings:

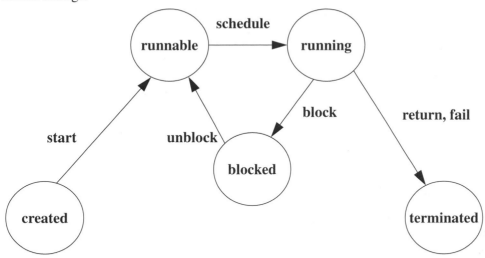

However, *permanent* or unbounded lack of progress is usually a serious problem. Examples of potentially permanent liveness failures described in more depth elsewhere in this book include:

Deadlock. Circular dependencies among locks. In the most common case, thread A holds a lock for object X and then tries to acquire the lock for object Y. Simultaneously, thread B already holds the lock for object Y and tries to acquire the lock for object X. Neither thread can ever make further progress (see §2.2.5).

Missed signals. A thread remains dormant because it started waiting *after* a notification to wake it up was produced (see §3.2.2).

Nested monitor lockouts. A waiting thread holds a lock that would be needed by any other thread attempting to wake it up (see §3.3.4).

Livelock. A continuously retried action continuously fails (see §2.4.4.2).

Starvation. The JVM/OS fails ever to allocate CPU time to a thread. This may be due to scheduling policies or even hostile denial-of-service attacks on the host computer (see §1.1.2.3 and §3.4.1.5).

Resource exhaustion. A group of threads together hold all of a finite number of resources. One of them needs additional resources, but no other thread will give one up (see §4.5.1).

Distributed failure. A remote machine connected by a socket serving as an InputStream crashes or becomes inaccessible (see §3.1).

1.3.3 Performance

Performance-based forces extend liveness concerns. In addition to demanding that every invoked method eventually execute, performance goals require them to execute soon and quickly. While we do not consider in this book hard real-time systems in which failure to execute within a given time interval can lead to catastrophic system errors, nearly all concurrent programs have implicit or explicit performance goals.

Meaningful performance requirements are stated in terms of measurable qualities, including the following metrics. Goals may be expressed for central tendencies (e.g., mean, median) of measurements, as well as their variability (e.g., range, standard deviation).

Throughput. The number of operations performed per unit time. The operations of interest may range from individual methods to entire program runs. Most often, throughput is reported not as a rate, but instead as the time taken to perform one operation.

Latency. The time elapsed between issuing a message (via for example a mouse click, method invocation, or incoming socket connection) and servicing it. In contexts where operations are uniform, single-threaded, and "continuously" requested, latency is just the inverse of throughput. But more typically, the latencies of interest reflect response times — the delays until *something* happens, not necessarily full completion of a method or service.

Capacity. The number of simultaneous activities that can be supported for a given target minimum throughput or maximum latency. Especially in networking applications, this can serve as a useful indicator of overall *availability*, since it reflects the number of clients that can be serviced without dropping connections due to time-outs or network queue overflows.

Efficiency. Throughput divided by the amount of computational resources (for example CPUs, memory, and IO devices) needed to obtain this throughput.

Scalability. The rate at which latency or throughput improves when resources (again, usually CPUs, memory, or devices) are added to a system. Related measures include *utilization* — the percentage of available resources that are applied to a task of interest.

Degradation. The rate at which latency or throughput worsens as more clients, activities, or operations are added without adding resources.

Most multithreaded designs implicitly accept a small trade-off of poorer computational efficiency to obtain better latency and scalability. Concurrency support introduces the following kinds of overhead and contention that can slow down programs:

Locks. A `synchronized` method typically requires greater call overhead than an unsynchronized method. Also, methods that frequently block waiting for locks (or for any other reason) proceed more slowly than those that do not.

Monitors. `Object.wait`, `Object.notify`, `Object.notifyAll`, and the methods derived from them (such as `Thread.join`) can be more expensive than other basic JVM run-time support operations.

Threads. Creating and starting a `Thread` is typically more expensive than creating an ordinary object and invoking a method on it.

Context-switching. The mapping of threads to CPUs encounters context-switch overhead when a JVM/OS saves the CPU state associated with one thread, selects another thread to run, and loads the associated CPU state.

Scheduling. Computations and underlying policies that select which eligible thread to run add overhead. These may further interact with other system chores such as processing asynchronous events and garbage collection.

Locality. On multiprocessors, when multiple threads running on different CPUs share access to the same objects, cache consistency hardware and low-level system software must communicate the associated values across processors.

Algorithmics. Some efficient sequential algorithms do not apply in concurrent settings. For example, some data structures that rely on caching work only if it is known that exactly one thread performs all operations. However, there are also efficient alternative concurrent algorithms for many problems, including those that open up the possibility of further speedups via parallelism.

The overheads associated with concurrency constructs steadily decrease as JVMs improve. For example, as of this writing, the overhead cost of a single uncontended `synchronized` method call with a no-op body on recent JVMs is on the order of a few unsynchronized no-op calls. (Since different kinds of calls, for example of static versus instance methods, can take different times and interact with other optimizations, it is not worth making this more precise.)

However, these overheads tend to degrade nonlinearly. For example, using one lock that is frequently contended by ten threads is likely to lead to much poorer overall performance than having each thread pass through ten uncontended locks. Also, because concurrency support entails underlying system resource management that is often optimized for given target loads, performance can dramatically degrade when too many locks, monitor operations, or threads are used.

Subsequent chapters include discussions of minimizing use of the associated constructs when necessary. However, bear in mind that performance problems of any kind can be remedied only after they are measured and isolated. Without empirical evidence, most guesses at the nature and source of performance problems are wrong. The most useful measurements are comparative, showing differences or trends under different designs, loads, or configurations.

1.3.4 Reusability

A class or object is reusable to the extent that it can be readily employed across different contexts, either as a black-box component or as the basis of white-box extension via subclassing and related techniques.

The interplay between safety and liveness concerns can significantly impact reusability. It is usually possible to design components to be safe across *all* possible contexts. For example, a `synchronized` method that refuses to commence until it possesses the synchronization lock will do this no matter how it is used. But in some of these contexts, programs using this safe component might encounter liveness failures (for example, deadlock). Conversely, the functionality surrounding a component using only unsynchronized methods will *always* be live (at least with respect to locking), but may encounter safety violations when multiple concurrent executions are allowed to occur.

The dualities of safety and liveness are reflected in some extreme views of design methodology. Some top-down design strategies take a pure safety-first approach: Ensure that each class and object is safe, and then later try to improve liveness as an optimization measure. An opposite, bottom-up approach is sometimes adopted in multithreaded systems programming: Ensure that code is live, and then try to layer on safety features, for example by adding locks. Neither extreme is especially successful in practice. It is too easy for top-down approaches to result in slow, deadlock-prone systems, and for bottom-up approaches to result in buggy code with unanticipated safety violations.

It is usually more productive to proceed with the understanding that some very useful and efficient components are not, and need not be, absolutely safe, and that useful services supported by some components are not absolutely live. Instead, they operate correctly only within certain restricted usage contexts. Therefore, establishing, documenting, advertising, and exploiting these contexts become central issues in concurrent software design.

There are two general approaches (and a range of intermediate choices) for dealing with context dependence: (1) Minimize uncertainty by closing off parts of systems, and (2) Establish policies and protocols that enable components to become or remain open. Many practical design efforts involve some of each.

1.3.4.1 Closed subsystems

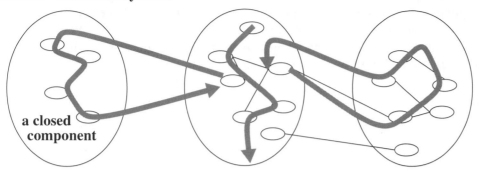

a closed component

An ideally closed system is one for which you have perfect static (design time) knowledge about all possible behaviors. This is typically both unattainable and undesirable. However, it is often still possible to close off parts of systems, in units ranging from individual classes to product-level components, by employing possibly extreme versions of OO encapsulation techniques:

Restricted external communication. All interactions, both inward and outward, occur through a narrow interface. In the most tractable case, the subsystem is *communication-closed*, never internally invoking methods on objects outside the subsystem.

Deterministic internal structure. The concrete nature (and ideally, number) of all objects and threads comprising the subsystem are statically known. The `final` and `private` keywords can be used to help enforce this.

In at least some such systems, you can in principle prove — informally, formally, or even mechanically — that no *internal* safety or liveness violations are possible within a closed component. Or, if they are possible, you can continue to refine designs and implementations until a component is provably correct. In the best cases, you can then apply this knowledge compositionally to analyze other parts of a system that rely on this component.

Perfect static information about objects, threads and interactions tells you not only what can happen, but also what cannot happen. For example, it may be the case that, even though two `synchronized` methods in two objects contain calls to each other, they can never be accessed simultaneously by different threads within the subsystem, so deadlock will never occur.

Closure may also provide further opportunities for manual or compiler-driven optimization; for example removing synchronization from methods that would ordinarily require it, or employing clever special-purpose algorithms that can be made to apply only by eliminating the possibility of unwanted interaction.

Embedded systems are often composed as collections of closed modules, in part to improve predictability, schedulability, and related performance analyses.

While closed subsystems are tractable, they can also be brittle. When the constraints and assumptions governing their internal structure change, these components are often thrown away and redeveloped from scratch.

1.3.4.2   Open systems

An ideal open system is infinitely extensible, across several dimensions. It may load unknown classes dynamically, allow subclasses to override just about any method, employ callbacks across objects within different subsystems, share common resources across threads, use reflection to discover and invoke methods on otherwise unknown objects, and so on. Unbounded openness is usually as unattainable and undesirable as complete closedness: If everything can change, then you cannot program anything. But most systems require at least some of this flexibility.

Full static analysis of open systems is not even possible since their nature and structure evolve across time. Instead, open systems must rely on documented *policies* and *protocols* that every component adheres to.

The Internet is among the best examples of an open system. It continually evolves, for example by adding new hosts, web pages, and services, requiring only that all participants obey a few network policies and protocols. As with other open systems, adherence to Internet policies and protocols is sometimes difficult to enforce. However, JVMs themselves arrange that non-conforming components cannot catastrophically damage system integrity.

Policy-driven design can work well at the much smaller level of typical concurrent systems, where policies and protocols often take the form of design rules. Examples of policy domains explored in more depth in subsequent chapters include:

Flow. For example, a rule of the form: Components of type A send messages to those of type B, but never vice versa.

Blocking. For example, a rule of the form: Methods of type A always immediately throw exceptions if resource R is not available, rather than blocking until it is available.

Notifications. For example, a rule of the form: Objects of type A always send change notifications to their listeners whenever updated.

Adoption of a relatively small number of policies simplifies design by minimizing the possibility of inconsistent case-by-case decisions. Component authors, perhaps with the help of code reviews and tools, need check only that they are obeying the relevant design rules, and can otherwise focus attention on the tasks at hand. Developers can think locally while still acting globally.

However, policy-driven design can become unmanageable when the number of policies grows large and the *programming obligations* they induce overwhelm developers. When even simple methods such as updating an account balance or printing "Hello, world" require dozens of lines of awkward, error-prone code to conform to design policies, it is time to take some kind of remedial action: Simplify or reduce the number of policies; or create tools that help automate code generation and/or check for conformance; or create domain-specific languages that enforce a given discipline; or create frameworks and utility libraries that reduce the need for so much support code to be written inside each method.

Policy choices need not be in any sense "optimal" to be effective, but they must be conformed to and believed in, the more fervently the better. Such policy choices form the basis of several frameworks and design patterns described throughout this book. It is likely that some of them will be inapplicable to your software projects, and may even strike you as wrong-headed ("I'd never do *that!*") because the underlying policies clash with others you have adopted.

While inducing greater closedness allows you to optimize for performance, inducing greater openness allows you to optimize for future change. These two kinds of tunings and refactorings are often equally challenging to carry out, but have opposite effects. Optimizing for performance usually entails exploiting special cases by hard-wiring design decisions. Optimizing for extensibility entails removing hard-wired decisions and instead allowing them to vary, for example by encapsulating them as overridable methods, supporting callback hooks, or abstracting functionality via `interfaces` that can be re-implemented in completely different ways by dynamically loaded components.

Because concurrent programs tend to include more in-the-small policy decisions than sequential ones, and because they tend to rely more heavily on invariants surrounding particular representation choices, classes involving concurrency constructs often turn out to require special attention in order to be readily extensible. This phenomenon is widespread enough to have been given a name, *the inheritance anomaly*, and is described in more detail in §3.3.3.3.

However, some other programming techniques needlessly restrict extensibility for the sake of performance. These tactics become more questionable as compilers and JVMs improve. For example, dynamic compilation allows many extensible components to be treated as if they are closed at class-loading time, leading to optimizations and specializations that exploit particular run-time contexts more effectively than any programmer could.

1.3.4.3 Documentation

When compositionality is context-dependent, it is vital for intended usage contexts and restrictions surrounding components to be well understood and well documented. When this information is not provided, use, reuse, maintenance, testing, configuration management, system evolution, and related software-engineering concerns are made much more difficult.

Documentation may be used to improve understandability by any of several audiences — other developers using a class as a black-box component, subclass authors, developers who later maintain, modify, or repair code, testers and code reviewers, and system users. Across these audiences, the first goal is to eliminate the need for extensive documentation by minimizing the unexpected, and thus reducing conceptual complexity via:

Standardization. Using common policies, protocols, and interfaces. For example:

- Adopting standard design patterns, and referencing books, web pages, or design documents that describe them more fully.

- Employing standard utility libraries and frameworks.

- Using standard coding idioms and naming conventions.

- Clearing against standard review checklists that enumerate common errors.

Clarity. Using the simplest, most self-evident code expressions. For example:

- Using exceptions to advertise checked conditions.

- Expressing internal restrictions via access qualifiers (such as `private`).

- Adopting common default naming and signature conventions, for example that, unless specified otherwise, methods that can block declare that they throw `InterruptedException`.

Auxiliary code. Supplying code that demonstrates intended usages. For example:

- Including sample or recommended usage examples.

- Providing code snippets that achieve non-obvious effects.

- Including methods designed to serve as self-tests.

After eliminating the need to explain the obvious via documentation, more useful forms of documentation can be used to clarify design *decisions*. The most critical details can be expressed in a systematic fashion, using semiformal annotations of the forms listed in the following table, which are used and further explained as needed throughout this book.

PRE	Precondition (not necessarily checked). `/** PRE:  Caller holds synch lock ...`
WHEN	Guard condition (always checked). `/** WHEN: not empty return oldest ...`
POST	Postcondition (normally unchecked). `/** POST: Resource r is released...`
OUT	Guaranteed message send (for example a callback). `/** OUT: c.process(buff) called after read...`
RELY	Required (normally unchecked) property of other objects or methods. `/** RELY: Must be awakened by x.signal()...`
INV	An object constraint true at the start and end of every public method. `/** INV:  x,y are valid screen coordinates...`
INIT	An object constraint that must hold upon construction. `/** INIT: bufferCapacity greater than zero...`

Additional, less structured documentation can be used to explain non-obvious constraints, contextual limitations, assumptions, and design decisions that impact use in a concurrent environment. It is impossible to provide a complete listing of constructions requiring this kind of documentation, but typical cases include:

- High-level design information about state and method constraints.

- Known safety limitations due to lack of locking in situations that would require it.

- The fact that a method may indefinitely block waiting for a condition, event, or resource.

- Methods designed to be called only from other methods, perhaps those in other classes.

This book, like most others, cannot serve as an especially good model for such documentation practices since most of these matters are discussed in the text rather than as sample code documentation.

1.3.5   Further Readings

Accounts of high-level object-oriented software analysis and design that cover at least some concurrency issues include:

Atkinson, Colin. *Object-Oriented Reuse, Concurrency and Distribution,* Addison-Wesley, 1991.

Booch, Grady. *Object Oriented Analysis and Design*, Benjamin Cummings, 1994.

Buhr, Ray J. A., and Ronald Casselman. *Use Case Maps for Object-Oriented Systems,* Prentice Hall, 1996. Buhr and Casselman generalize timethread diagrams similar to those used in this book to Use Case Maps.

Cook, Steve, and John Daniels. *Designing Object Systems: Object-Oriented Modelling With Syntropy,* Prentice Hall, 1994.

de Champeaux, Dennis, Doug Lea, and Penelope Faure. *Object Oriented System Development,* Addison-Wesley, 1993.

D'Souza, Desmond, and Alan Wills. *Objects, Components, and Frameworks with UML,* Addison-Wesley, 1999.

Reenskaug, Trygve. *Working with Objects,* Prentice Hall, 1995.

Rumbaugh, James, Michael Blaha, William Premerlani, Frederick Eddy, and William Lorensen. *Object-Oriented Modeling and Design*, Prentice Hall, 1991.

Accounts of concurrent software specification, analysis, design, and verification include:

Apt, Krzysztof and Ernst-Rudiger Olderog. *Verification of Sequential and Concurrent Programs,* Springer-Verlag, 1997.

Carriero, Nicholas, and David Gelernter. *How to Write Parallel Programs*, MIT Press, 1990.

Chandy, K. Mani, and Jayedev Misra. *Parallel Program Design*, Addison-Wesley, 1989.

Jackson, Michael. *Principles of Program Design*, Academic Press, 1975.

Jensen, Kurt, and Grzegorz Rozenberg (eds.). *High-level Petri Nets: Theory and Application*, Springer-Verlag, 1991.

Lamport, Leslie. *The Temporal Logic of Actions*, SRC Research Report 79, Digital Equipment Corp, 1991.

Leveson, Nancy. *Safeware: System Safety and Computers*, Addison-Wesley, 1995.

Manna, Zohar, and Amir Pneuli. *The Temporal Logic of Reactive and Concurrent Systems*, Springer-Verlag, 1991.

Several specialized fields of software development rely heavily on concurrency. For example, many simulation systems, telecommunications systems, and multimedia systems are highly multithreaded. While basic concurrency techniques form much of the basis for the design of such systems, this book stops short of describing large-scale software architectures or specialized programming techniques associated with particular concurrent applications. See, for example:

Fishwick, Paul. *Simulation Model Design and Execution,* Prentice Hall, 1995.

Gibbs. Simon and Dennis Tsichritzis. *Multimedia Programming*, Addison-Wesley, 1994.

Watkins, Kevin. *Discrete Event Simulation in C,* McGraw-Hill, 1993.

Technical issues are only one aspect of concurrent software development, which also entails testing, organization, management, human factors, maintenance, tools, and engineering discipline. For an introduction to basic engineering methods that can be applied to both everyday programming and larger efforts, see:

Humphrey, Watts. *A Discipline for Software Engineering*, Addison-Wesley, 1995.

For a completely different perspective, see:

Beck, Kent. *Extreme Programming Explained: Embrace Change*, Addison-Wesley, 1999.

For more information about integrating performance concerns into software engineering efforts, see for example:

Jain, Raj. *The Art of Computer Systems Performance Analysis*, Wiley, 1991.

Further distinctions between open and closed systems are discussed in:

Wegner, Peter. "Why Interaction Is More Powerful Than Algorithms", *Communications of the ACM*, May 1997.

1.4 Before/After Patterns

Many concurrent designs are best described as patterns. A pattern encapsulates a successful and common design form, usually an *object structure* (also known as a *micro-architecture)* consisting of one or more interfaces, classes, and/or objects that obey certain static and dynamic constraints and relationships. Patterns are an ideal vehicle for characterizing designs and techniques that need not be implemented in exactly the same way across different contexts, and thus cannot be usefully encapsulated as reusable components. Reusable components and frameworks can play a central role in concurrent software development. But much of concurrent OO programming entails the reuse, adaptation, and extension of recurring design forms and practices rather than of particular classes.

Unlike those in the pioneering *Design Patterns* book by Gamma, Helm, Johnson, and Vlissides (see Further Readings in §1.4.5), the patterns here are embedded within chapters discussing sets of related contexts and software design principles that generate the main forces and constraints resolved in the patterns. Many of these patterns are minor extensions or variants of other common OO layering and composition patterns. This section reviews some that are relied on heavily in subsequent chapters. Others are briefly described upon first encounter.

1.4.1 Layering

Layering policy control over mechanism is a common structuring principle in systems of all sorts. Many OO layering and composition techniques rely on sandwiching some method call or body of code between a given *before*-action and an *after*-action. All forms of before/after control arrange that a given *ground* method, say method, is intercepted so as always to execute in the sequence:

```
before(); method(); after();
```

Or, to ensure that *after*-actions are performed even if the ground methods encounter exceptions:

```
before();
try { method(); }
finally { after(); }
```

Most examples in this book of course revolve around concurrency control. For example, a `synchronized` method acquires a lock *before* executing the code inside the method, and releases the lock *after* the method otherwise completes. But the basic ideas of before/after patterns can be illustrated in conjunction with another useful practice in OO programming, self-checking code: The fields of any object should preserve all invariants whenever the object is not engaged in a public method (see §1.3.1). Invariants should be maintained even if these methods throw any of their declared exceptions, unless these exceptions denote corruption or program failure (as may be true for `RuntimeExceptions` and `Errors`).

Conformance to computable invariants can be tested dynamically by creating classes that check them both on entry to and on exit from every public method. Similar techniques apply to preconditions and postconditions, but for simplicity, we'll illustrate only with invariants.

As an example, suppose we'd like to create water tank classes that contain a self-check on the invariant that the volume is always between zero and the capacity. To do this, we can define a `checkVolumeInvariant` method and use it as both the *before* and *after* operation. We can first define an exception to throw if the invariant fails:

```
class AssertionError extends java.lang.Error {
  public AssertionError() { super(); }
  public AssertionError(String message) { super(message); }
}
```

It can be disruptive to insert these checks manually inside each method. Instead, one of three before/after design patterns can be used to separate the checks from the ground methods: adapter classes, subclass-based designs, and method adapter classes.

In all cases, the best way to set this up is to define an interface describing the basic functionality. Interfaces are almost always necessary when you need to give yourself enough room to vary implementations. Conversely, the lack of existing interfaces limits options when retrospectively applying before/after patterns.

Here is an interface describing a minor variant of the water tank class discussed in §1.2.4. Before/after techniques may be applied to check invariants around the `transferWater` operation.

```
interface Tank {
  float getCapacity();
  float getVolume();
  void  transferWater(float amount)
          throws OverflowException, UnderflowException;
}
```

1.4.2 Adapters

When standardized interfaces are defined after designing one or more concrete classes, these classes often do not quite implement the desired interface. For example, the names of their methods might be slightly different from those defined in the interface. If you cannot modify these concrete classes to fix such problems, you can still obtain the desired effect by building an Adapter class that translates away the incompatibilities.

Say you have a `Performer` class that supports method `perform` and meets all the qualifications of being usable as a `Runnable` except for the name mismatch. You can build an Adapter so it can be used in a thread by some other class:

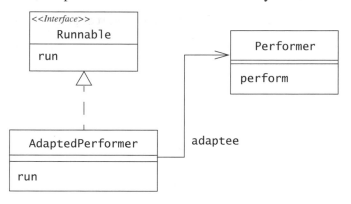

```
class AdaptedPerformer implements Runnable {
  private final Performer adaptee;

  public AdaptedPerformer(Performer p) { adaptee = p; }
  public void run() { adaptee.perform(); }
}
```

This is only one of many common contexts for building Adapters, which also form the basis of several related patterns presented in the *Design Patterns* book. A *Proxy* is an Adapter with the same interface as its delegate. A *Composite* maintains a collection of delegates, all supporting the same interface.

In this delegation-based style of composition, the publicly accessible host class forwards all methods to one or more delegates and relays back replies, perhaps doing some light translation (name changes, parameter coercion, result filtering, etc.) surrounding the delegate calls.

Adapters can be used to provide before/after control merely by wrapping the delegated call within the control actions. For example, assuming that we have an implementation class, say `TankImpl`, we can write the following `AdaptedTank` class. This class can be used instead of the original in some application by replacing all occurrences of:

    new TankImpl(...)

with:

    new AdaptedTank(new TankImpl(...)).

```
class AdaptedTank implements Tank {
  protected final Tank delegate;

  public AdaptedTank(Tank t) { delegate = t; }

  public float getCapacity() { return delegate.getCapacity(); }

  public float getVolume() { return delegate.getVolume(); }

  protected void checkVolumeInvariant() throws AssertionError {
    float v = getVolume();
    float c = getCapacity();
    if ( !(v >= 0.0 && v <= c) )
      throw new AssertionError();
  }

  public synchronized void transferWater(float amount)
   throws OverflowException, UnderflowException {

    checkVolumeInvariant();   // before-check

    try {
      delegate.transferWater(amount);
    }

    // The re-throws will be postponed until after-check
    //    in the finally clause

    catch (OverflowException ex)  { throw ex; }
    catch (UnderflowException ex) { throw ex; }

    finally {
      checkVolumeInvariant(); // after-check
    }
  }
}
```

1.4.3 Subclassing

In the normal case, when the intercepted before/after versions of methods have the same names and usages as base versions, subclassing can be a simpler alternative to the use of Adapters. Subclass versions of methods can interpose checks around calls to their `super` versions. For example:

```
class SubclassedTank extends TankImpl {

  protected void checkVolumeInvariant() throws AssertionError {
    // ... identical to AdaptedTank version ...
  }

  public synchronized void transferWater(float amount)
    throws OverflowException, UnderflowException {
    // identical to AdaptedTank version except for inner call:

    // ...
    try {
      super.transferWater(amount);
    }
    // ...
  }
}
```

Some choices between subclassing and Adapters are just a matter of style. Others reflect differences between delegation and inheritance.

    Adapters permit manipulations that escape subclassing rules. For example, you cannot override a `public` method as `private` in a subclass in order to disable access, but you can simply fail to relay the method in an Adapter. Various forms of delegation can even be used as a substitute of sorts for subclassing by having each "sub" class (Adapter) hold a reference to an instance of its "super" class (Adaptee), forwarding it all "inherited" operations. Such Adapters often have exactly the same interfaces as their delegates, in which case they are considered to be simple kinds of *Proxies*. Delegation can also be more flexible than subclassing, since "sub" objects can even change their "supers" (by reassigning the delegate reference) dynamically.

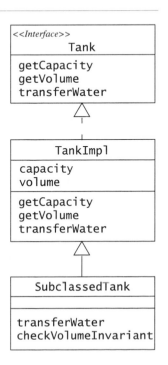

61

Delegation can also be used to obtain the effects of multiple code inheritance. For example, if a class must implement two unrelated interfaces, say `Tank` and `java.awt.event.ActionListener`, and there are two available superclasses providing the needed functionality, then one of these may be subclassed and the other delegated.

However, delegation is less powerful than subclassing in some other respects. For example, self-calls in "superclasses" are not automatically bound to the versions of methods that have been "overridden" in delegation-based "subclasses". Adapter designs can also run into snags revolving around the fact that the Adaptee and Adapter objects are different objects. For example, object reference equality tests must be performed more carefully since a test to see if you have the Adaptee version of an object fails if you have the Adapter version, and vice versa.

Most of these problems can be avoided via the extreme measure of declaring all methods in Adaptee classes to take an "apparent self" argument referring to the Adapter, and always using it instead of `this`, even for self-calls and identity checks (for example by overriding `Object.equals`). Some people reserve the term *delegation* for objects and classes written in this style rather than the forwarding techniques that are almost always used to implement simple Adapters.

1.4.3.1 Template methods

When you are pretty sure that you are going to rely on before/after control in a set of related classes, you can create an abstract class that automates the control sequence via an application of the *Template Method* pattern (which has nothing to do with C++ generic types).

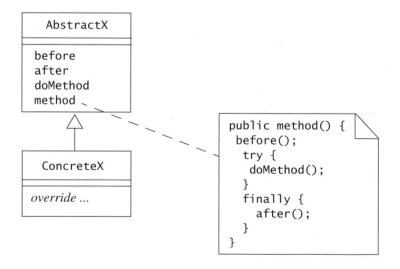

An abstract class supporting template methods sets up a framework facilitating construction of subclasses that may override the ground-level actions, the before/after methods, or both:

- Basic ground-level action code is defined in non-public methods. (By convention, we name the non-public version of any method method as doMethod.) Somewhat less flexibly, these methods need not be declared non-public if they are instead designed to be overridden in subclasses.

- Before and after operations are also defined as non-public methods.

- Public methods invoke the ground methods between the before and after methods.

Applying this to the Tank example leads to:

```
abstract class AbstractTank implements Tank {
  protected void checkVolumeInvariant() throws AssertionError {
    // ... identical to AdaptedTank version ...
  }

  protected abstract void doTransferWater(float amount)
    throws OverflowException, UnderflowException;

  public synchronized void transferWater(float amount)
    throws OverflowException, UnderflowException {
    // identical to AdaptedTank version except for inner call:

    // ...
    try {
      doTransferWater(amount);
    }
    // ...
  }
}

class ConcreteTank extends AbstractTank {
  protected final float capacity;
  protected float volume;
  // ...
  public float getVolume() { return volume; }
  public float getCapacity() { return capacity; }

  protected void doTransferWater(float amount)
    throws OverflowException, UnderflowException {
    // ... implementation code ...
  }
}
```

1.4.4   Method Adapters

The most flexible, but sometimes most awkward approach to before/after control is to define a class whose entire purpose is to invoke a particular method on a particular object. In the *Command Object* pattern and its many variants, instances of such classes can then be passed around, manipulated, and ultimately executed (here, between before/after operations).

Because of static typing rules, there must be a different kind of adapter class for each kind of method being wrapped. To avoid proliferation of all these types, most applications restrict attention to only one or a small set of generic interfaces, each defining a single method. For example, the Thread class and most other execution frameworks accept only instances of interface Runnable in order to invoke their argumentless, resultless, exceptionless run methods. Similarly, in §4.3.3.1, we define and use interface Callable containing only a method call that accepts one Object argument, returns an Object, and may throw any Exception.

In more focused applications, you can define any suitable single-method interface, instantiate an implementation — almost always via an anonymous inner class — and then pass it around for later execution. This technique is used extensively in the java.awt and javax.swing packages, which define interfaces and abstract classes associated with different kinds of event-handling methods. (In some other languages, *function pointers* and *closures* are defined and used to achieve some of these effects.)

We can apply a version of before/after layering based on method adapters here by first defining a TankOp interface:

```
interface TankOp {
  void op() throws OverflowException, UnderflowException;
}
```

In the following sample code, uncharacteristically, all uses of method adapters are local to the TankWithMethodAdapter class. Also, in this tiny example, there is only one wrappable method. However, the same scaffolding could be used for any other Tank methods defined in this class or its subclasses. Method adapters are much more common in applications where instances must be registered and/or passed around among multiple objects before being executed, which justifies the extra setup costs and programming obligations.

```
class TankWithMethodAdapter {
  // ...
  protected void checkVolumeInvariant() throws AssertionError {
    // ... identical to AdaptedTank version ...
  }

  protected void runWithinBeforeAfterChecks(TankOp cmd)
   throws OverflowException, UnderflowException {
    // identical to AdaptedTank.transferWater
    //    except for inner call:

    // ...
    try {
      cmd.op();
    }
    // ...
  }

  protected void doTransferWater(float amount)
   throws OverflowException, UnderflowException {
    // ... implementation code ...
  }

  public synchronized void transferWater(final float amount)
   throws OverflowException, UnderflowException {

    runWithinBeforeAfterChecks(new TankOp() {
      public void op()
       throws OverflowException, UnderflowException {
        doTransferWater(amount);
      }
    });
  }
}
```

Some applications of method adapters can be partially automated by using reflection facilities. A generic constructor can probe a class for a particular java.lang.reflect.Method, set up arguments for it, invoke it, and transfer back results. This comes at the price of weaker static guarantees, greater overhead, and the need to deal with the many exceptions that can arise. So this is generally only worthwhile when dealing with unknown dynamically loaded code.

More extreme and exotic reflective interception techniques are available if you escape the confines of the language. For example, it is possible to create and apply tools that splice bytecodes representing before and after actions into compiled class representations or do so upon class-loading.

1.4.5 Further Readings

There are many useful design patterns besides those that are particular to concurrent programming, and surely many others relating to concurrency that are not included in this book. Other books presenting patterns and pattern-related aspects of software design include:

Buschmann, Frank, Regine Meunier, Hans Rohnert, Peter Sommerlad, and Michael Stal. *Pattern-Oriented Software Architecture: A System of Patterns,* Wiley, 1996.

Coplien, James. *Advanced C++: Programming Styles and Idioms*, Addison-Wesley, 1992.

Fowler, Martin. Analysis Patterns, Addison-Wesley, 1997

Gamma, Erich, Richard Helm, Ralph Johnson, and John Vlissides. *Design Patterns,* Addison-Wesley, 1994. (The "Gang of Four" book.)

Rising, Linda. *The Patterns Handbook*, Cambridge University Press, 1998.

Shaw, Mary, and David Garlan. *Software Architecture*, Prentice Hall, 1996.

(Various editors) *Pattern Languages of Program Design,* Addison-Wesley. This series incorporates patterns presented at the annual Pattern Languages of Programming (*PLoP*) conference.

The OO language Self is among the few that directly support a pure delegation-based style of programming without requiring explicit message forwarding. See:

Ungar, David. "The Self Papers", *Lisp and Symbolic Computation*, 1991.

Reflective before/after techniques are often seen in Lisp, Scheme and CLOS (the Common Lisp Object System). See, for example:

Abelson, Harold, and Gerald Sussman. *Structure and Interpretation of Computer Programs*, MIT Press, 1996.

Kiczales, Gregor, Jim des Rivieres, and Daniel Bobrow. *The Art of the Metaobject Protocol,* MIT Press, 1993.

Additional layered synchronization design patterns are discussed in:

Rito Silva, António, João Pereira and José Alves Marques. "Object Synchronizer", in Neil Harrison, Brian Foote and Hans Rohnert (eds.), *Pattern Languages of Program Design, Volume 4*, Addison-Wesley, 1999.

A compositional approach to layering concurrency control is described in:

Holmes, David. *Synchronisation Rings: Composable Synchronisation for Concurrent Object Oriented Systems*, PhD Thesis, Macquarie University, 1999.

Composition of collections of before/after methods that deal with different aspects of functionality (for example, mixing synchronization control with persistence control) may require more elaborate frameworks than discussed here. One approach is to construct a *metaclass* framework that partially automates the interception and wrapping of methods by class objects. For an extensive analysis and discussion of the resulting composition techniques, see:

Forman, Ira, and Scott Danforth. *Putting Metaclasses to Work*, Addison-Wesley, 1999.

Aspect-oriented programming replaces layered before/after techniques with tools that weave together code dealing with different aspects of control. Reports on the language *AspectJ* include some examples from this book expressed in an aspect-oriented fashion. See:

Kiczales, Gregor, John Lamping, Anurag Mendhekar, Chris Maeda, Cristina Videira Lopes, Jean-Marc Loingtier, and John Irwin. "Aspect-Oriented Programming", *Proceedings of the European Conference on Object-Oriented Programming (ECOOP)*, 1997.

Several tools are available for partially automating invariant tests. See, for example:

Beck, Kent, and Erich Gamma. "Test Infected: Programmers Love Writing Tests", *The Java Report*, July 1998.

CHAPTER 2

Exclusion

$\mathbf{I}$N a safe system, every object protects itself from integrity violations. This sometimes requires the cooperation of other objects and their methods.

Exclusion techniques preserve object invariants and avoid effects that would result from acting upon even momentarily inconsistent state representations. Programming techniques and design patterns achieve exclusion by preventing multiple threads from concurrently modifying or acting upon object representations. All approaches rely on one or more of three basic strategies:

Eliminating the need for some or all exclusion control by ensuring that methods never modify an object's representation, so that the object cannot enter inconsistent states.

Dynamically ensuring that only one thread at a time can access object state, by protecting objects with locks and related constructs.

Structurally ensuring that only one thread (or only one thread at a time) can ever use a given object, by hiding or restricting access to it.

The first three sections of this chapter describe the central features and usage patterns surrounding each of these approaches — immutability (§2.1), synchronization (§2.2), and confinement (§2.3). Section §2.4 discusses some ways to combine these different approaches to improve safety, liveness, performance, and/or semantic guarantees. Section §2.5 shows how to use utility classes to obtain effects that are otherwise difficult to arrange using built-in constructs. Additionally, several of the classes, techniques, and utilities described in Chapter 3 can be used to ensure exclusion (see especially §3.3.2).

The *mandatory* use of these techniques represents an important difference between sequential and concurrent programming practices. To guarantee safety in a concurrent system, you must ensure that *all* objects accessible from multiple threads either are immutable or employ appropriate synchronization, and also must ensure that *no* other object ever becomes concurrently accessible by leaking out of its ownership domain. While the techniques that help maintain these guarantees are in many ways just extensions of other OO development practices, concurrent programs are typically less tolerant of error.

As discussed in §1.3.1, most of these matters cannot by nature be enforced by compilers or run-time systems. Analysis and testing tools may be helpful in detecting some kinds of failure, but the main responsibility for ensuring the safety of each class, component, subsystem, application, and system falls on its developers. Additionally, exclusion-related policies and design rules must be explicit and well advertised.

Much caution is needed when using code that was not designed to operate in multithreaded environments. Most classes in the `java.*` packages are designed to be thread-safe when applied in their intended usage contexts. (Some exceptions are noted as they arise in this book. Other limitations appear in class API documentation.) However, when constructing multithreaded applications, it is often necessary to rework or wrap (see §2.3.3.1) your own classes and packages that were originally designed only for use in single-threaded contexts.

2.1 Immutability

If an object cannot change state, then it can never encounter conflicts or inconsistencies when multiple activities attempt to change its state in incompatible ways.

Programs are much simpler to understand if existing objects are never changed, but instead new ones are continually created during the course of any computation. Unfortunately, such programs are generally unable to handle interaction via user interfaces, cooperating threads, and so on. However, selective use of immutability is a basic tool in concurrent OO programming.

The simplest immutable objects have no internal fields at all. Their methods are intrinsically *stateless* — they do not rely on any assignable fields of any object. For example, all possible uses of the following StatelessAdder class and its add method are obviously always safe and live:

```
class StatelessAdder {
  public int add(int a, int b) { return a + b; }
}
```

The same safety and liveness properties hold in classes possessing only final fields. Instances of immutable classes cannot experience low-level read-write or write-write conflicts (see §1.3.1), because values are never written. And as long as their initial values are established in a consistent, legal fashion, these objects cannot experience higher-level invariant failures. For example:

```
class ImmutableAdder {
  private final int offset;

  public ImmutableAdder(int a) { offset = a; }

  public int addOffset(int b) { return offset + b; }
}
```

2.1.1 Applications

It is of course possible to create immutable objects that contain more interesting structure and functionality than seen in ImmutableAdder. Applications include abstract data types, value containers, and shared state representations.

2.1.1.1 Abstract Data Types (ADTs)

Immutable objects can serve as instances of simple abstract data types representing values. Some common ones are already defined in the java.* packages. These include java.awt.Color, java.lang.Integer, java.math.BigDecimal, java.lang.String, and others[1]. It is easy to define your own ADT classes, for example, Fraction, Interval, ComplexFloat, and so on. Instances of such classes never alter their constructed field values, but may provide methods that create objects representing new values. For example:

```
class Fraction {                                          // Fragments
  protected final long numerator;
  protected final long denominator;

  public Fraction(long num, long den) {
    // normalize:
    boolean sameSign = (num >= 0) == (den >= 0);
    long n = (num >= 0)? num : -num;
    long d = (den >= 0)? den : -den;
    long g = gcd(n, d);
    numerator = (sameSign)? n / g : -n / g;
    denominator = d / g;
  }

  static long gcd(long a, long b) {
    // ... compute greatest common divisor ...
  }

  public Fraction plus(Fraction f) {
    return new Fraction(numerator * f.denominator +
                          f.numerator * denominator,
                        denominator * f.denominator);
  }

  public boolean equals(Object other) { // override default
    if (! (other instanceof Fraction) ) return false;
    Fraction f = (Fraction)(other);
    return numerator * f.denominator ==
           denominator * f.numerator;
  }

  public int hashCode() {                     // override default
    return (int) (numerator ^ denominator);
  }
}
```

---

[1] Note, however, that some other ADT-style classes in the java.* packages are not immutable, for example java.awt.Point.

Classes that represent immutable data abstractions have instances that serve only to encapsulate values, so their identities are not important. For example, two `java.awt.Color` objects that both represent black (via RGB value 0) are typically intended to be treated as equivalent. This is one reason why ADT-style classes should normally override methods `Object.equals` and `Object.hashCode` to reflect equality of abstract value, as illustrated in the `Fraction` class. The default implementations of these methods rely on the identities of objects maintaining these values. Masking identity by overriding `equals` enables multiple ADT objects to represent the same values and/or perform the same functionality without clients needing to know or care exactly which ADT object is being used at any given time.

You don't always have to commit to immutable representations of ADTs across an entire program. It is sometimes helpful to define different classes, supporting different usages, for the immutable versus updatable versions of some concept. For example, class `java.lang.String` is immutable, while class `java.lang.StringBuffer` is updatable, relying on `synchronized` methods.

2.1.1.2 Value containers

Immutable objects can be used when it is necessary or convenient to establish some consistent state once and then rely on it forever more. For example, an immutable `ProgramConfiguration` object may reflect all of the settings to be used during the execution of a given program.

Immutable value containers can also be useful whenever creating different variants, versions, or states of an object by creating new ones through partial copying is relatively rare or cheap. In these cases, the expense of copying may be outweighed by the benefits of never needing to synchronize state changes (see §2.4.4). The analog of a state change for an immutable object is to produce a new immutable object that differs from the original in some specified way.

2.1.1.3 Sharing

Immutability is a useful technical device when you would like to share objects for space efficiency, and still provide efficient access to these objects. One immutable object can be referenced by any number of other objects without concern for synchronization or access restriction. For example, many individual character (or glyph) objects may all share references to the same immutable font object. This is one application of the Flyweight pattern described in the *Design Patterns* book. Most Flyweights designs are simplest to establish by ensuring the immutability of shared representations.

Instances of many utility classes used in concurrent settings are intrinsically immutable and are shared by many other objects. For example:

```
class Relay {
  protected final Server server;

  Relay(Server s) { server = s; }

  void doIt() { server.doIt(); }
}
```

While purely immutable objects are simple, convenient, prevalent, and useful, many concurrent OO programs also rely on *partial* immutability — constancy for only some fields, or only after execution of a particular method, or only over some period of interest. Exploitation of immutability is a useful strategy for producing designs that would be difficult at best to realize using updatable objects. A number of such designs are presented in the course of this book, especially in §2.4.

2.1.2   Construction

To be effective, all design decisions relying on immutability must be enforced via appropriate use of the `final` keyword. Additionally, some care is required when initializing immutable objects (see §2.2.7). In particular, it is counterproductive to make an immutable object available to others before it has been fully initialized. As a general rule holding for any kind of class:

- **Do not allow fields to be accessed until construction is complete.**

This can be harder to ensure in concurrent settings than in sequential programs. Constructors should perform only actions directly related to field initialization. They should not invoke any other methods whose effects may rely on the object being fully constructed. Constructors should avoid recording a reference to the object being constructed in fields or tables accessible by others, avoid making calls to other methods with `this` as an argument, and more generally, avoid allowing the reference to `this` to *escape* (see §2.3). Without such precautions, other objects and methods running in other threads could instead access the default-initialized zeros (for scalar fields) or nulls (for reference fields) set by the JVM for each `Object` before its constructor is executed.

In some cases, the values of conceptually immutable fields cannot be fully initialized in constructors, for example, when they are incrementally initialized from files, or when there are interdependencies among multiple objects being constructed at the same time. Further care is needed to ensure that these objects are not made available for use by others until values are stable. This almost always requires use of synchronization (see for example §2.2.4 and §3.4.2).

2.2 Synchronization

Locking protects against low-level storage conflicts and corresponding high-level invariant failures. For example, consider the following class:

```
class Even {                              //  Do not use
  private int n = 0;
  public int next(){ // POST?: next is always even
    ++n;
    ++n;
    return n;
  }
}
```

Without locking, the desired postcondition may fail due to a storage conflict when two or more threads execute the `next` method of the same `Even` object. Here is one possible execution trace, showing only the reads and writes to variable `n` that would result from the `putfields` and `getfields` in compiled bytecode.

Thread A	Thread B
read 0	
write 1	
	read 1
	write 2
read 2	read 2
	write 3
write 3	return 3
return 3	

As is typical in concurrent programs, most traces of two threads concurrently executing `Even.next` do not display this safety violation. Programs using this version of `Even` are likely to pass some tests but are almost sure to break eventually. Such safety violations can be rare and difficult to test for, yet can have devastating effects. This motivates the careful, conservative design practices seen in reliable concurrent programs.

Declaring the `next` method as `synchronized` would preclude such conflicting traces. Locking *serializes* the execution of `synchronized` methods. So here, either thread A's `next` method would execute in full before thread B's, or vice versa.

2.2.1 Mechanics

As a preliminary to further discussions of design strategies based on locking, here is a summary of mechanics, as well as some usage notes surrounding the `synchronized` keyword.

2.2.1.1 Objects and locks

Every instance of class `Object` and its subclasses possesses a lock. Scalars of type `int`, `float`, etc., are not `Objects`. Scalar fields can be locked only via their enclosing objects. Individual fields cannot be marked as `synchronized`. Locking may be applied only to the *use* of fields within methods. However, as described in §2.2.7.4, fields can be declared as `volatile`, which affects atomicity, visibility, and ordering properties surrounding their use.

Similarly, array objects holding scalar elements possess locks, but their individual scalar elements do not. (Further, there is no way to declare array elements as `volatile`.) Locking an array of `Objects` does *not* automatically lock all its elements. There are no constructs for simultaneously locking multiple objects in a single atomic operation.

`Class` instances are `Objects`. As described below, the locks associated with `Class` objects are used in `static synchronized` methods.

2.2.1.2 Synchronized methods and blocks

There are two syntactic forms based on the `synchronized` keyword, blocks and methods. Block synchronization takes an argument of which object to lock. This allows any method to lock any object. The most common argument to `synchronized` blocks is `this`.

Block synchronization is considered more fundamental than method synchronization. A declaration:

```
synchronized void f() { /* body */ }
```
is equivalent to:
```
void f() { synchronized(this) { /* body */ } }
```

The `synchronized` keyword is not considered to be part of a method's signature. So the `synchronized` modifier is *not* automatically inherited when subclasses override superclass methods, and methods in `interfaces` cannot be declared as `synchronized`. Also, constructors cannot be qualified as `synchronized` (although block synchronization can be used within constructors).

Synchronized instance methods in subclasses employ the same lock as those in their superclasses. But synchronization in an *inner* class method is independent of its outer class. However, a non-static inner class method can lock its containing class, say `OuterClass`, via code blocks using:

```
synchronized(OuterClass.this) { /* body */ }.
```

2.2.1.3 Acquiring and releasing locks

Locking obeys a built-in acquire-release protocol controlled only by use of the `synchronized` keyword. All locking is block-structured. A lock is acquired on entry to a `synchronized` method or block, and released on exit, even if the exit occurs due to an exception. You cannot forget to release a lock.

Locks operate on a per-thread, not per-invocation basis. A thread hitting `synchronized` passes if the lock is free or the thread already possess the lock, and otherwise blocks. (This *reentrant* or *recursive* locking differs from the default policy used for example in POSIX threads.) Among other effects, this allows one `synchronized` method to make a self-call to another `synchronized` method on the same object without freezing up.

A `synchronized` method or block obeys the acquire-release protocol only with respect to other `synchronized` methods and blocks on the same target object. Methods that are not `synchronized` may still execute at any time, even if a `synchronized` method is in progress. In other words, `synchronized` is not equivalent to *atomic*, but synchronization can be used to achieve atomicity.

When one thread releases a lock, another thread may acquire it (perhaps the same thread, if it hits another `synchronized` method). But there is no guarantee about which of any blocked threads will acquire the lock next or when they will do so. (In particular, there are no *fairness* guarantees — see §3.4.1.5.) There is no mechanism to discover whether a given lock is being held by some thread.

As discussed in §2.2.7, in addition to controlling locking, `synchronized` also has the side-effect of synchronizing the underlying memory system.

2.2.1.4 Statics

Locking an object does *not* automatically protect access to `static` fields of that object's class or any of its superclasses. Access to `static` fields is instead protected via `synchronized static` methods and blocks. Static synchronization employs the lock possessed by the `Class` object associated with the class the static methods are declared in. The static lock for class `C` can also be accessed inside instance methods via:

```
synchronized(C.class) { /* body */ }
```

The static lock associated with each class is unrelated to that of any other class, including its superclasses. It is *not* effective to add a new `static synchronized` method in a subclass that attempts to protect `static` fields declared in a superclass. Use the explicit block version instead.

It is also poor practice to use constructions of the form:

```
synchronized(getClass()) { /* body */ }        // Do not use
```

This locks the actual class, which might be different from (a subclass of) the class defining the `static` fields that need protecting.

The JVM internally obtains and releases the locks for `Class` objects during class loading and initialization. Unless you are writing a special `ClassLoader` or holding multiple locks during `static` initialization sequences, these internal mechanics cannot interfere with the use of ordinary methods and blocks synchronized on `Class` objects. No other internal JVM actions independently acquire any locks for any objects of classes that you create and use. However, if you subclass `java.*` classes, you should be aware of the locking policies used in these classes.

2.2.2 Fully Synchronized Objects

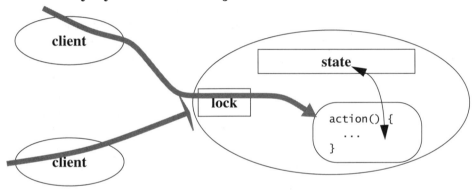

A lock is the most basic kind of message acceptance control mechanism. Locks may be used to block clients attempting to invoke a method on an object while another method or code block (running in a different thread) is in progress.

The safest (but not always the best) concurrent OO design strategy based on locking is to restrict attention to *fully synchronized* objects (also known as *atomic* objects) in which:

- All methods are `synchronized`.

- There are no public fields or other encapsulation violations.

- All methods are finite (no infinite loops or unbounded recursion), and so eventually release locks.

- All fields are initialized to a consistent state in constructors.

- The state of the object is consistent (obeys invariants) at both the beginning and end of each method, even in the presence of exceptions.

For example, consider the following `ExpandableArray` class, a simplified variant of `java.util.Vector`.

```
class ExpandableArray {

  protected Object[] data;  // the elements
  protected int size = 0;   // the number of array slots used
  // INV: 0 <= size <= data.length

  public ExpandableArray(int cap) {
    data = new Object[cap];
  }

  public synchronized int size() {
    return size;
  }

  public synchronized Object get(int i) // subscripted access
   throws NoSuchElementException {
    if (i < 0 || i >= size )
      throw new NoSuchElementException();

    return data[i];
  }

  public synchronized void add(Object x) { // add at end
    if (size == data.length) {          // need a bigger array
      Object[] olddata = data;
      data = new Object[3 * (size + 1) / 2];
      System.arraycopy(olddata, 0, data, 0, olddata.length);
    }
    data[size++] = x;
  }

  public synchronized void removeLast()
   throws NoSuchElementException {
    if (size == 0)
      throw new NoSuchElementException();

    data[--size] = null;
  }
}
```

Without synchronization, an instance of this class could not be used reliably in concurrent settings. For example, it could encounter a read/write conflict if processing the accessor at while in the midst of a `removeLast` operation. And it could encounter a write/write conflict if concurrently performing two add operations, in which case the state of the data array would be very difficult to predict.

2.2.3   Traversal

In fully synchronized classes, you can add another atomic operation just by encasing it in a `synchronized` method. For the sake of reusability and convenience, it is often a good idea to add small suites of such operations to general-purpose classes or their subclasses. This avoids making clients go through contortions trying to construct atomic versions of commonly used operations out of smaller components. For example, it would be useful to define `synchronized` versions of `removeFirst`, `prepend`, and similar methods to `ExpandableArray`, as found in `java.util.Vector` and other collection classes.

However, this strategy doesn't work for another common usage of collections, *traversal*. A traversal iterates through all elements of a collection and performs some operation on or using each element. Since there are an unbounded number of operations clients might want to apply to the elements of a collection, it is pointless to try to code all of them as `synchronized` methods.

There are three common solutions to this design problem, aggregate operations, indexed traversal, and versioned iterators, each of which reflect different design trade-offs. (See §2.4.1.3, §2.4.4, and §2.5.1.4 for additional strategies that apply to other kinds of collection classes.) The issues and trade-offs encountered in each approach are seen more generally in the design of many classes using locks.

2.2.3.1   Synchronized aggregate operations

One way to secure traversal is to abstract out the operation being applied to each element so that it can be sent as an argument to a single `synchronized` `applyToAll` method. For example:

```
interface Procedure {
  void apply(Object obj);
}

class ExpandableArrayWithApply extends ExpandableArray {

  public ExpandableArrayWithApply(int cap) { super(cap); }

  synchronized void applyToAll(Procedure p) {
    for (int i = 0; i < size; ++i)
      p.apply(data[i]);
  }
}
```

This could be used, for example, to print all elements in collection v:

```
v.applyToAll(new Procedure() {
  public void apply(Object obj) {
    System.out.println(obj)
  }
} );
```

This approach eliminates potential interference that could occur if other threads attempted to add or remove elements during traversal, but at the expense of possibly holding the lock on the collection for prolonged periods. While this is often acceptable, it may lead to the kinds of liveness and performance problems that motivated the default rule in §1.1.1.1 saying to release locks when making method calls (here, to apply).

2.2.3.2 Indexed traversal and client-side locking

A second traversal strategy available with ExpandableArray is to require clients to use the indexed accessor methods for traversal; for example:

```
for (int i = 0; i < v.size(); ++i)              // Do not use
  System.out.println(v.get(i));
```

This avoids holding the lock on v while performing each element operation, but at the expense of two synchronized operations (size and at) per element. More importantly, the loop must be rewritten to handle a potential interference problem resulting from the finer locking granularity: It is possible for the check of i < v.size() to succeed but for another thread to remove the current last element before the call to v.get(i). One way to deal with this is to employ *client-side locking* to preserve atomicity across the size check and access:

```
for (int i = 0; true; ++i) {                    // Limited utility
  Object obj = null;
  synchronized(v) {
    if (i < v.size())
      obj = v.get(i);
    else
      break;
  }
  System.out.println(obj);
}
```

However, even this can be problematic. For example, if the ExpandableArray class supported methods to rearrange elements, this loop could print the same element twice if v were modified between iterations.

81

As a more extreme measure, clients can surround the entire traversal with `synchronized(v)`. Again, this is often acceptable but can induce the long-term locking problems seen in `synchronized` aggregate methods. If the operations on elements are time-consuming, the client can instead first make a copy of the array for traversal purposes:

```
Object[] snapshot;
synchronized(v) {
  snapshot = new Object[v.size()];
  for (int i = 0; i < snapshot.length, ++i)
    snapshot[i] = v.get(i);
}

for (int i = 0; snapshot.length; ++i) {
  System.out.println(snapshot[i]);
}
```

Client-side locking tends to be used more extensively in non-object-oriented approaches to multithreaded programming. This style is sometimes more flexible, and can be useful in OO systems when instances of a class are designed to be embedded within others (see §2.4.5) and so must give up internal responsibility for synchronization decisions.

But client-side locking avoids potential interference problems at the expense of encapsulation breakdown. Correctness here relies on special knowledge of the inner workings of the `ExpandableArray` class that may fail to hold if the class is later modified. Still, this may be acceptable in closed subsystems. Client-side locking can also be a reasonable option when classes document these usages as sanctioned. This also constrains all future modifications and subclasses to support them as well.

2.2.3.3   Versioned iterators

A third approach to traversal is for a collection class to support *fast-fail* iterators that throw an exception if the collection is modified in the midst of a traversal. The simplest way to arrange this is to maintain a version number that is incremented upon each update to the collection. The iterator can then check this value whenever asked for the next element and throw an exception if it has changed. The version number field should be wide enough that it can never wrap around while a traversal is in progress. An `int` normally suffices.

This strategy is used in the `java.util.Iterator` classes in the collections framework. We can apply it here to a subclass of `ExpandableArray` that updates version numbers as an after-action (see §1.4.3):

```
class ExpandableArrayWithIterator extends ExpandableArray {
  protected int version = 0;

  public ExpandableArrayWithIterator(int cap) { super(cap); }

  public synchronized void removeLast()
   throws NoSuchElementException {
    super.removeLast();
    ++version;                  // advertise update
  }

  public synchronized void add(Object x) {
    super.add(x);
    ++version;
  }

  public synchronized Iterator iterator() {
    return new EAIterator();
  }

  protected class EAIterator implements Iterator {
    protected final int currentVersion;
    protected int currentIndex = 0;

    EAIterator() { currentVersion = version; }

    public Object next() {
      synchronized(ExpandableArrayWithIterator.this) {
        if (currentVersion != version)
          throw new ConcurrentModificationException();
        else if (currentIndex == size)
          throw new NoSuchElementException();
        else
          return data[currentIndex++];
      }
    }

    public boolean hasNext() {
      synchronized(ExpandableArrayWithIterator.this) {
        return (currentIndex < size);
      }
    }

    public void remove() {
      // similar
    }
  }
}
```

Here, the print loop would be expressed as:

```
for (Iterator it = v.iterator(); it.hasNext();) {
  try {
    System.out.println(it.next());
  }
  catch (NoSuchElementException ex) { /* ... fail ... */ }
  catch (ConcurrentModificationException ex) {
    /* ... fail ... */
  }
}
```

Even here, choices for dealing with failures are often very limited. A `ConcurrentModificationException` often signifies unplanned, unwanted interactions among threads that should be remedied rather than patched over.

The versioned iterator approach encapsulates the design choices underlying the data structure, at the price of occasionally undue conservatism. For example, an interleaved `add` operation would not interfere with the required semantics of a typical traversal, yet would cause an exception to be thrown here. Versioned iterators are still a good default choice for collection classes, in part because it is relatively easy to layer aggregate traversal or client-side locking on top of these iterators, but not vice versa.

2.2.3.4 Visitors

The *Visitor* pattern described in the *Design Patterns* book extends the notion of iterators to provide support for clients performing operations on sets of objects connected in arbitrary ways, thus forming the nodes of some kind of tree or graph rather than the sequential list seen in `ExpandableArray`. (Less relevantly here, the Visitor pattern also supports polymorphic operations on each node.)

The options and concerns for visitors and other extended senses of traversal are similar to, and can sometimes be reduced to, those seen in simple iterators. For example, you might first create a list of all nodes to traverse and then apply any of the above techniques for traversing the list. However, locks here would lock only the list, not the nodes themselves. This is usually the best policy. But if you need to ensure that all of the nodes are locked during the entire traversal, consider forms of confinement (see §2.3.3) or containment locking (see §2.4.5).

Conversely, if traversal is arranged by every node supporting a `nextNode` method, and you do not want to end up simultaneously holding all locks to all nodes encountered during traversal, synchronization of each node must be released before proceeding to the next node, as described in §2.4.1 and §2.5.1.4.

2.2.4 Statics and Singletons

As described in the *Design Patterns* book, a Singleton class intentionally supports
only one instance. It is convenient to declare that single instance as a `static`, in
which case both class and instance methods may use the same lock.

Here is one way to define a fully synchronized singleton class that postpones
construction of the instance until it is first accessed via the `instance` method.
This class represents a counter that could be used to assign global sequence numbers to objects, transactions, messages, etc., across different classes in an application. (Just to illustrate computation during initialization, the initial value is set to a
randomly chosen number with at least 2^{62} positive successors.)

```
class LazySingletonCounter {
  private final long initial;
  private long count;

  private LazySingletonCounter() {
    initial = Math.abs(new java.util.Random().nextLong() / 2);
    count = initial;
  }

  private static LazySingletonCounter s = null;

  private static final Object classLock =
                          LazySingletonCounter.class;

  public static LazySingletonCounter instance() {
    synchronized(classLock) {
      if (s == null)
        s = new LazySingletonCounter();
      return s;
    }
  }

  public long next() {
    synchronized(classLock) { return count++; }
  }

  public void reset() {
    synchronized(classLock) { count = initial; }
  }
}
```

The locking mechanics seen here (or any of several minor variants) prevent
situations in which two different threads invoke the `instance` method at about the
same time, causing two instances to be created. Only one of these instances would
be bound to s and returned the next time `instance` is invoked. As discussed in

§2.4.1, in a few cases this and other intentional semantic weakenings might be acceptable; in most cases, however, this would be a serious error.

An easier way to avoid this kind of error is to avoid lazy initialization. Because JVMs perform dynamic loading of classes, there is usually no need to support lazy initialization of singletons. A `static` field is not initialized until the class is loaded at runtime. While there are no guarantees about exactly when a class will be loaded (beyond that it will be loaded by the time it is accessed by executing code), full initialization of statics is less likely to impose significant start-up overhead than in most other languages. So, unless initialization is both very expensive and rarely needed, it is usually preferable to take the simpler approach of declaring a singleton as a `static final` field. For example:

```
class EagerSingletonCounter {
  private final long initial;
  private long count;

  private EagerSingletonCounter() {
    initial = Math.abs(new java.util.Random().nextLong() / 2);
    count = initial;
  }

  private static final EagerSingletonCounter s =
                              new EagerSingletonCounter();

  public static EagerSingletonCounter instance() { return s; }
  public synchronized long next() { return count++; }
  public synchronized void reset() { count = initial; }
}
```

Simpler yet, if there is no compelling reason to rely on instances, you can instead define and use a version with all `static` methods, as in:

```
class StaticCounter {
  private static final long initial =
              Math.abs(new java.util.Random().nextLong() / 2);
  private static long count = initial;
  private StaticCounter() { } // disable instance construction
  public static synchronized long next() { return count++; }
  public static synchronized void reset() { count = initial; }
}
```

Also, consider using `ThreadLocal` (see §2.3.2) rather than a Singleton in situations where it is more appropriate to create one instance of a class per thread than one instance per program.

2.2.5 Deadlock

Although fully synchronized atomic objects are always safe, threads using them
are not always live. Consider for example a `Cell` class containing a method that
swaps values with another `Cell`:

```
class Cell {                                               // Do not use
  private long value;
  synchronized long getValue() { return value; }
  synchronized void setValue(long v) { value = v; }

  synchronized void swapValue(Cell other) {
    long t = getValue();
    long v = other.getValue();
    setValue(v);
    other.setValue(t);
  }
}
```

`SwapValue` is a synchronized *multiparty* action — one that intrinsically acquires
locks on multiple objects. Without further precautions, it is possible for two different threads, one running `a.swapValue(b)`, and the other running
`b.swapValue(a)`, to *deadlock* when encountering the following trace:

Thread 1	Thread 2
acquire lock for a on entering `a.swapValue(b)`	
pass lock for a (since already held) on entering `t = getValue()`	acquire lock for b on entering `b.swapValue(a)`
block waiting for lock for b on entering `v = other.getValue()`	pass lock for b (since already held) on entering `t = getValue()`
	block waiting for lock for a on entering `v = other.getValue()`

At this point both threads block forever.

More generally, deadlock is possible when two or more objects are mutually
accessible from two or more threads, and each thread holds one lock while trying
to obtain another lock already held by another thread.

2.2.6   Resource Ordering

The need to preclude or recover from deadlocks and other liveness failures motivates the use of other exclusion techniques presented in this chapter. However, one simple technique, *resource ordering* can be applied to classes such as Cell without otherwise altering their structure.

The idea behind resource ordering is to associate a numerical (or any other strictly orderable data type) tag with each object that can be held in a nested synchronized block or method. If synchronization is always performed in least-first order with respect to object tags, then situations can never arise in which one thread has the synchronization lock for x while waiting for y and another has the lock for y while waiting for x. Instead, they will both obtain the locks in the same order, thus avoiding this form of deadlock. More generally, resource ordering can be used whenever there is a need to arbitrarily break symmetry or force precedence in a concurrent design.

In some contexts (see for example §2.4.5), there may be reasons to impose some specific ordering rules surrounding a set of locks. But in others, you can use any convenient tag for lock-ordering purposes. For example, you may be able to use the value returned by System.identityHashCode. This method always returns the default implementation of Object.hashCode, even if a class overrides the hashCode method. While there is no guarantee that identityHashCode is unique, in practice run-time systems rely on codes to be distinct with a very high probability. To be even safer about it, you could override method hashCode or introduce another tag method to ensure uniqueness in any classes employing resource ordering. For example, you could assign each object a sequence number using one of the classes in §2.2.4.

One further check, *alias detection*, can be applied in methods using nested synchronization to handle cases in which two (or more) of the references are actually bound to the same object. For example, in swapValue, you can check whether a Cell is being asked to swap with itself. This kind of check is strictly optional here (but see §2.5.1). Synchronization lock access is per-thread, not per-invocation. Additional attempts to synchronize on already held objects will still work. However, routine alias-checking is a useful way to forestall downstream functionality, efficiency, and synchronization-based complications. It may be applied before using synchronization surrounding two or more objects unless they are of distinct, unrelated types. (Two references of two unrelated declared types cannot possibly be referring to the same object anyway, so there is no reason to check.)

A better version of swapValue, applying both resource ordering and alias detection, can be written as:

```
public void swapValue(Cell other) {
  if (other == this) // alias check
    return;
  else if (System.identityHashCode(this) <
           System.identityHashCode(other))
    this.doSwapValue(other);
  else
    other.doSwapValue(this);
}

protected synchronized void doSwapValue(Cell other) {
  // same as original public version:
  long t = getValue();
  long v = other.getValue();
  setValue(v);
  other.setValue(t);
}
```

As a minor efficiency tweak, we could further streamline the code inside doSwapValue first to acquire the necessary locks, and then directly access the value fields. This avoids a self-call to a synchronized method while already holding the required lock, at the minor expense of adding lines of code that would need to be changed if the nature of the fields were ever modified:

```
// slightly faster version
protected synchronized void doSwapValue(Cell other) {
  synchronized(other) {
    long t = value;
    value = other.value;
    other.value = t;
  }
}
```

Note that the lock for this is obtained via the synchronized method qualifier, but the lock for other is explicitly acquired. A further, very tiny (perhaps nonexistent) performance improvement might be obtained by folding the code in doSwapValue into swapValue, remembering to acquire both locks explicitly.

Lock-ordering problems are by no means restricted to methods using nested synchronization. The issue arises in any code sequence in which a synchronized method holding the lock on one object in turn calls a synchronized method on another object. However, there is less opportunity to apply resource ordering in cascaded calls: In the general case, one object cannot know for sure which other objects will be involved in downstream calls and whether they require synchronization. This is one reason that deadlock can be such a hard problem in open systems (see §2.5) when you cannot release synchronization during calls (see §2.4.1).

2.2.7   The Java Memory Model

Consider the tiny class, defined without any synchronization:

```
final class SetCheck {
  private int  a = 0;
  private long b = 0;

  void set() {
    a =  1;
    b = -1;
  }

  boolean check() {
    return ((b ==   0) ||
            (b == -1 && a == 1));
  }
}
```

In a purely sequential language, the method `check` could never return `false`. This holds even though compilers, run-time systems, and hardware might process this code in a way that you might not intuitively expect. For example, any of the following might apply to the execution of method `set`:

- The compiler may rearrange the order of the statements, so b may be assigned before a. If the method is inlined, the compiler may further rearrange the orders with respect to yet other statements.

- The processor may rearrange the execution order of machine instructions corresponding to the statements, or even execute them at the same time.

- The memory system (as governed by cache control units) may rearrange the order in which writes are committed to memory cells corresponding to the variables. These writes may overlap with other computations and memory actions.

- The compiler, processor, and/or memory system may interleave the machine-level effects of the two statements. For example on a 32-bit machine, the high-order word of b may be written first, followed by the write to a, followed by the write to the low-order word of b.

- The compiler, processor, and/or memory system may cause the memory cells representing the variables not to be updated until sometime after (if ever) a subsequent check is called, but instead to maintain the corresponding values (for example in CPU registers) in such a way that the code still has the intended effect.

In a sequential language, none of this can matter so long as program execution obeys *as-if-serial* semantics[2]. Sequential programs cannot depend on the internal processing details of statements within simple code blocks, so they are free to be manipulated in all these ways. This provides essential flexibility for compilers and machines. Exploitation of such opportunities (via pipelined superscalar CPUs, multilevel caches, load/store balancing, interprocedural register allocation, and so on) is responsible for a significant amount of the massive improvements in execution speed seen in computing over the past decade. The as-if-serial property of these manipulations shields sequential programmers from needing to know if or how they take place. Programmers who never create their own threads are almost never impacted by these issues.

Things are different in concurrent programming. Here, it is entirely possible for check to be called in one thread while set is being executed in another, in which case the check might be "spying" on the optimized execution of set. And if any of the above manipulations occur, it is possible for check to return false. For example, as detailed below, check could read a value for the long b that is neither 0 nor -1, but instead a half-written in-between value. Also, out-of-order execution of the statements in set may cause check to read b as -1 but then read a as still 0.

In other words, not only may concurrent executions be interleaved, but they may also be reordered and otherwise manipulated in an optimized form that bears little resemblance to their source code. As compiler and run-time technology matures and multiprocessors become more prevalent, such phenomena become more common. They can lead to surprising results for programmers with backgrounds in sequential programming (in other words, just about all programmers) who have never been exposed to the underlying execution properties of allegedly sequential code. This can be the source of subtle concurrent programming errors.

In almost all cases, there is an obvious, simple way to avoid contemplation of all the complexities arising in concurrent programs due to optimized execution mechanics: *Use synchronization*. For example, if both methods in class SetCheck are declared as synchronized, then you can be sure that no internal processing details can affect the intended outcome of this code.

But sometimes you cannot or do not want to use synchronization. Or perhaps you must reason about someone else's code that does not use it. In these cases you must rely on the minimal guarantees about resulting semantics spelled out by the *Java Memory Model*. This model allows the kinds of manipulations listed above,

---

[2.] Somewhat more precisely, as-if-serial (also known as program order) semantics can be defined as any execution traversal of the graph formed by ordering only those operations that have value or control dependencies with respect to each other under a language's base expression and statement semantics.

but bounds their potential effects on execution semantics and additionally points to some techniques programmers can use to control some aspects of these semantics (most of which are discussed in §2.4).

The Java Memory Model is part of *The Java™ Language Specification*, described primarily in *JLS* chapter 17. Here, we discuss only the basic motivation, properties, and programming consequences of the model. The treatment here reflects a few clarifications and updates that are missing from the first edition of *JLS*[3].

The assumptions underlying the model can be viewed as an idealization of a standard SMP machine of the sort described in §1.2.4:

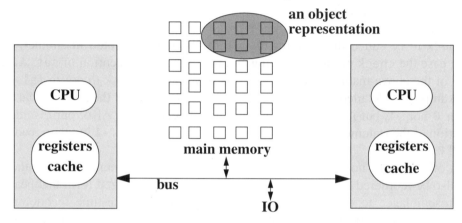

For purposes of the model, every thread can be thought of as running on a different CPU from any other thread. Even on multiprocessors, this is infrequent in practice, but the fact that this CPU-per-thread mapping is among the legal ways to implement threads accounts for some of the model's initially surprising properties. For example, because CPUs hold registers that cannot be directly accessed by other CPUs, the model must allow for cases in which one thread does not know about values being manipulated by another thread. However, the impact of the model is by no means restricted to multiprocessors. The actions of compilers and processors can lead to identical concerns even on single-CPU systems.

The model does not specifically address whether the kinds of execution tactics discussed above are performed by compilers, CPUs, cache controllers, or any other mechanism. It does not even discuss them in terms of classes, objects, and methods familiar to programmers. Instead, the model defines an abstract relation between threads and main memory. Every thread is defined to have a *working*

---

[3]. As of this writing, the memory model and other relevant sections of *JLS* are still being updated to cover the Java 2 Platform. Please check the online supplement for any changes that impact the material in this section.

memory (an abstraction of caches and registers) in which to store values. The model guarantees a few properties surrounding the interactions of instruction sequences corresponding to methods and memory cells corresponding to fields. Most rules are phrased in terms of when values must be transferred between the main memory and per-thread working memory. The rules address three intertwined issues:

Atomicity. Which instructions must have indivisible effects. For purposes of the model, these rules need to be stated only for simple reads and writes of memory cells representing fields — instance and static variables, also including array elements, but not including local variables inside methods.

Visibility. Under what conditions the effects of one thread are visible to another. The effects of interest here are writes to fields, as seen via reads of those fields.

Ordering. Under what conditions the effects of operations can appear out of order to any given thread. The main ordering issues surround reads and writes associated with sequences of assignment statements.

When synchronization is used consistently, each of these properties has a simple characterization: All changes made in one `synchronized` method or block are atomic and visible with respect to other `synchronized` methods and blocks employing the same lock, and processing of `synchronized` methods or blocks within any given thread is in program-specified order. Even though processing of statements *within* blocks may be out of order, this cannot matter to other threads employing synchronization.

When synchronization is not used or is used inconsistently, answers become more complex. The guarantees made by the memory model are weaker than most programmers intuitively expect, and are also weaker than those typically provided on any given JVM implementation. This imposes additional obligations on programmers attempting to ensure the object consistency relations that lie at the heart of exclusion practices: Objects must maintain invariants as seen by all threads that rely on them, not just by the thread performing any given state modification.

The most important rules and properties specified by the model are discussed below.

2.2.7.1 Atomicity

Accesses and updates to the memory cells corresponding to fields of any type except `long` or `double` are guaranteed to be atomic. This includes fields serving as references to other objects. Additionally, atomicity extends to `volatile long` and `double`. (Even though non-volatile `long`s and `double`s are not guaranteed atomic, they are of course allowed to be.)

Atomicity guarantees ensure that when a non-`long`/`double` field is used in an expression, you will obtain either its initial value or some value that was written by some thread, but not some jumble of bits resulting from two or more threads both trying to write values at the same time. However, as seen below, atomicity alone does not guarantee that you will get the value most recently written by any thread. For this reason, atomicity guarantees *per se* normally have little impact on concurrent program design.

2.2.7.2   Visibility

Changes to fields made by one thread are *guaranteed* to be visible to other threads only under the following conditions:

1. A writing thread releases a synchronization lock and a reading thread subsequently acquires that same synchronization lock.

   In essence, releasing a lock forces a flush of all writes from working memory employed by the thread, and acquiring a lock forces a (re)load of the values of accessible fields. While lock actions provide exclusion only for the operations performed within a `synchronized` method or block, these memory effects are defined to cover all fields used by the thread performing the action.

   Note the double meaning of `synchronized`: it deals with locks that permit higher-level synchronization protocols, while at the same time dealing with the memory system (sometimes via low-level *memory barrier* machine instructions) to keep value representations in synch across threads. This reflects one way in which concurrent programming bears more similarity to distributed programming than to sequential programming. The latter sense of `synchronized` may be viewed as a mechanism by which a method running in one thread indicates that it is willing to send and/or receive changes to variables to and from methods running in other threads. From this point of view, using locks and passing messages might be seen merely as syntactic variants of each other.

2. If a field is declared as `volatile`, any value written to it is flushed and made visible by the writer thread before the writer thread performs any further memory operation (i.e., for the purposes at hand it is flushed immediately). Reader threads must reload the values of `volatile` fields upon each access.

3. The first time a thread accesses a field of an object, it sees either the initial value[4] of the field or a value since written by some other thread.

   Among other consequences, it is bad practice to make available the reference to an incompletely constructed object (see §2.1.2). It can also be risky to start new threads inside a constructor, especially in a class that may be subclassed. `Thread.start` has the same memory effects as a lock release by the thread calling `start`, followed by a lock acquire by the started thread. If a `Runnable` superclass invokes `new Thread(this).start()` before subclass constructors execute, then the object might not be fully initialized when the run method executes. Similarly, if you create and start a new thread T and then create an object X used by thread T, you cannot be sure that the fields of X will be visible to T unless you employ synchronization surrounding all references to object X. Or, when applicable, you can create X before starting T.

4. As a thread terminates, all written variables are flushed to main memory.

   For example, if one thread synchronizes on the termination of another thread using `Thread.join`, then it is guaranteed to see the effects made by that thread (see §4.3.2).

Note that visibility problems *never* arise when passing references to objects across methods in the *same* thread.

The memory model guarantees that, given the eventual occurrence of the above operations, a particular update to a particular field made by one thread will eventually be visible to another. But *eventually* can be an arbitrarily long time. Long stretches of code in threads that use no synchronization can be hopelessly out of synch with other threads with respect to values of fields. In particular, it is always wrong to write loops waiting for values written by other threads unless the fields are `volatile` or accessed via synchronization (see §3.2.6).

The model also allows inconsistent visibility in the absence of synchronization. For example, it is possible to obtain a fresh value for one field of an object, but a stale value for another. Similarly, it is possible to read a fresh, updated value of a reference variable, but a stale value of one of the fields of the object now being referenced.

However, the rules do not require visibility failures across threads, they merely allow these failures to occur. This is one aspect of the fact that not using synchronization in multithreaded code doesn't guarantee safety violations, it just allows them. On most current JVM implementations and platforms, even those employing multiple processors, detectable visibility failures rarely occur. The use of common caches across threads sharing a CPU, the lack of aggressive compiler-based optimizations, and the presence of strong cache consistency hardware often cause values to act as if they propagate immediately among threads. This makes

---

[4.] As of this writing, the *JLS* does not yet clearly state that the visible initial value read for an initialized `final` field is the value assigned in its initializer or constructor. However, this anticipated clarification is assumed throughout this book. The visible initial default values of non-final fields are zero for scalars and `null` for references.

testing for freedom from visibility-based errors impractical, since such errors might occur extremely rarely, or only on platforms you do not have access to, or only on those that have not even been built yet. These same comments apply to multithreaded safety failures more generally. Concurrent programs that do not use synchronization fail for many reasons, including memory consistency problems.

2.2.7.3   Ordering

Ordering rules fall under two cases, within-thread and between-thread:

- From the point of view of the thread performing the actions in a method, instructions proceed in the normal as-if-serial manner that applies in sequential programming languages.

- From the point of view of other threads that might be "spying" on this thread by concurrently running unsynchronized methods, almost anything can happen. The only useful constraint is that the relative orderings of `synchronized` methods and blocks, as well as operations on `volatile` fields, are always preserved.

Again, these are only the minimal guaranteed properties. In any given program or platform, you may find stricter orderings. But you cannot rely on them, and you may find it difficult to test for code that would fail on JVM implementations that have different properties but still conform to the rules.

Note that the within-thread point of view is implicitly adopted in all other discussions of semantics in *JLS*. For example, arithmetic expression evaluation is performed in left-to-right order (*JLS* section 15.6) as viewed by the thread performing the operations, but not necessarily as viewed by other threads.

The within-thread as-if-serial property is helpful only when only one thread at a time is manipulating variables, due to synchronization, structural exclusion, or pure chance. When multiple threads are all running unsynchronized code that reads and writes common fields, then arbitrary interleavings, atomicity failures, race conditions, and visibility failures may result in execution patterns that make the notion of as-if-serial just about meaningless with respect to any given thread.

Even though *JLS* addresses some particular legal and illegal reorderings that can occur, interactions with these other issues reduce practical guarantees to saying that the results may reflect just about any possible interleaving of just about any possible reordering. So there is no point in trying to reason about the ordering properties of such code.

2.2.7.4 Volatile

In terms of atomicity, visibility, and ordering, declaring a field as `volatile` is nearly identical in effect to using a little fully synchronized class protecting only that field via get/set methods, as in:

```
final class VFloat {
  private float value;

  final synchronized void  set(float f) { value = f; }
  final synchronized float get()        { return value; }
}
```

Declaring a field as `volatile` differs only in that no locking is involved. In particular, composite read/write operations such as the "++" operation on `volatile` variables are *not* performed atomically.

Also, ordering and visibility effects surround only the single access or update to the `volatile` field itself. Declaring a reference field as `volatile` does not ensure visibility of *non*-`volatile` fields that are accessed via this reference. Similarly, declaring an array field as `volatile` does not ensure visibility of its elements. Volatility cannot be manually propagated for arrays because array elements themselves cannot be declared as `volatile`.

Because no locking is involved, declaring fields as `volatile` is likely to be cheaper than using synchronization, or at least no more expensive. However, if `volatile` fields are accessed frequently inside methods, their use is likely to lead to slower performance than would locking the entire methods.

Declaring fields as `volatile` can be useful when you do not need locking for any other reason, yet values must be accurately accessible across multiple threads. This may occur when:

- The field need not obey any invariants with respect to others.

- Writes to the field do not depend on its current value.

- No thread ever writes an illegal value with respect to intended semantics.

- The actions of readers do not depend on values of other non-volatile fields.

Using `volatile` fields can make sense when it is somehow known that only one thread can change a field, but many other threads are allowed to read it at any time. For example, a `Thermometer` class might declare its `temperature` field as `volatile`. As discussed in §3.4.2, a `volatile` can be useful as a completion flag. Additional examples are illustrated in §4.4, where the use of lightweight executable frameworks automates some aspects of synchronization, but `volatile` declarations are needed to ensure that result field values are visible across tasks.

2.2.8   Further Readings

Features of computer architectures that impact multithreaded programs are described in:

Schimmel, Curt. *UNIX Systems for Modern Architectures Symmetric Multiprocessing and Caching for Kernel Programmers*, Addison-Wesley, 1994.

Patterson, David, and John Hennessy. *Computer Organization and Design: The Hardware/Software Interface*, Morgan Kaufmann, 1997. See also its online supplement with links to further resources on specific machine architectures.

Memory consistency models are the subject of increasing attention as both multiprocessors and multithreaded programs become more common and their interactions become more of a concern. At least with respect to locking, the Java memory model is closest to the family of *release consistency* models. For an overview, see:

Adve, Sarita and K. Gharachorloo. "Shared Memory Consistency Models: A Tutorial", *IEEE Computer*, December 1996, 66-76. See also follow-ups, including: "Recent Advances in Memory Consistency Models for Hardware Shared-Memory Systems" *Proceedings of the IEEE*, special issue on distributed shared memory, 1999.

2.3 Confinement

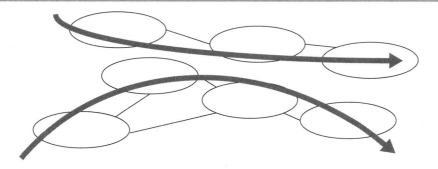

Confinement employs encapsulation techniques to structurally guarantee that at most one activity at a time can possibly access a given object. This statically ensures that the accessibility of a given object is *unique* to a single thread without needing to rely on dynamic locking on each access. The main tactic is to define methods and classes that establish leak-proof *ownership* domains guaranteeing that only one thread, or one thread at a time, can ever access a confined object.

Confinement practices are similar to other security measures that guarantee that no sensitive information ever escapes from a domain. The information leakage of interest here is access to objects, almost always via references to these objects. This issue poses the same kinds of challenges seen in other aspects of security: It is sometimes difficult to demonstrate that not even one leak is possible, yet confinement cannot be relied on unless a design is proven leak-proof. However, this task is less critical than in some other aspects of security, since there are backup strategies. Thus, when you cannot ensure confinement, you can employ other exclusion techniques described in this chapter.

Confinement relies on the scoping, access control, and security features of a given language that support data hiding and encapsulation. However, the senses of confinement needed to ensure uniqueness cannot be completely enforced by language mechanisms. There are four categories to check to see if a reference r to an object x can *escape* from a method m executing within some activity:

- m passes r as an argument in a method invocation or object constructor.

- m passes r as the return value from a method invocation.

- m records r in some field that is accessible from another activity (in the most flagrant case, `static` fields that are accessible anywhere).

- m releases (in any of the above ways) another reference that can in turn be traversed to access r.

Selected leakages can sometimes be tolerated if you can somehow guarantee that escapes are allowed only to methods that cannot cause state changes (field assignments) in the objects of interest (see §2.4.3).

In some closed classes and subsystems (see §1.3.4), these matters can be exhaustively checked. In open systems, most constraints can only be maintained as design rules, as assisted by tools and reviews.

This section discusses four sorts of confinement. The first and simplest, *method* confinement, involves ordinary programming practices surrounding local variables. The second, *thread* confinement, introduces techniques for restricting access within threads. The third, *object* confinement, uses OO encapsulation techniques to provide the stronger guarantees needed to ensure uniqueness of access for methods entering objects. The fourth, *group* confinement, extends these techniques to collaborating sets of objects operating across multiple threads.

2.3.1 Confinement Across Methods

If a given method invocation creates an object and does not let it escape, then it can be sure that no other threads will interfere with (or even know about) its use of that object. Hiding access within local scopes is a common encapsulation tactic in all forms of programming.

With only a modicum of care, these techniques can be extended to *sequences* of method invocations. For example, consider the following class that uses `java.awt.Point`. This `Point` class is defined as a simple record-style class with `public` x and y fields, so it would be unwise to share instances across threads.

```
class Plotter {                                          // Fragments
  // ...

  public void showNextPoint() {
    Point p = new Point();
    p.x = computeX();
    p.y = computeY();
    display(p);
  }

  protected void display(Point p) {
    // somehow arrange to show p.
  }
}
```

Here the `showNextPoint` method creates a local `Point`. It allows the `Point` to escape into `display(p)` only in a *tail call*, after `showNextPoint` is sure never to access it again, even if the `Point` is later accessed from another thread. (Access

100

from another thread *could* occur here: Essentially all graphics-based programs somehow rely on the AWT event thread — see §1.1.1.3 and §4.1.4 — although it is unlikely that the thread would modify the `Point` object.)

This is an example of a *hand-off* protocol that ensures that, at any given time, at most one actively executing method can access an object. This tail-call version is the simplest and usually best form. Similar usages are seen in *factory* methods that construct and initialize an object and finally return it, as seen for example in the `ParticleApplet.makeThread` method in §1.1.1.3.

2.3.1.1 Sessions

Many hand-off sequences are structured as *sessions* in which some public entry method constructs objects that will be confined to a sequence of operations comprising a service. This entry method should also be responsible for any cleanup operations required upon completion of the sequence. For example:

```
class SessionBasedService {                              // Fragments
  // ...
  public void service() {
    OutputStream output = null;
    try {
      output = new FileOutputStream("...");
      doService(output);
    }
    catch (IOException e) {
      handleIOFailure();
    }
    finally {
      try { if (output != null) output.close(); }
      catch (IOException ignore) {} // ignore exception in close
    }
  }


  void doService(OutputStream s) throws IOException {
    s.write(...);
    // ... possibly more handoffs ...
  }
}
```

When you have a choice between them, it is almost always preferable to perform cleanup in `finally` clauses rather than relying on finalization (i.e., overriding `Object.finalize`). Use of `finally` provides a stronger guarantee about when cleanup will take place, which helps conserve possibly scarce resources such as files. In contrast, finalizers generally trigger asynchronously as a result of garbage collection, if ever.

2.3.1.2 Alternative protocols

Tail-call hand-offs do not apply if a method must access an object after a call or must make multiple calls. Additional design rules are needed to cover cases such as a revised `Plotter` class with method:

```
public void showNextPointV2() {
   Point p = new Point();
   p.x = computeX();
   p.y = computeY();
   display(p);
   recordDistance(p); // added
}
```

Options include:

Caller copies. When the objects being passed around represent data values such as points in which object identity does not matter, then the caller can make a copy of the object for use by the receiver. Here, for example,
```
display(p);
```
would be replaced by:
```
display(new Point(p.x, p.y));
```

Receiver copies. If a method knows nothing about the usage constraints surrounding an object reference sent as an argument (and again, if object identity does not matter), it can conservatively make a copy for its own local use. Here for example, the `display` method could have as its first line:
```
Point localPoint = new Point(p.x, p.y);
```

Using scalar arguments. Uncertainties about caller and receiver responsibilities can be eliminated by not sending references at all, but instead sending scalar arguments providing enough information for the receiver to construct an object if desired. Here, for example, we could reparameterize `display` to:
```
protected void display(int xcoord, int ycoord) { ... }
```
and the call to:
```
display(p.x, p.y);
```

Trust. A receiver (or rather its author) may promise not to modify or transmit objects accessible via reference arguments. It must in turn ensure lack of unwanted access in any downstream calls.

If none of these can be arranged, then pure confinement is not guaranteed to succeed, and other solutions described in this chapter should be applied. For example, if use of `java.awt.Point` were not required here, you could instead use an `ImmutablePoint` class to ensure lack of modification (see §2.4.4).

2.3.2 Confinement Within Threads

Thread-based confinement techniques[5] extend those for method sequences. In fact, the simplest and often best technique is to use a thread-per-session design (see §4.1) that is otherwise identical to session-based confinement. For example, you can initialize hand-offs in the base of a run method:

```
class ThreadPerSessionBasedService { // fragments
  // ...
  public void service() {
    Runnable r = new Runnable() {
      public void run() {
        OutputStream output = null;
        try {
          output = new FileOutputStream("...");
          doService(output);
        }
        catch (IOException e) {
          handleIOFailure();
        }
        finally {
          try { if (output != null) output.close(); }
          catch (IOException ignore) {}
        }
      }
    };
    new Thread(r).start();
  }

  void doService(OutputStream s) throws IOException {
    s.write(...);
    // ... possibly more hand-offs ...
  }
}
```

Some approaches to concurrent software design (such as CSP — see §4.5.1) arrange or require that *all* fields accessible within a thread be strictly confined to that thread. This mimics the enforced isolation of address spaces seen in process — versus thread — based concurrent programming (see §1.2.2).

However, note that it is generally impossible to confine access to *every* object used in a given thread. All threads running on a given JVM must ultimately share access to at least some underlying resources, for example those controlled via methods in the java.lang.System class.

[5.] Even though this section presupposes only knowledge of the basic Thread usages presented in Chapter 1, you may find a cursory glance through Chapter 4 helpful.

2.3.2.1   Thread-specific fields

In addition to receiving confined references along call chains, the method invocations executing within a single thread can access the `Thread` object representing the thread they are running in, and any further information traversable from there. The static method `Thread.currentThread()` can be called from any method and returns the `Thread` object of the caller.

You can exploit this by adding fields to `Thread` subclasses and supplying methods to access them *only* from within the current thread. For example:

```
class ThreadWithOutputStream extends Thread {
  private OutputStream output;

  ThreadWithOutputStream(Runnable r, OutputStream s) {
    super(r);
    output = s;
  }

  static ThreadWithOutputStream current()
   throws ClassCastException {
    return (ThreadWithOutputStream) (currentThread());
  }

  static OutputStream getOutput() { return current().output; }

  static void setOutput(OutputStream s) { current().output = s;}
}
```

This class could be used, for example, in:

```
class ServiceUsingThreadWithOutputStream {          // Fragments
  // ...
  public void service() throws IOException {
    OutputStream output = new FileOutputStream("...");
    Runnable r = new Runnable() {
      public void run() {
        try { doService(); } catch (IOException e) { ... }
      }
    };
    new ThreadWithOutputStream(r, output).start();
  }

  void doService() throws IOException {
    ThreadWithOutputStream.current().getOutput().write(...);
    // ...
  }
}
```

2.3.2.2 ThreadLocal

The java.lang.ThreadLocal utility class removes one obstacle to using thread-specific techniques, their reliance on special Thread subclasses. This class allows thread-specific variables to be added in an ad-hoc fashion to just about any code.

The ThreadLocal class internally maintains a table associating data (Object references) with Thread instances. ThreadLocal supports set and get methods to access data held by the current Thread. The java.lang.InheritableThreadLocal class extends ThreadLocal to automatically propagate per-thread variables to any threads that are in turn created by the current thread.

Most designs employing ThreadLocal may be seen as extensions of the Singleton (see §2.2.4) pattern. Rather than constructing one instance of a resource per program, most applications of ThreadLocals construct one instance per thread. ThreadLocal variables are normally declared as static, and usually have package-scoped visibility so they may be accessed by any of a set of methods running in a given thread.

A ThreadLocal could be used in our running example as follows:

```
class ServiceUsingThreadLocal {                         // Fragments
  static ThreadLocal output = new ThreadLocal();

  public void service() {
    try {
      final OutputStream s = new FileOutputStream("...");
      Runnable r = new Runnable() {
        public void run() {
          output.set(s);
          try { doService(); }
          catch (IOException e) { ... }
          finally {
            try { s.close(); }
            catch (IOException ignore) {}
          }
        }
      };
      new Thread(r).start();
    }
    catch (IOException e) { ...}
  }

  void doService() throws IOException {
    ((OutputStream)(output.get())).write(...);
    // ...
  }
}
```

105

2.3.2.3 Applications and consequences

`ThreadLocals` and `Thread` subclasses holding thread-specific fields are typically used only when there is no other good option available. Advantages and disadvantages compared to other approaches such as session-based designs include:

- Housing object references in (or associated with) `Thread` objects allows methods running in the same thread to share them freely without needing to pass them explicitly as parameters. This can be a good option for maintaining contextual information such as the `AccessControlContext` of the current thread (as is done in the `java.security` packages) or the current working directory to be used for opening a set of related files. `ThreadLocal` can also be useful for constructing per-thread resource pools (see §3.4.1.2).

- The use of thread-specific variables tends to hide parameters that influence behavior and can make it harder to check for errors or leakage. In this sense, thread-specific variables present the same, although less extreme, traceability problems as static global variables.

- It is simple to guarantee that a status change to a thread-specific variable (for example, closing one output file and opening another) affects all relevant code. On the other hand, it can be difficult to guarantee that all such changes are properly coordinated.

- No synchronization is necessary for either reads or writes to thread-specific fields from within the thread. However, the access paths via `currentThread` or internal `ThreadLocal` tables are not likely to be any cheaper than uncontended `synchronized` method calls. So the use of thread-specific techniques generally improves performance only when objects would otherwise need to be shared and heavily contended for across threads.

- Use of thread-specific variables can detract from reusability by increasing code dependencies. This is a more serious problem under the `Thread` subclass approach. For example, the `doService` method is unusable unless run within a `ThreadWithOutputStream`. Any attempted use outside this context will result in a `ClassCastException` when invoking method `current`.

- Adding context information via `ThreadLocal` is sometimes the only way to let components work with existing code that does not propagate required information along call sequences (see §3.6.2).

- It is difficult to associate data with execution contexts when using lightweight executable frameworks that are only indirectly based upon class `Thread`, in particular, worker thread pools (see §4.1.4).

2.3.3 Confinement Within Objects

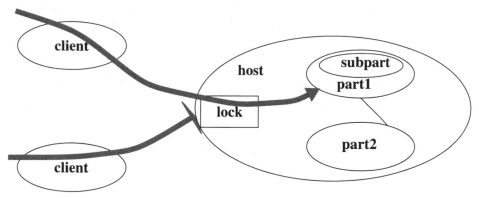

Even when you cannot confine access to an object within a particular method or thread, and so must use dynamic locking, you can confine all accesses *internal* to that object so that no *additional* locking is necessary once a thread enters one of its methods. In this way, the exclusion control for the outer *Host* container object automatically propagates to its internal *Parts*. For this to work, references to the Parts must not be leaked. (See §2.4.5 for strategies that may apply when leakage from containers cannot be precluded.)

Object confinement is seen in OO programs of all kinds. The main added requirement in concurrent contexts is to ensure synchronization at all entry points into the Host object. This employs the same techniques used when building fully synchronized objects (§2.2.2) holding instances of primitive scalar types such as double. But here they are applied to classes holding *references* to other objects.

In confinement-based designs, the Host object may be thought of as *owning* the inner Parts. Conversely, the Part objects may be thought of as being "physically" contained in their Host:

- The Host object constructs new instances of each Part object upon its own construction, assigning references to non-public fields. Fresh construction guarantees that references to the Part objects are not shared by any other object. Alternatively, the constructor can act as a hand-off point.

- As in any confinement technique, the Host object must never leak references to any Part object: It must never pass the references as arguments or return values of any method, and must ensure that the fields holding the references are inaccessible. Additionally, the Part objects must not leak their own identities, for example by sending this as a callback argument (see §4.3.1) to an external method. This guarantees that the Part objects are externally accessible only via methods on the Host object.

107

- In the most conservative variant, *fixed containment*, the Host object never reassigns reference fields pointing to the inner Part objects. This avoids the need for synchronization surrounding field updates in the Host object. Fixed containment implements the main sense of *aggregation* discussed in the *Design Patterns* book and denoted by UML diamond symbols.

- Unless the Host object is in turn confined within another, all appropriate methods of the host object are synchronized. (See §2.3.3.2 for one approach to defining both synchronized and unsynchronized versions of classes.) This guarantees that all accesses to the Parts (and all objects recursively constructed within them) maintain exclusion. Note that the Parts recursively held in a single confinement domain can invoke methods on one another without employing synchronization; only external accesses require synchronization.

Despite the demanding (and sometimes difficult to check) constraints that they must fulfill, object confinement techniques are very common, in part due to their utility in constructing Adapters and other delegation-based designs.

2.3.3.1 Adapters

Adapters (see §1.4.2) can be used to wrap bare unsynchronized *ground* objects within fully synchronized host objects. This leads to the simplest possible delegation-style designs: those in which the Adapters just forward all messages on to their delegates. Synchronized Adapters can be used to enclose "legacy" code originally written for sequential settings, as well as dynamically loaded code that you do not trust to be safe in multithreaded contexts.

An Adapter can also provide a single safe entry point into a heavily optimized (perhaps even into `native` code), computationally intensive set of functionality that, for the sake of efficiency, performs no internal concurrency control. Note, however, that no amount of wrapping can deal with `native` code that internally accesses fields unsafely across different threads.

Given one or more unprotected *ground* classes, you can define a synchronized Adapter class with a field, say `delegate`, holding a reference to a ground object, to which it forwards requests and relays replies. (Note that if any ground method contains a reply of the form `return this`, it should be translated as `return this` in the Adapter.) Delegate references need not be `final`, but if they are assignable, care must be taken that the Adapter obtains exclusive access. For example, an Adapter might occasionally assign the reference to a new internally constructed delegate.

As mentioned in §1.4, when it is important to ensure that Adapters are treated as identical to their internally held ground objects, you can override the `equals` and `hashCode` methods accordingly. However, there is no reason to do so in confinement-based designs since the internal objects are never leaked out, so will never be compared.

As one simple application, synchronized Adapters can be used to place synchronized access and update methods around a class containing `public` instance variables, such as a wide-open point class:

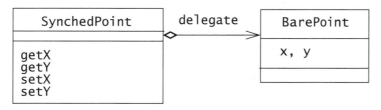

```
class BarePoint {
  public double x;
  public double y;
}

class SynchedPoint {

  protected final BarePoint delegate = new BarePoint();

  public synchronized double getX() { return delegate.x;}
  public synchronized double getY() { return delegate.y; }
  public synchronized void setX(double v) { delegate.x = v; }
  public synchronized void setY(double v) { delegate.y = v; }
}
```

The `java.util.Collection` framework uses an Adapter-based scheme to allow layered synchronization of collection classes. Except for `Vector` and `Hashtable`, the basic collection classes (such as `java.util.ArrayList`) are unsynchronized. However, anonymous synchronized Adapter classes can be constructed around the basic classes using for example:

```
List l = Collections.synchronizedList(new ArrayList());
```

2.3.3.2 Subclassing

When instances of a given class are always
intended to be confined within others, there is
no reason to synchronize their methods. But
when some instances are confined and some
are not, the safest practice is to synchronize
them appropriately, even though locking is not
required in all usage contexts. (See, however,
§2.4.5 and §3.3.4 for situations in which other
tactics may apply.)

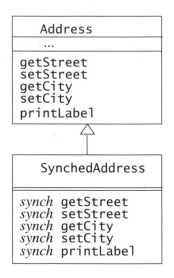

As compilers, tools, and run-time systems
continue to improve, they are increasingly able
to optimize away or minimize the overhead of
superfluous locking. However, when necessary
or desirable, you can arrange this manually by
defining multiple versions of a class and then
instantiating the appropriate version for a
given usage context. Among the simplest options is subclassing (see §1.4.3): creating an unprotected base class and then overriding each method m as a synchronized method calling super.m. For example:

```
class Address {                                                    // Fragments
  protected String street;
  protected String city;

  public String getStreet() { return street; }
  public void setStreet(String s) { street = s; }
  // ...
  public void printLabel(OutputStream s) { ... }
}

class SynchronizedAddress extends Address {
  // ...
  public synchronized String getStreet() {
    return super.getStreet();
  }
  public synchronized void setStreet(String s) {
    super.setStreet(s);
  }

  public synchronized void printLabel(OutputStream s) {
    super.printLabel(s);
  }
}
```

2.3.4 Confinement Within Groups

Groups of objects accessible across multiple threads can together ensure that only one of them at a time can access a given *resource* object. Here each resource is always owned by only one object, but ownership may change hands over time. Protocols for maintaining exclusive ownership are similar to those for handing off references across method invocations discussed in §2.3.1, but require more structure to manage conformance across groups of objects and threads.

Exclusively held resources are analogs of physical objects in the sense that:

- If you have one, then you can do something (with it) that you couldn't do otherwise.

- If you have it, then no one else has it.

- If you give it to someone else, then you no longer have it.

- If you destroy it, then no one will ever have it.

Any kind of object can be viewed as a resource if it is used in this manner. A more concrete way of characterizing this policy is that at most one field of one object refers to any exclusive resource at any given time. This fact can be exploited to ensure confinement within any given activity, thus reducing the need for dynamic synchronization on resource objects.

In some contexts and senses, protocols involving exclusive resources have been termed *tokens, batons, linear objects, capabilities,* and sometimes just *resources.* Several concurrent and distributed algorithms hinge on the idea that only one object at a time possesses a token. For a hardware-based example, token-ring networks maintain a single token that is continually circulated among the nodes. Each node may send messages only when it has the token.

While most transfer protocols are very simple, implementation can be error-prone: Fields containing references to objects just don't act much like physical objects when it comes to the notion of possession. For example, statements of the form x.r = y.s. do not cause owner y containing field s to lose possession after completion of the operation. The assignment instead results in both r and s still being bound. (This state of affairs is analogous to real-life problems in dealing with intellectual property rights and other forms of permission that do not intrinsically entail physical transfer operations.) This problem has led to a vast array of solutions, ranging from informal conventions to arbitrarily heavy legal apparatus.

To improve reliability, you can encapsulate protocols in methods performing the following operations, for distinct `Resource` objects r and s, and `Owner` objects x and y that may hold them in field `ref`. For emphasis, required locks are shown using `synchronized` blocks:

Acquire. Owner x establishes initial possession of r. This is usually the result of constructing or otherwise initializing r and setting:
```
synchronized(this) { ref = r; }
```

Forget. Owner x causes Resource r not to be possessed by any Owner. This is usually accomplished by the current Owner performing:
```
synchronized(this) { ref = null; }
```

Put (give). Owner y sends Owner x a message containing a reference to Resource r as an argument, after which y no longer has possession of r but x does.

```
        x                              y
void put(Resource s) {       void anAction(Owner x) { //...
  synchronized(this) {         Resource s;
    ref = s;                   synchronized(this) {
  }                              s = ref;
}                                ref = null;
                               }
                               x.put(s);
                             }
```

Take. Owner y requests a Resource from Owner x, which then sends r as the return value, relinquishing possession.

```
        x                              y
Resource take() {            void anAction(Owner x) { //...
  synchronized(this) {         Resource r = x.take();
    Resource r = ref;          synchronized(this) {
    ref = null;                  ref = r;
    return r;                  }
  }                          }
}
```

Exchange. Owner y trades its Resource s for Owner x's Resource r. This operation can also be used to perform a take via s = exchange(null), or a put via exchange(r), ignoring the result.

```
        x                              y
Resource exchange(Resource s){  void anAction(Owner x) { //...
  synchronized(this) {            synchronized(this) {
    Resource r = ref;               ref = x.exchange(ref);
    ref = s;                      }
    return r;                   }
  }
}
```

One application of such protocols arises when one object, say an `Output-Stream`, is *almost* completely confined within its host object, but must be used occasionally by other clients. In these cases, you can allow clients to `take` the internal object, operate on it, then `put` it back. In the meantime the host object will be temporarily crippled, but at least you are sure not to encounter integrity violations.

2.3.4.1 Rings

In the general case, resource management may involve maintaining pools (see §3.4.1), using message-passing networks that adopt particular exchange (see §3.4.3) or flow (see §4.2) policies, or adopting protocols that help avoid deadlock and resource exhaustion (see §4.5.1). But simpler transfer protocols can be used when you just need to ensure that an interconnected group of cooperating objects together strictly confines a resource. One way to implement this is to arrange a set of peer objects in a ring in which each node communicates only with a single neighbor.

As an unrealistically simplified example, consider a set of `PrintService` objects arranged as nodes in a ring, passing around rights to use a `Printer`. If a node is asked to print but does not currently have access, it tries to take it from its neighbor. This request cascades down to a node that has a printer. Defining the relevant methods as `synchronized` ensures that nodes do not give up the printer until they are finished with it. Here is a snapshot of one possible configuration.

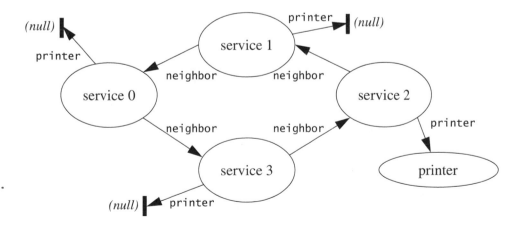

This design produces the desired effects only if all nodes obey the transfer protocol, the connections are set up appropriately, and at least one node has a printer. A sample start-up method shows one way to establish the required structure. Many additional extensions would be needed to allow dynamic connections of new `PrintService` objects, to support more than one `Printer`, and to deal with situations in which no `Printer` at all is available.

```
class Printer {
  public void printDocument(byte[] doc) { /* ... */ }
  // ...
}

class PrintService {

  protected PrintService neighbor = null; // node to take from
  protected Printer printer = null;

  public synchronized void print(byte[] doc) {
    getPrinter().printDocument(doc);
  }

  protected Printer getPrinter() {     // PRE: synch lock held
    if (printer == null)   // need to take from neighbor
      printer = neighbor.takePrinter();
    return printer;
  }

  synchronized Printer takePrinter() { // called from others
    if (printer != null) {
      Printer p = printer; // implement take protocol
      printer = null;
      return p;
    }
    else
      return neighbor.takePrinter(); // propagate
  }

  // initialization methods called only during start-up

  synchronized void setNeighbor(PrintService n) {
    neighbor = n;
  }

  synchronized void givePrinter(Printer p) {
    printer = p;
  }
```

```
// Sample code to initialize a ring of new services

public static void startUpServices(int nServices, Printer p)
  throws IllegalArgumentException {

  if (nServices <= 0 || p == null)
    throw new IllegalArgumentException();

  PrintService first = new PrintService();
  PrintService pred = first;

  for (int i = 1; i < nServices; ++i) {
    PrintService s = new PrintService();
    s.setNeighbor(pred);
    pred = s;
  }

  first.setNeighbor(pred);
  first.givePrinter(p);
  }
}
```

2.3.5 Further Readings

The Hermes programming language pioneered several language constructs and techniques for structuring concurrent and distributed programs, including reference transfer as a primitive. See:

Strom, Robert, David Bacon, Arthur Goldberg, Andy Lowry, Daniel Yellin, and Shaula Yemini. *Hermes: A Language for Distributed Computing*, Prentice Hall, 1991.

The Spring operating system interface definition language embedded hand-off policies as argument qualifiers for methods. See:

A Spring Collection, SunSoft Press, 1994.

Techniques based on unique references have also played roles in other OO design and analysis methods. See, for example:

Hogg, John, Doug Lea, R. C. Holt, Alan Wills, and Dennis de Champeaux. "The Geneva Convention on the Treatment of Object Aliasing", *OOPS Messenger,* April 1992.

For a formal approach to confinement in distributed systems, see:

Cardelli, Luca, and Andrew Gordon. "Mobile Ambients", in Maurice Nivat (ed.), *Foundations of Software Science and Computational Structures,* Springer LNCS 1378, 1998.

2.4   Structuring and Refactoring Classes

It can be difficult to balance the design forces surrounding exclusive access control during initial class design. Most classes used in concurrent programs undergo iterative refactorings to address concerns such as:

- Using only a few entry-point locks, as seen in most confinement-based designs, tends to work well when there are few threads, due to reduced overhead. But performance can quickly degrade under contention, especially on multiprocessors. When many threads all contend for the same entry-point lock, most threads will spend most of their time waiting for the lock, increasing latencies and limiting opportunities for parallelism. Most systems evolve to use finer-granularity locks as they grow. The best known cases are operating systems that once used a single *giant lock* as the entry point to a kernel, but increasingly use narrowly-scoped, briefly-held locks, in part for better support of multiprocessing.

- Using too many locks can add overhead and increase the chances of unanticipated liveness failures.

- Using one lock to protect more than one aspect of functionality can result in unnecessary contention.

- Holding locks for long periods invites liveness and performance problems, and complicates exception processing.

- Locking individual methods does not always maintain intended semantics. For example when two related attributes are obtained by calling two different locked accessors, the values obtained might not obey intended relationships if a state transition occurs between calls.

There is no single optimal strategy. However, several techniques and patterns can be used to provide better balance among such forces. This section describes strategies for removing unnecessary synchronization, splitting synchronization to match functionality, exporting read-only operations via adapters, isolating state representations to reduce access costs or improve potential parallelism, and grouping objects to use common locks so as to mirror layered designs. While any of these could be used during the initial design of classes, several of them rely on technical manipulations that are difficult (and sometimes unwise) to exploit during early design efforts.

2.4.1   Reducing Synchronization

When locking presents liveness or performance problems for a given class or program, usually the best solution is to refactor the design to use one or more of the other approaches presented in this chapter. However, there are cases where the basic logic of a synchronization-based design can be maintained even when some of the `synchronized` method qualifiers or blocks are removed, although sometimes at the expense of weakened semantic guarantees.

2.4.1.1   Accessors

Synchronizing a field accessor method sometimes (but by no means always) adds noticeable overhead to programs. Two considerations enter into any decision about whether synchronization of an accessor method can be removed:

Legality. The value of the underlying field never assumes an illegal value; that is, you can ensure that the field never, even momentarily, breaks invariants. (This by definition excludes fields of type `long` and `double`.)

Staleness. Clients do not necessarily require the most recently updated value of a field, but can live with possibly stale values (see §2.2.7).

If a field is *not* always legal, then the choices are:

- Synchronize the accessor (as well as all update methods).

- Ensure somehow that clients realize when they have obtained an illegal value and take evasive action (for example via *double-checks* — see §2.4.1.2).

- Omit the accessor method. This applies surprisingly often. Ask yourself why any client would want to know the value of a field and what they could do with this value. Because object attributes can change asynchronously in concurrent programs, a value obtained by a client in one line of code may have changed before the next line of code is executed. Thus, accessor methods are not frequently useful in concurrent programs. Moreover, because they are not *frequently* useful, synchronization is unlikely to be a performance concern even if you do not remove the accessor methods in such cases.

If a field is always legal but staleness is not acceptable, then you have the additional choice:

- Remove synchronization from the accessor, and qualify the instance variable as `volatile`. However, this works as expected only for scalar types, not references to arrays or `Objects` that help maintain object representations: accessing a `volatile` reference does not automatically ensure visibility of the fields or elements accessible from that reference. (In the case of `Object` references, you can if necessary further ensure that the accessed fields are themselves `volatile`.) The main disadvantage of this approach is that `volatile` declarations impede compiler optimizations of methods using these fields, and so can lead to a net performance loss.

If a field is always legal and staleness is acceptable, then you also have the choices:

- Remove synchronization from the accessor without any further alteration.

- If you like to live dangerously, just make the field `public`.

As an example, consider the `size()` method of the `ExpandableArray` class (§2.2.2), that returns the value of the `size` field. Inspection of all methods reveals that the value of the `size` field is always legal — it never assumes a value outside the range `0..data.length`. (This would not be true if, for example, `size` were temporarily set to `-1` as a resize indicator flag inside the `add` method.) Assuming that this constraint is documented as an internal requirement for all subclasses and future modifications, then synchronization can be removed from the accessor.

The decision about staleness and need for `volatile` is a matter of judgment about possible usage contexts that here interacts with (among other issues) choice of traversal strategies. If clients mainly traverse elements using indexed loops:

```
for (int i = 0; i < v.size(); ++i)        // questionable
    System.out.println(v.get(i));
```

then obtaining stale values of `size` is not likely to be acceptable. For example, a client might obtain the value zero even when there are many elements in the array, thus skipping the loop entirely. Note that if the loop ran at all, the synchronization performed in the first invocation of method `get` would force a fresher value of `size` to be returned on the *second* and subsequent calls to `size()`. (Also recall from §2.2.3 that clients must in any case be prepared for the size to change between the index check and the element access, so this traversal style is problematic at best anyway.)

However, if either aggregates or iterators are used, each performing internal synchronization, then you could make an argument for leaving the `size()` method unsynchronized and the `size` field non-volatile, and advertising the method as only a heuristic estimate of the current number of elements. Still, this is unlikely to be acceptable to clients of a general-purpose class such as `ExpandableArray`. But similar reasoning may be invoked when it is acceptable for clients to obtain values that are guaranteed to be only as recent as the last synchronization points of reading and writing threads.

2.4.1.2 Double-check

If callers of unsynchronized field accessors can somehow realize when they have just read an illegal value, they can sometimes take evasive action. One such action is to re-access the field under synchronization, determine its most current value, and then take appropriate action. This is the essence of the double-check idiom.

Double-check and its variants (including looping versions sometimes called *test-and-test-and-set*) are seen in latches (see §3.4.2), spin locks (see §3.2.6), and caching protocols. But the most common application of double-check is to conditionally relax synchronization surrounding initialization checks. When an uninitialized value (for scalars, a default zero value) is encountered, the accessing method acquires a lock, rechecks to see if initialization is really necessary (as opposed to having read a stale value), and if so performs the initialization while still under the synchronization lock, to prevent multiple instantiations. For example:

```
class AnimationApplet extends Applet {              // Fragments
  // ...
  int framesPerSecond; // default zero is illegal value

  void animate() {
    // ...
    if (framesPerSecond == 0) { // the unsynchronized check
      synchronized(this) {
        if (framesPerSecond == 0) { // the double-check
          String param = getParameter("fps");
          framesPerSecond = Integer.parseInt(param);
        }
      }
    }

    // ... actions using framesPerSecond ...
  }
}
```

While there are several legitimate uses, double-check is extremely delicate:

- It is generally unwise to use double-check for fields containing references to objects or arrays. Visibility of a reference read without synchronization does not guarantee visibility of non-volatile fields accessible from the reference (see §2.2.7). Even if such a reference is non-null, fields accessed via the reference without synchronization may obtain stale values.

- It is difficult at best to use a single flag field as an indicator that a whole set of fields must be initialized. The as-if-serial reorderings discussed in §2.2.7 may cause the flag to be visibly set before the other fields are visibly initialized.

120

Remedies to both of these problems almost always require some sort of locking. So, these considerations usually lead to avoidance of double-checked lazy initialization, and adoption of schemes that instead either eagerly initialize or rely on fully synchronized checks (as seen for example in the Singleton classes in §2.2.4).

However, in a few other cases you may be able to use an even weaker technique, *single-check*. Here, the check, initialization, and field binding are all performed *without* synchronization, and thus depend on the vagaries of unsynchronized field access. This opens up the possibility for multiple instantiations. This is a plausible option only if initialization is side-effect-free and need not otherwise entail synchronization, and use of multiple threads is rare.

2.4.1.3 Open calls

As discussed in §2.1, a method is *stateless* if it does not access or rely on any mutable object fields. Methods on fully immutable objects are by necessity stateless, but stateless methods can occur in other kinds of classes as well, for example in purely computational utility methods and during method invocations made to *acquaintances* (as opposed to representational support objects — see §1.3.1.2).

You do not need to synchronize stateless parts of methods. This allows other calls to `synchronized` methods to execute during unsynchronized sections, improving performance and reducing lock interference. However, synchronization can be split only when the different parts of the method are not in any way dependent, so that it is acceptable for other methods to "see" and use the object before full method completion.

To illustrate, consider the following generic server class. If `helper.operation` takes a long time, then calls to `synchronized` methods such as `getState` might block for an unacceptable time waiting for the method to be available.

```
class ServerWithStateUpdate {
  protected double state;
  protected final Helper helper = new Helper();

  public synchronized void service() {
    state = ...; // set to some new value
    helper.operation();
  }

  public synchronized double getState() { return state; }
}
```

If `helper` represents some aspect of the host's state, or the call to `helper.operation` relies on or modifies host state, then the entire `service` method must employ synchronization. However, if `helper.operation` is otherwise independent of the host, then the `service` method can be structured in the form suggested by the default rules in §1.1.1.1:

- First, update state (holding locks).

- Then, send messages (without holding locks).

Messages sent without holding locks are also known as *open calls*. As discussed in §4.1 and §4.2, classes with methods of this form are among the most well-behaved and readily composable components in concurrent and event-based systems. For example, assuming that `helper.operation` meets our criteria, the above class can be rewritten as:

```
class ServerWithOpenCall {
  protected double state;
  protected final Helper helper = new Helper();

  protected synchronized void updateState() {
    state =   ...; // set to some new value
  }

  public void service() {
    updateState();
    helper.operation();
  }
}
```

It is still possible to use open calls here even if the `helper` reference field is mutable; for example, using block synchronization:

```
class ServerWithAssignableHelper {
  protected double state;
  protected Helper helper = new Helper();
  synchronized void setHelper(Helper h) { helper = h; }

  public void service() {
    Helper h;
    synchronized(this) {
      state = ...
      h = helper;
    }
    h.operation();
  }

  public synchronized void synchedService() { // see below
    service();
  }
}
```

The synchedService method here reveals a weakness in any technique involving open calls. The call to service from within synchedService results in the lock being held throughout the duration of service, including the call to h.operation. This defeats the purpose of the method restructurings. Avoiding such problems requires documentation of the intentional *lack* of synchronization in classes used in concurrent settings.

Data structures that are linked via immutable references are often amenable to these kinds of manipulations. For example, consider a LinkedCell class in which each cell contains a reference to a successor cell, and for which we require that successor cell references be fixed upon construction. This is a common requirement for cells serving as Lisp-style lists. Methods and sections of methods solely involving the successor need not be synchronized, which speeds up traversal. For clarity and emphasis, the methods here use recursion; in practice you would probably use iteration instead:

```
class LinkedCell {
  protected int value;
  protected final LinkedCell next;

  public LinkedCell(int v, LinkedCell t) {
    value = v;
    next = t;
  }

  public synchronized int value() { return value; }
  public synchronized void setValue(int v) { value = v; }

  public int sum() {                    // add up all element values
    return (next == null) ? value() : value() + next.sum();
  }

  public boolean includes(int x) { // search for x
    return (value() == x) ? true:
           (next == null)? false : next.includes(x);
  }
}
```

Again note that an object remains locked when a synchronized method calls an unsynchronized one. So it would *not* avoid synchronization to write sum as:

```
synchronized int ineffectivelyUnsynchedSum() {    // bad idea
  return value + nextSum();       // synch still held on call
}
int nextSum() { return (next == null)? 0: next.sum(); }
```

2.4.2 Splitting Synchronization

When the representations and behavior of one class can be partitioned into independent, non-interacting, or just non-conflicting subsets, it is almost always worth
refactoring the class to use distinct finer-granularity helper objects whose actions
are delegated by the host.

    This rule of thumb holds in object-oriented design generally. But it carries
much more force in concurrent OO programming. A set of `synchronized` operations might deadlock or present other liveness or lock-based performance problems if they were all waiting for the single synchronization lock associated with a
single object. But they might be deadlock-free and/or run more efficiently if they
are waiting on multiple distinct locks. As a general rule, the more finely you can
subdivide the internal synchronization of a given class, the better will be its liveness properties across a wider range of contexts. However, this sometimes comes
at the expense of greater complexity and potential for error.

2.4.2.1 Splitting classes

Consider a simplified `Shape` class that maintains both location and dimension
information, along with time-consuming methods `adjustLocation` and `adjust-`
`Dimensions` that independently alter them:

```
class Shape {                                        // Incomplete
  protected double x = 0.0;
  protected double y = 0.0;
  protected double width = 0.0;
  protected double height = 0.0;

  public synchronized double x()       { return x;}
  public synchronized double y()       { return y; }
  public synchronized double width()   { return width;}
  public synchronized double height()  { return height; }

  public synchronized void adjustLocation() {
    x = longCalculation1();
    y = longCalculation2();
  }

  public synchronized void adjustDimensions() {
    width = longCalculation3();
    height = longCalculation4();
  }

  // ...
}
```

Under the assumptions that `adjustLocation` never deals with dimension information and `adjustDimensions` never deals with location, better performance could be obtained by revising this class so that callers of `adjustLocation` need not wait for those calling `adjustDimensions` and vice versa.

Splitting classes to reduce granularity is a straightforward exercise in class refactoring:

- Partition some functionality of a `Host` class into another class, say `Helper`.

- In the `Host` class, declare a `final` unique field referencing a helper that is initialized to a new `Helper` in the constructor. (In other words, strictly confine each helper in its host.)

- In the `Host` class, forward all appropriate methods to the `Helper` as open calls, using unsynchronized methods. This works because the methods are stateless with respect to the `Host` class.

The most extreme result of these steps is a *Pass-Through Host* design in which *all* messages are relayed as open calls via simple unsynchronized methods:

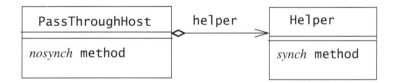

For example, here is a pass-through version of the `Shape` class:

```
class PassThroughShape {

    protected final AdjustableLoc loc = new AdjustableLoc(0, 0);
    protected final AdjustableDim dim = new AdjustableDim(0, 0);

    public double x()                { return loc.x(); }
    public double y()                { return loc.y(); }

    public double width()            { return dim.width(); }
    public double height()           { return dim.height(); }

    public void adjustLocation()     { loc.adjust(); }
    public void adjustDimensions()   { dim.adjust(); }
}
```

```
class AdjustableLoc {
  protected double x;
  protected double y;

  public AdjustableLoc(double initX, double initY) {
    x = initX;
    y = initY;
  }

  public synchronized double x() { return x;}
  public synchronized double y() { return y; }

  public synchronized void adjust() {
    x = longCalculation1();
    y = longCalculation2();
  }

  protected double longCalculation1() { /* ... */ }
  protected double longCalculation2() { /* ... */ }

}


class AdjustableDim {
  protected double width;
  protected double height;

  public AdjustableDim(double initW, double initH) {
    width = initW;
    height = initH;
  }

  public synchronized double width() { return width;}
  public synchronized double height() { return height; }

  public synchronized void adjust() {
    width = longCalculation3();
    height = longCalculation4();
  }

  protected double longCalculation3() { /* ... */ }
  protected double longCalculation4() { /* ... */ }

}
```

2.4.2.2 Splitting locks

Even if you do not want to or cannot split a class, you can still split the synchronization locks associated with each subset of functionality. This technique is equivalent to one in which you first split a class into helpers and then fold all representations and methods of the helpers *except* their synchronization locks back into the host class. However, there is no need to proceed in exactly this way.

Stripped of all but its synchronization lock, any class is reduced to just `java.lang.Object`. This fact accounts for the idiomatic practice of using instances of class `Object` as synchronization aids.

To recover the underlying design whenever you see an `Object` used for a synchronization lock, you might ask yourself what kind of helper object a particular lock is a stand-in for. In the case of lock-splitting, each `Object` controls access to a subset of methods, so each method in each subset is block-synchronized on a common lock object.

The basic steps for splitting locks are similar to those for splitting objects:

- For each *independent* subset of functionality, declare a `final` object, say `lock`, initialized in the constructor for the `Host` class and never reassigned:

  - The lock object can be of any subclass of class `Object`. If it will not be used for any other purpose, it might as well be of class `Object` itself.

  - If a subset is uniquely associated with some existing object uniquely referenced from a field, you may use that object as the lock.

  - One of these locks can be associated with the `Host` object (`this`) itself.

- Declare all methods corresponding to each subset as unsynchronized, but surround all code with `synchronized(lock) { ... }`.

Among the applications of lock splitting are fixed-size hash tables, in which each bin of the table possesses its own lock. (This strategy cannot easily be applied to dynamically resizable hash tables such as those used in `java.util.Hashtable`, since they cannot rely on immutability of the lock objects.) Lock splitting is also seen in classes that carefully manage waiting and notification operations, as discussed in §3.7.2. For a simpler example, here is a split version of the `Shape` class:

```
class LockSplitShape {                                    // Incomplete
  protected double x = 0.0;
  protected double y = 0.0;
  protected double width = 0.0;
  protected double height = 0.0;

  protected final Object locationLock = new Object();
  protected final Object dimensionLock = new Object();

  public double x() {
    synchronized(locationLock) {
      return x;
    }
  }

  public double y() {
    synchronized(locationLock) {
      return y;
    }
  }

  public void adjustLocation() {
    synchronized(locationLock) {
      x = longCalculation1();
      y = longCalculation2();
    }
  }

  // and so on

}
```

2.4.2.3   Isolating fields

Some classes manage sets of independent properties and attributes, each of which can be manipulated in isolation of the others. For example, a Person class may have age, income and isMarried fields that can be changed regardless of any other actions being performed on the Person object as a whole. The decision about whether this is acceptable of course rests on the intended usage semantics of a given class.

You cannot just declare such fields as volatile if you need synchronization protection to avoid conflicts among concurrent attempts to update them. However, you can use a simple form of splitting to offload synchronization protection to objects used solely to protect basic operations on basic types. Such classes play a similar role as classes java.lang.Double and java.lang.Integer, except that instead of promising immutability, they promise atomicity. For example, you can create a class such as:

```
class SynchronizedInt {
  private int value;

  public SynchronizedInt(int v) { value = v; }

  public synchronized int get() { return value; }

  public synchronized int set(int v) { // returns previous value
    int oldValue = value;
    value = v;
    return oldValue;
  }

  public synchronized int increment() { return ++value; }

  // and so on

}
```

(The util.concurrent package available from the online supplement contains a set of such classes, one for each basic type, that also support other utility operations such as the commit method described in §2.4.4.2.)

These classes could be used, for example, in:

```
class Person {                                           // Fragments
  // ...

  protected final SynchronizedInt age = new SynchronizedInt(0);

  protected final SynchronizedBoolean isMarried =
                          new SynchronizedBoolean(false);

  protected final SynchronizedDouble income =
                          new SynchronizedDouble(0.0);

  public int getAge() { return age.get(); }

  public void birthday() { age.increment(); }

  // ...
}
```

2.4.2.4 Linked data structures

Lock-splitting techniques can minimize access contention to objects serving as entry points into linked data structures, by finding a middle ground between the extreme strategies of fully synchronizing the entry classes (which can limit concurrency) and fully synchronizing all the linked node objects being controlled (which can be inefficient and can lead to liveness problems).

As with all lock-splitting techniques, the main goal is to associate different locks with different methods. But in the case of linked structures, this often leads to further adjustments in the data structures and algorithms themselves. There are no universally applicable recipes for splitting synchronization in classes controlling access to linked structures, but the following class illustrates some common tactics.

The following `LinkedQueue` class can serve as a generic unbounded first-in-first-out (FIFO) queue. It maintains separate synchronization for `put` and `poll`. The `putLock` lock ensures that only one `put` operation at a time can proceed. The `pollLock` lock similarly ensures that only one `poll` operation at a time can proceed. A `head` node always exists in this implementation so that a `put` and a `poll` can normally proceed independently. After each `poll`, the previous first node becomes the new head. Additionally, the accessed nodes themselves must be locked to prevent conflicts when a `put` and a `poll` are both simultaneously executing on a queue that was previously empty or is about to become empty, in which case `head` and `last` both refer to the same header node.

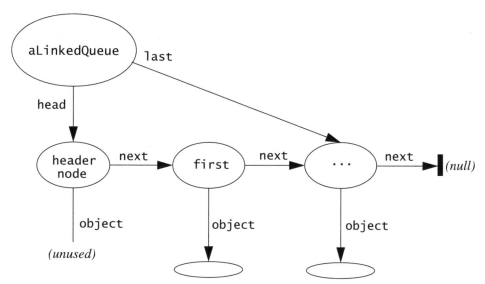

```
class LinkedQueue {
  protected Node head = new Node(null);
  protected Node last = head;

  protected final Object pollLock = new Object();
  protected final Object putLock = new Object();

  public void put(Object x) {
    Node node = new Node(x);
    synchronized (putLock) {         // insert at end of list
      synchronized (last) {
        last.next = node;            // extend list
        last = node;
      }
    }
  }

  public Object poll() {             // returns null if empty
    synchronized (pollLock) {
      synchronized (head) {
        Object x = null;
        Node first = head.next;      // get to first real node
        if (first != null) {
          x = first.object;
          first.object = null;       // forget old object
          head = first;              // first becomes new head
        }
        return x;
      }
    }
  }

  static class Node {                // local node class for queue
    Object object;
    Node next = null;

    Node(Object x) { object = x; }
  }
}
```

The online supplement includes queue classes that further refine, extend, and optimize this basic design.

2.4.3   Read-Only Adapters

In confinement-based designs (see §2.3.3), a Host object cannot reveal the identity of any of its Part objects. This eliminates the choice of returning references to parts in any accessor or property inspection method.

One alternative is instead to return a copy of the Part. For example, class Syn-chedPoint (§2.3.3) could add a method:

```
public synchronized BarePoint getPoint() {
  return new BarePoint(delegate.x, delegate.y);
}
```

When Parts are instances of classes known to implement an appropriate clone method, you can instead return part.clone(). And, when you need to return arbitrary sets of values, you can use an ad-hoc array, for example:

```
public synchronized double[] getXY() {
  return new double[] { delegate.x, delegate.y } ;
}
```

However, copying can be too expensive when dealing with some objects, and does not make sense when dealing with others; for example, objects that maintain references to files, threads or other resources that should not themselves be copied. In many cases you can instead selectively permit some leakage by constructing and returning an Adapter object surrounding the part that exposes only those operations that clients may use without introducing any potential interference — generally, read-only operations. Unless these methods deal only with immutable state, they require synchronization.

The most secure version of this scheme takes a bit of work to set up:

- Define a base interface describing some non-mutative functionality.

- Optionally, define a subinterface that supports additional update methods used in the normal mutable implementation class.

- Define a read-only adapter that forwards only the exported operations. For added security, declare that the immutable class is final. The use of final means that when you think you have an immutable object, you really do — it's not of some subclass that supports mutable operations as well.

These steps can be applied to the following simple Account class. Even though accounts in this example are held only by AccountHolders, the general-purpose mutable UpdatableAccount implementation employs synchronization.

```
class InsufficientFunds extends Exception {}

interface Account {
  long balance();
}

interface UpdatableAccount extends Account {
  void credit(long amount) throws InsufficientFunds;
  void debit(long amount) throws InsufficientFunds;
}

// Sample implementation of updatable version
class UpdatableAccountImpl implements UpdatableAccount {
  private long currentBalance;

  public UpdatableAccountImpl(long initialBalance) {
    currentBalance = initialBalance;
  }

  public synchronized long balance() {
    return currentBalance;
  }

  public synchronized void credit(long amount)
   throws InsufficientFunds {
    if (amount >= 0 || currentBalance >= -amount)
      currentBalance += amount;
    else
      throw new InsufficientFunds();
  }

  public synchronized void debit(long amount)
   throws InsufficientFunds {
    credit(-amount);
  }
}

final class ImmutableAccount implements Account {
  private Account delegate;

  public ImmutableAccount(long initialBalance) {
    delegate = new UpdatableAccountImpl(initialBalance);
  }

  ImmutableAccount(Account acct) { delegate = acct; }

  public long balance() { // forward the immutable method
    return delegate.balance();
  }
}
```

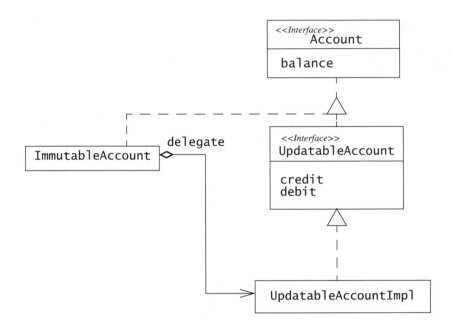

These classes could be used, for example, in:

```
class AccountRecorder { // A logging facility
  public void recordBalance(Account a) {
    System.out.println(a.balance()); // or record in file
  }
}

class AccountHolder {
  private UpdatableAccount acct = new UpdatableAccountImpl(0);
  private AccountRecorder recorder;

  public AccountHolder(AccountRecorder r) {
    recorder = r;
  }

  public synchronized void acceptMoney(long amount) {
    try {
      acct.credit(amount);
      recorder.recordBalance(new ImmutableAccount(acct));//(*)
    }
    catch (InsufficientFunds ex) {
      System.out.println("Cannot accept negative amount.");
    }
  }
}
```

Use of a read-only wrapper at line (*) might seem an unnecessary precaution. But it guards against what might happen if someone were to write the following subclass and use it in conjunction with `AccountHolder`:

```
class EvilAccountRecorder extends AccountRecorder {
  private long embezzlement;
  // ...
  public void recordBalance(Account a) {
    super.recordBalance(a);

    if (a instanceof UpdatableAccount) {
      UpdatableAccount u = (UpdatableAccount)a;
      try {
        u.debit(10);
        embezzlement += 10;
      }
      catch (InsufficientFunds quietlyignore) {}
    }
  }
}
```

The `java.util.Collection` framework uses a variant of this scheme. Rather than declaring a separate immutable interface, the main `Collection` interface permits mutative methods to throw `UnsupportedOperationExceptions`. Anonymous read-only adapter classes throw these exceptions on all attempted update operations. They can be constructed via, for example:

```
List l = new ArrayList();
// ...
untrustedObject.use(Collections.unmodifiableList(l));
```

2.4.4 Copy-on-Write

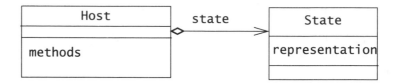

When a set of fields comprising the state of an object must maintain a set of inter-related invariants, you can isolate these fields in another object that preserves the intended semantic guarantees.

A good way to go about this is to rely on immutable representation objects that at all times maintain consistent snapshots of legal object states. Relying on immutability eliminates the need to otherwise coordinate separate readings of related attributes. It also normally eliminates the need to hide these representations from clients.

For example, in §1.1.1.1, we had to take special precautions involving block synchronization in order to guarantee that consistent (x, y) coordinates of Parti-cles were always displayed correctly. And the Shape classes described in §2.4.2 do not even provide a mechanism for doing this. One solution is to employ a sepa-rate ImmutablePoint class that maintains location information that is at all times consistent:

```
class ImmutablePoint {
  private final int x;
  private final int y;

  public ImmutablePoint(int initX, int initY) {
    x = initX;
    y = initY;
  }

  public int x() { return x; }
  public int y() { return y; }
}
```

ImmutablePoints could be used in the following Dot class that is otherwise similar to the Particle class in §1.1.1.1. This class illustrates the general tech-niques surrounding copy-on-write updates, in which state changes do not directly update fields, but instead construct and attach new representation objects.

Note that synchronization of some form is required here. Even though the point representation objects are immutable, the loc reference is mutable. While synchronization of the accessor method location might be loosened in accord with the considerations in §2.4.1, the shiftX method must be synchronized (or perhaps otherwise modified) in order to preclude multiple concurrent executions in which different versions of `loc` are obtained when accessing `loc.x()` and `loc.y()`.

```
class Dot {
  protected ImmutablePoint loc;

  public Dot(int x, int y) {
    loc = new ImmutablePoint(x, y);
  }

  public synchronized ImmutablePoint location() { return loc; }

  protected synchronized void updateLoc(ImmutablePoint newLoc) {
    loc = newLoc;
  }

  public void moveTo(int x, int y) {
    updateLoc(new ImmutablePoint(x, y));
  }

  public synchronized void shiftX(int delta) {
    updateLoc(new ImmutablePoint(loc.x() + delta,
                                 loc.y()));
  }
}
```

2.4.4.1 Internal copy-on-write

When state representations are strictly internal to an object, there is no compelling reason to create new classes just to enforce immutable access. Copy-on-write can be applied whenever the need to obtain consistent representations quickly and effortlessly overwhelms construction costs. It requires at most one synchronized operation to access all of the state held by an immutable representation object. Additionally, in some contexts, it is convenient to obtain a single snapshot rather than one that reflects any state modifications made during the use of that snapshot.

For example, copy-on-write collection objects can be very useful for maintaining collections of listeners in event and multicast frameworks (see §4.1). Here objects maintain lists of listeners or handlers that must receive notifications of state changes or other events of interest. These lists rarely change, but may be traversed very frequently. Also, when objects receiving notifications make changes in the list of notifyees, they are almost always intended to take effect the *next* time a notification is issued, not in the current round.

While there are other good choices for the underlying data structure (including the special-purpose tree-based structure used in `java.awt.EventMulti-`

caster, and more elaborate structures maintaining edit-records from a common base), an array-based copy-on-write collection class is suitable for most applications. Traversal via iterators is not only fast but also avoids ConcurrentModificationExceptions that can occur in some other approaches to traversal (see §2.2.3).

```
class CopyOnWriteArrayList {                                    // Incomplete
  protected Object[] array = new Object[0];

  protected synchronized Object[] getArray() { return array; }

  public synchronized void add(Object element) {
    int len = array.length;
    Object[] newArray = new Object[len+1];
    System.arraycopy(array, 0, newArray, 0, len);
    newArray[len] = element;
    array = newArray;
  }

  public Iterator iterator() {
    return new Iterator() {
      protected final Object[] snapshot = getArray();
      protected int cursor = 0;

      public boolean hasNext() {
        return cursor < snapshot.length;
      }

      public Object next() {
        try {
          return snapshot[cursor++];
        }
        catch (IndexOutOfBoundsException ex) {
          throw new NoSuchElementException();
        }
      }
    };
  }
}
```

(The util.concurrent package available from the online supplement contains a version of this class that conforms to the java.util.List interface.)

This class would be horribly inefficient if used in contexts involving frequent modifications of large collections, but it is well suited for most multicast applications, as illustrated in §3.5.2 and §3.6.4.

2.4.4.2 Optimistic Updates

Optimistic updates employ a weaker protocol than other copy-on-write techniques: Rather than engaging locks for the entire duration of state update methods, they employ synchronization only at the beginnings and ends of update methods. Typically, each method takes the form:

1. Get a copy of the current state representation (while holding a lock).

2. Construct a new state representation (without holding any locks).

3. *Commit* to the new state only if the old state has not changed since obtaining it.

Optimistic update techniques limit synchronization to very brief intervals — just long enough to access and later update state representations. Tnis tends to provide very good performance on multiprocessors, at least under appropriate usage conditions.

The main added requirement here over conventional copy-on-write techniques is dealing with the possibility that Step 3 will *fail* because some other thread has independently updated the state representation before the current thread has had a chance to do so. The potential for failure introduces two concerns (discussed in more detail in §3.1.1) that limit the range of applicability of optimistic update techniques:

Failure protocols. The choices are either to retry the entire method sequence or to propagate the failure back to a client, which can then take evasive action. The most common choice is to retry. However, this can lead to *livelock* — the optimistic analog of indefinite blocking in which methods continuously spin without making any further progress. While the probability of livelock is normally vanishingly small, the action may never complete and may expend a lot of CPU resources repeatedly attempting to do so. For this reason, optimistic update techniques are bad choices for classes used in contexts that may encounter massive thread contention of unbounded duration. However, some specialized *wait-free* optimistic algorithms have been *proven* to succeed after a bounded number of attempts regardless of contention (see Further Readings).

Side effects. Because they may fail, the actions performed while constructing new state representations cannot include any irrevocable side effects. For example, they should not write to files, create threads, or draw to GUIs unless these actions can themselves be meaningfully *cancelled* upon failure (see §3.1.2).

2.4.4.3 Atomic commitment

The heart of any optimistic technique is an atomic commitment method that is used instead of assignment statements. It must conditionally swap in a new state representation only if the existing state representation is the one expected by the caller. There are many ways to distinguish and track different state representations, for example, using version numbers, transaction identifiers, time stamps, and signature codes. But it is by far most convenient and most common to simply rely on the reference identity of the state object. Here is a generic example:

```
class Optimistic {                            // Generic code sketch

  private State state; // reference to representation object

  private synchronized State getState() { return state; }

  private synchronized boolean commit(State assumed,
                                      State next) {
    if (state == assumed) {
      state = next;
      return true;
    }
    else
      return false;
  }
}
```

There are several common minor variations in how the `commit` method is defined. For example, the version usually named `compareAndSwap` returns the current value, which may be either the new or the old value depending on whether the operation committed successfully. The increasing popularity of optimistic techniques in systems-level concurrent programming is in part due to (and in part the cause of) the fact that most modern processors include an efficient built-in `compareAndSwap` instruction or one of its variants. While these are not directly accessible from the Java programming language, it is in principle possible for optimizing compilers to map constructs to use such instructions. (Even if not, optimistic updates are still efficient.)

In a purely optimistic class, most update methods take a standard form: getting the initial state, building a new state representation, and then committing if possible, else looping or throwing an exception. However, methods that do not rely on any particular initial states can be written more simply, unconditionally swapping in the new state. For example, here is an optimistic version of the `Dot` class:

```
class OptimisticDot {
  protected ImmutablePoint loc;

  public OptimisticDot(int x, int y) {
    loc = new ImmutablePoint(x, y);
  }

  public synchronized ImmutablePoint location() { return loc; }

  protected synchronized boolean commit(ImmutablePoint assumed,
                                        ImmutablePoint next) {
    if (loc == assumed) {
      loc = next;
      return true;
    }
    else
      return false;
  }

  public synchronized void moveTo(int x, int y) {
    // bypass commit since the operation is unconditional
    loc = new ImmutablePoint(x, y);
  }

  public void shiftX(int delta) {
    boolean success = false;
    do {
      ImmutablePoint old = location();
      ImmutablePoint next = new ImmutablePoint(old.x() + delta,
                                               old.y());
      success = commit(old, next);
    } while (!success);
  }

}
```

If the potential for prolonged interference is a concern, rather than simply spinning, the loop in shiftX can use an exponential back-off scheme as discussed in §3.1.1.5.

141

2.4.5 Open Containers

Ordered *hierarchical* locking techniques may be applied when you have a layered containment design (§2.3.3) but cannot, or do not want to, strictly hide all of the Part objects from other clients.

If Parts are visible to clients, they must employ synchronization. But when these parts frequently invoke methods on other parts, the resulting designs may be prone to deadlock. For example, suppose one thread holds the lock on `part1` which in turn makes a call to `part2`, while another thread is doing the opposite:

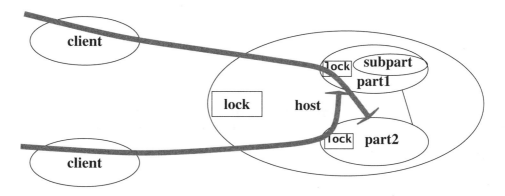

You can eliminate this form of deadlock by using the strategy seen in strict object confinement designs: arrange that the Part objects rely on the Host lock for their synchronization control. If clients must first obtain the host lock, then this form of deadlock cannot occur:

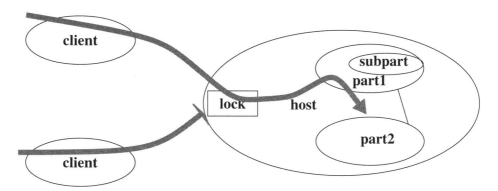

This solution suffices for most containment designs involving visible components (see also §2.5.1.3 for an additional variant). Obtaining outermost locks of containers before operating on parts represents a structured approach to applying the resource-ordering techniques discussed in §2.2.6. However, without confinement, there is no simple strategy that *enforces* this solution. Classes (and their authors) must know the rules and stick to them. The main policy choice concerns who should know these rules, the internal parts or the external clients. Neither choice is at all perfect, but one must be adopted:

- Internal locking is difficult to retrofit to existing classes and can increase the dependence of a class on its context.

- External locking fails if any client forgets to use the protocol.

2.4.5.1 Internal disciplines

Under internal containment locking, each Part uses its container's synchronization lock for all methods requiring dynamic exclusion control. In the most efficient case, each Part has a `final` field that is initialized upon construction and then used for all locking. Additional unrelated locking inside the Part methods may also be acceptable (but see §3.3.4).

For example:

```
class Part {                                // Code sketch
  protected final Object lock;
  // ...

  public Part(Object owner) { lock = owner; }

  public Part() { lock = this; } // if no owner, use self

  public void anAction() {
    synchronized(lock) {
      anotherPart.help();
      // ...
    }
  }
}
```

As a matter of design policy, you can define most or all classes in this way in order to accommodate usage in various container-based frameworks. However, these designs are more difficult to manage when the ownership of a Part can change dynamically. In this case you must additionally synchronize access to the lock field itself (normally using `synchronized(this)`) before using it to control access to the body of a method.

A simpler structure is available when you can arrange that each Part class be declared as an *inner* class of its Host. In this case, you can use `synchronized` blocks with `Host.this` as an argument:

```
class Host {                                                    // code sketch
  // ...

  class Part {
    // ...
    public void anAction() {
      synchronized(Host.this) {
        anotherPart.help();
        // ...
      }
    }
  }
}
```

2.4.5.2   External disciplines

In the most extreme, unstructured version of external locking, each caller of each method on each Part must somehow know which lock to acquire before making the call:

```
synchronized(someLock) { aPart.anAction(); }
```

In finite, closed systems, developers can even create a list defining which locks are to be associated with which objects and then require code authors to conform to these rules. This tactic can be defensible for small non-extensible embedded systems that might otherwise be prone to deadlock.

However, this solution of course does not scale well. In even slightly larger contexts, client code must be able to programmatically determine which lock to use. One way to arrange this is to construct tables that maintain the required associations between objects and locks. A slightly more structured strategy is to include in each Part class a method, say `getLock`, that returns the lock to use for synchronization control. Clients can then make calls using:

```
synchronized(aPart.getLock()) { aPart.anAction(); }
```

This approach is used in the `java.awt` package (at least up through release 1.2). Each `java.awt.Component` supports method `getTreeLock` that returns the lock to be used for controlling synchronized operations on the current container (for example, a `Frame`). Choice of how and when to use this lock is then left to client code. This introduces opportunities for ad-hoc extensibility and can result in minor performance improvements compared to internal locking disciplines. For example, a client need not reacquire the lock if it is known to be held already. But this form of external locking also introduces more opportunities for error, as well as the need for extensive documentation — clients must know enough about operations to determine whether and how locks should be used.

2.4.5.3 Multilevel containment

Both approaches to hierarchical containment locking can be extended past two levels. Each layer of the hierarchy must have an associated lock. Code must pass through the locks at all layers, in outermost-to-innermost order, before invoking update methods. Support for an *arbitrary* level of nested locks is exceedingly awkward to set up using `synchronized` blocks or methods, but may be approachable using lock utility classes and managers (see §2.5.1).

2.4.6 Further Readings

A general account of refactoring classes is:

Fowler, Martin. *Refactoring*, Addison-Wesley, 1999.

Optimistic update algorithms that can be proven to succeed eventually include the class of *wait-free* algorithms in which no thread ever blocks on a condition that can be satisfied only by the action of some other thread. In wait-free algorithms, every thread succeeds after a finite number of attempts, regardless of what other threads do or do not do. Most algorithms employ the notion of *helping:* when a thread cannot continue, it takes some action to help another thread complete its task. The theory of wait-free algorithms is described in:

Herlihy, Maurice. "Wait-free synchronization", *ACM Transactions on Programming Languages and Systems*, vol. 13, no. 1, 1991.

Practical wait-free update algorithms are known for only a small number of common data structures, for example queues and lists. However, these algorithms are increasingly used in underlying run-time support in operating system kernels and JVM implementations. The online supplement contains an adaptation of a wait-free queue class described in the following paper, as well as links to descriptions of wait-free algorithms implemented in other languages.

Michael, Maged and Michael Scott. "Simple, fast, and practical non-blocking and blocking concurrent queue algorithms", *Proceedings, 15th ACM Symposium on Principles of Distributed Computing, ACM*, 1996.

2.5 Using Lock Utilities

Built-in `synchronized` methods and blocks suffice for many lock-based applications, but they have the following limitations:

- There is no way to back off from an attempt to acquire a lock if it is already held, to give up after waiting for a specified time, or to cancel a lock attempt after an interrupt. This can make it difficult to recover from liveness problems.

- There is no way to alter the semantics of a lock, for example with respect to reentrancy, read versus write protection, or fairness.

- There is no access control for synchronization. Any method can perform `synchronized(obj)` for any accessible object, thus leading to potential denial-of-service problems caused by the holding of needed locks.

- Synchronization within methods and blocks limits use to strict block-structured locking. For example, you cannot acquire a lock in one method and release it in another.

These problems can be overcome by using utility classes to control locking. Such classes can be constructed using the techniques described in §3.7. Here, we restrict attention to their use in implementing lock-based designs. While it is possible to create lock classes providing just about any desired semantics and usage properties, we illustrate only two common ones, mutual exclusion locks and read-write locks. For the sake of concreteness, presentations rely on the versions of these classes in the `util.concurrent` package available from the online supplement. However, similar remarks hold for just about any kind of lock utility class that you could construct.

All lock-based designs discussed previously in this chapter can, if desired, be re-implemented using lock utilities rather than built-in `synchronized` methods and blocks. (Additional examples may be found in most of the concurrent systems programming texts listed in §1.2.5.) This section focuses on usages that are otherwise difficult to arrange.

The solutions provided by lock utility classes come at the price of more awkward coding idioms and less automatic enforcement of correct usage. Using lock utilities requires more care and discipline than typically necessary when using `synchronized` methods and blocks. These constructions may also entail greater overhead since they are less readily optimized than are uses of built-in synchronization.

2.5.1 Mutexes

A Mutex (short for *mutual exclusion lock*) class can be defined as (omitting implementation code):

```
public class Mutex implements Sync {
  public void acquire() throws InterruptedException;
  public void release();
  public boolean attempt(long msec) throws InterruptedException;
}
```

(In the util.concurrent version, Mutex implements interface Sync, a standardized interface for all classes obeying acquire-release protocols.)

As you might expect, acquire is analogous to the operations performed on entry into a synchronized block, and release is analogous to the operations performed on exit from a block. The attempt operation returns true only if the lock is acquired within the specified time (at least to the best of the implementation's ability to measure this time and react in a timely manner — see §3.2.5). Zero is a legal argument, meaning do not wait at all if the lock is not available.

Also, unlike built-in synchronization, the acquire and attempt methods throw InterruptedException if the current thread has been interrupted while trying to obtain the lock. This complicates usage, but makes possible the development of responsive and robust code in the face of cancellation. The range of reasonable responses to InterruptedException is discussed in more detail in §3.1.2; here we illustrate only the most common options.

A Mutex can be used in the same way as a built-in lock by replacing blocks of the form:

```
synchronized(lock) { /* body */ }
```

with the more verbose and awkward before/after construction:

```
try {
  mutex.acquire();
  try {
    /* body */
  }
  finally {
    mutex.release();
  }
}
catch (InterruptedException ie) {
  /* response to thread cancellation during acquire */
}
```

Unlike synchronized blocks, locking in standard Mutex classes is non-reentrant. If the lock is held, even by the thread performing the acquire, the thread will block. While it is possible to define and use a ReentrantLock as well, a simple Mutex class suffices in many locking applications. For example, we can use it to re-implement the Particle class from §1.1.1.1:

```
class ParticleUsingMutex {
  protected int x;
  protected int y;
  protected final Random rng = new Random();
  protected final Mutex mutex = new Mutex();

  public ParticleUsingMutex(int initialX, int initialY) {
    x = initialX;
    y = initialY;
  }

  public void move() {
    try {
      mutex.acquire();
      try {
        x += rng.nextInt(10) - 5;
        y += rng.nextInt(20) - 10;
      }
      finally { mutex.release(); }
    }
    catch (InterruptedException ie) {
      Thread.currentThread().interrupt();
    }
  }

  public void draw(Graphics g) {
    int lx, ly;

    try {
      mutex.acquire();
      try {
        lx = x; ly = y;
      }
      finally { mutex.release(); }
    }
    catch (InterruptedException ie) {
      Thread.currentThread().interrupt();
      return;
    }

    g.drawRect(lx, ly, 10, 10);
  }
}
```

The try/finally constructions surrounding the operation bodies mimic the behavior of synchronized blocks in which locks are released no matter how the body exits, even if via an uncaught exception. As a design rule, it is a good idea to use try/finally even if you believe that the body cannot throw any exceptions.

The move and draw methods both return immediately without performing any action if the thread was interrupted during lock acquisition. This is a simple and appropriate response to cancellation. However, as discussed in §3.1.2, the catch clauses are also obligated to propagate cancellation status via Thread.current-Thread().interrupt().

The ParticleUsingMutex class is more resistant to hostile denial-of-service attacks than is the original. Since the built-in synchronized lock is not used, it doesn't matter if anyone holds it. (Note, however, that no such problems could occur in ParticleApplet anyway because all references are confined to the applet.) If we were even more paranoid, we might declare mutex as private. But in most cases, this would needlessly preclude extensibility. Since any plausible subclass would also need to access the lock, declaring mutex as private is nearly equivalent to declaring the class itself as final.

2.5.1.1 Method adapters

Better structure and discipline surrounding locks can be arranged via any of the before/after patterns discussed in §1.4. For example, the use of method adapters supports definition of generic wrappers that can run any code within any lock. A wrapper can be defined either as method of a class using locking or as a separate utility class. An example of the latter is:

```
class WithMutex {
  private final Mutex mutex;
  public WithMutex(Mutex m) { mutex = m; }

  public void perform(Runnable r) throws InterruptedException {
    mutex.acquire();
    try      { r.run(); }
    finally { mutex.release(); }
  }
}
```

This could be used by classes that separate out bare actions as internal methods, invoked within wrappers by public methods, for example:

```
class ParticleUsingWrapper {                              // Incomplete
  // ...
  protected final WithMutex withMutex =
                                    new WithMutex(new Mutex());

  protected void doMove() {
    x += rng.nextInt(10) - 5;
    y += rng.nextInt(20) - 10;
  }

  public void move() {
    try {
      withMutex.perform(new Runnable() {
        public void run() { doMove(); }
      });
    }
    catch (InterruptedException ie) {
      Thread.currentThread().interrupt();
    }
  }
  // ...
}
```

This design encounters somewhat greater overhead, so it is mainly applicable in classes protecting relatively time-consuming actions. Also, the illustrated version applies only to internal actions that can be expressed as argumentless, resultless Runnables. So, for example, it cannot be used with the draw method. However, this scheme can be extended by defining additional method adapters that accept other arguments and/or return results, as described in §1.4.4.

2.5.1.2 Back-offs

The attempt method is useful for recovery from deadlocks and other liveness problems involving multiple locks. When you cannot ensure that lockups are impossible (as is the case for at least some components in most open systems), you can routinely use attempt instead of acquire, providing a heuristic time-out value (for example a few seconds) to indicate possible lockups, and then take evasive action upon failure (see §3.2.5).

The attempt method can also be used in more specialized constructions to deal with particular deadlock-prone constructions. For example, here is another version of the Cell class from §2.2.5, that backs out and retries upon discovering a potential deadlock. As a heuristic, it includes a short delay between retries. Because it relies on retries, it can livelock. This may be acceptable if you can convince yourself that the probability of infinite livelock is, say, less than the probability of a random hardware failure.

151

Note that alias checking is needed here and in all similar constructions involving non-reentrant locks to avoid lockups while trying to re-acquire a lock that is already held (see §2.2.6).

```
class CellUsingBackoff {
  private long value;
  private final Mutex mutex = new Mutex();

  void swapValue(CellUsingBackoff other) {
    if (this == other) return;    // alias check required here
    for (;;) {
      try {
        mutex.acquire();
        try {
          if (other.mutex.attempt(0)) {
            try {
              long t = value;
              value = other.value;
              other.value = t;
              return;
            }
            finally {
              other.mutex.release();
            }
          }
        }
        finally {
          mutex.release();
        };
        Thread.sleep(100);
      }
      catch (InterruptedException ie) {
        Thread.currentThread().interrupt();
        return;
      }
    }
  }
}
```

2.5.1.3 Reorderings

Back-off techniques may be used as safeguards in designs employing lock ordering techniques (see §2.2.6 and §2.4.5) in which there are relatively rare exceptions to a given locking hierarchy. In these cases, code requiring multiple locks can try one ordering, and if it fails, release all locks and try a different ordering. This strategy can extend the range of applicability of containment-based locking schemes. You do not need to be absolutely certain that all locking maintains the desired ordering if you can arrange a somewhat more expensive fallback strategy to deal with exceptional cases. This might occur, for example, in hierarchical containment designs employing callbacks or collection traversals in which it is not possible to ensure conformance to a given set of lock ordering rules.

To illustrate basic techniques, here is a Cell class that employs such a deadlock-avoidance shuffle for swapValue. Upon getting stuck, it attempts to lock the two objects from the opposite direction:

```java
class CellUsingReorderedBackoff {
  private long value;
  private final Mutex mutex = new Mutex();

  private static boolean trySwap(CellUsingReorderedBackoff a,
                                 CellUsingReorderedBackoff b)
    throws InterruptedException {
    boolean success = false;

    if (a.mutex.attempt(0)) {
      try {
        if (b.mutex.attempt(0)) {
          try {
            long t = a.value;
            a.value = b.value;
            b.value = t;
            success = true;
          }
          finally {
            b.mutex.release();
          }
        }
      }
      finally {
        a.mutex.release();
      }
    }
    return success;
  }

  void swapValue(CellUsingReorderedBackoff other) {
    if (this == other) return;      // alias check required here
    try {
      while (!trySwap(this, other) &&
             !trySwap(other, this))
        Thread.sleep(100);
    }
    catch (InterruptedException ex) {
      Thread.currentThread().interrupt();
    }
  }
}
```

2.5.1.4 Non-block-structured locking

A Mutex may be used in constructions that cannot be expressed using synchronized blocks because the acquire/release pairs do not occur in the same method or code block.

For example, you can use a Mutex for hand-over-hand locking (also known as lock coupling) across the nodes of a linked list during traversal. Here, the lock for the next node must be obtained while the lock for the current node is still being held. But after acquiring the next lock, the current lock may be released.

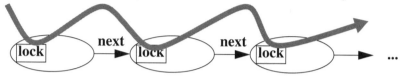

Hand-over-hand traversal allows extremely fine-grained locking and thus increases potential concurrency, but at the cost of additional complexity and overhead that would normally be worthwhile only in cases of extreme contention.

```
class ListUsingMutex {

  static class Node {
    Object item;
    Node next;
    Mutex lock = new Mutex(); // each node keeps its own lock
    Node(Object x, Node n) { item = x; next = n; }
  }

  protected Node head; // pointer to first node of list

  // Use plain synchronization to protect head field.
  //   (We could instead use a Mutex here too but there is no
  //   reason to do so.)

  protected synchronized Node getHead() { return head; }

  public synchronized void add(Object x) { // simple prepend

    // for simplicity here, do not allow null elements
    if (x == null) throw new IllegalArgumentException();

    // The use of synchronized here protects only head field.
    // The method does not need to wait out other traversers
    // that have already made it past head node.

    head = new Node(x, head);
  }
```

```
boolean search(Object x) throws InterruptedException {
  Node p = getHead();

  if (p == null || x == null) return false;

  p.lock.acquire();  // Prime loop by acquiring first lock.

  // If above acquire fails due to interrupt, the method will
  //   throw InterruptedException now, so there is no need for
  //   further cleanup.

  for (;;) {
    Node nextp = null;
    boolean found;

    try {
      found = x.equals(p.item);
      if (!found) {
        nextp = p.next;
        if (nextp != null) {
          try {              // Acquire next lock
                             //   while still holding current
            nextp.lock.acquire();
          }
          catch (InterruptedException ie) {
            throw ie;        // Note that finally clause will
                             //   execute before the throw
          }
        }
      }
    }
    finally {           // release old lock regardless of outcome
      p.lock.release();
    }

    if (found)
      return true;
    else if (nextp == null)
      return false;
    else
      p = nextp;
  }
}

// ...  other similar traversal and update methods ...
}
```

Another application of `Mutex` that exploits the lack of required block structuring is the construction of condition variable objects, discussed in §3.4.4.

2.5.1.5   Lock Ordering Managers

When multiple locks must be obtained in some particular order, for example in the hierarchical containment schemes discussed in §2.4.5 and the general resource-ordering techniques discussed in §2.2.6, you can help ensure conformance by centralizing the ordering methods in a lock manager class.

There are numerous techniques for structuring the kinds of locks used, defining their ordering rules, and establishing the responsibilities of the manager class. However, nearly any design contains methods of the following form, which illustrates the care required to ensure that locks will be released no matter what exceptions occur:

```
class LockManager {                                    // Code sketch
  // ...
  protected void sortLocks(Sync[] locks) { /* ... */ }

  public void runWithinLocks(Runnable op, Sync[] locks)
   throws InterruptedException {

    sortLocks(locks);

    // for help in recovering from exceptions
    int lastlocked = -1;
    InterruptedException caught = null;

    try {
      for (int i = 0; i < locks.length; ++i) {
        locks[i].acquire();
        lastLocked = i;
      }

      op.run();

    }

    catch (InterruptedException ie) {
      caught = ie;
    }

    finally {
      for (int j = lastlocked; j >= 0; --j)
        locks[j].release();

      if (caught != null)
        throw caught;
    }
  }
}
```

2.5.2   Read-Write Locks

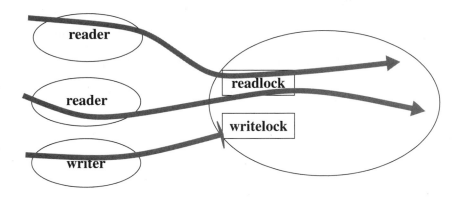

`ReadWriteLocks` maintain a pair of associated locks. One way to define them is:

```
interface ReadWriteLock {
  Sync readLock();
  Sync writelock();
}
```

The locks returned by the two methods here obey the same `Sync` interface as `Mutex` (see §2.5.1), supporting methods `acquire`, `release`, and `attempt`.

As discussed in §3.3.3, there are a number of ways to implement this interface, depending on selection of the desired policies surrounding their use. For the sake of illustration, we will assume definition of a generic implementation class `RWLock`.

The idea behind read-write locks is that the `readLock` may be held simultaneously by multiple reader threads, so long as there are no writers. The `writeLock` is exclusive. Read-Write locks are generally preferable to plain locks when:

- The methods in a class can be cleanly separated into those that only access (read) internally held data and those that modify (write).

- Reading is not permitted while writing methods are in progress. (If reads are permitted during writes, you may instead rely on unsynchronized read methods or copy-on-write updates — see §2.4.)

- Target applications generally have more readers than writers.

- The methods are relatively time-consuming, so it pays to introduce a bit more overhead associated with read-write locks compared to simpler techniques in order to allow concurrency among reader threads.

Read-write locks are often used in classes that provide access to large collections of data, where methods are structured as:

```
class DataRepository {                                  // Code sketch

  protected final ReadWriteLock rw = new RWLock();

  public void access() throws InterruptedException {
    rw.readLock().acquire();
    try {
      /* read data */
    }
    finally {
      rw.readLock().release();
    }
  }

  public void modify() throws InterruptedException {
    rw.writeLock().acquire();
    try {
      /* write data */
    }
    finally {
      rw.writeLock().release();
    }
  }

}
```

Read-write locks can be useful in some applications of ordinary collection classes. The `util.concurrent` package available from the online supplement contains a set of adapter classes that can be used with `java.util.Collection` classes, placing read-locks around purely inspective methods (such as `contains`) and write-locks around update methods (such as `add`).

2.5.3 Further Readings

A set of patterns for using different styles of locks can be found in:

McKenney, Paul. "Selecting Locking Primitives for Parallel Programming", *Communications of the ACM*, 39(10): 75-82, 1996.

CHAPTER 3

State Dependence

TWO kinds of enabling conditions are generally needed to perform any action:

External. An object receives a message requesting that an action be performed.

Internal. The object is in an appropriate state to perform the action.

As a non-programming example, suppose you are asked to write down a telephone message. To do this, you need to have a pencil and paper (or some other recording device).

Exclusion techniques are mainly concerned with maintaining invariants. State-dependent concurrency control imposes additional concerns surrounding *preconditions* and *postconditions*. Actions may have state-based preconditions that need not always hold when clients invoke methods on the host object. Conversely, actions may have postconditions that are unattainable when the host object is not in a proper state, when the actions of other objects it relies on fail to achieve their own postconditions, or when the actions of other threads have changed the states of other objects being relied on.

Most design issues for classes with state-dependent actions revolve around the considerations necessary to *complete* a design so that you take into account all possible combinations of messages and states, as in:

	have pencil	do not have pencil
phone ring	answer phone	answer phone
take message	write message	?

As hinted in the table, designs usually need to take into account situations in which the object is not in a state that permits any "normal" action. In an ideal system, all methods would have no state-based preconditions and would always fulfill their postconditions. When sensible, classes and methods should be written in this fashion, thus avoiding nearly all the issues discussed in this chapter. But many activities are intrinsically state-dependent and just cannot be programmed to achieve postconditions in all states.

There are two general approaches to the design and implementation of any state-dependent action, that stem from liveness-first versus safety-first design perspectives:

Optimistic *try-and-see* methods can always be tried when invoked, but do not always succeed, and thus may have to deal with failure.

Conservative *check-and-act* methods refuse to proceed unless preconditions hold. When preconditions do hold, the actions always succeed.

If methods check neither their preconditions nor their postconditions, they can be called only in contexts in which the preconditions are somehow known to hold. Reliance on such practices in concurrent systems is problematic at best.

Optimistic and conservative approaches are about equally prevalent, and appropriate forms of them may be equally good or bad with respect to various design forces. But since their general forms are governed by issues that may be outside of your control, the two are not always interchangeable. Optimistic approaches rely on the existence of exceptions and related mechanism that indicate when postconditions do not hold. Conservative approaches rely on the availability of guard constructions that indicate when preconditions hold and guarantee that they continue to hold across the course of an action relying on them. Mixtures are of course possible and are in fact common. In particular, many conservative designs contain code that may encounter exceptions, and thus must be prepared to deal with failure.

Concurrency control measures that deal with state-dependent actions can require significant effort and attention in concurrent programming. This chapter divides coverage as follows:

- §3.1 discusses exceptions and cancellation.

- §3.2 introduces the guard constructions used in conservative designs, along with the mechanics used to implement them.

- §3.3 presents structural patterns for classes employing concurrency control.

- §3.4 shows how utility classes can reduce complexity while improving reliability, performance, and flexibility.

- §3.5 extends problems and solutions to deal with *joint actions* — those depending on the states of multiple participants.

- §3.6 provides a brief overview of transactional concurrency control.

- §3.7 concludes with some techniques seen in the construction of concurrency control utility classes.

3.1 Dealing with Failure

Pure optimistic control designs originate from optimistic update and transaction protocols. But optimistic approaches of some sort are seen in just about any code making calls to methods that may encounter failures. Try-and-see designs attempt actions without first ensuring that they will succeed, often because the constraints that would ensure success cannot be checked. However, optimistic methods always check postconditions (often by catching failure exceptions) and, if they fail to hold, apply a chosen failure policy.

The need for try-and-see approaches usually stems from inability or unwillingness to check preconditions and related constraints. This can arise in the following ways:

- Some conditions cannot be computed using the constructs available in a given language or execution context. For example, it is not possible to check whether a given lock is being held or a given reference is unique (see §2.3).

- In concurrent programs, preconditions may have temporal scopes (in which case they are sometimes called *activation constraints*). If a constraint is not under the control of the host object, then even if it is known to hold momentarily, it need not hold throughout the course of an action relying on it. For example, your pencil may break while you are writing a message. A file system that is known at entry to a method to have enough space to write a file may run out of space (due to the actions of other independent programs) before the method finishes writing the file. Similarly, the fact that a given remote machine is currently available says nothing about whether it will crash or become unreachable in the course of a method relying on it.

- Some conditions change due to the signaling actions of other threads. The most common example is cancellation status, which may asynchronously become true while any thread is performing any action (see §3.1.2).

- Some constraints are too computationally expensive to check, for example a requirement that a matrix be normalized in upper-triangular form. When actions are simple and easy to undo or the chances of failure are extremely low, it might not be worth computing even simple preconditions, instead relying on fallback strategies upon later detection of failure.

In all these cases, the lack of provisions that would ensure success forces methods to detect and deal with potential failures to achieve postconditions.

3.1.1 Exceptions

Accommodations for failure infiltrate the design of multithreaded programs. Concurrency introduces the possibility that one part of a program will fail while others continue. But without care, a failing action may leave objects in states such that other threads cannot succeed.

Methods may throw exceptions (as well as set status indicators or issue notifications) when they have detected that their intended effects or postconditions cannot be attained. There are six general responses to such failed actions: abrupt termination, continuation (ignoring failures), rollback, roll-forward, retry, and delegation to handlers. Abrupt termination and continuation are the two most extreme responses. Rollback and roll-forward are intermediate options that ensure that objects maintain consistent states. Retries locally contain failure points. Delegation allows cooperative responses to failure across objects and activities.

Choices among these options must be agreed upon and advertised. It is sometimes possible to support multiple policies and let client code decide which one to use — for example via dialogs asking users whether to retry reading from a disk. Additional examples of these options are illustrated throughout this book.

3.1.1.1 Abrupt termination

An extreme response to failure is to let a method die immediately, returning (usually via an exception) regardless of the state of the current object or status of the current activity. This may apply if you are certain that local failure forces failure of the entire activity *and* that the objects engaged in the activity will never be used again (for example if they are completely confined within a session — see §2.3.1). For example, this might be the case in a file-conversion component that fails to open the file to be converted.

Abrupt termination is also the default strategy for uncaught (and undeclared) `RuntimeExceptions`, such as `NullPointerException`, that most often indicate programming errors. When a normally recoverable failure cannot be dealt with, you can force more extreme responses by escalating it to a throw of a `RuntimeException` or `Error`.

Short of full program termination (via `System.exit`), options for further recovery from such errors are often very limited. When objects are intrinsically shared across activities, and there is no way to re-establish consistent object states upon failure, and there is no possible (or practical) way to back out of a failing operation, then the only recourse is to set a `broken` or `corrupted` flag in the object encountering the failure and then abruptly terminate. Such a flag should cause all future operations to fail until the object is somehow repaired, perhaps via the actions of an error handler object.

3.1.1.2 Continuation

If a failed invocation has no bearing on either the state of the caller object or the overall functionality requirements of the current activity, then it may be acceptable just to ignore the exception and continue forward. While it is ordinarily too irresponsible to contemplate, this option may apply in event frameworks and one-way messaging protocols (see §4.1). For example, a failed invocation of a change-notification method on a listener object might at worst cause some parts of an animation sequence to be skipped, without any other long-term consequences.

Continuation policies are also seen within other error handlers (and inside most `finally` clauses) that ignore other incidental exceptions occurring while they are trying to deal with the failure that triggered them, for example ignoring exceptions while closing files. They may also be used in threads that should never shut down, and thus try their best to continue in the face of exceptions.

3.1.1.3 Rollback

The most desirable semantics in optimistic designs are *clean-fail* guarantees: Either the operation succeeds completely, or it fails in a way that leaves the object in exactly the same state as before the operation was attempted. The optimistic update techniques in §2.4.4.2 demonstrate one form of this approach in which the success criterion is lack of interference by other threads trying to perform updates.

There are two complementary styles for maintaining state representations that can be used in rollbacks:

Provisional action. Before attempting updates, construct a new representation that will, upon success, be swapped in as the current state. Methods perform updates on the tentative new version of the state representations, but do not commit to the new version until success is assured. This way, nothing needs to be undone upon failure.

Checkpointing. Before attempting updates, record the current state of the object in a history variable, perhaps in the form of a Memento (see the *Design Patterns* book). Methods directly perform updates on the current representation. But upon failure, fields can be reverted to the old values.

Provisional action is usually necessary when actions are not otherwise fully synchronized. Provisional action eliminates the possibility that other threads will see inconsistent, partially updated representations. It is also more efficient when reads are much more common than writes. Checkpointing is usually simpler to arrange and is thus often preferable in other situations. In either approach, it is not always necessary to create new representation objects to record state: often, a few extra fields in the object, or local variables inside the methods, suffice.

Situation-specific rollback techniques are needed for actions other than state updates that must be undone upon failure, including actions resulting from sending other messages. Every message sent within such a method should have an inverse *antimessage*. For example, a `credit` operation might be undone via `debit`. This idea can be extended to maintaining undo-lists associated with sequences of actions, in order to allow rollback to any given point.

Some kinds of operations can neither be provisionally attempted nor undone via antimessages, and thus cannot employ rollback techniques. This rules out methods with externally visible effects that irrevocably change the real world by performing IO or actuating physical devices unless it is possible to undo the actions without harm. In the case of IO, conventions can be adopted to allow the conceptual equivalent of rollback. For example, if methods log actions in a log file and the log file supports a "please disregard log entry XYZ" option, then this can be invoked in case of failure.

However, as discussed further in §3.1.2.2, rollback of most IO objects (such as `InputStreams`) themselves is typically not possible. There are no control methods to revert the internal buffers or other fields of most IO objects back to the values they held at some arbitrary point. Typically, the best you can do is close the IO objects and construct new ones bound to the same files, devices, or network connections.

3.1.1.4   Roll-forward

When rollback is impossible or undesirable but full continuation is also impossible, you may instead push ahead as conservatively as possible to re-establish some guaranteed legal, consistent state that may be different from the one holding upon entry to the method. Roll-forward (sometimes known simply as *recovery*) is often perfectly acceptable as far as other objects, methods, and threads are concerned; in many cases, they cannot even distinguish it from rollback.

Some such actions may be placed in `finally` clauses that perform minimal cleanup (for example closing files, cancelling other activities) necessary to reach *safe points* of program execution. Most roll-forward techniques otherwise take forms similar to rollback techniques. But because they do not require full representations of saved or provisional state, they are usually slightly easier to arrange.

Some methods can be divided into two conceptual parts: a preliminary part that can roll back easily (for example, by either returning or rethrowing the exception immediately), and the part occurring after a *point of no return,* at which some unrecoverable action has already begun, that must be advanced to a safe point even upon failure. For example, a method may reach a point in a protocol at which an acknowledgment *must* be sent or received (see §3.4.1.4).

3.1.1.5 Retry

You can contain local failure to the current method, rather than throwing exceptions back to clients, if you have reason to believe that retrying an action will succeed. Retries are in general only possible when local rollback options can be applied, so that the state of the object and status of the activity remain the same at the beginning of each retry attempt.

Retry-based tactics may be used when failure is due to other independent objects that may have been in temporarily bad or undesired states; for example, when dealing with IO devices and remote machines. As seen in §2.4.4.2, optimistic state update methods also typically rely on retries, since interference patterns are extremely unlikely to persist indefinitely. Retries are also common in polling designs, for example those discussed in §4.1.5. Variants of retries are seen in cascading algorithms that first try the most desirable of several alternative actions, and if that fails, try a series of less desirable alternatives until one succeeds.

Without care, retries can consume unbounded amounts of CPU time (see §3.2.6). You can minimize the likelihood of repeated contention-based failures, as well as reduce CPU wastage, by inserting heuristic delays between attempts. One popular strategy (seen for example in Ethernet protocols) is exponential backoff, in which each delay is proportionally longer than the last one.

For example, you could use the following method to connect to a server that sometimes refuses connections because it is overloaded. The retry loop backs off for a longer time after each failure. However, it fails upon thread interruption (see §3.1.2) since there is no point in continuing if the current thread has been cancelled. (As noted in §3.1.2.2, on some releases of JDK, you may need to modify this to catch `InterruptedIOException` and rethrow `InterrruptedException`.)

```
class ClientUsingSocket {                          // Code sketch
  // ...
  Socket retryUntilConnected() throws InterruptedException {
    // first delay is randomly chosen between 5 and 10secs
    long delayTime = 5000 + (long)(Math.random() * 5000);
    for (;;) {
      try {
        return new Socket(server, portnumber);
      }
      catch (IOException ex) {
        Thread.sleep(delayTime);
        delayTime = delayTime * 3 / 2 + 1; // increase 50%
      }
    }
  }
}
```

3.1.1.6 Handlers

Calls, callbacks, or notifications to error-handling objects can be useful when you need to offload error processing operations to centralized handlers because an exception in one thread or one part of a system requires compensating actions in other threads or other parts of a system that wouldn't otherwise be known to the method catching the exception. They can also be used to make code more extensible and more resilient when used by clients that cannot be expected to know how to respond to failures. However, some care is needed when replacing exceptions with callbacks, events, and related notification techniques. When they escape the stack-based flow-of-control rules of exceptions, their use can make it more difficult to predict and manage responses to failure across different parts of a system.

One way to set up a handler is to create a before/after class (see §1.4) that deals with exceptions as its *after*-action. For example, suppose you have an interface describing a service that can throw a `ServiceException`, and an interface describing handlers for the resulting exceptions. Implementations of `ServiceExceptionHandler` serve here as Strategy objects, as discussed in the *Design Patterns* book. You can then make a proxy for use by clients that do not handle `ServiceException` themselves. For example:

```
interface ServerWithException {
  void service() throws ServiceException;
}

interface ServiceExceptionHandler {
  void handle(ServiceException e);
}

class HandledService implements ServerWithException {
  final ServerWithException server = new ServerImpl();
  final ServiceExceptionHandler handler = new HandlerImpl();

  public void service() { // no throw clause
    try {
      server.service();
    }
    catch (ServiceException e) {
      handler.handle(e);
    }
  }
}
```

Note that while it is legal to declare that `HandledService` implements `ServerWithException`, all usages that rely on handlers would need to be statically typed to use `HandledService`, not the generic `ServerWithException` type.

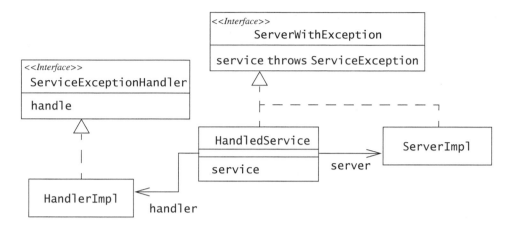

A handler object can perform any action that any code in a catch clause can, including shutting down processing in one or more threads or starting up other cleanup threads. The handler call can also somehow communicate the problem to error handling facilities occurring in a different thread, engage in some interactive protocol, rethrow the exception as a RuntimeException or Error, wrap it in an InvocationTargetException to indicate cascaded failures (see §4.3.3.1), and so on.

You can set up services in which clients *always* use handlers by supplying callback arguments to service methods. Callback-based handling may also apply when the service itself does not even know which exception it should throw upon failure. This can be set up via:

```
interface ServerUsingCallback {
  void anotherservice(ServiceFailureHandler handler);
}
```

Here all callers must supply a callback target (which may just be themselves) to be invoked in exceptional situations. Further details, alternatives, and variants are discussed in §4.3.1.

Handlers may also be used when converting one style of messaging protocol to another (see §4.1.1). For example, when using event-based frameworks, a service may generate and issue a new ExceptionEvent that is processed by an ExceptionEventListener. The following ServiceIssuingExceptionEvent class shows one way to set this up. It uses the CopyOnWriteArrayList from §2.4.4 for managing lists of handlers. Alternatively, the events could be issued asynchronously (see §4.1).

```
class ExceptionEvent extends java.util.EventObject {
  public final Throwable theException;

  public ExceptionEvent(Object src, Throwable ex) {
    super(src);
    theException = ex;
  }
}


class ExceptionEventListener {                    // Incomplete
  public void exceptionOccured(ExceptionEvent ee) {
    // ... respond to exception...
  }
}

class ServiceIssuingExceptionEvent {              // Incomplete
  // ...
  private final CopyOnWriteArrayList handlers =
                               new CopyOnWriteArrayList();

  public void addHandler(ExceptionEventListener h) {
    handlers.add(h);
  }

  public void service() {
    // ...
    if ( /* failed */ ) {
      Throwable ex = new ServiceException();
      ExceptionEvent ee = new ExceptionEvent(this, ex);

      for (Iterator it = handlers.iterator(); it.hasNext();) {
        ExceptionEventListener l =
                      (ExceptionEventListener)(it.next());
        l.exceptionOccured(ee);
      }
    }
  }
}
```

An inverse style of conversion, of events to exceptions, is used in the java.beans package, as described in §3.6.4.

3.1.2 Cancellation

When activities in one thread fail or change course, it may be necessary or desirable to cancel activities in other threads, regardless of what they are doing. Cancellation requests introduce inherently unforeseeable failure conditions for running threads. The asynchronous nature of cancellation[1] leads to design tactics reminiscent of those in distributed systems where failures may occur at any time due to crashes and disconnections. Concurrent programs have the additional obligation to ensure consistent states of internal objects participating in other threads.

Cancellation is a natural occurrence in most multithreaded programs, seen in:

- Nearly any activity associated with a GUI *CANCEL* button.

- Media presentations (for example animation loops) associated with normally terminating activities.

- Threads that produce results that are no longer needed. For example, when multiple threads are used to search a database, once one thread returns an answer, the others may be cancelled.

- Sets of activities that cannot continue because one or more of them encounter unexpected errors or exceptions.

3.1.2.1 Interruption

The best-supported techniques for approaching cancellation rely on per-thread interruption[2] status that is set by method `Thread.interrupt`, inspected by `Thread.isInterrupted`, cleared (and inspected) by `Thread.interrupted`, and sometimes responded to by throwing `InterruptedException`.

Thread interrupts serve as requests that activities be cancelled. Nothing stops anyone from using interrupts for other purposes, but this is the intended convention. Interrupt-based cancellation relies on a protocol between cancellers and cancellees to ensure that objects that might be used across multiple threads do not become damaged when cancelled threads terminate. Most (ideally all) classes in the `java.*` packages conform to this protocol.

In almost all circumstances, cancelling the activity associated with a thread should cause the thread to terminate. But there is nothing about `interrupt` that *forces* immediate termination. This gives any interrupted thread a chance to clean up before dying, but also imposes obligations for code to check interruption status and take appropriate action on a timely basis.

[1.] The two-*l* spelling of *cancellation* seems to be most common in concurrent programming.

[2.] Interruption facilities were not supported in JDK 1.0. Changes in policies and mechanisms across releases account for some of the irregularities in cancellation support.

This ability to postpone or even ignore cancellation requests provides a mechanism for writing code that is both very responsive and very robust. Lack of interruption may be used as a precondition checked at safe points before doing anything that would be difficult or impossible to undo later. The range of available responses includes most of the options discussed in §3.1.1:

- Continuation (ignoring or clearing interruptions) may apply to threads that are intended *not* to terminate; for example, those that perform database management services essential to a program's basic functionality. Upon interrupt, the particular task being performed by the thread can be aborted, allowing the thread to continue to process other tasks. However, even here, it can be more manageable instead to replace the thread with a fresh one starting off in a known good initial state.

- Abrupt termination (for example throwing `Error`) generally applies to threads that provide isolated services that do not require any cleanup beyond that provided in a `finally` clause at the base of a `run` method. However, when threads are performing services relied on by other threads (see §4.3), they should also somehow alert them or set status indicators. (Exceptions themselves are not automatically propagated across threads.)

- Rollback or roll-forward techniques must be applied in threads using objects that are also relied on by other threads.

You can control how responsive your code is to interrupts in part by deciding how often to check status via `Thread.currentThread().isInterrupted()`. Checks need not occur especially frequently to be effective. For example, if it takes on the order of 10,000 instructions to perform all the actions associated with the cancellation and you check for cancellation about every 10,000 instructions, then on average, it would take 15,000 instructions total from cancellation request to shutdown. So long as it is not actually dangerous to continue activities, this order of magnitude suffices for the majority of applications. Typically, such reasoning leads you to place interrupt-detection code at only at those program points where it is both most convenient and most important to check cancellation. In performance-critical applications, it may be worthwhile to construct analytic models or collect empirical measurements to determine more accurately the best trade-offs between responsiveness and throughput (see also §4.4.1.7).

Checks for interruption are performed automatically within `Object.wait` `Thread.join`, `Thread.sleep`, and their derivatives. These methods abort upon interrupt by throwing `InterruptedException`, allowing threads to wake up and apply cancellation code.

By convention, interruption status is cleared when `InterruptedException` is thrown. This is sometimes necessary to support clean-up efforts, but it can also be the source of error and confusion. When you need to propagate interruption status after handling an `InterruptedException`, you must either rethrow the exception or reset the status via `Thread.currentThread().interrupt()`. If code in threads you create calls other code that does not properly preserve interruption status (for example, ignoring `InterruptedException` without resetting status), you may be able to circumvent problems by maintaining a field that remembers cancellation status, setting it whenever calling `interrupt` and checking it upon return from these problematic calls.

There are two situations in which threads remain dormant without being able to check interruption status or receive `InterruptedException`: blocking on synchronized locks and on IO. Threads do not respond to interrupts while waiting for a lock used in a `synchronized` method or block. However, as discussed in §2.5, lock utility classes can be used when you need to drastically reduce the possibility of getting stuck waiting for locks during cancellation. Code using lock classes dormantly blocks only to access the lock objects themselves, but not the code they protect. These blockages are intrinsically very brief (although times cannot be strictly guaranteed).

3.1.2.2 IO and resource revocation

Some IO support classes (notably `java.net.Socket` and related classes) provide optional means to time out on blocked reads, in which case you can check for interruption on time-out.

An alternative approach is adopted in other `java.io` classes — a particular form of *resource revocation*. If one thread performs `s.close()` on an IO object (for example, an `InputStream`) `s`, then any other thread attempting to use `s` (for example, `s.read()`) will receive an `IOException`. Revocation affects *all* threads using the closed IO objects and causes the IO objects to be unusable. If necessary, new IO objects can be created to replace them.

This ties in well with other uses of resource revocation (for example, for security purposes). The policy also protects applications from having a possibly shared IO object automatically rendered unusable by the act of cancelling only one of the threads using it. Most classes in `java.io` do not, and cannot, clean-fail upon IO exceptions. For example, if a low-level IO exception occurs in the midst of a `StreamTokenizer` or `ObjectInputStream` operation, there is no sensible recovery action that will preserve the intended guarantees. So, as a matter of policy, JVMs do not automatically interrupt IO operations.

This imposes an additional obligation on code dealing with cancellation. If a thread may be performing IO, any attempt to cancel it in the midst of IO operations must be aware of the IO object being used and must be willing to close the

IO object. If this is acceptable, you may instigate cancellation by both closing the
IO object and interrupting the thread. For example:

```
class CancellableReader {                                // Incomplete
  private Thread readerThread; // only one at a time supported
  private FileInputStream dataFile;

  public synchronized void startReaderThread()
   throws IllegalStateException, FileNotFoundException {
    if (readerThread != null) throw new IllegalStateException();
    dataFile = new FileInputStream("data");
    readerThread = new Thread(new Runnable() {
      public void run() { doRead(); }
    });
    readerThread.start();
  }

  protected synchronized void closeFile() { // utility method
    if (dataFile != null) {
      try { dataFile.close(); }
      catch (IOException ignore) {}
      dataFile = null;
    }
  }

  protected void doRead() {
    try {
      while (!Thread.interrupted()) {
        try {
          int c = dataFile.read();
          if (c == -1) break;
          else process(c);
        }
        catch (IOException ex) {
          break; // perhaps first do other cleanup
        }
      }
    }
    finally {
      closeFile();
      synchronized(this) { readerThread = null; }
    }
  }

  public synchronized void cancelReaderThread() {
    if (readerThread != null) readerThread.interrupt();
    closeFile();
  }
}
```

Most other cases[3] of cancelled IO arise from the need to interrupt threads waiting for input that you somehow know will not arrive, or will not arrive in time to do anything about. With most socket-based streams, you can manage this by setting socket time-out parameters. With others, you can rely on `Input-Stream.available`, and hand-craft your own timed polling loop to avoid blocking in IO during a time-out (see §4.1.5). These constructions can use a timed back-off retry protocol similar to the one described in §3.1.1.5. For example:

```
class ReaderWithTimeout {                      // Generic code sketch
  // ...
  void attemptRead(InputStream stream, long timeout) throws... {
    long startTime = System.currentTimeMillis();
    try {
      for (;;) {
        if (stream.available() > 0) {
          int c = stream.read();
          if (c != -1) process(c);
          else break; // eof
        }
        else {
          try {
            Thread.sleep(100); // arbitrary fixed back-off time
          }
          catch (InterruptedException ie) {
            /* ... quietly wrap up and return ... */
          }
          long now = System.currentTimeMillis();
          if (now - startTime >= timeout) {
            /* ... fail ...*/
          }
        }
      }
    }
    catch (IOException ex) { /* ... fail ... */ }
  }
}
```

---

3. Some JDK releases also supported `InterruptedIOException`, but it was only partially implemented, and only on some platforms. As of this writing, future releases are projected to discontinue support, due in part to its undesirable consequence of rendering IO objects unusable. But since `InterruptedIOException` was defined as a subclass of `IOException`, the constructions here work approximately as described on releases that include `InterruptedIOException` support, although with an additional uncertainty: An interrupt may show up as either an `InterruptedIOException` or `InterruptedException`. One partial solution is to catch `InterruptedIOException` and then rethrow it as `InterruptedException`.

3.1.2.3 Asynchronous termination

The `stop` method was originally included in class `Thread`, but its use has since been *deprecated*. `Thread.stop` causes a thread to abruptly throw a `ThreadDeath` exception regardless of what it is doing. (Like `interrupt`, `stop` does not abort waits for locks or IO. But, unlike `interrupt`, it is not strictly guaranteed to abort `wait`, `sleep`, or `join`.)

This can be an arbitrarily dangerous operation. Because `Thread.stop` generates asynchronous signals, activities can be terminated while they are in the midst of operations or code segments that absolutely must roll back or roll forward for the sake of program safety and object consistency. For a bare generic example, consider:

```
class C {                                                  // Fragments
  private int v;   // invariant: v >= 0

  synchronized void f() {
    v = -1  ;    // temporarily set to illegal value as flag
    compute();   // possible stop point (*)
    v = 1;       // set to legal value
  }

  synchronized void g() {
    while (v != 0) {
      --v;
      something();
    }
  }
}
```

If a `Thread.stop` happens to cause termination at line (*), then the object will be broken: Upon thread termination, it will remain in an inconsistent state because variable `v` is set to an illegal value. Any calls on the object from other threads might make it perform undesired or dangerous actions. For example, here the loop in method `g` will spin `2*Integer.MAX_VALUE` times as `v` wraps around the negatives.

The use of `stop` makes it extremely difficult to apply rollback or roll-forward recovery techniques. At first glance, this problem might not seem so serious — after all, any uncaught exception thrown by the call to `compute` would also corrupt state. However, the effects of `Thread.stop` are more insidious since there is nothing you can do in these methods that would eliminate the `ThreadDeath` exception (thrown by `Thread.stop`) while still propagating cancellation requests. Further, unless you place a `catch(ThreadDeath)` after every line of code, you cannot reconstruct the current object state precisely enough to recover, and so you may encounter undetected corruption. In contrast, you can usually bullet-proof code to eliminate or deal with other kinds of run-time exceptions without such heroic efforts.

In other words, the reason for deprecating `Thread.stop` was not to fix its faulty logic, but to correct for misjudgments about its utility. It is humanly impossible to write all methods in ways that allow a cancellation exception to occur at every bytecode. (This fact is well known to developers of low-level operating system code. Programming even those few, very short routines that must be *asynch-cancel-safe* can be a major undertaking.)

Note that any executing method is allowed to `catch` and then ignore the `ThreadDeath` exception thrown by `stop`. Thus, `stop` is no more guaranteed to terminate a thread than is `interrupt`, it is merely more dangerous. Any use of `stop` implicitly reflects an assessment that the potential damage of attempting to abruptly terminate an activity is less than the potential damage of not doing so.

3.1.2.4 Resource control

Cancellation may play a part in the design of any system that loads and executes foreign code. Attempts to cancel code that does not conform to standard protocols face a difficult problem. The code may just ignore all interrupts, and even catch and discard `ThreadDeath` exceptions, in which case invocations of `Thread.interrupt` and `Thread.stop` will have no effect.

You cannot control exactly what foreign code does or how long it does it. But you can and should apply standard security measures to limit undesirable effects. One approach is to create and use a `SecurityManager` and related classes that deny all checked resource requests when a thread has run too long. (Details go beyond the scope of this book; see Further Readings.) This form of *resource denial*, in conjunction with *resource revocation* strategies discussed in §3.1.2.2 can together prevent foreign code from taking any actions that might otherwise contend for resources with other threads that should continue. As a byproduct, these measures often eventually cause threads to fail due to exceptions.

Additionally, you can minimize contention for CPU resources by invoking `setPriority(Thread.MIN_PRIORITY)` for a thread. A `SecurityManager` may be used to prevent the thread from re-raising its priority.

3.1.2.5 Multiphase cancellation

Sometimes, even ordinary code must be cancelled with more extreme prejudice than you would ordinarily like. To deal with such possibilities, you can set up a generic multiphase cancellation facility that tries to cancel tasks in the least disruptive manner possible and, if they do not terminate soon, tries a more disruptive technique.

Multiphase cancellation is a pattern seen at the process level in most operating systems. For example, it is used in Unix shutdowns, which first try to terminate tasks using `kill -1`, followed if necessary by `kill -9`. An analogous strategy is used by the task managers in most window systems.

Here is a sketch of sample version. (More details on the use of `Thread.join` seen here may be found in §4.3.2.)

```
class Terminator {

  // Try to kill; return true if known to be dead

  static boolean terminate(Thread t, long maxWaitToDie) {

    if (!t.isAlive()) return true;   // already dead

    // phase 1 -- graceful cancellation

    t.interrupt();
    try { t.join(maxWaitToDie); }
    catch(InterruptedException e){} //  ignore

    if (!t.isAlive()) return true;   // success

    // phase 2 -- trap all security checks

    theSecurityMgr.denyAllChecksFor(t); // a made-up method
    try { t.join(maxWaitToDie); }
    catch(InterruptedException ex) {}

    if (!t.isAlive()) return true;

    // phase 3 -- minimize damage

    t.setPriority(Thread.MIN_PRIORITY);
    return false;
  }

}
```

Notice here that the `terminate` method itself ignores interrupts. This reflects the policy choice that cancellation attempts must continue once they have begun. Cancelling a cancellation otherwise invites problems in dealing with code that has already started termination-related cleanup.

Because of variations in the behavior of `Thread.isAlive` on different JVM implementations (see §1.1.2), it is possible for this method to return `true` before all traces of the killed thread have disappeared.

3.1.3 Further Readings

A pattern-based account of exception handling may be found in:

Renzel, Klaus. "Error Detection", in Frank Buschmann and Dirk Riehle (eds.) *Proceedings of the 1997 European Pattern Languages of Programming Conference*, Irsee, Germany, Siemens Technical Report 120/SW1/FB, 1997.

Some low-level techniques for protecting code from asynchronous cancellation or interruption (e.g., masking hardware interrupts) are not available or appropriate in the Java programming language. But even many systems-level developers avoid asynchronous cancellation at all costs. See for example Butenhof's book listed in §1.2.5. Similar concerns are expressed about concurrent object-oriented programs in:

Fleiner, Claudio, Jerry Feldman, and David Stoutamire. "Killing Threads Considered Dangerous", *Proceedings of the POOMA '96 Conference*, 1996.

Detecting and responding to termination of a *group* of threads can require more complex protocols when applied in less structured contexts than seen in most concurrent programs. General-purpose termination detection algorithms are discussed in several of the sources on concurrent and distributed programming listed in §1.2.5.

Security management is described in:

Gong, Li. *Inside Java™ 2 Platform Security*, Addison-Wesley, 1999.

A resource control framework is described in:

Czajkowski, Grzegorz, and Thorsten von Eicken. "JRes: A Resource Accounting Interface for Java", *Proceedings of 1998 ACM OOPSLA Conference*, ACM, 1998.

3.2 Guarded Methods

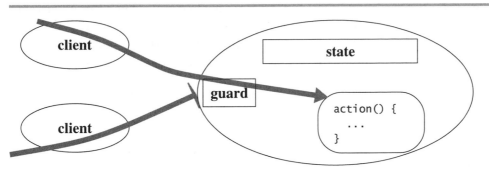

Conservative check-and-act methods refuse to perform actions unless they can ensure that these actions will succeed, in part by first checking their preconditions. The three basic flavors reflect policy decisions surrounding failed preconditions:

Balking. Throwing an exception if the precondition fails. The exceptions thrown are conceptually different from those seen in optimistic methods: here, an exception indicates refusal, not failure. But these exceptions usually have the same consequences to clients.

Guarded suspension. Suspending the current method invocation (and its associated thread) until the precondition becomes true.

Time-outs. The range of cases falling between balking and suspension, where an upper bound is placed on how long to wait for the precondition to become true.

There is no universally best policy choice among these options. As illustrated in §3.4.1, it is often possible to create multiple methods that support multiple policies among which clients may choose.

Balking is common in both sequential and concurrent programs. Refusal is the only sensible strategy when there is no reason to believe that a precondition will ever become true if it is not true already. For example, `Thread.start` throws `IllegalThreadStateException` if a thread is already started (see §1.1.2), since it can never again enter an unstarted state once started. Refusal is also the best choice for nearly all argument-based preconditions. For example, a graphics method might throw an `IllegalArgumentException` when asked to draw something with a negative size. Balking is also useful whenever a method is intended to have *now-or-never* semantics associated with the availability of resources. When refusal is not considered to be exceptional, a balking method need not throw an exception. This is seen for example in the `ParticleApplet.stop` method in §1.1.1.3, that quietly ignores attempts to stop the applet if it is not running.

3.2.1 Guarded Suspension

Guarded suspension and time-outs have no analog in sequential programs, but play central roles in concurrent software. This is reflected in the wide range of approaches to conceptualizing guards and in the many different notations and constructs available for designing concurrent software using guards. Before delving into implementation matters, it is worth stepping back to consider higher-level approaches and constructs that help organize designs relying on guarded suspension.

As fodder, consider the following toy BoundedCounter example, expressed for now only as an interface. The idea here is that implementations of Bounded-Counter are obligated to maintain a count between MIN and MAX:

```
interface BoundedCounter {
  static final long MIN = 0;   // minimum allowed value
  static final long MAX = 10;  // maximum allowed value

  long count();           // INV:  MIN <= count() <= MAX
                          // INIT: count() == MIN

  void inc();             // only allowed when count() < MAX

  void dec();             // only allowed when count() > MIN

}
```

3.2.1.1 Guards

In one sense, guarded methods are customizable extensions of synchronized methods, providing extended forms of exclusion. The "guard" for a plain synchronized method is just that an object is in the *Ready* execution state; i.e., is not engaged in any activity. At the implementation level, this means that the current thread is in possession of the object's synchronization lock. Guarded methods further partition the *Ready* state by adding state-based conditions (for example that count() < MAX) that are logically necessary for an action to proceed.

Guards may also be considered as special forms of conditionals. In sequential programs, an if statement can check whether a condition holds upon entry to a method. When the condition is false, there is no point in waiting for it to be true; it can never become true since no other concurrent activities could cause the condition to change. But in concurrent programs, asynchronous state changes can happen all the time.

Guarded methods thus pose liveness issues that simple conditionals do not encounter. Any guard implicitly asserts that, eventually, some other thread(s) will cause the required state changes to occur, or, if they do not, that it would be best never to proceed with the current activity. Time-outs are a way of softening such assertions, using a balking policy as a backup if the wait continues too long.

Some high-level design methods express conditional waits using an if-like construct called *WHEN* (also known as *AWAIT*) that can be useful in designing guarded methods. For example, here is a pseudocode version of the counter class using *WHEN*:

```
pseudoclass BoundedCounterWithWhen {              // Pseudocode
  protected long count = MIN;

  public long count() { return count; }

  public void inc() {
    WHEN (count < MAX) {
      ++count;
    }
  }

  public void dec()
    WHEN (count > MIN) {
      --count;
    }
  }
}
```

The *WHEN* constructs here express the idea that the `BoundedCounter` is obligated to keep the `count` between `MIN` and `MAX`. If a `dec` message is received but the count cannot be decremented because it is already at `MIN`, the thread is blocked, resuming sometime later if and when the count becomes greater than `MIN` via an `inc` message invoked by some method running in some other thread.

3.2.1.2 State-based message acceptance

Actions in guarded methods trigger only when both a certain message is received *and* the object is in a certain state. Because neither the message nor the state is necessarily primary, you can design abstract versions of methods with the two parts inverted. This state-based style can be easier to use when designing classes in which several different methods are all triggered in the same states, for example when the object is assuming a particular role. This form also more clearly reflects state-based notations used in several popular high-level OO analysis and design methods.

Ada concurrency constructs can be used to define methods in this fashion. Expressed in Ada-like pseudocode, the `BoundedCounter` is:

```
pseudoclass BoundedCounterWithAccept {                        // Pseudocode
  protected long count = MIN;

  WHEN (true) ACCEPT public long count() {
    return count;
  }

  WHEN (count < MAX) ACCEPT public void inc()  {
    ++count;
  }

  WHEN (count > MIN) ACCEPT public void dec()  {
    --count;
  }
}
```

Going to the extreme, some designs are easier to reason about if you think of actions as *always* being requested, but triggered only when the object makes a particular state transition. Some looping methods take this form. For example, you might design a special counter with a continuously enabled mechanism that resets the count to zero whenever it reaches a threshold. This style is sometimes called *concurrent constraint programming*, where actions can be triggered only by state changes since there are no messages.

3.2.1.3 Defining logical control state

Many objects maintain attributes that together constitute a very large (or for all practical purposes infinite) state space, but maintain only a small logical state space for purposes of guarding actions. For example, for purposes of `inc` and `dec`, `BoundedCounters` have only three logical states, not one state per value of their count:

State	Condition	`inc`	`dec`
top	`count == MAX`	no	yes
middle	`MIN < count < MAX`	yes	yes
bottom	`count == MIN`	yes	no

A bit of care is needed in characterizing these states. For example, if MAX is equal to MIN+1, then there is no distinct middle state. And if MIN is equal to MAX, then there is no way to distinguish top from bottom: neither method should ever fire.

As seen in the table, logical states are normally defined in terms of predicates — boolean expressions that distinguish particular ranges, values and/ or other computable properties of fields. They can be coded either as free-standing internal boolean methods or simply as boolean conditions written inside methods relying on them. When state analysis becomes too big and unwieldy for such techniques, you can design and encode states using *StateCharts*, tables, decision trees, automata, and related tools of the trade for dealing with state machines (see the Further Readings in §1.3.5).

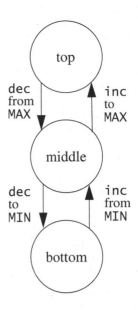

Instead of relying on predicate expressions, you can represent logical state explicitly in a variable. Each distinct state can be labeled as an integer or any other discrete data type. The field representing state must be re-evaluated upon each update so that it is always accurate (see §3.3.1). It is not strictly necessary to use a single variable — multiple variables can be used if object state can be partitioned on several independent dimensions. Special cases include:

- *Role variables* control responses to all of a related set of methods (often those declared in a single interface). When objects may alternate among roles, a single variable suffices to direct appropriate behavior. For example, an object may alternate between being a Producer and a Consumer. When in one role, it may ignore or delay responses to messages associated with the other.

- Rather than coding state as a value, you can code it as a reference to a *state-object*. For each state, you can write a class describing the behavior of the object when it is in that state. The main class then contains a reference field, say stateObject, that is always bound to the appropriate delegate. This is an application of the *States as Objects* pattern in the *Design Patterns* book; a variant is described in §3.7.2.

3.2.2   Monitor Mechanics

There are at least as many ways to implement guarded methods as there are ways to design them. But nearly all these techniques can be considered specializations of the following strategy employing methods `Object.wait`, `Object.notify`, and `Object.notifyAll`:

- For each condition that needs to be waited on, write a guarded `wait` loop that causes the current thread to block if the guard condition is false.

- Ensure that every method causing state changes that affect the truth value of any waited-for condition notifies threads waiting for state changes, causing them to wake up and recheck their guard conditions.

As a preliminary to discussing such techniques, here is a summary of the properties of waiting and notification methods.

In the same way that every `Object` has a lock (see §2.2.1), every `Object` has a *wait set* that is manipulated only by methods `wait`, `notify`, `notifyAll`, and `Thread.interrupt`. Entities possessing both locks and wait sets are generally called *monitors* (although almost every language defines details somewhat differently). Any `Object` can serve as a monitor.

The wait set for each object is maintained internally by the JVM. Each set holds threads blocked by `wait` on the object until corresponding notifications are invoked or the waits are otherwise released.

Because of the way in which wait sets interact with locks, the methods `wait`, `notify`, and `notifyAll` may be invoked only when the synchronization lock is held on their targets. Compliance generally cannot be verified at compile time. Failure to comply causes these operations to throw an `IllegalMonitorState-Exception` at run time.

The actions of these methods are as follows:

Wait. A `wait` invocation results in the following actions:

- If the current thread has been interrupted, then the method exits immediately, throwing an `InterruptedException`. Otherwise, the current thread is blocked.

- The JVM places the thread in the internal and otherwise inaccessible wait set associated with the target object.

- The synchronization lock for the target object is released, but all other locks held by the thread are retained. A full release is obtained even if the lock is re-entrantly held due to nested synchronized calls on the target object. Upon later resumption, the lock status is fully restored.

Notify. A `notify` invocation results in the following actions:

- If one exists, an arbitrarily chosen thread, say *T*, is removed by the JVM from the internal wait set associated with the target object. There is no guarantee about which waiting thread will be selected when the wait set contains more than one thread — see §3.4.1.5.

- *T* must re-obtain the synchronization lock for the target object, which will *always* cause it to block at least until the thread calling `notify` releases the lock. It will continue to block if some other thread obtains the lock first.

- *T* is then resumed from the point of its `wait`.

NotifyAll. A `notifyAll` works in the same way as `notify` except that the steps occur (in effect, simultaneously) for *all* threads in the wait set for the object. However, because they must acquire the lock, threads continue one at a time.

Interrupt. If `Thread.interrupt` is invoked for a thread suspended in a `wait`, the same `notify` mechanics apply, except that after re-acquiring the lock, the method throws an `InterruptedException` and the thread's interruption status is set to `false`. If an `interrupt` and a `notify` occur at about the same time, there is no guarantee about which action has precedence, so either result is possible. (Future revisions of *JLS* may introduce deterministic guarantees about these outcomes.)

Timed Waits. The timed versions of the `wait` method, `wait(long msecs)` and `wait(long msecs, int nanosecs)`, take arguments specifying the desired maximum time to remain in the wait set. They operate in the same way as the untimed version except that if a wait has not been notified before its time bound, it is released automatically. There is no status indication differentiating waits that return via notifications versus time-outs. Counterintuitively, `wait(0)` and `wait(0, 0)` both have the special meaning of being equivalent to an ordinary untimed `wait()`.

A timed wait may resume an arbitrary amount of time after the requested bound due to thread contention, scheduling policies, and timer granularities. (There is no guarantee about granularity. Most JVM implementations have observed response times in the 1-20ms range for arguments less than 1ms.)

The `Thread.sleep(long msecs)` method uses a timed wait, but does not tie up the current object's synchronization lock. It acts as if it were defined as:

```
if (msecs != 0)  {
  Object s = new Object();
  synchronized(s) { s.wait(msecs); }
}
```

185

Of course, a system need not implement `sleep` in exactly this way. Note that `sleep(0)` pauses for at least no time, whatever that means.

To illustrate some of the underlying mechanics, consider the following useless class that blindly issues `wait` and `notifyAll`:

```
class X {
  synchronized void w() throws InterruptedException {
    before(); wait(); after();
  }
  synchronized void n() { notifyAll(); }
  void before() {}
  void after() {}
}
```

Here is one possible outcome of three threads invoking methods on a common x. Notice that even though T1 began waiting before T2, T2 resumed before T1. It could have been otherwise; there are no guarantees.

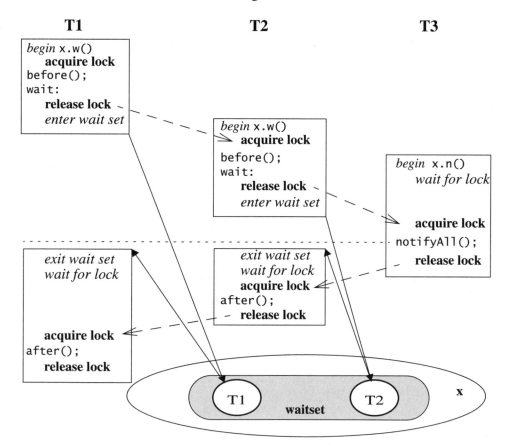

3.2.3 Guarded Waits

The standard coding idiom for expressing guarded methods is a simple `while` loop invoking `wait`. For example, the `inc` method of a `BoundedCounter` implementation might start out as:

```
synchronized void inc() throws InterruptedException {
  while (count >= MAX) wait();
  ++count;
  // ...
}
```

To ensure that guards are implemented correctly, it is sometimes helpful to encapsulate each guard in its own method. For a generic example:

```
class GuardedClass {                      // Generic code sketch
  protected boolean cond = false;

  // PRE: lock held
  protected void awaitCond() throws InterruptedException {
    while (!cond) wait();
  }

  public synchronized void guardedAction() {
    try {
      awaitCond();
    }
    catch (InterruptedException ie) {
      // fail
    }

    // actions
  }
}
```

Condition checks must be placed in `while` loops. When an action is resumed, the waiting task doesn't know whether the condition it is waiting for is actually true; it only knows that it has been woken up. So, in order to maintain safety properties, it must check again.

As a matter of programming practice, this style should be used even if the class contains only a single instance of `wait` that waits for a single condition. It is never acceptable to write code that assumes an object is in some particular state when it resumes after a given `wait`. One reason is that such code could fail just because some other unrelated object invoked `notify` or `notifyAll` on the target object by mistake. (These are `public` methods defined on all objects.) Additionally, it is wise to avoid breakage in the case of *spurious wakeups* in which waits are released by the system without any explicit call to a notification method[4]. However, a more important consideration is that without re-evaluation, such code will start failing in peculiar ways if people define additional methods (perhaps in subclasses of your class) that also use waits and notifications for other purposes.

Objects with guarded waits can be harder to think about than simple fully synchronized objects (§2.2.2). Methods with guarded waits are not completely atomic. A waiting method suspends without retaining its synchronization lock, thus allowing any other thread to begin executing any `synchronized` method on that object. (And, as usual, other unsynchronized methods can still execute at any time.)

Guarded methods thus need to be written so that objects are in consistent states upon entering `wait`. The best strategy for ensuring this stems from the general idea of check-and-act policies. If you place a guarded `wait` as the first statement in a method and do not change state in the process of checking it, then you cannot have changed state in any inconsistent way when entering `wait`.

3.2.3.1 Interrupted waits

A `wait` will be broken (or will not start at all) if the waiting thread has been interrupted. This enables blocked threads to respond to thread cancellation. In this sense, guarded methods are similar to try-and-see methods — attempts to pass preconditions may themselves fail — and the failure policies and implementations described in §3.1 apply.

By far the most common policy applied in guarded methods is just to rethrow `InterruptedException` to denote failure to the client, which will then need to deal with it. Assuming that guarded waits appear at the beginnings of methods, no further local cleanup is necessary.

The routine practice of rethrowing `InterruptedException` (or, in the usual case, merely not catching it) and thus including `throws InterruptedException` in method signatures also serves as a simple declarative assertion that a method employs a guarded wait or derivative. This can be vital information for potential users of a class (see especially §3.3.4).

[4.] As of this writing, the *JLS* does not specifically acknowledge that spurious wakeups may occur. However, many JVM implementations are constructed using system routines (for example POSIX thread libraries) in which spurious wakeups are permitted and are known to occur.

3.2.4 Notifications

Wait-based constructions make up the bulk of the safety side of guard implementation. To ensure liveness, classes must also contain code to wake up waiting threads when the conditions they are waiting for change. Every time the value of any field mentioned in a guard changes in a way that might affect the truth value of the condition, waiting tasks must be awakened so they can recheck guard conditions.

The simplest way to arrange that blocked threads eventually recheck conditions is to insert `notifyAll` in methods that cause relevant state changes. In turn, the simplest way to do this is to define utility methods that encapsulate assignment, issuing a notification upon any change in value. This may lead to useless signals and poor performance (due to context switching overhead) in classes that perform lots of assignments. However, as a design practice, it is occasionally a good idea to start out using blanket notifications within assignment methods, and then to minimize and reorganize them as discussed in later sections of this chapter. For example, here is a first pass at `BoundedCounter`:

```
class SimpleBoundedCounter {
  protected long count = MIN;

  public synchronized long count() { return count; }

  public synchronized void inc() throws InterruptedException {
    awaitUnderMax();
    setCount(count + 1);
  }

  public synchronized void dec() throws InterruptedException {
    awaitOverMin();
    setCount(count - 1);
  }

  protected void setCount(long newValue) { // PRE: lock held
    count = newValue;
    notifyAll(); // wake up any thread depending on new value
  }

  protected void awaitUnderMax() throws InterruptedException {
    while (count == MAX) wait();
  }

  protected void awaitOverMin() throws InterruptedException {
    while (count == MIN) wait();
  }
}
```

3.2.4.1   Slipped conditions and missed signals

In `SimpleBoundedCounter`, the calls to `awaitUnderMax` and `setCount` in method `inc` are performed under the same synchronized lock scope. It would not suffice to separately synchronize `awaitUnderMax` and `setCount` but not `inc`. This could encounter a safety violation. Expanding these out:

```
void badInc() throws InterruptedException {    // Do not use
  synchronized(this) { while (count >= MAX) wait(); }
  // (*)
  synchronized(this) { ++count; notifyAll(); }
}
```

This version may encounter a *slipped condition* in which the condition changes due to the actions of some other thread executing at point (*) — between the time the lock is released after the wait and then reacquired before incrementing the count. This could result in the action being performed even if the guard is now false, possibly breaking the object by causing the required invariant to become false.

Additionally, a liveness failure could result if `setCount` were written in a non-atomic fashion, in particular as:

```
void badSetCount(long newValue) {                // Do not use
  synchronized(this) { notifyAll(); }
  // (**)
  synchronized(this) { count = newValue; }
}
```

Here, the method first acquires the lock to perform `notifyAll`, then releases it, and then re-acquires it to change `count`. This could result in a *missed signal*: A thread executing at point (**) might start waiting *after* the signal intended to wake it up was issued but *before* the condition was changed. This thread will wait forever, or at least until the next notification is somehow produced.

Note that *within* `synchronized` methods, the order in which a `notifyAll` is placed does not matter. No awakened threads will be able to continue until the synchronization lock is released. Just as a matter of style, most people put notifications last in method bodies.

The mistakes leading to missed signals and slipped conditions illustrated here may seem farfetched. But they can be common sources of error in designs making more extensive use of waiting and notification techniques (see for example §3.7.2).

3.2.4.2 Single notifications

The SimpleBoundedCounter class uses notifyAll because threads may be waiting for the count either to be greater than MIN or less than MAX. It would not suffice here to use notify, which wakes up only one thread (if one exists). The JVM might pick a thread waiting for a condition that does not hold without picking the possibly many that could continue. This might happen, for example, if there are several threads all trying to increment and several all trying to decrement. (Consider for example the case where MAX == MIN+1.)

However, in some other classes, you can reduce the context-switch overhead associated with notifications by using a single notify rather than notifyAll. Single notifications can be used to improve performance when you are sure that at most one thread needs to be woken. This applies when:

- All possible waiting threads are necessarily waiting for conditions relying on the same notifications, usually the exact same condition.

- Each notification intrinsically enables at most a single thread to continue. Thus it would be useless to wake up others.

- You can accommodate uncertainties surrounding the possibility that an interrupt and a notify may occur at about the same time. In this case, the one thread that was notified is about to terminate. You might want another thread to receive notification instead, but this is not automatically arranged. (The issue does not arise with notifyAll since all threads are woken.)

To illustrate the relation between notify and notifyAll, the following GuardedClassUsingNotify class uses notify to approximate the effects of notifyAll by adding instrumentation to helper methods that encapsulate guards. Here, adding an *execution state* variable to track the number of waiting threads allows construction of a loop that broadcasts a notification to all waiting threads, thus simulating notifyAll (although only approximately — notifyAll is a primitive built-in operation).

The odd-looking catch clause seen here ensures that if a cancelled thread receives a notify, it relays that notification to some other waiting thread (if one exists). This safeguard is not really needed here since all waiting threads are being awakened anyway, but the technique should be employed in any code using notify in which interruptions do not necessarily shut down an entire program.

Note that the extra call to notify inside the catch clause may cause the count of waiting threads to overestimate the number of notifications necessary to wake up all threads. This in turn may cause more than the minimal number of calls to notify to be issued. This fact underscores the need to place waits in guard loops, even when using notify.

```
class GuardedClassUsingNotify {
  protected boolean cond = false;
  protected int nWaiting = 0; // count waiting threads

  protected synchronized void awaitCond()
    throws InterruptedException {
    while (!cond) {
      ++nWaiting;       // record fact that a thread is waiting
      try {
        wait();
      }
      catch (InterruptedException ie) {
        notify();       // relay to non-cancelled thread
        throw ie;
      }
      finally {
        --nWaiting;   // no longer waiting
      }
    }
  }

  protected synchronized void signalCond() {
    if (cond) {                      // simulate notifyAll
      for (int i = nWaiting; i > 0; --i) notify();
    }
  }
}
```

In open, extensible designs (see §1.3.4), the conditions under which notify apply are rather special and fragile. The use of notify, and optimizations of guarded constructions more generally, are common sources of error. As a general design tactic, it is a better idea to isolate uses of notify to concurrency control utility classes (see §3.4) that can be heavily optimized and carefully reviewed and tested. We adopt this approach throughout the remainder of this chapter.

The conditions for using notify hold much more frequently in closed designs, where you are in full control of all participating threads. For example, the following sketch of a closed-system two-player game uses waits for turn-taking. A single notify suffices to wake the only thread that can possibly be awaiting its turn. On the other hand, because there is only one thread waiting anyway, the performance differences between this version and one using notifyAll are probably too small to measure — the main overhead associated with notifyAll is context switching, not the call to notifyAll itself.

Note that giveTurn is invoked as an open call (see §2.4.1.3) in method Game-Player.releaseTurn. It is good practice to release as much synchronization as possible when performing notifications (see §3.7.2).

```
class GamePlayer implements Runnable {            // Incomplete
  protected GamePlayer other;
  protected boolean myturn = false;

  protected synchronized void setOther(GamePlayer p) {
    other = p;
  }

  synchronized void giveTurn() { // called by other player
    myturn = true;
    notify();                         // unblock thread
  }

  void releaseTurn() {
    GamePlayer p;
    synchronized(this) {
      myturn = false;
      p = other;
    }
    p.giveTurn(); // open call
  }

  synchronized void awaitTurn() throws InterruptedException {
    while (!myturn) wait();
  }

  void move() { /*... perform one move ... */ }

  public void run() {
    try {
      for (;;) {
        awaitTurn();
        move();
        releaseTurn();
      }
    }
    catch (InterruptedException ie) {} // die
  }

  public static void main(String[] args) {
    GamePlayer one = new GamePlayer();
    GamePlayer two = new GamePlayer();
    one.setOther(two);
    two.setOther(one);
    one.giveTurn();
    new Thread(one).start();
    new Thread(two).start();
  }
}
```

3.2.5 Timed Waits

Rather than waiting forever for a condition to become true in a guarded method, time-out designs place a bound on how long any given `wait` should remain suspended.

Responses to time-outs are of course situation-dependent. When time-outs are used heuristically, the fact that a predicate does not hold may be only of informational value. In other cases, time-outs force cancellation of attempted actions, in which case it is often appropriate to declare a `TimeoutException` as a subclass of `InterruptedException`.

Time-outs are typically more useful than other techniques that detect unanticipated liveness problems (such as deadlock[5]) because they make fewer assumptions about contexts — *any* stall that causes unacceptably long blockages can be detected by a time-out that then triggers failure responses (see §3.1.1). Since most responses to delays of any kind are the same, they can all be triggered by time-out exceptions or related notification techniques.

The parameters controlling wait time and condition re-evaluation are sometimes completely arbitrary, and often require some trial and error. Usually, it is not too hard to provide values that will catch true liveness problems without false-alarming on waits that just happen to be slow. Since many such failures will at some point require human intervention, policies can be backed up via mechanisms that query users about remedial actions.

Time-outs are somewhat awkward to express using `wait(msec)`. In the following `TimeoutBoundedCounter` class, the `wait` is placed in a loop in order to deal with the fact that unrelated notifications may occur. This loop is slightly messy but has the identical rationale as versions without time-outs. The condition being waited on is always checked first after waking up from the `wait`, before checking for time-out. This helps avoid programming errors stemming from cases in which a wait is released by a time-out, but other contending threads execute before the timed-out thread gets a chance to resume. One of those other threads could have changed the condition, in which case it would not be necessary or appropriate to return a failure indication. If the condition does not hold, the time-out value is checked and adjusted for use in the next iteration.

You could change this code to make the opposite decision about ordering the condition check and time check if time-outs are always considered to denote failure, even if the condition does hold upon resumption from the time-out.

---

5. Deadlock detection algorithms are discussed, for example, in the texts by Andrews and by Bernstein and Lewis listed in the Further Readings in §1.2.5. Implementation requires use of special lock classes. However, some run-time systems and debuggers contain features allowing detection of deadlocks involving built-in synchronization.

```
class TimeoutException extends InterruptedException { ... }

class TimeOutBoundedCounter {
  protected long count = 0;

  protected long TIMEOUT = 5000; // for illustration

  // ...
  synchronized void inc() throws InterruptedException {

    if (count >= MAX) {
      long start = System.currentTimeMillis();
      long waitTime = TIMEOUT;

      for (;;) {
        if (waitTime <= 0)
          throw new TimeoutException();
        else {
          try {
            wait(waitTime);
          }
          catch (InterruptedException ie) {
            throw ie;  // coded this way just for emphasis
          }
          if (count < MAX)
            break;
          else {
            long now = System.currentTimeMillis();
            waitTime = TIMEOUT - (now - start);
          }
        }
      }
    }

    ++count;
    notifyAll();
  }

  synchronized void dec() throws InterruptedException {
    // ... similar ...
  }

}
```

3.2.6   Busy Waits

Implementing guards via waiting and notification methods is nearly always superior to using an optimistic-retry-style busy-wait "spinloop" of the form:

```
protected void busyWaitUntilCond() {
  while (!cond)
    Thread.yield();
}
```

Busy-waits have drawbacks that make them poor choices for implementing most guarded actions. The contrasts between the two techniques help explain why suspension-based waiting and notification methods are defined as they are.

3.2.6.1   Efficiency

Busy-waits can waste an unbounded amount of CPU time spinning uselessly. The `wait`-based version rechecks conditions only when some other thread provides a notification that the object's state has changed, thus possibly affecting the guard condition. Even if notifications are sometimes sent when enabling conditions do not hold, conditions are likely to be unproductively rechecked far less often than in a spinloop that continually, blindly rechecks.

The main exceptions are those cases in which you somehow know that the condition must become true within some *very* short, bounded amount of time. In such cases, the time wasted spinning might be less than the time required to suspend and resume threads. This may apply to operations associated with device control. Bounded spins, followed by suspensions, are also sometimes used inside run-time systems as an optimization for "adaptive" locks that are usually held only briefly.

3.2.6.2   Scheduling

The `yield` in the spinloop version is only a hint (see §1.1.2) and is not guaranteed effective in allowing other threads to execute so they can change the condition. Thus the utility of busy-waits is more dependent on the policies of a particular JVM, and may interact with other aspects of scheduling. For example, if the spinning task is running at a high priority but the threads that change the condition run at low priority, the spinning task may still crowd the others out. In the `wait`-based version, the waiting task does not run at all, and thus cannot encounter such scheduling problems (although other scheduling problems can of course still arise).

Some of the most plausible situations for using spinloops are those in which some other action can be taken within the loop if the condition is not true, rather than just yielding. This helps limit CPU wastage and interacts better with common scheduling policies. If spinning is for some reason necessary and no other alternatives apply, you can reduce CPU costs and scheduling uncertainties by using the timed back-off techniques described in §3.1.1.5.

3.2.6.3 Triggering

Unlike wait-based constructions, methods with spinloops need not be paired with methods that provide notifications to trigger checks. Spinloops are sometimes used in desperation when no such signaling method exists or can be written. But busy waits can miss opportunities to fire if they happen not to be scheduled to execute during times when the condition is momentarily true.

Note however, that similar phenomena also occur in `wait`-based constructions: A condition signaled by a `notify` or `notifyAll` may later change due to the action of some other thread occurring before the notified thread gets a chance to continue. This is one reason to guard all forms of waits.

Additionally, neither technique alone automatically guarantees *fairness* — that each potentially enabled thread eventually proceeds. Even in wait-based constructions, it could happen that one particular looping thread that repeatedly encounters the guard is always the one that proceeds, starving out all others (see §3.4.1.5).

3.2.6.4 Synchronizing actions

It can be difficult to synchronize spinloops in the desired manner. For example, it wouldn't always work to declare the method `busyWaitUntilCond` as `synchronized`, since this does not allow any other `synchronized` method to change the condition. Minimally, `cond` needs to be declared as `volatile` and/or accessed and set in its own `synchronized` methods. However, without synchronization of an entire check-act sequence, you cannot in general ensure that an object remains in the same state between the condition test and the associated action.

As described in §3.4.2.1, reliable use of unsynchronized busy-waits in guarded methods is generally restricted to *latching* predicates that are somehow guaranteed to remain true forever once set. In contrast, the `wait`-based version automatically relinquishes the synchronization lock (for the host object only) upon `wait` and re-obtains the lock upon waking up. So long as both the guard and the action are enclosed within a common lock, and the guard references only variables protected by that lock, there is no danger of slipped conditions. This is one reason that `wait` statements can be used only under synchronization. However, the fact that waiting tasks hold any locks at all can be the source of logistical difficulties, including the *nested monitor problem* discussed in §3.3.4.

3.2.6.5 Implementations

In those rare cases in which you have no alternative to busy-waits, you can use a class such as the following SpinLock. There is never any reason to use this class for locking (see §2.5.1), but it is a simple vehicle for illustrating constructions that can be applied in other contexts.

The release method here is synchronized as an assurance that a memory synchronization occurs upon lock release, as would be necessary in nearly any use of this class (see §2.2.7). The escalation rules for failed checks are uncomfortably dependent on settings that are intrinsically platform- and application-specific (for example, the pure yield-less spin phase is plausible only on multiprocessors), and can be difficult to tune effectively even with empirical feedback.

```
class SpinLock {                        // Avoid needing to use this

  private volatile boolean busy = false;

  synchronized void release() { busy = false; }

  void acquire() throws InterruptedException {
    int spinsBeforeYield = 100;     // 100 is arbitrary
    int spinsBeforeSleep = 200;     // 200 is arbitrary
    long sleepTime = 1;             // 1msec is arbitrary
    int spins = 0;
    for (;;) {
      if (!busy) {                  // test-and-test-and-set
        synchronized(this) {
          if (!busy) {
            busy = true;
            return;
          }
        }
      }

      if (spins < spinsBeforeYield) {        // spin phase
        ++spins;
      }
      else if (spins < spinsBeforeSleep) {  // yield phase
        ++spins;
        Thread.yield();
      }
      else {                                 // back-off phase
        Thread.sleep(sleepTime);
        sleepTime =  3 * sleepTime / 2 + 1; // 50% is arbitrary
      }
    }
  }
}
```

3.3 Structuring and Refactoring Classes

The basic waiting and notification techniques described in §3.2 can be combined with other design strategies to improve reusability and/or performance, as well as to obtain finer-grained control over actions. This section surveys some common patterns, techniques, and problems seen when tracking logical state and execution state, wrapping control in overridable methods, and creating confinement-based designs.

3.3.1 Tracking State

The most conservative strategy for writing guarded methods is to call `notifyAll` every time you change the value of any instance variable. This strategy is highly extensible. If all changes to all instance variables generate `notifyAll`, then any method in the class and all of its possible subclasses can define a guard clause that waits for any particular state. On the other hand, this practice can be inefficient when it generates notifications that cannot possibly affect the guard conditions of any waiting thread. Often, some or all of these useless notifications can be eliminated via logical state analysis. Rather than issuing notifications upon all changes in instance variables, you can arrange to issue notifications only upon transitions out of the logical states in which threads can wait. The following examples illustrate techniques.

3.3.1.1 Channels and bounded buffers

Channel abstractions play central roles in several styles of concurrent software design (see §1.2.4 and §4.1). A `Channel` interface may be defined as:

```
interface Channel {
  void    put(Object x) throws InterruptedException;
  Object  take()        throws InterruptedException;
}
```

Methods `take` and `put` may be viewed as data-carrying analogs of `Sync` `acquire` and `release` operations (see §2.5.1), non-IO-based versions of stream `read` and `write` operations, encapsulated forms of transfer operations (see §2.3.4), and when channel elements represent messages, message `receive` and `send` operations (see §4.1.1).

199

A bounded buffer can be used as a channel (see §3.4.1 for some other alternatives). Bounded buffers have the same overall structure as bounded counters. In addition to a size (count), a buffer maintains a fixed array of elements. Instead of inc, it supports put, and instead of dec, it supports take. Also, the MIN is simply zero and the MAX is the capacity (declared as int to simplify use in array indexing).

```
interface BoundedBuffer extends Channel {
    int capacity();     // INV: 0 < capacity
    int size();         // INV: 0 <= size <= capacity
}
```

As described in just about any data structures textbook, implementations of BoundedBuffers can employ a fixed-sized array along with two indices that circularly traverse the array, keeping track of the next positions to put and take respectively. The logical states and transitions defined for a BoundedBuffer are similar to those for a BoundedCounter:

State	Condition	put	take
full	size == capacity	no	yes
partial	0 < size < capacity	yes	yes
empty	size == 0	yes	no

Notice that the only transitions that can possibly affect *waiting* threads are those that step away from states empty and full; that is, increment the size up from zero or decrement it down from the capacity.

These observations lead to the following implementation of BoundedBuffer in which notifications are issued only when transitions are made out of the empty and full states. (Part of the conciseness of the code is due to the convenience of *post*-increment and *post*-decrement coding idioms.)

This version can generate far fewer notifications than a version in which every change to size results in a notification, thus uselessly waking up threads. In cases where evaluating guards is itself computationally expensive, minimizing rechecks in this fashion results in even greater efficiency improvements.

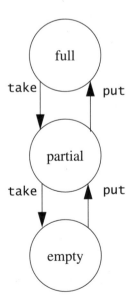

```
class BoundedBufferWithStateTracking {
  protected final Object[]  array;      // the elements
  protected int putPtr = 0;             // circular indices
  protected int takePtr = 0;
  protected int usedSlots = 0;          // the count

  public BoundedBufferWithStateTracking(int capacity)
   throws IllegalArgumentException {
    if (capacity <= 0) throw new IllegalArgumentException();
    array = new Object[capacity];
  }

  public synchronized int size() { return usedSlots; }

  public int capacity() { return array.length; }

  public synchronized void put(Object x)
   throws InterruptedException {

    while (usedSlots == array.length) // wait until not full
      wait();

    array[putPtr] = x;
    putPtr = (putPtr + 1) % array.length; // cyclically inc

    if (usedSlots++ == 0)                 // signal if was empty
      notifyAll();
  }

  public synchronized Object take()
   throws InterruptedException{

    while (usedSlots == 0)               // wait until not empty
      wait();

    Object x = array[takePtr];
    array[takePtr] = null;
    takePtr = (takePtr + 1) % array.length;

    if (usedSlots-- == array.length) // signal if was full
      notifyAll();
    return x;
  }

}
```

3.3.1.2 State variables

State tracking can sometimes be simplified and better encapsulated by using state variables that represent the entire logical state of an object in a single field (see §3.2.1.3). Usually, a state variable takes on values of an enumerated type. The variable is re-evaluated after any update to relevant fields. This re-evaluation may then be isolated in a single method, say `updateState`, called after each update method. After re-evaluating state, `updateState` issues notifications associated with the state change. For example, using a state variable in a `BoundedCounter` (a `BoundedBuffer` would work similarly) leads to:

```
class BoundedCounterWithStateVariable  {
  static final int BOTTOM = 0, MIDDLE = 1, TOP = 2;
  protected int state = BOTTOM;  // the state variable
  protected long count = MIN;

  protected void updateState() { // PRE: synch lock held
    int oldState = state;
    if      (count == MIN) state = BOTTOM;
    else if (count == MAX) state = TOP;
    else                   state = MIDDLE;
    if (state != oldState && oldState != MIDDLE)
      notifyAll();                // notify on transition
  }

  public synchronized long count() { return count; }

  public synchronized void inc() throws InterruptedException {
    while (state == TOP) wait();
    ++count;
    updateState();
  }

  public synchronized void dec() throws InterruptedException {
    while (state == BOTTOM) wait();
    --count;
    updateState();
  }
}
```

Instead of using `updateState` to reassess state, you can arrange that each method that performs updates also determines the correct next state and sends it as an argument to `updateState`, which can then still perform notifications upon change. (However, this may compound the fragility problems discussed in §3.3.3.3.) As the number of states grows, you can employ heavier machinery, such as finite-state machines or decision tables (see Further Readings).

3.3.2 Conflict Sets

Classes that track the execution state of underlying operations can use this information to decide what to do about new incoming requests. One of the main applications is construction of custom-made exclusion policies that provide more fine-grained exclusion control than seen in Chapter 2.

To illustrate, consider an `Inventory` class with methods to `store` and `retrieve` objects, each of which has a unique description. Suppose that these operations are somewhat time-consuming, but are implemented in a way that does not necessarily require low-level synchronization. In this case, we can allow those operations that do not semantically conflict with each other to execute at the same time, thus permitting more concurrency than possible in a fully synchronized version of the class.

In the classic context of this form of policy control, basic functionality is arranged via database transactions, but we will illustrate using `java.util.Hashtable`. Even though the fully synchronized `Hashtable` class allows an `Inventory` class to be defined without worrying about some low-level synchronization details, we still want to place some semantic constraints on the `store` and `retrieve` operations. One policy choice is:

- A `retrieve` operation should not run concurrently with a `store` operation since the `store` might be in the process of adding exactly the item requested, in which case you don't want to return a failure indication.

- Two or more `retrieve` operations should not execute at the same time, since one may be in the process of removing the item requested by the others.

We could have made other decisions here, for example even allowing all operations to operate concurrently, thus allowing failures. Also, we could have based the policies on the internal implementation details of the operations. For example, the above choices would also hold here if the `retrieve` method were programmed in a way that required exclusion, but `store` did not.

Several formal and semiformal notations have been devised to help represent this kind of information. The most widely used method, which suffices for most concurrency control problems of this kind, is based on *conflict sets* — sets of pairs of actions that cannot co-occur. For example, here the conflict set is merely:

```
{ (store, retrieve), (retrieve, retrieve) }.
```

This information can serve both as documentation of class semantics and as a guide for implementing these semantics via execution-state tracking.

3.3.2.1 Implementation

Classes based on conflict sets can employ before/after designs (see §1.4) in which ground actions are surrounded by code that maintains the intended exclusion relations. The following mechanics can be implemented via any before/after pattern:

- For each method, declare a counter field representing whether or not the method is in progress.

- Isolate each ground action in a non-public method.

- Write public versions of the methods that surround the ground action with before/after control:

  - Each synchronized before-action first waits until all non-conflicting methods have terminated, as indicated by counters. It then increments the counter associated with the method.

  - Each synchronized after-action decrements the method counter and performs notifications to wake up other waiting methods.

Applying these steps directly to the methods of an `Inventory` class leads to:

```
class Inventory {

  protected final Hashtable items = new Hashtable();
  protected final Hashtable suppliers = new Hashtable();

  // execution state tracking variables:

  protected int storing = 0;    // number of in-progress stores
  protected int retrieving = 0; // number of retrieves

  // ground actions:

  protected void doStore(String description, Object item,
                         String supplier) {
    items.put(description, item);
    suppliers.put(supplier, description);
  }

  protected Object doRetrieve(String description) {
    Object x = items.get(description);
    if (x != null)
      items.remove(description);
    return x;
  }
```

```
public void store(String description,
                  Object item,
                  String supplier)
 throws InterruptedException {

  synchronized(this) {                      // before-action
    while (retrieving != 0) // don't overlap with retrieves
      wait();
    ++storing;                              // record exec state
  }

  try {
    doStore(description, item, supplier); // ground action
  }

  finally {                                 // after-action
    synchronized(this) {                    // signal retrieves
      if (--storing == 0) // only necessary when hit zero
        notifyAll();
    }
  }
}

public Object retrieve(String description)
 throws InterruptedException {

  synchronized(this) {                      // before-action
    // wait until no stores or retrieves
    while (storing != 0 || retrieving != 0)
      wait();
    ++retrieving;
  }

  try {
    return doRetrieve(description);         // ground action
  }

  finally {
    synchronized(this) {                    // after-action
      if (--retrieving == 0)
        notifyAll();
    }
  }
}
}
```

(Because of the nature of the conflict set here, the notifyAll in the retrieve method happens always to be enabled. However, more generally the notifications should take the conditional form shown:)

3.3.2.2   Variants and extensions

The ideas seen in the above `Inventory` example also apply to optimistic methods, in which case conflicts are often termed *invalidation relations*. These are implemented by aborting conflicting operations before commitment rather than waiting until it is safe to perform them (see §3.6).

More extensive notation can be used to represent conflict at an arbitrarily fine level of detail, covering cases such as those in which, say, some `methodA` conflicts with `methodB` only if it occurs after `methodC`. Similarly, in the `Inventory` class, we might want to use a more precise notation in order to state that a `store` operation can commence if a `retrieve` is in progress, but not vice versa. A range of notation has been devised for such purposes (see the Further Readings in §1.2.5 and §3.3.5), enabling more detailed representation of conflicts while still allowing semi-automatic implementation via execution-state tracking variables. However, in the extreme, it may be that nothing short of a full history log suffices to implement a given policy.

The techniques described in §3.4 and §3.7 can be used to reduce the number of notifications and context switches in most classes relying on conflict sets.

Implementations based on execution-state tracking and conflict sets can suffer fragility and non-extensibility problems. Since conflict sets are based on the methods actually defined in a class rather than on logical representations of their semantics or underlying state invariants, they are difficult to extend when changing or adding methods in subclasses. For example, if a `sort` method is introduced to re-order the items in some fashion, or a `search` method to check if an item exists, they might conflict in different ways from those currently handled, requiring rework.

The Readers and Writers pattern and related constructions described in §3.3.3 alleviate some of these problems by classifying operations into extensible categories. The Readers and Writers pattern also addresses matters of precedence and scheduling that are not covered by conflict notations. For example, in `Inventory`, we might want to add a provision that if there are multiple waiting threads, threads waiting to perform `retrieve` operations are preferred over those waiting to perform `store` operations, or vice versa.

3.3.3 Subclassing

Subclassing can be used to layer different control policies over existing mechanism, or even vice versa. This practice extends the applications of subclassing seen in §2.3.3.2 that layer locking over bare functionality.

3.3.3.1 Readers and Writers

The Readers and Writers pattern is a family of concurrency control designs having a common basis but differing in matters of policy governing control of threads invoking accessors ("Readers") versus those invoking mutative, state-changing operations ("Writers").

In §2.5.2, we saw a version of this pattern encapsulated as a utility class. Here we show a subclassable before/after version using the template method pattern (see §1.4.3). Beyond its intrinsic utility, this design is a good model for any kind of policy that can be implemented by mixing together subclass-based before/after concurrency control and counters recording messages and activities. For example, very similar techniques apply to classes that require certain categories of messages to occur in ordered pairs (as in enforcing, say, `read`, `write`, `read`, `write`, and so on). They also apply to extended schemes supporting *intention locks* that reserve the option to later acquire (or upgrade to) read or write locks for any of a set of objects reachable from a given container (see §2.4.5).

Before putting control mechanisms in place, you must first establish a set of policies governing their use. Readers and Writers policies are generalizations of the kinds of concurrency-control policies seen, for example, in the `Inventory` class in §3.3.2. But rather than dealing with particular methods, they deal with all methods having the semantics of reading versus writing. However, the details are still situation-dependent. Considerations include:

- If there are already one or more active (executing) Readers, can a newly arriving Reader immediately join them even if there is also a waiting Writer? If so, a continuous stream of entering Readers will cause Writers to starve. If not, the throughput of Readers decreases.

- If both some Readers and some Writers are waiting for an active Writer to finish, should you bias the policy toward allowing Readers? a Writer? Earliest first? Random? Alternate? Similar choices are available after termination of Readers.

- Do you need a way to allow Writers to downgrade access to be Readers without having to give up locks?

Although there are no right answers to these policy matters, there are some standard solutions and corresponding implementations. We'll illustrate with a common set of choices: Readers are blocked if there are waiting Writers, waiting Writers are chosen arbitrarily (just relying on the order in which the underlying JVM scheduler happens to resume unblocked threads), and there are no downgrade mechanisms.

Implementing this concurrency control policy requires execution state tracking. Like most policies, it can be established by maintaining counts of threads that are actively engaged in the read and write operations, plus those that are waiting to do so. Tracking *waiting* threads is the main extension here of the techniques seen in typical implementations of conflict sets.

To structure the corresponding implementations, control code can be factored out into method pairs that surround the actual read and write code, which must be defined in subclasses. This before/after design (see §1.4.3) allows construction of any number of public read-style and write-style methods, where each public method invokes the non-public one within the pairs.

The following version is written in a generic fashion, so that minor variants are simple to implement in subclasses. In particular, the count of waiting readers is not really necessary in this version, since no policy depends on its value. However, its presence allows you to adjust policies by changing the predicates in the `allowReader` and `allowWriter` methods to rely on them in some way. For example, you might alter the conditionals to give preference to whichever count is greater.

```
abstract class ReadWrite {
  protected int activeReaders = 0;   // threads executing read
  protected int activeWriters = 0;   // always zero or one

  protected int waitingReaders = 0;  // threads not yet in read
  protected int waitingWriters = 0;  // same for write

  protected abstract void doRead();  // implement in subclasses
  protected abstract void doWrite();

  public void read() throws InterruptedException {
    beforeRead();
    try     { doRead(); }
    finally { afterRead(); }
  }

  public void write() throws InterruptedException {
    beforeWrite();
    try     { doWrite(); }
    finally { afterWrite(); }
  }
```

```
  protected boolean allowReader() {
    return waitingWriters == 0 && activeWriters == 0;
  }

  protected boolean allowWriter() {
    return activeReaders == 0 && activeWriters == 0;
  }

  protected synchronized void beforeRead()
   throws InterruptedException {
    ++waitingReaders;
    while (!allowReader()) {
      try { wait(); }
      catch (InterruptedException ie) {
        --waitingReaders; // roll back state
        throw ie;
      }
    }
    --waitingReaders;
    ++activeReaders;
  }

  protected synchronized void afterRead()  {
    --activeReaders;
    notifyAll();
  }

  protected synchronized void beforeWrite()
   throws InterruptedException {
    ++waitingWriters;
    while (!allowWriter()) {
      try { wait(); }
      catch (InterruptedException ie) {
        --waitingWriters;
        throw ie;
      }
    }
    --waitingWriters;
    ++activeWriters;
  }

  protected synchronized void afterWrite() {
    --activeWriters;
    notifyAll();
  }
}
```

This class or its subclasses may also be repackaged to support the Read-WriteLock interface discussed in §2.5.2. This can be done using inner classes. (A similar strategy is used by the util.concurrent versions of ReadWriteLock, which also include some optimizations discussed in §3.7 to minimize unnecessary notifications.) For example:

```
class RWLock extends ReadWrite implements ReadWriteLock {
  class RLock implements Sync {
    public void acquire() throws InterruptedException {
      beforeRead();
    }

    public void release() {
      afterRead();
    }

    public boolean attempt(long msecs)
     throws InterruptedException{
       return beforeRead(msecs);
    }
  }

  class WLock implements Sync {
    public void acquire() throws InterruptedException {
      beforeWrite();
    }

    public void release() {
      afterWrite();
    }

    public boolean attempt(long msecs)
     throws InterruptedException{
       return beforeWrite(msecs);
    }
  }

  protected final RLock rlock = new RLock();
  protected final WLock wlock = new WLock();

  public Sync readLock()  { return rlock; }
  public Sync writeLock() { return wlock; }

  public boolean beforeRead(long msecs)
   throws InterruptedException {
    // ... time-out version of beforeRead ...
  }

  public boolean beforeWrite(long msecs)
   throws InterruptedException {
    // ... time-out version of beforeWrite ...
  }
}
```

3.3.3.2 Layering Guards

Guards may be added to basic data structure classes that were originally written in balking form. For example, consider a simple `Stack`:

```
class StackEmptyException extends Exception { }

class Stack {                                        // Fragments

  public synchronized boolean isEmpty() { /* ... */ }

  public synchronized void push(Object x) { /* ... */ }

  public synchronized Object pop() throws StackEmptyException {
    if (isEmpty())
      throw new StackEmptyException();
    // else ...
  }
}
```

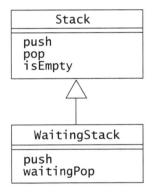

Balking on attempts to `pop` an element from an empty stack is attractive since it makes the class usable in sequential settings where it would be pointless to wait for a `pop`: if no other threads can add an element, the program will just stall forever. On the other hand, some clients of a `Stack` in concurrent contexts might want to hold up and wait for an element to appear. One inefficient approach is to try to perform `pop` and if a `StackEmptyException` is caught, to try again. This is a disguised form of busy-waiting.

A version that directly supports guarded usage can be built using a straightforward subclass-based design introducing methods that provide further coordination. However, it is not a particularly good idea to *override* method `pop` here. Among other considerations, the different policies of balking versus waiting are reflected in the different signatures of the methods: The balking form of `pop` can throw `StackEmptyException`, but a waiting version never can; conversely, a waiting version can throw `InterruptedException`, but a balking version never can. While these could be merged under some blander interface, it is more manageable all around to define them as separate methods.

Even so, it is possible to add method `waitingPop` in the subclass without needing to rewrite all of the internals of `pop`. Notice, however, that this also requires overriding `push` to provide notifications for threads blocked in `waiting-Pop`. (The `notifyAll` here could be further optimized.)

```
class WaitingStack extends Stack {

  public synchronized void push(Object x) {
    super.push(x);
    notifyAll();
  }

  public synchronized Object waitingPop()
   throws InterruptedException {

    while (isEmpty()) {
      wait();
    }

    try {
      return super.pop();
    }
    catch (StackEmptyException cannothappen) {
      // only possible if pop contains a programming error
      throw new Error("Internal implementation error");
    }
  }
}
```

3.3.3.3 Inheritance anomalies

Some concurrent OO programming languages (see Further Readings) syntacti-
cally require separation between non-public methods defining functionality and
public methods defining concurrency control policies; that is, they mandate the
kind of separation seen in the template method version of class ReadWrite. Even
when separation is not strictly required, it is an attractive option:

- It enables either action code or concurrency control code to be varied independently in subclasses, avoiding constructions that would make it impossible
  for the subclass to obtain desired functionality without rewriting nearly every
  method.

- It avoids the need to mix variables used solely for purposes of synchronization
  with logical state variables required for base functionality. Instead, these variables can be introduced in subclasses.

- It avoids problems surrounding exclusive control, access to internal variables
  and methods, object identity, nested monitors (§3.3.4), and interface adaptation encountered with other layering techniques. Subclassing extends objects
  rather than composing them. For example, no special considerations are
  needed to guarantee unique ownership of the superclass "part" of an object.

So long as all relevant variables and methods are declared as protected, a subclass can usually perform necessary modifications to base-level code in order to support a desired policy. Despite the best intentions of class authors, extensive surgery on method code in a subclass is sometimes the only way to salvage a class so that it obeys a given policy. Although protected access has some clear drawbacks as a design convention, in concurrent settings the resulting ability for subclasses to alter policy control can outweigh concerns about abuse of superclass representations.

For this to work, necessary invariants must be well documented. Superclasses relying on protected fields and methods and documented constraints are more likely to be correctly extended than those that publicly expose all fields (even via get/set methods), hoping that external clients can figure out how to preserve consistency, semantic invariants, and atomicity requirements for new actions or new policies.

But this form of subclassing does have its limitations. When people first started using experimental concurrent OO languages, several researchers noticed that it can be difficult or even impossible to define subclasses that add or extend commonly desired functionality or policy to superclasses. Similar concerns have been expressed in accounts of high-level OO analysis and design methods.

Some constructions in purely sequential classes are hard to extend as well, for example those declaring methods as final for no good reason. But enough additional snags are encountered in concurrent OO programming for this state of affairs to have been labeled the *inheritance anomaly*. The issues and problems covered by this term are only loosely related. Examples include:

- If a subclass includes guarded waits on conditions about which superclass methods do not provide notifications, then these methods must be recoded. This is seen in class WaitingStack (§3.3.3.2), where push is overridden solely in order to provide notifications for the new method waitingPop.

- Similarly, if a superclass uses notify instead of notifyAll, and a subclass adds features that cause the conditions for using notify no longer to hold, then all methods performing notifications must be recoded.

- If a superclass does not explicitly represent and track aspects of its logical or execution state on which subclass methods depend, then all methods that need to track and check that state must be recoded.

- Using state variables (§3.3.1.2) restricts subclasses to those in which synchronization depends only on the logical states or subdivisions of these states defined in the superclass. Thus, subclasses must conform to the same abstract specifications with respect to logical state. This practice is recommended in several accounts of high-level OO analysis and design, but can impede subclassing efforts. For example, suppose you want to extend class `Bounded-CounterWithStateVariable` to add a `disable` method that causes `inc` and `dec` to block, and an `enable` method that allows them to continue. Support for these additional methods introduces a new dimension to logical state that alters both the guard and the notification conditions for the base methods.

Taken together, these kinds of problems serve as a warning that, without more care than is usually necessary in sequential settings, you are likely to write concurrent classes that programmers (including you) will not be able to extend easily or usefully. Although they have no catchy name, similar obstacles may be encountered when trying to aggregate, compose, and delegate to objects.

An approach that avoids some of the most common extensibility problems is to encapsulate both guards and notifications in overridable methods and then structure public actions as:

```
public synchronized void anAction() {
  awaitGuardsForThisAction();
  doAction();
  notifyOtherGuardsAffectedByThisAction();
}
```

However, just as in sequential OO programming, there are no universally valid rules for making classes that can serve as useful superclasses for all possible extensions or can be used without modification in all possible contexts. Most guidelines for writing classes that avoid obstacles boil down to two well-known design rules:

1. Avoid premature optimization.

2. Encapsulate design decisions.

Both of these rules can be surprisingly hard to follow. More often than not, avoiding optimization requires more abstraction and scaffolding than optimizing for known situations. Similarly, you cannot encapsulate a design decision unless you are aware that a decision has been made. This requires contemplation of alternatives that may not occur to you upon first writing a class.

Rules such as these are perhaps most commonly applied retrospectively, during cleanup of existing code in efforts to make it more reusable. In an ideal world, you might be able to anticipate all the ways a purportedly reusable class must be opened up to make it more extensible. The world is almost never this ideal. Retrospective refactorings and iterative reworkings are honorable and routine aspects of software development.

3.3.4 Confinement and Nested Monitors

As discussed in §2.3.3 and §2.4.5, it is generally acceptable to confine synchronized Part objects within synchronized Host objects — at worst, you may encounter some superfluous locking overhead. However, this story becomes significantly
more complicated for Parts that employ waiting and notification methods. The
associated issues are usually described as *the nested monitor problem*. To illustrate the potential for lockout, consider the following minimal classes:

```
class PartWithGuard {
  protected boolean cond = false;

  synchronized void await() throws InterruptedException {
    while (!cond)
      wait();
    // any other code
  }

  synchronized void signal(boolean c) {
    cond = c;
    notifyAll();
  }
}

class Host {
  protected final PartWithGuard part = new PartWithGuard();

  synchronized void rely() throws InterruptedException {
    part.await();
  }

  synchronized void set(boolean c) {
    part.signal(c);
  }
}
```

Guarded suspension makes sense when you believe that other threads can
eventually unblock a wait. But here, the Host class structurally precludes other
threads from executing code that could do so. Problems here stem from the fact
that any thread waiting in a wait set retains all of its locks except that of the object
in whose wait set it was placed. For example, suppose that in thread *T* a call is
made to host.rely causing it to block within part. The lock to host is retained
while *T* is blocked: no other thread will ever get a chance to unblock it via
host.set.

These nesting constraints can lead to unexpected lockouts when otherwise
ordinary-looking synchronized methods invoke other equally ordinary-looking

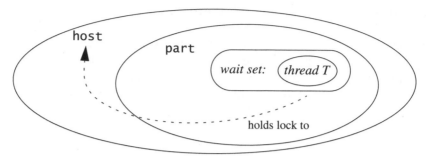

synchronized methods that employ `wait`. As with all policies for handling state-dependent behavior, you need to document and advertise the wait policies employed in a class so that people trying to use them have a chance to address potential problems. Simply adding `InterruptedException` to the signatures of guarded methods is a good start.

There are two general approaches to avoiding nested monitor lockouts. The first and simplest (in fact, just an application of our default rules in §1.1.1.1) is not to employ Host synchronization in the Host methods that relay to Part methods. This applies whenever the call is stateless with respect to the Host (see §2.4.1).

In other cases, where Part methods must access locked Host state, you can redefine Part classes to use an extended form of hierarchical containment locking (see §2.4.5) employing the Host as the monitor. For example:

```
class OwnedPartWithGuard {                              // Code sketch
  protected boolean cond = false;
  final Object lock;
  OwnedPartWithGuard(Object owner) { lock = owner; }

  void await() throws InterruptedException {
    synchronized(lock) {
      while (!cond)
        lock.wait();
      // ...
    }
  }

  void signal(boolean c) {
    synchronized(lock) {
      cond = c;
      lock.notifyAll();
    }
  }
}
```

3.3.5 Further Readings

More thorough discussions and further examples of inheritance anomalies can be found in the collection edited by Agha, Wegner, and Yonezawa listed in §1.2.5, as well as in papers presented at recent OO conferences such as *ECOOP*, the thesis by David Holmes listed in §1.4.5, and in:

McHale, Ciaran. *Synchronization in Concurrent Object-Oriented Languages*, PhD Thesis, Trinity College, Ireland, 1994.

The *Composition-Filters* system is an example of an OO development framework that requires separation of functionality from synchronization control. It also includes a more extensive notation than conflict sets for representing concurrency control constraints. See for example, papers by Mehmet Aksit and others in the collection edited by Guerraoui, Nierstrasz, and Riveill listed in §1.2.5.

Techniques for representing states and transitions (for example using finite state machines) are described in most accounts of OO and concurrent software design listed in §1.3.5. Additional patterns are discussed in:

Dyson, Paul, and Bruce Anderson. "State Patterns", in Robert Martin, Dirk Riehle, and Frank Buschmann (eds.), *Pattern Languages of Program Design, Volume 3*, Addison-Wesley, 1998.

The inner classes used in RWLock illustrate a simple, non-queryable version of the Extension Object pattern. See:

Gamma, Erich. "Extension Object", in Robert Martin, Dirk Riehle, and Frank Buschmann (eds.), *Pattern Languages of Program Design, Volume 3*, Addison-Wesley, 1998.

3.4 Using Concurrency Control Utilities

Built-in waiting and notification methods provide sufficient mechanisms for implementing any kind of state-dependent coordination scheme. But they present three related obstacles:

- The requirements and properties of waiting and notification methods often intrude into apparently unrelated aspects of class design, leading to unnecessary conceptual overhead and code complexity. For example, while the template-method version of Readers and Writers in §3.3.3 is sound and flexible, using it requires more understanding of the underlying design than does the version supporting the ReadWriteLock interface in §2.5.2.

- While simple applications of monitor methods are indeed simple, the chances for error (for example slipped conditions) can increase dramatically when additional factors are addressed, especially performance and robustness in the face of thread cancellation. When solutions are encapsulated as utility classes, the hard work of putting them together need be done only once. This may be worthwhile even when the resulting classes impose additional programming obligations on their users, as long as reusing classes is not more difficult and error-prone than re-inventing them. To improve software quality, utility classes (of any sort) should encapsulate not-so-simple implementations of simple ideas and impose minimal obstacles surrounding their use.

- While an unbounded number of designs can in principle be implemented via guarded methods, a large fraction of those used in practice fall under a small number of general categories. Much of the code for these can be reused, rather than rewritten from scratch inside each class using them. This also provides a clearer separation between the choice of a particular concurrency control policy and its implementation.

This section discusses four representative examples of utilities and their applications, including the construction of larger utilities out of more basic ones. A few others are introduced later in this book. For concreteness, descriptions focus on the versions available in the util.concurrent package, but nearly all discussions apply to any others you could construct. Most implementation details surrounding these classes are postponed to §3.7 (which is probably of interest only to developers creating their own customized versions of such utilities).

3.4.1   Semaphores

Semaphores (specifically, *counting semaphores*) are classic concurrency control constructs. Like many other utilities, they conform to an acquire-release protocol, and thus support the same Sync interface as class Mutex in §2.5.

Conceptually, a semaphore maintains a set of *permits* initialized in a constructor. Each acquire blocks if necessary until a permit is available, and then takes it. Method attempt is the same except that it fails upon time-out. Each release adds a permit. However, no actual permit-objects are used; the semaphore just keeps track of the number available and acts accordingly.

There are other ways to describe semaphores as well, including those based on their original motivating metaphor: the signaling flags used to prevent railroad collisions.

3.4.1.1   Mutual exclusion locks

Semaphores can be used to implement mutual exclusion locks simply by initializing the number of permits to 1. For example, a Mutex class could be defined as:

```
class Mutex implements Sync {
  private Semaphore s = new Semaphore(1);

  public void acquire() throws InterruptedException {
    s.acquire();
  }

  public void release(); {
    s.release();
  }

  public boolean attempt(long ms) throws InterruptedException {
    return s.attempt(ms);
  }
}
```

This kind of lock is also known as a *binary semaphore*, since the counter should only take on the values zero and one. One minor detail that is not (but could be) addressed here is that by the most common convention, releasing a Mutex that is not held has no effect. (A less common alternative convention is to throw an exception.) Otherwise, there is no strict need to define a Mutex class at all. A Semaphore initialized to 1 can be used directly as a lock, in which case "extra" releases are remembered and thus allow extra acquires. While this property is not at all desirable here, in contexts unrelated to locking it can be exploited as a cure for missed signals (see §3.2.4.1).

Because semaphores can be used as locks as well as other forms of concurrency control, they suffice as a single primitive concurrency control construct. For example, it is possible to implement the equivalents of `synchronized` method locks, `wait`, `notify`, and `notifyAll` operations out of semaphores rather than vice versa. (For details, see for example Andrews's book listed in the Further Readings in §1.2.5.)

Several systems and languages have in fact offered semaphores as their sole concurrency control construct. However, overreliance on bare semaphores for mutual exclusion purposes tends to be more complex and error-prone than block-structured locking, as enforced by `synchronized` methods and blocks and assisted by before/after constructions surrounding the use of `Mutex`. Semaphores are much more valuable in contexts that exploit their counting and signaling capabilities rather than their use as locks.

3.4.1.2 Resource pools

Semaphores are specialized counters, and so are natural choices for concurrency control in many classes involving counts. For example, pool classes of various kinds normally keep counts of resource items (e.g., file descriptors, printers, buffers, large graphical objects) that clients can check out and later check back in.

The following `Pool` class illustrates the basic structure of most resource pools. This class contains only one of several common and useful safeguards, ensuring that items checked back into the pool had actually been checked out. Others could be added, for example, checks to make sure that callers are eligible to obtain items.

To aid conformance to this check-out/check-in protocol, users of pools should normally employ before/after constructions, as in:

```
try {
  Object r = pool.getItem();
  try { use(r); }
  finally { pool.returnItem(r); }
}
catch (InterruptedException ie) {
  // deal with interrupt while trying to obtain item
}
```

The `Pool` class displays a layered structure characteristic of nearly all classes using concurrency control utilities: public unsynchronized control methods surround internal `synchronized` helper methods. Exclusion is needed in methods `doGet` and `doReturn` because multiple clients may pass `available.acquire`. Without locking, several threads could operate concurrently on the underlying lists. On the other hand, it would be a mistake to declare the `getItem` and `retur-`

nItem methods as synchronized. Not only would this make no sense, it can also cause a form of nested monitor lockout (see §3.3.4) when a thread waiting in acquire holds the lock needed by any thread that could perform a release.

```
class Pool {                                            // Incomplete
  protected java.util.ArrayList items = new ArrayList();
  protected java.util.HashSet busy = new HashSet();

  protected final Semaphore available;

  public Pool(int n) {
    available = new Semaphore(n);
    initializeItems(n);
  }

  public Object getItem() throws InterruptedException {
    available.acquire();
    return doGet();
  }

  public void returnItem(Object x) {
    if (doReturn(x))
      available.release();
  }

  protected synchronized Object doGet() {
    Object x = items.remove(items.size()-1);
    busy.add(x); // put in set to check returns
    return x;
  }

  protected synchronized boolean doReturn(Object x) {
    if (busy.remove(x)) {
      items.add(x); // put back into available item list
      return true;
    }
    else return false;
  }

  protected void initializeItems(int n) {
    // Somehow create the resource objects
    //    and place them in items list.
  }
}
```

Note that the use of HashSet here requires that the classes defining resource items *not* override method equals in a way that disrupts the identity-based comparisons (see §2.1.1) needed for pool maintenance.

3.4.1.3 Bounded buffers

Semaphores are useful tools whenever you can conceptualize a design in terms of *permits*. For example, we can design a BoundedBuffer based on the idea that:

- Initially, for a buffer of size n, there are n put-permits and 0 take-permits.

- A take operation must acquire a take-permit and then release a put-permit.

- A put operation must acquire a put-permit and then release a take-permit.

To exploit this, it is convenient to isolate the underlying array operations in a simple BufferArray helper class. (In fact, as illustrated in §4.3.4, a completely different underlying data structure such as a linked list can be used without otherwise altering the logic of this design.) The BufferArray class uses synchronized methods, maintaining exclusion when multiple clients receive permits and could otherwise insert or extract elements concurrently.

```
class BufferArray {
  protected final Object[]  array;       // the elements
  protected int putPtr = 0;              // circular indices
  protected int takePtr = 0;
  BufferArray(int n) { array = new Object[n]; }

  synchronized void insert(Object x) {  // put mechanics
    array[putPtr] = x;
    putPtr = (putPtr + 1) % array.length;
  }

  synchronized Object extract() {        // take mechanics
    Object x = array[takePtr];
    array[takePtr] = null;
    takePtr = (takePtr + 1) % array.length;
    return x;
  }
}
```

The corresponding BoundedBufferWithSemaphores class surrounds buffer operations with semaphore operations to implement put and take. Even though each method starts with an acquire and ends with a release, they follow a different usage pattern than seen with locks in §2.5. The release is on a different semaphore from the acquire, and is performed only after the element is successfully inserted or extracted. So, among other consequences, these releases are not placed in finally clauses: If there were any chance that buffer operations could fail, some recovery actions would be needed, but these trailing release statements are not among them.

```
class BoundedBufferWithSemaphores {
  protected final BufferArray buff;
  protected final Semaphore putPermits;
  protected final Semaphore takePermits;

  public BoundedBufferWithSemaphores(int capacity) {
    if (capacity <= 0) throw new IllegalArgumentException();
    buff = new BufferArray(capacity);
    putPermits = new Semaphore(capacity);
    takePermits = new Semaphore(0);
  }

  public void put(Object x) throws InterruptedException {
    putPermits.acquire();
    buff.insert(x);
    takePermits.release();
  }

  public Object take() throws InterruptedException {
    takePermits.acquire();
    Object x = buff.extract();
    putPermits.release();
    return x;
  }

  public Object poll(long msecs) throws InterruptedException {
    if (!takePermits.attempt(msecs)) return null;
    Object x = buff.extract();
    putPermits.release();
    return x;
  }

  public boolean offer(Object x, long msecs)
   throws InterruptedException {
    if (!putPermits.attempt(msecs)) return false;
    buff.insert(x);
    takePermits.release();
    return true;
  }
}
```

This class also includes variants of put and take, called offer and poll, that support balking (when msecs is 0) or time-out policies. These methods are implemented using Semaphore.attempt, which handles the messy time-based constructions described in §3.2.5. Methods offer and poll allow clients to choose the guarding policy most appropriate for their needs. However, clients must still pick compatible policies. For example, if a producer relied solely on offer(x, 0) and its only consumer used poll(0), items would rarely be transferred.

The BoundedBufferWithSemaphores class is likely to run more efficiently than the BoundedBufferWithStateTracking class in §3.3.1 when there are many threads all using the buffer. BoundedBufferWithSemaphores relies on two different underlying wait sets. The BoundedBufferWithStateTracking class gets by with only one, so any empty-to-partial or full-to-partial state transition causes all waiting threads to wake up, including those waiting for the other logical condition and those that will immediately rewait because some other thread took the only item or filled the only available slot.

The BoundedBufferWithSemaphores class isolates the monitors for these two conditions. This can be exploited by the underlying Semaphore implementation (see §3.7.1) to eliminate unnecessary context switching by using notify instead of notifyAll. This reduces the worst-case number of wakeups from being a quadratic function of the number of invocations to being linear. More generally, whenever you can isolate a condition using a semaphore, you can usually improve performance as compared to notifyAll-based solutions.

3.4.1.4 Synchronous channels

As mentioned in §3.3.1, the interface for BoundedBuffer can be broadened to describe any kind of Channel that supports a put and a take operation:

```
interface Channel {                                      // Repeated
  void  put(Object x) throws InterruptedException;
  Object take()        throws InterruptedException;
}
```

(The util.concurrent version of this interface also includes the offer and poll methods that support time-outs, and declares it to extend interfaces Puttable and Takable to allow type enforcement of one-sided usages.)

There are many possible semantics that you might attach to a Channel. For example, the queue class in §2.4.2 has unbounded capacity (at least conceptually — failing only when a system runs out of memory), while bounded buffers have finite predetermined capacity. A limiting case is the idea of a *synchronous channel* that has *no* internal capacity. With synchronous channels, every thread attempting a put must wait for a thread attempting a take, and vice versa. This allows the precise control over thread interaction needed in several of the design frameworks and patterns discussed in §4.1.4 and §4.5.1.

Semaphores can be used to implement synchronous channels. Here, we can use the same approach as with bounded buffers, adding another semaphore that permits a put to continue only after its offered item has been taken. However, this introduces a new problem. So far, we have used only blocking constructions that can throw InterruptedExceptions as the first lines of methods, allowing simple clean exit upon interruption. But here, we need to do a second `acquire` at the end of the `put` method. Aborting at this point of no return would break the protocol. While it is possible to define a version of this class that performs full rollback, the simplest solution here is to roll forward (see §3.1.1.4), ignoring any interrupt until after the second `acquire` completes:

```
class SynchronousChannel implements Channel {

  protected Object item = null; // to hold while in transit

  protected final Semaphore putPermit;
  protected final Semaphore takePermit;
  protected final Semaphore taken;

  public SynchronousChannel() {
    putPermit = new Semaphore(1);
    takePermit = new Semaphore(0);
    taken = new Semaphore(0);
  }

  public void put(Object x) throws InterruptedException {
    putPermit.acquire();
    item = x;
    takePermit.release();

    // Must wait until signaled by taker
    InterruptedException caught = null;
    for (;;) {
      try {
        taken.acquire();
        break;
      }
      catch(InterruptedException ie) { caught = ie; }
    }

    if (caught != null) throw caught; // can now rethrow
  }

  public Object take() throws InterruptedException {
    takePermit.acquire();
    Object x = item;
    item = null;
    putPermit.release();
    taken.release();
    return x;
  }
}
```

3.4.1.5 Fairness and scheduling

Built-in waiting and notification methods do not provide any fairness guarantees. They make no promises about which of the threads in a wait set will be chosen in a `notify` operation, or which thread will grab the lock first and be able to proceed (thus excluding others) in a `notifyAll` operation.

This flexibility in JVM implementations permitted by the *JLS* makes it all but impossible to *prove* particular liveness properties of a system. But this is not a practical concern in most contexts. For example, in most buffer applications, it doesn't matter at all which of the several threads trying to `take` an item actually do so. On the other hand, in a resource pool management class, it is prudent to ensure that threads waiting for needed resource items don't continually get pushed aside by others because of unfairness in how the underlying `notify` operations choose which threads to unblock. Similar concerns arise in many applications of synchronous channels.

It is not possible to change the semantics of `notify`, but it is possible to implement `Semaphore` (sub)class `acquire` operations to provide stronger fairness properties. A range of policies can be supported, varying in exactly how fairness is defined.

The best-known policy is First-In-First-Out (FIFO), in which the thread that has been waiting the longest is always selected. This is intuitively desirable, but can be unnecessarily demanding and even somewhat arbitrary on multiprocessors where different threads on different processors start waiting at (approximately) the same time. However, various weakenings of and approximations to FIFO are available that provide sufficient fairness for applications that need to avoid indefinite postponement.

There are, however, some intrinsic limitations to such guarantees: There is no way to ensure that an underlying system will ever actually execute a given runnable process or thread unless the system provides guarantees that go beyond the minimal requirements stated in the *JLS*. However, this is unlikely to be a significant pragmatic issue. Most if not all JVM implementations strive to provide sensible scheduling policies that extend well beyond minimal requirements. They display some sort of weak, restricted, or probabilistic fairness properties with respect to executing runnable threads. However, it is difficult for a language specification to state all the reasonable ways in which this may occur. The matter is left as a quality-of-implementation issue in the *JLS*.

Utility classes such as semaphores are convenient vehicles for establishing different fairness policies, modulo these scheduling caveats. For example, §3.7.3 describes implementation of a `FIFOSemaphore` class that maintains FIFO notification order. Applications such as the `Pool` class can use this or other implementations of semaphores that provide any supported fairness properties, at the potential cost of additional overhead.

3.4.1.6 Priorities

In addition to addressing fairness, semaphore implementation classes can pay attention to thread priorities. The `notify` method is not guaranteed to do so, but it is of course allowed to, and does so on some JVM implementations.

Priority settings (see §1.1.2.3) tend to be of value only when there may be many more runnable threads than CPUs, and the tasks running in these threads intrinsically have different urgencies or importances. This occurs most commonly in embedded (soft) real-time systems where a single small processor must carry out many tasks that interact with its environment.

Reliance on priority settings can complicate notification policies. Even if notifications unblock (and run) threads in highest-priority-first order, systems may still encounter *priority inversions*. A priority inversion occurs when a high-priority thread becomes blocked waiting for a low-priority thread to complete and then release a lock or change a condition needed by the high-priority thread. In a system using strict priority scheduling, this can cause the high-priority thread to starve if the low-priority thread does not get a chance to run.

One solution is to use special semaphore classes or lock classes constructed via such semaphores. Here, the concurrency control objects themselves manipulate priorities. When a high-priority thread becomes blocked, the concurrency control object can temporarily raise the priority of a low-priority thread that could unblock it. This reflects the fact that proceeding to a release point is a high-priority action (see Further Readings in §1.2.5). For this to work, *all* relevant synchronization and locking must rely on such priority-adjusting utility classes.

Further, this tactic is guaranteed to maintain the intended properties only on particular JVM implementations that use strict priority scheduling. In practice, any usable JVM implementation supporting strict priority scheduling is sure to apply priority adjustment for built-in lock and monitor operations. Doing otherwise would defeat most of the rationale for adopting strict priority scheduling in the first place.

The main practical consequence is that programs that absolutely rely on strict priority scheduling sacrifice portability. They need additional JVM implementation-specific guarantees that may be bolstered via construction and use of additional concurrency control utilities. In other more portable programs, semaphore classes and related utilities that prefer higher-priority threads can still be used occasionally as devices for heuristically improving responsiveness.

3.4.2 Latches

A latching variable or condition is one that eventually receives a value from which it never again changes. A *binary* latching variable or condition (normally just called a *latch*, also known as a *one-shot*) can change value only once, from its initial state to its final state.

Concurrency control techniques surrounding latches can be encapsulated using a simple `Latch` class that again obeys the usual acquire-release interface, but with the semantics that a *single* `release` permits all previous and future `acquire` operations to proceed.

Latches help structure solutions to initialization problems (see §2.4.1) where you do not want a set of activities to proceed until all objects and threads have been completely constructed. For example, a more ambitious game-playing application than shown in §3.2.4 might need to ensure that all players wait until the game officially begins. This could be arranged using code such as:

```
class Player implements Runnable {              // Code sketch
  // ...
  protected final Latch startSignal;

  Player(Latch l) { startSignal = l; }

  public void run() {
    try {
      startSignal.acquire();
      play();
    }
    catch(InterruptedException ie) { return; }
  }
  // ...
}

class Game {
  // ...
  void begin(int nplayers) {
    Latch startSignal = new Latch();

    for (int i = 0; i < nplayers; ++i)
      new Thread(new Player(startSignal)).start();

    startSignal.release();
  }
}
```

Extended forms of latches include *countdowns*, which allow `acquire` to proceed when a fixed number of `releases` occur, not just one. Latches, countdowns, and other simple utilities built on top of them can be used to coordinate responses to conditions involving:

Completion indicators. For example, to force a set of threads to wait until some other activity completes.

Timing thresholds. For example, to trigger a set of threads at a certain date.

Event indications. For example, to trigger processing that cannot occur until a certain packet is received or button is clicked.

Error indications. For example, to trigger a set of threads to proceed with global shut-down tasks.

3.4.2.1 Latching variables and predicates

While utility classes are convenient for most one-shot triggering applications, latching fields (also known as *permanent* variables) and predicates can improve reliability, simplify usage, and improve efficiency in other contexts as well.

Among their other properties, latching predicates (including the common special case of threshold indicators) are among the very few conditions for which unsynchronized busy-wait loops (see §3.2.6) may be a possible (although rarely taken) implementation option for guarded methods. If a predicate is known to latch, then there is no risk that it will slip (see §3.2.4.1). Its value cannot change between the check to see if it is true and a subsequent action that requires it to remain true. For example:

```
class LatchingThermometer {                          // Seldom useful
  private volatile boolean ready; // latching
  private volatile float temperature;

  public double getReading() {
    while (!ready)
      Thread.yield();
    return temperature;
  }

  void sense(float t) { // called from sensor
    temperature = t;
    ready = true;
  }
}
```

Note that this kind of construction is confined to classes in which *all* relevant variables are either declared as volatile or are read and written only under synchronization (see §2.2.7).

3.4.3 Exchangers

An exchanger acts as a synchronous channel (see §3.4.1.4) except that instead of supporting two methods, `put` and `take`, it supports only one method, `rendezvous` (sometimes just called `exchange`) that combines their effects (see §2.3.4). This operation takes an argument representing an `Object` offered by one thread to another, and returns the `Object` offered by the other thread.

Exchangers can be generalized to more than two parties, and can be further generalized to apply arbitrary functions on arguments rather than simply exchanging them. These capabilities are supported by the `Rendezvous` class in `util.concurrent`. But the majority of applications are restricted to the exchange of resource objects among two threads (as arranged below by using only the default two-party constructor for `Rendezvous`).

Exchange-based protocols extend those described in §2.3.4 to serve as alternatives to resource pools (see §3.4.1.2). They can be used when two or more tasks running in different threads at all times *each* maintain one resource. When one thread is finished with one resource and needs another, it exchanges with another thread. The most common application of this protocol is buffer exchange. Here, one thread fills up a buffer (for example by reading in data). When the buffer is full, it exchanges it with a thread that processes the buffer, thereby emptying it. In this way, only two buffers are ever used, no copying is needed, and a resource management pool becomes unnecessary.

The following `FillAndEmpty` class gives a glimpse of the additional exception-handling obligations required with exchangers. Because the protocol is symmetric, cancellation or time-out of one party in the midst of an attempted exchange must lead to an exception (here, `BrokenBarrierException`) in the other party. In the example below, this is handled simply by returning from the run method. A more realistic version would entail further cleanup, including additional adjustments to deal with incompletely filled or emptied buffers upon termination, as well as to deal with IO exceptions and end-of-file conditions surrounding the `readByte` method.

```
class FillAndEmpty {                              // Incomplete
  static final int SIZE = 1024; // buffer size, for demo
  protected Rendezvous exchanger = new Rendezvous(2);

  protected byte readByte() { /* ... */; }
  protected void useByte(byte b) { /* ... */ }

  public void start() {
    new Thread(new FillingLoop()).start();
    new Thread(new EmptyingLoop()).start();
  }
```

```
class FillingLoop implements Runnable { // inner class
  public void run() {
    byte[] buffer = new byte[SIZE];
    int position = 0;

    try {
      for (;;) {

        if (position == SIZE) {
          buffer = (byte[])(exchanger.rendezvous(buffer));
          position = 0;
        }

        buffer[position++] = readByte();
      }
    }
    catch (BrokenBarrierException ex) {} // die
    catch (InterruptedException ie) {} // die
  }
}

class EmptyingLoop implements Runnable { // inner class
  public void run() {
    byte[] buffer = new byte[SIZE];
    int position = SIZE;   // force exchange first time through

    try {
      for (;;) {

        if (position == SIZE) {
          buffer = (byte[])(exchanger.rendezvous(buffer));
          position = 0;
        }

        useByte(buffer[position++]);
      }
    }
    catch (BrokenBarrierException ex) {} // die
    catch (InterruptedException ex) {} // die
  }
}

}
```

The use of exchangers here illustrates one of the design advantages of utility classes that replace concerns surrounding the fields of objects with those surrounding the passing of messages. This can be much easier to deal with as coordination schemes scale up (see Chapter 4).

3.4.4   Condition Variables

Monitor operations in the Java programming language maintain a single wait set for each object. Some other languages and thread libraries (in particular POSIX pthreads) include support for multiple wait sets associated with multiple *condition variables* managed under a common object or lock.

While any design requiring multiple wait sets can be implemented using other constructions such as semaphores, it is possible to create utilities that mimic the condition variables found in other systems. In fact, support for pthreads-style *condvars* leads to usage patterns that are almost identical to those in concurrent C and C++ programs.

A `CondVar` class can be used to represent a condition variable that is managed in conjunction with a given `Mutex`, where this `Mutex` is also (unenforceably) used for all exclusion locking in the associated class(es). Thus, classes using `CondVar` must also rely on the "manual" locking techniques discussed in §2.5.1. More than one `CondVar` can use the same `Mutex`[6].

The class supports analogs of the standard waiting and notification methods, here given names based on those in pthreads:

```
class CondVar {                            // Implementation omitted
  protected final Sync mutex;
  public CondVar(Sync lock) { mutex = lock; }

  public void await() throws InterruptedException;
  public boolean timedwait(long ms) throws InterruptedException;
  public void signal();              // analog of notify
  public void broadcast();           // analog of notifyAll
}
```

(In the `util.concurrent` version, the nuances of these operations also mirror those in pthreads. For example, unlike `notify`, `signal` does not require the lock to be held.)

The main applications of such a class lie not in original design efforts, but in adapting code originally written using other languages and systems. In other respects, a `CondVar` may be employed in the same design patterns, encountering the same design issues, as discussed in §3.3. For example, here is another bounded buffer class. Except for the structured exception handling, this version almost looks as if it came out of a pthreads programming book (see Further Readings in §1.2.5).

[6.] The converse that more than one `Mutex` serve the same condition variable is logically possible but usually reflects a programming error and is not supported by this class.

```
class PThreadsStyleBuffer {
  private final Mutex mutex = new Mutex();
  private final CondVar notFull = new CondVar(mutex);
  private final CondVar notEmpty = new CondVar(mutex);
  private int count = 0;
  private int takePtr = 0;
  private int putPtr = 0;
  private final Object[] array;

  public PThreadsStyleBuffer(int capacity) {
    array = new Object[capacity];
  }

  public void put(Object x) throws InterruptedException {
    mutex.acquire();
    try {
      while (count == array.length)
        notFull.await();

      array[putPtr] = x;
      putPtr = (putPtr + 1) % array.length;
      ++count;
      notEmpty.signal();
    }
    finally {
      mutex.release();
    }
  }

  public Object take() throws InterruptedException {
    Object x = null;
    mutex.acquire();
    try {
      while (count == 0)
        notEmpty.await();

      x = array[takePtr];
      array[takePtr] = null;
      takePtr = (takePtr + 1) % array.length;
      --count;
      notFull.signal();
    }
    finally {
      mutex.release();
    }
    return x;
  }
}
```

3.4.5 Further Readings

Additional discussions and examples of semaphores and condition variables can be found in almost any book on concurrent programming (see §1.2.5).

Resource pools can be extended into more general Object Manager classes. See:

Sommerlad, Peter. "Manager", in Robert Martin, Dirk Riehle, and Frank Buschmann (eds.), *Pattern Languages of Program Design, Volume 3*, Addison-Wesley, 1998.

Exchangers are described in more detail in:

Sane, Aamod, and Roy Campbell. "Resource Exchanger", in John Vlissides, James Coplien, and Norman Kerth (eds.), *Pattern Languages of Program Design, Volume 2*, Addison-Wesley, 1996.

The approximate fairness of some commonly used scheduling policies is discussed in:

Epema, Dick H. J. "Decay-Usage Scheduling in Multiprocessors", *ACM Transactions on Computer Systems*, Vol. 16, 367-415, 1998.

3.5 Joint Actions

So far, this chapter has confined itself mainly to discussions of guarded actions that rely on the state of a single object. *Joint action* frameworks provide a more general setting to attack more general design problems. From a high-level design perspective, joint actions are atomic guarded methods that involve conditions and actions among multiple, otherwise independent *participant* objects. They can be described abstractly as *atomic* methods involving two or more objects:

```
void jointAction(A a, B b) {                       // Pseudocode
  WHEN (canPerformAction(a, b))
    performAction(a, b);
}
```

Problems taking this general, unconstrained form are encountered in distributed protocol development, databases, and concurrent constraint programming. As seen in §3.5.2, even some ordinary-looking design patterns relying on delegation require this kind of treatment when otherwise independent actions in otherwise independent objects must be coordinated.

Unless you have a special-purpose solution, the first order of business in dealing with joint actions is translating vague intentions or declarative specifications into something you can actually program. Considerations include:

Allocating responsibility. Which object has responsibility for executing the action? One of the participants? All of them? A separate coordinator?

Detecting conditions. How can you tell when the participants are in the right state to perform the action? Do you ask them by invoking accessors? Do they tell you whenever they are in the right state? Do they tell you whenever they *might* be in the right state?

Programming actions. How are actions in multiple objects arranged? Do they need to be atomic? What if one or more of them fails?

Linking conditions to actions. How do you make sure that the actions occur only under the right conditions? Are false alarms acceptable? Do you need to prevent one or more participants from changing state between testing the condition and performing the action? Do the actions need to be performed when the participants enter the appropriate states, or merely whenever the conditions are noticed to hold? Do you need to prevent multiple objects from attempting to perform the action at the same time?

3.5.1   General Solutions

No small set of solutions addresses all issues across all contexts. But the most widely applicable general approach is to create designs in which participants tell one another when they are (or may be) in appropriate states for a joint action, while at the same time preventing themselves from changing state again until the action is performed.

These designs provide efficient solutions to joint action problems. However, they can be fragile and non-extensible, and can lead to high coupling of participants. They are potentially applicable when you can build special subclasses or versions of each of the participant classes to add particular notifications and actions, and when you can prevent or recover from deadlocks that are otherwise intrinsic in many joint action designs.

The main goal is to define notifications and actions within synchronized code that nests correctly across embedded calls, in a style otherwise reminiscent of *double-dispatching* and the Visitor pattern (see the *Design Patterns* book). Very often, good solutions rely on exploiting special properties of participants and their interactions. The combination of direct coupling and the need to exploit any available constraints to avoid liveness failures accounts for the high context dependence of many joint action designs. This in turn can lead to classes with so much special-purpose code that they must be marked as `final`.

3.5.1.1   Structure

For concreteness, the following descriptions are specific to the two-party case (for classes A and B), but can be generalized to more than two. Here, state changes in either participant can lead to notifications to the other. These notifications can in turn lead to coordinated actions in either or both participants.

Designs can take either of two characteristic forms. *Flat* versions couple participant objects directly:

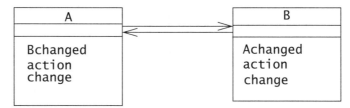

Explicitly *coordinated* versions route some or all messages and notifications through a third object (a form of *Mediator* — see the *Design Patterns* book) that may also play some role in the associated actions. Coordination through third parties is rarely an absolute necessity, but can add flexibility and can be used to initialize objects and connections:

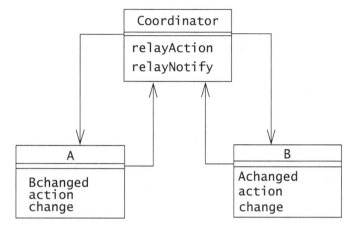

3.5.1.2 Classes and methods

The following generic steps can be applied when constructing the corresponding classes and methods:

- Define versions (often subclasses) of A and B that maintain references to each other, along with any other values and references needed to check their parts in triggering conditions and/or to perform the associated actions. Alternatively, link participants indirectly with the help of a coordinator class.

- Write one or more methods that perform the main actions. This can be done by choosing one of the classes to house the main action method, which in turn calls secondary helper methods in the other. Alternatively, the main action can be defined in the coordinator class, in turn calling helper methods in A and B.

- In both classes, write `synchronized` methods designed to be called when the *other* object changes state. For example, in class A, write method `Bchanged`, and in class B, write `Achanged`. In each, write code to check if the host object is also in the correct state. If the resulting actions involve both participants, they must be performed *without* losing either synchronization lock.

- In both classes, arrange that the other's `changed` method is called upon any change that may trigger the action. When necessary, ensure that the state-change code that leads to the notification is appropriately synchronized, guaranteeing that the entire check-and-act sequence is performed before breaking the locks held on both of the participants at the onset of the change.

- Ensure that connections and states are initialized before instances of A and B are allowed to receive messages that result in interactions. This can be arranged most easily via a coordinator class.

These steps are almost always somehow simplified or combined by exploiting available situation-dependent constraints. For example, several substeps disappear when notifications and/or actions are always based in only one of the participants. Similarly, if the changed conditions involve simple latching predicates (see §3.4.2), then there is typically no need for synchronization to bridge notifications and actions. And if it is permissible to establish a common lock in the coordinator class and use it for *all* methods in classes A and B (see §2.4.5), you can remove all other synchronization, and then treat this as a disguised form of a single-object concurrency control problem, using techniques from §3.2-§3.4.

3.5.1.3 Liveness

When all notifications and actions are symmetrical across participants, the above steps normally yield designs that have the potential for deadlock. A sequence starting with an action issuing `Achanged` can deadlock against one issuing `Bchanged`. While there is no universal solution, *conflict-resolution strategies* for addressing deadlock problems include the following approaches. Some of these remedies require extensive reworking and iterative refinement.

Forcing directionality. For example, requiring that all changes occur via one of the participants. This is possible only if you are allowed to change the interfaces of the participants.

Precedence. For example, using resource ordering (see §2.2.6) to avoid conflicting sequences.

Back-offs. For example, ignoring an update obligation if one is already in progress. As illustrated in the example below, update contention can often be simply detected and safely ignored. In other cases, detection may require the use of utility classes supporting time-outs, and semantics may require that a participant retry the update upon failure.

Token passing. For example, enabling action only by a participant that holds a certain resource, controlled via ownership-transfer protocols (see §2.3.4).

Weakening semantics. For example, loosening atomicity guarantees when they turn out not to impact broader functionality (see §3.5.2).

Explicit scheduling. For example, representing and managing activities as tasks, as described in §4.3.4.

3.5.1.4 Example

To illustrate some common techniques, consider a service that automatically transfers money from a savings account to a checking account whenever the checking balance falls below some threshold, but only if the savings account is not overdrawn. This operation can be expressed as a pseudocode joint action:

```
void autoTransfer(BankAccount checking,        // Pseudocode
                  BankAccount savings,
                  long threshold,
                  long maxTransfer) {
  WHEN (checking.balance() < threshold &&
        savings.balance() >= 0) {
    long amount = savings.balance();
    if (amount > maxTransfer) amount = maxTransfer;
    savings.withdraw(amount);
    checking.deposit(amount);
  }
}
```

We'll base a solution on a simple BankAccount class:

```
class BankAccount {
  protected long balance = 0;

  public synchronized long balance() {
    return balance;
  }

  public synchronized void deposit(long amount)
   throws InsufficientFunds {
    if (balance + amount < 0)
      throw new InsufficientFunds();
    else
      balance += amount;
  }

  public void withdraw(long amount) throws InsufficientFunds {
    deposit(-amount);
  }
}
```

Here are some observations that lead to a solution:

- There is no compelling reason to add an explicit coordinator class. The required interactions can be defined in special subclasses of BankAccount.

- The action can be performed if the checking balance decreases or the savings balance increases. The only operation that causes either one to change is

241

deposit (since withdraw is here defined to call deposit), so versions of this method in each class initiate all transfers.

* Only a checking account needs to know about the threshold, and only a savings account needs to know about the maxTransfer amount. (Other reasonable factorings would lead to slightly different implementations.)

* On the savings side, the condition check and action code can be rolled together by defining the single method transferOut to return zero if there is nothing to transfer, and otherwise to deduct and return the amount.

* On the checking side, a single method tryTransfer can be used to handle both checking-initiated and savings-initiated changes.

Without further care, the resulting code would be deadlock-prone. This problem is intrinsic in symmetrical joint actions in which changes in either object could lead to an action. Here, both a savings account and a checking account can start their deposit sequences at the same time. We need a way to break the cycle that could lead to both being blocked while trying to invoke each other's methods. (Note that deadlock would never occur if we require only that the action take place when checking balances decrease. This would in turn lead to a simpler solution all around.)

For illustration, potential deadlock is addressed here in a common (although of course not universally applicable) fashion, via a simple untimed *back-off* protocol. The tryTransfer method uses a boolean utility class supporting a testAndSet method that atomically sets its value to true and reports its previous value. (Alternatively, the attempt method of a Mutex could be used here.)

```
class TSBoolean {
  private boolean value = false;

  // set to true; return old value
  public synchronized boolean testAndSet() {
    boolean oldValue = value;
    value = true;
    return oldValue;
  }

  public synchronized void clear() {
    value = false;
  }
}
```

An instance of this class is used to control entry into the synchronized part of the main checking-side method tryTransfer, which is the potential deadlock point in this design. If another transfer is attempted by a savings account while one is executing (always, in this case, one that is initiated by the checking account), then it is just ignored without deadlocking. This is acceptable here since the executing `tryTransfer` and `transferOut` operations are based on the most recently updated savings balance anyway.

All this leads to the following very special subclasses of `BankAccount`, tuned to work only in their given context. Both classes rely upon an (unshown) initialization process to establish interconnections.

The decision on whether to mark the classes as `final` is a close call. However, there is just enough latitude for minor variation in the methods and protocols not to preclude knowledgeable subclass authors from, say, modifying the transfer conditions in `shouldTry` or the amount to transfer in `transferOut`.

```
class ATCheckingAccount extends BankAccount {
  protected ATSavingsAccount savings;
  protected long threshold;
  protected TSBoolean transferInProgress = new TSBoolean();

  public ATCheckingAccount(long t) { threshold = t; }

  // called only upon initialization
  synchronized void initSavings(ATSavingsAccount s) {
    savings = s;
  }

  protected boolean shouldTry() { return balance < threshold; }

  void tryTransfer() { // called internally or from savings
    if (!transferInProgress.testAndSet()) { // if not busy ...
      try {
        synchronized(this) {
          if (shouldTry()) balance += savings.transferOut();
        }
      }
      finally { transferInProgress.clear(); }
    }
  }

  public synchronized void deposit(long amount)
   throws InsufficientFunds {
    if (balance + amount < 0)
      throw new InsufficientFunds();
    else {
      balance += amount;
      tryTransfer();
    }
  }
}
```

```
class ATSavingsAccount extends BankAccount {

  protected ATCheckingAccount checking;
  protected long maxTransfer;

  public ATSavingsAccount(long max) {
    maxTransfer = max;
  }

  // called only upon initialization
  synchronized void initChecking(ATCheckingAccount c) {
    checking = c;
  }

  synchronized long transferOut() { // called only from checking
    long amount = balance;
    if (amount > maxTransfer)
      amount = maxTransfer;
    if (amount >= 0)
      balance -= amount;
    return amount;
  }

  public synchronized void deposit(long amount)
   throws InsufficientFunds {
    if (balance + amount < 0)
      throw new InsufficientFunds();
    else {
      balance += amount;
      checking.tryTransfer();
    }
  }

}
```

3.5.2 Decoupling Observers

The best way to avoid the design and implementation issues surrounding full joint-action designs is not to insist that operations spanning multiple independent objects be atomic in the first place. Full atomicity is rarely necessary, and can introduce additional downstream design problems that impede use and reuse of classes.

To illustrate, consider the *Observer* pattern from the *Design Patterns* book:

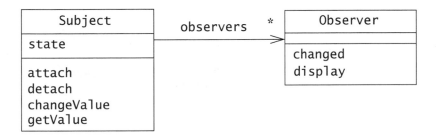

In the Observer pattern, Subjects (sometimes called *Observables*) represent the state of whatever they are modeling (for example a Temperature) and have operations to reveal and change this state. Observers somehow display or otherwise use the state represented by Subjects (for example by drawing different styles of Thermometers). When a Subject's state is changed, it merely informs its Observers that it has changed. Observers are then responsible for probing Subjects to determine the nature of the changes via callbacks checking whether, for example, Subject representations need to be re-displayed on a screen.

The Observer pattern is seen in some GUI frameworks, publish-subscribe systems, and constraint-based programs. A version is defined in classes java.util.Observable and

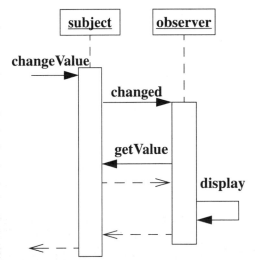

`java.util.Observer`, but they are not as of this writing used in AWT or Swing (see §4.1.4).

It is all too easy to code an Observer design as a synchronized joint action by mistake, without noticing the resulting potential liveness problems. For example, if all methods in both classes are declared as `synchronized` and `Observer.changed` can ever be called from outside of the `Subject.changeValue` method, then it would be possible for these calls to deadlock:

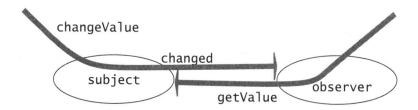

This problem could be solved by one of the techniques discussed in §3.5.1. However, it is easier and better just to avoid it. There is no reason to synchronize operations surrounding change notifications unless you really need `Observer` actions to occur atomically in conjunction with any change in the `Subject`. In fact, this requirement would defeat most of the reasons for using the Observer pattern in the first place.

Instead, here you can apply our default rules from §1.1.1.1 and release unnecessary locks when making calls from `Subject`s to `Observer`s, which serves to implement the desired decoupling. This permits scenarios in which a `Subject` changes state more than once before the change is noticed by an `Observer`, as well as scenarios in which the `Observer` doesn't notice any change when invoking `getValue`. Normally, these semantic weakenings are perfectly acceptable and even desirable.

Here is a sample implementation in which `Subject` just uses a double as an example of modeled state. It uses the `CopyOnWriteArrayList` class described in §2.4.4 to maintain its `observers` list. This avoids any need for locking during traversal, which helps satisfy the design goals. For simplicity of illustration, `Observer` here is defined as a concrete class (rather than as an `interface` with multiple implementations) and can deal with only a single `Subject`.

```
class Subject {

   protected double val = 0.0;          // modeled state
   protected final CopyOnWriteArrayList observers =
                               new CopyOnWriteArrayList();

   public synchronized double getValue() { return val; }
   protected synchronized void setValue(double d) { val = d; }

   public void attach(Observer o) { observers.add(o); }
   public void detach(Observer o) { observers.remove(o); }

   public void changeValue(double newstate) {
     setValue(newstate);
     for (Iterator it = observers.iterator(); it.hasNext();)
       ((Observer)(it.next())).changed(this);
   }

}

class Observer {

   protected double cachedState;        // last known state
   protected final Subject subj;        // only one allowed here

   public Observer(Subject s) {
     subj = s;
     cachedState = s.getValue();
     display();
   }

   public synchronized void changed(Subject s){
     if (s != subj) return;       // only one subject

     double oldState = cachedState;
     cachedState = subj.getValue(); // probe
     if (oldState != cachedState)
       display();
   }

   protected void display() {
     // somehow display subject state; for example just:
     System.out.println(cachedState);
   }

}
```

3.5.3 Further Readings

Joint actions serve as a unifying framework for characterizing multiparty actions in the DisCo modeling and specification language:

Jarvinen, Hannu-Matti, Reino Kurki-Suonio, Markku Sakkinen and Kari Systa. "Object-Oriented Specification of Reactive Systems", *Proceedings, 1990 International Conference on Software Engineering,* IEEE, 1990.

They are further pursued in a slightly different context in IP, which also addresses different senses of *fairness* that may apply to joint action designs. For example, designs for some problems avoid conspiracies among some participants to starve out others. See:

Francez, Nissim, and Ira Forman. *Interacting Processes*, ACM Press, 1996.

For a wide-ranging survey of other approaches to task coordination among objects and processes, see:

Malone, Thomas, and Kevin Crowston. "The Interdisciplinary Study of Coordination", *ACM Computing Surveys*, March 1994.

Joint action frameworks can provide the basis for implementing the internal mechanisms supporting distributed protocols. For some forward-looking presentations and analyses of protocols among concurrent and distributed objects, see:

Rosenschein, Jeffrey, and Gilad Zlotkin. *Rules of Encounter: Designing Conventions for Automated Negotiation Among Computers*, MIT Press, 1994.

Fagin, Ronald, Joseph Halpern, Yoram Moses, and Moshe Vardi. *Reasoning about Knowledge*, MIT Press, 1995.

A joint action framework that accommodates failures among participants is described in:

Stroud, Robert, and Avelino Zorzo. "A Distributed Object-Oriented Framework for Dependable Multiparty Interactions", *Proceedings of OOPSLA*, ACM, 1999.

3.6 Transactions

In the context of concurrent OO programming, a *transaction* is an operation performed by an arbitrary client that invokes an arbitrary set of methods on an arbitrary set of participant objects, all without interference from other activities.

The arbitrariness of both the participants and the action sequences requires extensions of the joint action control strategies discussed in §3.5. Transaction techniques extend delegation-based synchronization and control to situations in which each participant may be unaware of the atomicity constraints placed on its actions, and cannot rely on more efficient structural solutions. In transaction frameworks, each participant (and each client) gives up its local autonomy in deciding how to perform concurrency control. Participants must instead reach *consensus* deciding how and when to perform actions and/or to commit to their effects.

Transaction frameworks are among the most famous examples of how providing components that implement valuable general-purpose functionality sometimes has the price of introducing a large number of programmer obligations. Classes supporting transaction protocols can be highly usable and reusable. Transaction frameworks can be used to tackle most of the concurrency problems discussed in this book. But they rely on designs in which each class, at each layer of functionality, supports a standardized transaction protocol that propagates control down through successive layers. The heaviness of transaction frameworks usually restricts their use to contexts in which you really need to set up objects so as to guarantee atomicity of arbitrary code sequences.

For example, you may be able to bypass transactional control if you know all the call-sequences that will ever be encountered in a component or application. In this case, you can specifically design support for each one (using whatever techniques happen to apply) without having to address the general case. This is a perhaps extreme extension of the idea (see §2.2.2) of padding reusable synchronized objects with atomic versions of frequently needed convenience methods. This is sometimes a plausible alternative, in the spirit of doing the simplest and surest thing that could possibly work. Similarly, you may be able to rely entirely on client-side locking (see §2.2.3) in cases where clients somehow know to obtain all locks required for a given action and how to avoid any potential deadlocks.

This section provides a brief overview of transaction based techniques applicable in general-purpose concurrent programming contexts. The designs presented here deal only with internal concurrency, and not explicitly with databases or distribution. Because even lightweight (at least in a relative sense) internal transaction frameworks are normally tied to other application-specific constraints

249

and features, you are unlikely to use the exact interfaces and classes described here (although most are simplified variants of those in the net.jini package). And if you instead rely on a standardized transaction framework such as JDBC or JTS, you will encounter additional issues tied to persistence support and related services that fall outside the scope of this book. However, the final example in this section (§3.6.4) illustrates how the ideas behind transactions can help structure more ordinary concurrent OO designs. Thus, the main goals of this section are to give a brief synopsis of how transaction systems extend other approaches to concurrency control, and to present techniques that may be scaled down as needed to apply to other concurrency problems.

As a running example, consider again writing a transfer operation for the BankAccount class in §3.5.1. From a transactional point of view, a stand-alone transfer operation (without any provisions for *automatic* transfers) looks like:

```
pseudoclass AccountUser {                               // Pseudocode

  TransactionLogger log; // any kind of logging facility
  // ...

  // Attempt transfer; return true if successful
  public boolean transfer(long amount,
                          BankAccount source,
                          BankAccount destination) {
    TRANSACTIONALLY {
      if (source.balance() >= amount) {
        log.logTransfer(amount, source, destination);
        source.withdraw(amount);
        destination.deposit(amount);
        return true;
      }
      else
        return false;
    }
  }
}
```

The *TRANSACTIONALLY* pseudo-qualifier indicates that we'd like this code to be executed in an all-or-none fashion without any possibility of interference from other activities. Once implemented, this operation could be used in an automated transfer scheme of the sort described in §3.5.1. Additionally, the transactional approach permits greater flexibility than seen in our specific solution, although with significantly greater overhead. Once classes are fitted with transactional apparatus, it becomes possible to associate transactionality with any sequence of operations involving bank accounts.

3.6.1 Transaction Protocols

Transaction frameworks rely on extended forms of the before/after tactics characteristic of most concurrency control strategies. Here, the before-action is typically called *join* (or sometimes, *begin*) and the after-action is called *commit*. The main differences between join/commit and operations such as lock acquire/release stem from the fact that join/commit require *consensus* among the set of participating objects: All participants must agree to begin and end transactions. This leads to *two-phase* protocols surrounding join and/or commit — first to obtain consensus and then to act. If any participant disagrees about joining or committing, the attempted transaction is *aborted*. The most straightforward version of the basic protocol is:

1. For each participant p, if p cannot join, abort.

2. For each participant p, tentatively execute p's action.

3. For each participant p, if p cannot commit, abort.

4. For each participant p, commit p's effects of the transaction.

As in most concurrency control contexts, two complementary sets of policies can be applied to this protocol. In the purest form of *optimistic transactions*, participants can always join, but cannot always commit. In the purest form of *conservative transactions*, participants cannot always join, but if they do, they can always commit. Optimistic approaches apply best when the likelihood of contention is low enough to outweigh rollback costs. Conservative approaches apply best when it is difficult or impossible to undo actions performed during transactions. However, it is rare to find pure forms of each, and it is not hard to create frameworks that permit mixtures.

The most classic forms of conservative transactions can be implemented only if the identities of all participants can be known before any actions are taken. This is not always possible. In an OO system, the participants are just those objects whose methods are invoked during some call sequence that is wrapped as a transaction. Because of polymorphism, dynamic loading, etc., it is generally impossible to identify them all beforehand; instead, their identities become known only as the action unfolds. Still, in many cases, at least some participants are known beforehand and they can be probed before starting to engage in any unrecoverable action.

However, in most approaches to conservative OO transactions, participants join only tentatively. They can still later refuse to commit, using approximately the same strategy seen in optimistic transactions. Conversely, full rollback is not always necessary in optimistic approaches. Some roll-forward operations may be allowed if they do not impact overall functionality.

3.6.2   Transaction Participants

In addition to supporting methods for joining, committing, aborting, and (when necessary) creating transactions, each class in a structured transaction framework must declare all of its public methods to add a transaction control argument to its set of normal arguments.

A method invocation supplying a given transaction argument serves as a request to perform the associated action on behalf of the given transaction, but without committing to its effects until requested to do so. Methods take the form:

```
ReturnType aMethod(Transaction t, ArgType args) throws...
```

For example, `BankAccount.deposit` would be declared as:

```
void deposit(Transaction t, long amount) throws ...
```

`Transaction` is any type that supplies the necessary control information. This transaction information must be propagated throughout all methods invoked in the course of a particular transaction, including nested calls to helper objects. The simplest kind of transaction argument is a transaction *key* that uniquely identifies each transaction. Each method in each participating object is then responsible for using this key to manage and isolate actions in accord with the given transaction policy. Alternatively, a transaction argument may refer to a special control or coordinator object possessing methods that help participants perform their roles in transactions.

It is, however, possible to cheat here, and many transaction frameworks do. For example, transaction identifiers can be hidden as thread-specific data (see §2.3.2). Before/after control can be restricted to intercepted entry points into sessions performing services provided by components. Participants can be determined via reflection or scanning bytecodes. And rollback obligations can be semi-automated by serializing the entire state of a component and/or acquiring locks on entry into a service session. These kinds of tactics can help hide the details of transactional control from application writers. This comes at the expense overhead and usage restrictions that are not generally worthwhile in lightweight transaction frameworks performing internal concurrency control.

3.6.2.1 Interfaces

Participant classes must implement interfaces defining the methods used in transaction control. Here is a simple but representative interface:

```
class Failure extends Exception {}

interface Transactor {

  // Enter a new transaction and return true, if possible
  public boolean join(Transaction t);

  // Return true if this transaction can be committed
  public boolean canCommit(Transaction t);

  // Update state to reflect current transaction
  public void commit(Transaction t) throws Failure;

  // Roll back state (No exception; ignore if inapplicable)
  public void abort(Transaction t);

}
```

Among many other variants, it is possible to split the join phase similarly to
the commit phase — a preliminary `canJoin` followed by a required `join`. The
`canCommit` method is most often named `prepare` in transaction frameworks.

For simplicity of illustration, a single `Failure` exception type is associated
with these operations, as well as all others in this series of examples. Participant
objects are allowed to raise exceptions when they encounter actual or potential
conflicts and when they are requested to participate in transactions they do not
know about. Of course in practice, you'd want to subclass these exception types
and use them to provide additional information to clients in cases of failure.

A second interface or class is needed to describe `Transaction` objects themselves. In discussing basic operations, we can use a no-op version:

```
class Transaction {
  // add anything you want here
}
```

Again, it is not even necessary to associate an object with a transaction. A
simple unique `long transactionKey` argument may suffice in place of all uses of
`Transaction`. At the other extreme, you may need a `TransactionFactory` for
creating all `Transactions`. This allows different kinds of `Transaction` objects
to be associated with different styles of transactions.

3.6.2.2 Implementations

Participants in transactions must support both a transaction participant interface and an interface describing their basic actions. For example:

```
interface TransBankAccount extends Transactor {

  public long balance(Transaction t) throws Failure;

  public void deposit(Transaction t, long amount)
    throws InsufficientFunds, Failure;

  public void withdraw(Transaction t, long amount)
    throws InsufficientFunds, Failure;

}
```

However, it is not always necessary to provide transactional signatures for pure accessor methods such as `balance` here. Instead (or in addition to transactional versions), such methods can return the most recently committed value when called from clients that are not participating in transactions. Alternatively, a special null-transaction type (or just passing `null` for the `Transaction` argument) can be used to denote one-shot invocations of transactional methods.

The most common approach to implementing transactional classes entails first splitting out underlying state representations into separate helper classes using either a provisional action or checkpointing approach (see §2.4.4 and §3.1.1.3). This makes it easier to perform virtual state changes that are updated only after `commit` operations and/or reverted from during `abort` operations. This approach is especially appropriate in transaction frameworks supporting persistence, which often require representations to be isolated anyway in order to be efficiently read from and written to disks and other media.

While this is by far the most tractable option, it leads to a sometimes-uncomfortable coding style in which objects must pretend to be in the states maintained by representations associated with particular transactions. Each normal public method performs operations only on the state representation associated with the given transaction, and invokes methods on other objects that are doing likewise.

Implementations of transactional methods (both control methods and base actions) can span the range from optimistic to conservative tactics. The following table sketches some highlights of the end-points for methods invoked with `Transaction` argument tx:

Method	Optimistic	Conservative
join	• Create a copy of state and associate it with `tx` (for example in a hash table), along with some record of the version of the state it originated with. • Return true.	• Return false if already participating in conflicting transaction, optionally first trying a timed wait for it to complete. • Ask all other objects referenced in action methods if they can join; return false if any cannot. • Make a backup copy of current state to recover to in the case of an abort. • Record that `tx` is current transaction; return true.
action methods	• If tx is not a known transaction, then first join `tx`, failing if the join fails. • Perform base action on current state and/or by calling other methods on other objects with argument `tx`, recording identity of all such objects. • On any failure, mark `tx` as not committable.	• If `tx` is not current transaction, fail. • Perform base action on current state and/or by calling other methods on other joined objects with argument `tx`. • On any failure, mark current transaction as not committable.
abort	• Throw away all bookkeeping associated with `tx`. • Propagate to all other known participants.	• If `tx` is current transaction, reset state to backup copy and record that there is no current transaction. • Propagate to all other known participants.

Method	Optimistic	Conservative
commit	• Save representation associated with `tx` as current state. • Propagate to all known participants.	• Throw away backup; record that there is no current transaction. • Propagate to all known participants.
canCommit	• Return false if any conflicting commit occurred since joining `tx`, or if any other conflicting transaction has already promised to commit. • Ask all other objects referenced in the course of actions if they can commit; return false if any cannot. • Record that `tx` has promised to commit; return true.	• Ask other participants, return false if any cannot. • Return true unless a local failure occurred during an action.

When applied to the `BankAccount` class, taking the simplest possible option at each step leads to a mixed-strategy version that is probably not fit for serious use. Among other scale-downs, it maintains only a single backup copy of state (as a single field), so can be used only for non-overlapping transactions. But this version suffices to illustrate the general structure of transactional classes and also, implicitly, how much more code would be required to build a more useful version:

```java
class SimpleTransBankAccount implements TransBankAccount {

  protected long balance = 0;
  protected long workingBalance = 0; // single shadow copy
  protected Transaction currentTx = null; // single transaction

  public synchronized long balance(Transaction t) throws Failure {
    if (t != currentTx) throw new Failure();
    return workingBalance;
  }

  public synchronized void deposit(Transaction t, long amount)
    throws InsufficientFunds, Failure {
    if (t != currentTx) throw new Failure();
    if (workingBalance < -amount)
      throw new InsufficientFunds();
    workingBalance += amount;
  }

  public synchronized void withdraw(Transaction t, long amount)
    throws InsufficientFunds, Failure {
    deposit(t, -amount);
  }

  public synchronized boolean join(Transaction t) {
    if (currentTx != null) return false;
    currentTx = t;
    workingBalance = balance;
    return true;
  }

  public synchronized boolean canCommit(Transaction t) {
    return (t == currentTx);
  }

  public synchronized void abort(Transaction t) {
    if (t == currentTx)
      currentTx = null;
  }

  public synchronized void commit(Transaction t) throws Failure{
    if (t != currentTx) throw new Failure();
    balance = workingBalance;
    currentTx = null;
  }

}
```

Classes obeying the `Transactor` interface can also employ arbitrary sharing of references among participants. For example, you can construct a Proxy account that forwards messages to another unrelated and otherwise uncontrolled account.

```
class ProxyAccount implements TransBankAccount {
  private TransBankAccount delegate;

  public boolean join(Transaction t) {
    return delegate.join(t);
  }


  public long balance(Transaction t) throws Failure {
    return delegate.balance(t);
  }

  // and so on...
}
```

3.6.3   Creating Transactions

Transactions that employ participants obeying the `Transactor` interface take a standard form, performing the following steps:

- Create a new `Transaction`.

- Invoke `join` on all (initially known) participants, failing immediately if any cannot join.

- Try the entire action, aborting all participants on any failure and also rolling back any other auxiliary actions.

- Upon completion, collect votes using `canCommit` and then `commit` or `abort`.

In most applications, it simplifies matters if the classes initiating transactions also support the `Transactor` interface. They may also support other methods that set up logging and related bookkeeping matters.

It is possible to automate many aspects of this protocol, redistribute or centralize functionality, and incorporate additional features. For example, an arbitrary amount of effort can be expended computing whether a transaction can be joined and/or committed in order to minimize the probability and expense of aborts. The actions and participant structure of potentially conflicting transactions can be analyzed and manipulated (for example, via use of conflict sets — see §3.3.2) to allow overlaps in cases when you can determine that no conflicts are possible.

Similarly, locking strategies can be refined to use read and write locks, or even further refined to support lock upgrades and intention locks (see §3.3.3.1).

3.6.3.1 Example

The following version of the `transfer` operation deals with several kinds of potential failures:

Semantic failure. There may not be sufficient funds in the accounts, in which case the method returns `false`. In this example, there is not even a pre-check that the source holds a sufficient balance. Even if it reported true, the `withdraw` attempt may fail anyway. Similarly, since the `amount` is allowed to be negative, `destination.deposit` may fail even if `source.withdraw` succeeds. (For a negative amount, a deposit acts like a withdraw and vice versa.) Additional exceptions could be caught here to deal with other errors encountered within these methods.

Interference. If either account cannot join or cannot commit to this transaction due to interference by another concurrent transaction, an exception is thrown indicating that the action is retryable.

Transaction error. Unrecoverable, catastrophic operation failure can occur if objects fail to commit after they say they can. Of course, these methods should do everything within their power to avoid commitment failure, since there is nothing to be done about this internal error. Here, the exception is propagated back to clients. In a more realistic version, this might in turn trigger a recovery from the last recorded persistent record of the object's state.

The recovery action for each of these cases happens to be identical in this example (and is factored into a helper method). The `abort` clauses perform the state rollbacks. But the log must be cancelled independently.

```
class FailedTransferException extends Exception {}
class RetryableTransferException extends Exception {}

class AccountUser {
  TransactionLogger log;                    // a made-up class

  // helper method called on any failure
  void rollback(Transaction t, long amount,
              TransBankAccount src, TransBankAccount dst) {
    log.cancelLogEntry(t, amount, src, dst);
    src.abort(t);
    dst.abort(t);
  }
```

```
  public boolean transfer(long amount,
                          TransBankAccount src,
                          TransBankAccount dst)
    throws FailedTransferException, RetryableTransferException {

    if (src == null || dst == null)          // screen arguments
      throw new IllegalArgumentException();
    if (src == dst) return true;             // avoid aliasing

    Transaction t = new Transaction();
    log.logTransfer(t, amount, src, dst);   // record

    if (!src.join(t) || !dst.join(t)) {     // cannot join
      rollback(t, amount, src, dst);
      throw new RetryableTransferException();
    }

    try {
      src.withdraw(t, amount);
      dst.deposit(t, amount);
    }
    catch (InsufficientFunds ex) {           // semantic failure
      rollback(t, amount, src, dst);
      return false;
    }
    catch (Failure k) {                      // transaction error
      rollback(t, amount, src, dst);
      throw new RetryableTransferException();
    }

    if (!src.canCommit(t) || !dst.canCommit(t)) { // interference
      rollback(t, amount, src, dst);
      throw new RetryableTransferException();
    }

    try {
      src.commit(t);
      dst.commit(t);
      log.logCompletedTransfer(t, amount, src, dst);
      return true;
    }
    catch(Failure k) {                       // commitment failure
      rollback(t, amount, src, dst);
      throw new FailedTransferException();
    }

  }
}
```

3.6.4 Vetoable Changes

The fact that transaction frameworks can become almost arbitrarily heavy some-times makes developers neglect simpler transactional solutions in smaller-scale concurrent design efforts. We conclude this section with a more ordinary-sound-ing design problem that is readily solved in a transactional fashion.

In the JavaBeans™ framework, component objects have sets of *properties* — fields that support `get` and `set` methods. *Constrained* properties may support *vetoable* `set` methods. A host component may have a list of listeners to which it sends vetoable change events in the course of a vetoable `set` method. If any lis-tener responds to an event with a `PropertyVetoException`, then an attempted set of the property must be cancelled.

Some components express many of their operations as vetoable property changes. For example, an attempt to exit an editor application may be imple-mented as a `set` method, vetoable by any documents that have not yet been saved, as well as by confirmation dialogs.

Vetoable changes employ a slimmed-down transaction protocol that has only one active participant, but possibly several passive participants that must be polled for consensus. This can be done in either a conservative (i.e., before performing the update) or optimistic (i.e., after tentatively performing the update) fashion.

Here are some background notes about `java.beans` support needed to con-struct any solution:

- Listeners are normally structured identically to the Observers discussed in §3.5.2 except that they are triggered via events that contain information about changes. In the normal case discussed here, the event-based method `veto-ableChange(PropertyChangeEvent evt)` is invoked directly for each lis-tener rather than being held in queues described in §4.1.

- The `VetoableChangeSupport` and `PropertyChangeSupport` classes in the `java.beans` package can be used to manage multicasts to listeners. But, as usual, we'll adopt copy-on-write versions that allow lock-free multicasting. The version below uses `VetoableChangeMulticaster` and `Property-ChangeMulticaster` from `util.concurrent`, both of which support the same interfaces as `java.beans` versions. They provide methods to attach and detach listeners similar to those described in §2.4.4.

- The `VetoableChangeMulticaster.fireVetoableChange` method con-structs and multicasts a `PropertyChangeEvent` with event fields indicating the name of the property, its old value, and its proposed new value.

As a bland example illustrating basic techniques, consider a `ColoredThing` component with a vetoable `color` property. Each `ColoredThing` may have several vetoers, as well as several ordinary listeners that are notified upon every update. We'll use a simple conservative-style solution.

When a `ColoredThing` receives a request to `setColor(Color newColor)`, it performs the following steps:

1. Check to see if another attempted `setColor` operation is already in progress, if so throwing a `PropertyVetoException`. To manage this, the class maintains a boolean execution state variable indicating whether a change is pending. A fancier (but probably less desirable) version could instead wait out other transactions using a `wait/notifyAll` construction based on `changePending`.

2. Check to see if the argument is null, in which case also refuse to change the property. This illustrates how a component can, in a sense, veto its own changes.

3. Invoke `fireVetoableChange`, which multicasts to vetoers.

4. If a `PropertyVetoException` results from the change event, abort and rethrow the exception. Otherwise, update the color field, clear the pending flag, and send a change event to all property listeners. As an extra safeguard here, the method maintains a `completed` variable used for detecting run-time exceptions. The `finally` clause makes sure that the `changePending` flag is reset properly if the method encounters such an exception.

```
class ColoredThing {

  protected Color myColor = Color.red; // the sample property
  protected boolean changePending;

  // vetoable listeners:
  protected final VetoableChangeMulticaster vetoers =
    new VetoableChangeMulticaster(this);

  // also some ordinary listeners:
  protected final PropertyChangeMulticaster listeners =
    new PropertyChangeMulticaster(this);

  // registration methods, including:
  void addVetoer(VetoableChangeListener l) {
    vetoers.addVetoableChangeListener(l);
  }

  public synchronized Color getColor() { // property accessor
    return myColor;
  }
```

```
  // internal helper methods
  protected synchronized void commitColor(Color newColor) {
    myColor = newColor;
    changePending = false;
  }

  protected synchronized void abortSetColor() {
    changePending = false;
  }

  public void setColor(Color newColor)
   throws PropertyVetoException {
   Color oldColor = null;
   boolean completed = false;

   synchronized (this) {

     if (changePending) { // allow only one transaction at a time
       throw new PropertyVetoException(
         "Concurrent modification", null);
     }
     else if (newColor == null) {   // Argument screening
       throw new PropertyVetoException(
         "Cannot change color to Null", null);
     }
     else {
       changePending = true;
       oldColor = myColor;
     }
   }

   try {
     vetoers.fireVetoableChange("color", oldColor, newColor);
     // fall through if no exception:
     commitColor(newColor);
     completed = true;
     // notify other listeners that change is committed
     listeners.firePropertyChange("color", oldColor, newColor);
   }
   catch(PropertyVetoException ex) { // abort on veto
     abortSetColor();
     completed = true;
     throw ex;
   }
   finally {                        // trap any unchecked exception
     if (!completed) abortSetColor();
   }
  }
}
```

3.6.5 Further Readings

More thorough accounts of transactions in database systems may be found in:

Bacon, Jean. *Concurrent Systems,* Addison-Wesley, 1993.

Cellary, Wojciech, E. Gelenbe, and Tadeusz Morzy, *Concurrency Control in Distributed Database Systems,* North-Holland, 1988.

Gray, Jim, and Andreas Reuter. *Transaction Processing: Concepts and Techniques*, Morgan Kaufmann, 1993.

Khoshafian, Setrag. *Object-Oriented Databases,* Wiley, 1993.

Lynch, Nancy, Michael Merritt, William Weihl, and Alan Fekete. *Atomic Transactions*, Morgan Kaufmann, 1994.

The following covers database programming using JDBC:

White, Seth, Maydene Fisher, Rick Cattell, Graham Hamilton, and Mark Hapner. *JDBC™ API Tutorial and Reference, Second Edition*, Addison-Wesley, 1999.

3.7 Implementing Utilities

Utility classes and methods can encapsulate efficient, reliable, general-purpose implementations of concurrency control constructs in a way that lets them be used almost as if they were part of the language proper. These classes can capture clever, complex, error-prone constructions and efficiently exploit special cases, packaging the results so that programs using them can be written more simply, reliably, and often with better performance. It is worth the development effort to arrive at such classes only once, and only when justified by real design concerns.

This section illustrates some techniques used in the construction of common utilities. All of them rely on general design and implementation tactics described previously in this book, but also introduce a few additional specialized constructions that typically arise only when building support classes.

The section starts by illustrating how to package acquire-release protocols under a common interface. This is followed by an example showing how to apply joint action design techniques to split classes into parts for the sake of obtaining necessary concurrency control, and then recombining them to improve efficiency. Finally, it discusses how to isolate waiting threads in order to manage notifications.

3.7.1 Acquire-Release Protocols

As discussed in §2.5.1 and §3.4.1, many concurrency control constructs conform to an acquire-release protocol that can be encompassed under the simple interface:

```
interface Sync {
  void acquire() throws InterruptedException;
  void release();
  boolean attempt(long msec) throws InterruptedException;
}
```

Supporting this interface under a given semantics (for example, locks, semaphores, latches) requires that the internal state representations that drive waits and notifications be managed by the Sync objects, not the classes using them. Additionally, all control must be placed within the exported methods; it cannot be strewn around other methods in client classes, and it is a bad idea to introduce other methods that clients must use in a special, non-standard way to obtain desired behavior.

Most of the resulting issues and concerns can be illustrated with a sample implementation of the basic `Semaphore` class discussed in §3.4.1. Implementations of other `Sync` classes follow similar patterns. (In fact, as shown in §3.4.1, classes such as `Mutex` can in turn be defined using semaphores.)

Both at the conceptual and representational level, a semaphore maintains a count of the number of permits that it manages. The basic idea is that an `acquire` should wait (if necessary) until there is at least one permit, and that a `release` should increment the number of permits and provide notifications to any waiting threads. Here are some other observations and choices that lead to an implementation:

- Since all waiting threads are waiting for permits, and since a `release` adds one permit, we can use `notify` rather than `notifyAll`, leading to cheaper notifications. Also, the extra-notify-on-interrupt technique described in §3.2.4.2 is available to avoid lossage when threads are interrupted at just the wrong time.

- Because this is intended to be a general-purpose class, we should play it safe and use `long` (not `int`) for counts. This avoids all practical possibility of value overflow and costs almost nothing compared to monitor overhead.

- To maintain responsiveness, we should check to make sure that the current thread has not been interrupted before acquiring any locks. This minimizes windows of vulnerability for client threads getting stuck waiting for locks when they should be cancelling themselves (see §3.1.2). It also provides a more uniform guarantee that `InterruptedException` will be thrown if the thread enters in an interrupted state, rather than having the exception thrown only if the thread happens to block on the internal `wait`.

```
class Semaphore implements Sync  {

  protected long permits; // current number of available permits

  public Semaphore(long initialPermits) {
    permits = initialPermits;
  }

  public synchronized void release() {
    ++permits;
    notify();
  }
```

```
public void acquire() throws InterruptedException {
  if (Thread.interrupted()) throw new InterruptedException();
  synchronized(this) {
    try {
      while (permits <= 0) wait();
      --permits;
    }
    catch (InterruptedException ie) {
      notify();
      throw ie;
    }
  }
}

public boolean attempt(long msecs)throws InterruptedException{
  if (Thread.interrupted()) throw new InterruptedException();
  synchronized(this) {
    if (permits > 0) {          // same as acquire but messier
      --permits;
      return true;
    }
    else if (msecs <= 0)    // avoid timed wait if not needed
      return false;
    else {
      try {
        long startTime = System.currentTimeMillis();
        long waitTime = msecs;

        for (;;) {
          wait(waitTime);
          if (permits > 0) {
            --permits;
            return true;
          }
          else {                        // check for time-out
            long now = System.currentTimeMillis();
            waitTime = msecs - (now - startTime);
            if (waitTime <= 0)
              return false;
          }
        }
      }
      catch(InterruptedException ie) {
        notify();
        throw ie;
      }
    }
  }
}
}
```

3.7.2 Delegated Actions

Joint action designs can be used to address a potential source of inefficiency in guarded methods in which different threads in a wait set are waiting for different logical conditions. A `notifyAll` intended to alert threads about one condition also wakes up threads waiting for completely unrelated conditions. Useless signals, and the resulting "thundering herds" of context switches can be minimized by delegating operations with different wait conditions to different helper objects.

We achieved this effect with almost no effort using semaphores in §3.4.1. Here, we will proceed from the ground up, potentially achieving better performance by exploiting the special properties of particular design problems. The techniques here are worth using only when a design problem is amenable to optimizations that can be applied only to bare waiting and notification mechanics.

Splitting classes with state-dependent actions extends ideas seen in §2.4.2 for splitting objects with respect to locks, as well as some from the States as Objects pattern (see *Design Patterns*). However, the design space is restricted to a narrow range of constructions because of constraints including:

- Since helpers must access common state, you cannot fully isolate each helper along with its own self-contained representation. Independent access to common representations across helpers requires appropriate synchronization.

- Each of the helpers that might affect guard conditions for another must provide it with effective notifications while avoiding liveness problems.

- Synchronization of helper methods involving `wait` mechanics must avoid nested monitor problems (§3.3.4).

3.7.2.1 Design steps

A general approach to these constraints is first to decompose the `Host` class into its smallest possible pieces: one class for the shared state representation and one each per kind of helper. You can then deal with the resulting coordinated joint action design problem. Finally, you can organize the pieces into useful classes:

- Define a class, say `Representation`, to hold fields used across more than one method. This is just a record-style class with non-private fields, allowing arbitrary accesses and updates to be performed within special synchronized blocks.

- Define a `Helper` class for each set of functionality that shares the same wait conditions. Each `Helper` class requires instance variables referencing the host and the representation (this reference may be indirect via the host).

- Define the `Host` class as a pass-through. Each public `Host` method should be an unsynchronized forwarding method. Also, define unsynchronized methods designed to be called by helpers whenever they change states in ways that may affect other helpers. Relay the associated `notify` or `notifyAll` calls. (Alternatively, these notifications can be sent directly among helpers.) The host should also initialize all helper objects in its constructor.

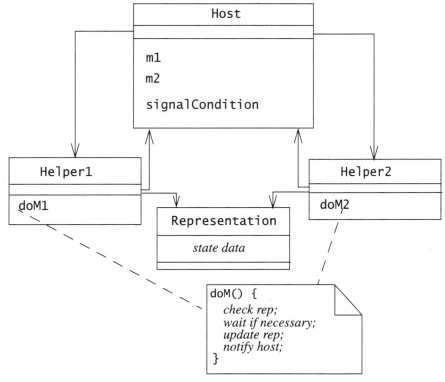

- Each helper method must avoid liveness failures while still preserving safety. In particular:

  - If the condition checks involve the shared representation, they must be performed while both the representation and helper are locked.

  - The representation lock must be released before entering any `wait`, but the lock on the helper must be retained to avoid missed signals (see §3.2.4) in which waits are started after notifications have already occurred.

  - Notification relays must be initiated without synchronization to avoid potential deadlocks.

  A generic helper method can take the form:

```
void doM() throws InterruptedException {
  for(;;) {                          // wait loop
    synchronized(this) {        // check->wait must lock this
      synchronized(rep) {       // check->act must lock rep
        boolean canAct = inRightState(rep);
        if (canAct) {
          update(rep);              // the guarded action
          break;
        }
      }                             // release rep lock before wait
      wait();                       // fall-through if !canAct
    }                               // release lock before signal
  }
  host.signalChange();
}
```

3.7.2.2 Bounded buffers

As our last examples of BoundedBuffer, we will create delegated versions that also exploit special characteristics of the underlying data structure and algorithm to obtain better performance. The final result is just slightly faster than previous versions, but serves to exemplify techniques.

First, we need to split up helper objects to do put and take. Delegation designs normally require a helper class per method. But here, we can get away with only one helper class (with two instances) by exploiting an observation about ownership transfers. As noted in §2.3.4, the single operation exchange can be used for both put-style and take-style transfers. For example, exchange(null) accomplishes a take. The buffer-based version of exchange replaces the old value with the argument at the current array slot and then circularly advances to the next array position.

It is convenient to define the helper class Exchanger as an inner class to gain access to the host and the array serving as the shared representation. We also need a slot counter variable to indicate when an exchange operation must stall because there are no more items. For the helper doing put, the counter starts off at capacity; for take, it starts off at zero. An exchange operation can proceed only if the number of slots is greater than zero.

Each successful exchange operation decrements the count. Waits on zero counts can be released only by the helper performing the complementary operation, which must provide a notification. This is implemented by issuing an added-SlotNotification to the other exchanger, as relayed through the host.

Another special consideration in this particular design leads to another minor economy. Even though the data array must be shared across the two helpers, it does not need synchronization protection so long as put and take are the *only* operations supported. This can be ensured by declaring the host class final. We can make do without a synchronization lock because, in this algorithm, any executing put *must* be operating on a different array slot than the one being accessed by any executing take. Additionally, the outer synchronizations suffice to preclude memory visibility problems (see §2.2.7). In contrast, the BoundedBuffer-WithSemaphores class requires locking around array operations because it does not otherwise restrict at most one put or take to occur at any given time.

As a further performance enhancement, notifications here use notify, since the conditions for its use (discussed in §3.2.4.2) are met: (1) Each waiting task in each helper is waiting on the same logical condition (non-emptiness for take, and non-fullness for put). (2) Each notification enables at most a single thread to continue — each put enables one take, and each take enables one put. (3) We can re-notify to deal with interruptions.

And to squeeze another bit of efficiency out of this, it is simple here to (conservatively) track whether there are any waiting threads, and issue notify only if there can be threads that need notifying. The performance effect of this tactic varies across JVM implementations. As notify operations become increasingly cheap, the minor bookkeeping overhead here to avoid calls becomes decreasingly worthwhile.

```
final class BoundedBufferWithDelegates {
  private Object[] array;
  private Exchanger putter;
  private Exchanger taker;

  public BoundedBufferWithDelegates(int capacity)
   throws IllegalArgumentException {
    if (capacity <= 0) throw new IllegalArgumentException();
    array = new Object[capacity];
    putter = new Exchanger(capacity);
    taker = new Exchanger(0);
  }


  public void put(Object x) throws InterruptedException {
    putter.exchange(x);
  }

  public Object take() throws InterruptedException {
    return taker.exchange(null);
  }

  void removedSlotNotification(Exchanger h) { // relay
    if (h == putter)  taker.addedSlotNotification();
    else              putter.addedSlotNotification();
  }
```

```
    protected class Exchanger {                    // Inner class
      protected int ptr = 0;           // circular index
      protected int slots;             // number of usable slots
      protected int waiting = 0;       // number of waiting threads

      Exchanger(int n) { slots = n; }

      synchronized void addedSlotNotification() {
        ++slots;
        if (waiting > 0) // unblock a single waiting thread
          notify();
      }

      Object exchange(Object x) throws InterruptedException {
        Object old = null; // return value

        synchronized(this) {
          while (slots <= 0) { // wait for slot
            ++waiting;
            try {
              wait();
            }
            catch(InterruptedException ie) {
              notify();
              throw ie;
            }
            finally {
              --waiting;
            }
          }

          --slots;                  // use slot
          old = array[ptr];
          array[ptr] = x;
          ptr = (ptr + 1) % array.length; // advance position
        }

        removedSlotNotification(this); // notify of change
        return old;
      }
    }
  }
}
```

3.7.2.3 Collapsing classes

Synchronization splitting of all kinds can be accomplished in two ways. In the case of lock-splitting (§2.4.2), you can either create new helper classes and forward operations from the host, or you can just keep the methods in the host but invoke them under synchronization of Objects that conceptually represent the different helpers.

The same principle holds when splitting state-dependent actions. Rather than delegating actions to helpers, you can keep the methods in the host class, adding Objects that conceptually represent the helpers. Objects used solely for synchronization serve as locks. Those used for waiting and notification serve as monitors — places to put threads that need to wait and be notified.

Combining helpers into a host class makes the host class more complex but also potentially more efficient, due to short-circuited method calls and the like. Performing such simplifications along the way, we can define a more concise, slightly more efficient, and surely more frightening version of BoundedBuffer:

```
final class BoundedBufferWithMonitorObjects {
  private final Object[] array;    // the elements

  private int putPtr = 0;          // circular indices
  private int takePtr = 0;

  private int emptySlots;          // slot counts
  private int usedSlots = 0;

  private int waitingPuts = 0;     // counts of waiting threads
  private int waitingTakes = 0;

  private final Object putMonitor = new Object();
  private final Object takeMonitor = new Object();

  public BoundedBufferWithMonitorObjects(int capacity)
   throws IllegalArgumentException {
    if (capacity <= 0)
      throw new IllegalArgumentException();

    array = new Object[capacity];
    emptySlots = capacity;
  }
```

```java
public void put(Object x) throws InterruptedException {
  synchronized(putMonitor) {
    while (emptySlots <= 0) {
      ++waitingPuts;
      try { putMonitor.wait(); }
      catch(InterruptedException ie) {
        putMonitor.notify();
        throw ie;
      }
      finally { --waitingPuts; }
    }
    --emptySlots;
    array[putPtr] = x;
    putPtr = (putPtr + 1) % array.length;
  }
  synchronized(takeMonitor) { // directly notify
    ++usedSlots;
    if (waitingTakes > 0)
      takeMonitor.notify();
  }
}

public Object take() throws InterruptedException {
  Object old = null;
  synchronized(takeMonitor) {
    while (usedSlots <= 0) {
      ++waitingTakes;
      try { takeMonitor.wait(); }
      catch(InterruptedException ie) {
        takeMonitor.notify();
        throw ie;
      }
      finally { --waitingTakes; }
    }
    --usedSlots;
    old = array[takePtr];
    array[takePtr] = null;
    takePtr = (takePtr + 1) % array.length;
  }
  synchronized(putMonitor) {
    ++emptySlots;
    if (waitingPuts > 0)
      putMonitor.notify();
  }
  return old;
}

}
```

3.7.3 Specific Notifications

Instead of treating the little helper `Objects` in classes such as `BoundedBuffer-WithMonitorObjects` as the culmination of design efforts, you can treat them as tools for implementing any design problem amenable to solution via split monitors. The Specific Notification pattern devised by Tom Cargill takes precisely this tactic.

The basic idea is to put tasks to sleep via `waits` in monitors — ordinary `Objects` (or more typically, instances of simple classes that help with bookkeeping) used solely for their wait sets. One monitor is used for each task or set of tasks that must be individually notified. In most cases, this requires one monitor per thread; in others, a group of threads that should all be awakened at once can use the same monitor. These monitors serve similar purposes to the *condition queues* that are natively supported in some monitor-based concurrent programming languages (see §3.4.4). The main difference is that, without native support, these helper monitors must be dealt with more carefully to avoid nesting problems.

Specific notifications may be useful whenever you need threads to `wait` and the notification policy does not dynamically depend on the properties of the threads. Once a thread is put in its wait set, it is impossible to access it in any way other than to wake it up. Among the common applications to which these constraints apply are:

- Supporting specific scheduling policies through the use of an explicit queue (for example FIFO, LIFO, priority).

- Dividing incoming tasks into different queues depending on the method they are waiting to perform. This can be used to extend techniques based on conflict sets (see §3.3.2).

However, while it may be tempting to combine support for scheduling constraints such as FIFO with constraints based on logical state or execution state, interactions between these two applications usually lead to both conceptual and logistical problems. For example, you need to consider cases where thread A should be enabled before thread B because it arrived earlier, but thread B is logically able to proceed while thread A is not. This may necessitate elaborate apparatus to requeue threads, manage locking orders, and arbitrarily handle corner cases.

3.7.3.1   Design steps

The main design steps are specializations of those described in §3.7.2.1. Create or modify a class, say Host, as follows:

- For each thread or set of threads that needs specific notification, create an object serving as a monitor. These monitors may be arranged in arrays or other collections, or dynamically created during execution.

- Set up bookkeeping in the classes serving as monitors to manage waiting and notification operations and their interactions with time-out and interruption policies. As shown in the WaitNode class in §3.7.3.2, this usually entails maintaining a released field to remember if a waiting thread has been released due to notification, interruption, or time-out. These classes may then support methods, say doWait, doTimedWait, doNotify, and doNotifyAll, that perform *reliable* waiting and notification and deal with interrupts and time-outs in the desired fashion. If you cannot add bookkeeping to the classes serving as monitors, then these matters need to be addressed in the Host class methods.

- In each Host method in which tasks are to be suspended, use monitor.doWait() with the appropriate monitor object. This code must avoid nested monitor problems by ensuring that the wait is performed within code regions that are *not* synchronized on the host object. The simplest and most desirable form is:

```
boolean needToWait;    // to remember value after synch exit
synchronized (this) {
  needToWait = ...;
  if (needToWait)
    enqueue(monitor); // or any similar bookkeeping
}
if (needToWait) monitor.doWait();
```

- In each method in which tasks are to be resumed, use monitor.doNotify(), also handling the consequences of time-out or interruption.

276

3.7.3.2 FIFO semaphores

Specific notifications can be used to implement the kinds of First-In-First-Out semaphore classes discussed in §3.4.1.5. FIFO semaphores can in turn be used to build other utilities that rely on FIFO properties.

The following `FIFOSemaphore` class (a streamlined version of one in `util.concurrent`) is defined as a subclass of the generic `Semaphore` class from §3.7.1. The `FIFOSemaphore` class maintains a linked `WaitQueue` holding `Wait-Nodes`, each serving as a monitor. An `acquire` operation that cannot immediately obtain a permit enqueues a new monitor object that enters a `wait`. The `release` operation dequeues the oldest waiting node and notifies it.

A `released` field in each `WaitNode` helps manage interactions between notifications and interruptions. During a `release`, any monitor that has aborted due to interruption is skipped over. Conversely, an interrupted `wait` first checks to see if it has been notified in addition to being interrupted. If so, it must roll forward, ignoring the exception but resetting interrupt status (see §3.1.2) to preserve cancellation status. (An unshown `doTimedWait` method can be implemented similarly, by setting `released` status upon time-out.) The potential for interruptions at inconvenient times accounts for the retry loop in `release`.

The interactions among `FIFOSemaphore`, `WaitQueue`, and `WaitNode` ensure the necessary atomicity while avoiding nested monitor problems. They also demonstrate some of the arbitrariness of decisions surrounding support of FIFO policies. We can promise only that the semaphore is FIFO with respect to an arbitrary start point and end point. The start point commences with the `synchronized(this)` in `acquire`. The end point normally occurs upon release from a `wait` due to `notify`. Two threads entering `acquire` might obtain the lock in different orders from their arrivals, for example if the first one is scheduled out by the JVM before it hits the `synchronized(this)` statement. Similarly, a thread released before another might finally return to its caller after the other. Especially on multiprocessors, the class provides as strong a guarantee as users of the class should expect.

The scheduling rules can be changed by substituting a different kind of queue here; for example one based on `Thread.getPriority`. However, it is trickier to adapt this class to handle semantic restrictions based on execution or logical state. Most semantic restrictions require notified or interrupted threads to acquire additional locks. This would introduce complications to the scheme here that exploits the fact that awakened threads need not access the main lock. These would need to be resolved in an application-specific manner.

```
class FIFOSemaphore extends Semaphore {

  protected final WaitQueue queue = new WaitQueue();

  public FIFOSemaphore(long initialPermits) {
    super(initialPermits);
  }

  public void acquire() throws InterruptedException {
    if (Thread.interrupted()) throw new InterruptedException();

    WaitNode node = null;

    synchronized(this) {
      if (permits > 0) {      // no need to queue
        --permits;
        return;
      }
      else {
        node = new WaitNode();
        queue.enq(node);
      }
    }

    // must release lock before node wait

    node.doWait();
  }

  public synchronized void release() {
    for (;;) {                      // retry until success
      WaitNode node = queue.deq();

      if (node == null) {     // queue is empty
        ++permits;
        return;
      }
      else if (node.doNotify())
        return;

      // else node was already released due to
      //   interruption or time-out, so must retry
    }
  }
}
```

```
// Queue node class. Each node serves as a monitor.

protected static class WaitNode {
  boolean released = false;
  WaitNode next = null;        // to arrange in linked list

  synchronized void doWait() throws InterruptedException {
    try {
      while (!released)
        wait();
    }
    catch (InterruptedException ie) {

      if (!released) {          // interrupted before notified
        // Suppress future notifications:
        released = true;
        throw ie;
      }
      else {                    // interrupted after notified
        // ignore exception but propagate status:
        Thread.currentThread().interrupt();
      }

    }
  }

  synchronized boolean doNotify() { // return true if notified

    if (released)               // was interrupted or timed out
      return false;
    else {
      released = true;
      notify();
      return true;
    }
  }

  synchronized boolean doTimedWait(long msecs)
   throws InterruptedException {
    // similar
  }
}
```

```
// Standard linked queue class.
// Used only when holding Semaphore lock.

protected static class WaitQueue {
  protected WaitNode head = null;
  protected WaitNode last = null;

  protected void enq(WaitNode node) {
    if (last == null)
      head = last = node;
    else {
      last.next = node;
      last = node;
    }
  }

  protected WaitNode deq() {
    WaitNode node = head;
    if (node != null) {
      head = node.next;
      if (head == null) last = null;
      node.next = null;
    }
    return node;
  }
}
}
```

3.7.4 Further Readings

Techniques for implementing elementary locks using, for example, Dekker's algorithm and ticket-based algorithms are presented in the concurrent programming texts by Andrews and others listed in §1.2.5. However, there is no reason to base general-purpose concurrency control utilities on such techniques rather than on built-in `synchronized` methods and blocks.

The Specific Notification pattern was first described in:

Cargill, Thomas. "Specific Notification for Java Thread Synchronization", *Proceedings of the Pattern Languages of Programming Conference*, 1996.

An alternative account of refining `notifyAll` constructions using specific notifications can be found in:

Mizuno, Masaaki. "A Structured Approach for Developing Concurrent Programs in Java", *Information Processing Letters*, 1999.

Further examples and extensions of the techniques described in this section may be found in the online supplement.

CHAPTER 4

Creating Threads

IT is impossible to categorize all the ways to exploit the functionality associated with threads. But two general approaches can be distinguished by their points of view on the statement:

```
new Thread(aRunnable).start();
```

Is this a fancy way to invoke a method (i.e., a `Runnable`'s `run` method), or is it a way to create a fancy object (i.e., a new instance of class `Thread`)? Clearly it is both, but focusing on one aspect versus the other leads to two approaches to using threads that were implicit in discussions in Chapter 1:

Task-based. Here, the main reason to use a thread is to asynchronously invoke a method that performs some task. The task might range from a single method to an entire session. Thread-based techniques can support message-passing schemes that escape the limitations of pure procedural calls. Task-based designs are seen in event frameworks, parallel computation, and IO-intensive systems.

Actor-based. Here, the main reason to use a thread is to create and set into motion a new autonomous, active, process-like object. This object may in turn react to external events, interact with other actors, and so on. Actor-based designs are seen in reactive, control, and distributed systems. They are also the focus of most formal approaches to concurrency.

(Both the terms *task* and *actor* have many overloaded meanings and near-synonyms. We'll confine usage to the above senses.)

In task-based systems, passive objects sometimes send active (thread-propelled) messages, while in actor-based systems, active objects normally send passive messages. As is usually the case for artificial dichotomies, neither approach is always best, and there is a huge middle ground that can be designed from either or both perspectives.

Actor-based approaches are commonly used in the construction of daemons that interact with other systems. They are also employed when defining intrinsically active entities, for example the `GamePlayer` in §3.2.4. Their main methods often take a reactive looping form:

```
for(;;) { acceptAndProcessCommand(); }
```

Task-based approaches are commonly used when there is some conceptual or performance-based reason to execute a given task, service, or computation asynchronously rather than relying on direct procedural invocation. Task-based designs provide a separation of concerns between logical asynchrony and mappings to threads and thread-based constructions. They receive the bulk of discussion in this chapter.

As an initial example, here is one way to approach a common thread-based design, a web service. Here, a running `WebService` is a "daemon process" actor-style thread — it continuously interacts with its environment by listening for new incoming requests. But invocations to `handler.process` are issued in a task-based manner — a new task is set in motion to handle each incoming request. Here, for the sake of concise illustration, the request is simply a number, and the handler just returns the negation of the number back to the client.

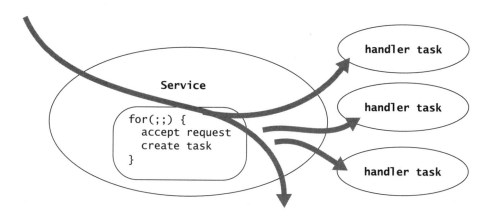

```java
class WebService implements Runnable {
  static final int PORT = 1040;    // just for demo
  Handler handler = new Handler();

  public void run() {
    try {
      ServerSocket socket = new ServerSocket(PORT);
      for (;;) {
        final Socket connection = socket.accept();
        new Thread(new Runnable() {
          public void run() {
            handler.process(connection);
          }}).start();
      }
    }
    catch(Exception e) { } // die
  }

  public static void main(String[] args) {
    new Thread(new WebService()).start();
  }
}


class Handler {

  void process(Socket s) {
    DataInputStream in = null;
    DataOutputStream out = null;
    try {
      in = new DataInputStream(s.getInputStream());
      out = new DataOutputStream(s.getOutputStream());
      int request = in.readInt();
      int result = -request;      // return negation to client
      out.writeInt(result);
    }
    catch(IOException ex) {}      // fall through

    finally {                     // clean up
      try { if (in != null) in.close(); }
      catch (IOException ignore) {}
      try { if (out != null) out.close(); }
      catch (IOException ignore) {}
      try  { s.close(); }
      catch (IOException ignore) {}
    }
  }

}
```

This chapter divides coverage of thread construction and structuring techniques as follows:

- §4.1 presents a series of options for implementing conceptually oneway messages, sometimes by asynchronously initiating tasks using threads or thread-based lightweight execution frameworks.

- §4.2 discusses the design of systems in which networks of components employ oneway messaging strategies.

- §4.3 presents alternatives for constructing threads that compute results or provide services to clients that initiate them.

- §4.4 examines problem decomposition techniques that can be used to improve performance by exploiting multiprocessors.

- §4.5 provides an overview of constructs and frameworks for designing systems of active objects, illustrated in part using CSP.

Many of the designs presented in this chapter straddle the borders among concurrent, distributed, and parallel programming. Presentations focus on concurrent, single-JVM solutions. But they include constructions often seen when developing the plumbing support for systems and frameworks involving multiple processes or computers.

4.1   Oneway Messages

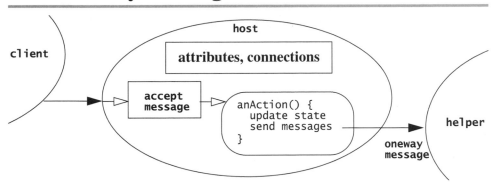

A host object issues a logically oneway message to one or more recipients without depending on the consequences of that message. Sending a oneway message somehow results in some task being performed. The task might consist of only a single line of code, or might represent a session that entails acquisition of many resources and hours of computation. But the outcome of the thread issuing a one-way message does not rely on the task's outcome, or on when the task completes, or (normally) on whether it *ever* completes. Common examples include:

Events	Mouse clicks, etc.
Notifications	Status change alerts
Postings	Mail messages, stock quotes, etc.
Activations	Creating Applets, daemons, etc.
Commands	Print requests, etc.
Relays	Message forwardings and dispatchings

Oneway interactions between senders and recipients need not be strictly asynchronous. For example, the sender may be responsible for ensuring that a recipient actually receives the message. Also, the sender or another object may later wish to cancel or roll back the effects of the resulting task (which is of course not always possible, for example if the task has already completed — see §3.1.2).

If every task could run instantaneously, you might trigger oneway messages via procedural invocations in which the caller waits out the task triggered by the message, even though it has no reason to do so. But there are often performance-based, conceptual, and logistical reasons to issue some of these messages via thread-based constructions in which the associated tasks proceed independently.

4.1.1   Message Formats

Many different styles of invocation are encompassed under the notion of oneway message passing. While some of them are more closely associated with distributed or multiprocess applications (see §1.2.2), any of them can be used in conjunction with the constructions discussed in this section. In addition to direct method invocations, message formats may include:

Command strings. The recipient must parse, decode, and then dispatch the associated task. Command string messages are widely used in socket-based and pipe-based communication, especially in web services.

Event objects. The message contains a structured description of an event. The recipient then dispatches some arbitrary handling task that it associates with the event. Event objects are used extensively in GUI frameworks such as `java.awt`, as well as component frameworks supported by `java.beans`.

Request objects. The message contains an encoding of a method name and (*marshalled* or *serialized*) arguments. The recipient issues the corresponding method call to a helper object that performs this method. Request objects are used in distributed object support systems such as those in `java.rmi` and `org.omg.corba`. Variants are used in Ada tasking.

Class objects. The message is a representation of a class (for example via a `.class` file) which the recipient then instantiates. This scheme is used in the `java.applet` framework, as well as in remote activation protocols.

Runnable objects. The message consists of some code that the recipient executes. Mixed forms of *runnable events* (which include both an event description and an associated action) are used in some event frameworks. Extended forms employing serialized runnable objects are seen in mobile agent frameworks.

Arbitrary objects. A sender may treat any kind of object as a message by including it as method argument or passing it through a `Channel` (see §4.2.1). For example, in the JavaSpaces™ framework, senders may post any serialized object as a message (also known as an *entry*). Recipients accept only those entries with types and field values that conform to a specified set of matching criteria. Recipients then process these objects in any appropriate manner.

Differences among these formats reflect (among other things) how much the caller knows about the code the recipient needs to run to perform its task. It is often both most convenient and most efficient to use runnable objects, especially in thread-based frameworks that use instances of class `Runnable` as arguments in `Thread` constructors. We'll focus on this form, but occasionally illustrate others.

4.1.2 Open Calls

Consider the central Host object in a call chain in which the Host receives `req` requests from any number of Clients and, in the course of processing them, must issue logically oneway `handle` messages to one or more Helper objects. Again, we'll ignore the facts that an arbitrary amount of effort might be needed to decode the request before acting upon it, that the request might actually be read from a socket as seen in the `WebService` class, and so on. Also, all classes discussed in this section can be extended to issue multicasts to multiple helpers using the constructions described in §2.4.4 and §3.5.2.

The main design force here is latency. If a Host is busy servicing requests, then it cannot accept new ones. This adds response time to new requests from Clients, reducing overall service availability.

Some aspects of latency can be addressed simply by using the pass-through and open call designs described in §2.4:

```
class OpenCallHost {                       // Generic code sketch
   protected long localState;
   protected final Helper helper = new Helper();

   protected synchronized void updateState(...) {
      localState = ...;
   }

   public void req(...) {
      updateState(...);
      helper.handle(...);
   }
}
```

Here, even if the `helper.handle` call is relatively time-consuming, the Host object will still be able to accept new requests from clients running in different threads. The request acceptance rate is bounded only by the time it takes to update local state.

The use of open calls typically eliminates bottleneck points surrounding a given Host, but does not address the broader question of how to introduce concurrency into a system to begin with. Open calls are useful only when clients somehow already know enough to use some other approach that permits independent execution when necessary or desired.

4.1.3 Thread-Per-Message

Concurrency can be introduced into oneway messaging designs by issuing a message in its own thread, as in:

```
class ThreadPerMessageHost {                    // Generic code sketch
  protected long localState;
  protected final Helper helper = new Helper();

  protected synchronized void updateState() {
    localState = ...;
  }

  public void req(...) {
    updateState(...);
    new Thread(new Runnable() {
      public void run() {
        helper.handle(...);
      }
    }).start();
  }
}
```

This strategy improves throughput when multiple parallel tasks can run faster than a sequence of them could, normally because they are either IO-bound or are compute-bound and running on a multiprocessor. It can also enhance fairness and improve availability if clients need not wait for each other's tasks to complete.

Decisions about whether to create and start threads to perform tasks are not too different from decisions about whether to create other kinds of objects or send other kinds of messages: The benefits must outweigh the costs.

Thread-per-message designs introduce response latency because thread creation is more expensive than direct method invocation. When tasks are time-consuming compared to thread construction time, are session-based, need to be isolated from other independent activities, or can exploit IO or CPU parallelism, the trade-offs are generally worth it. But performance problems can emerge even when construction latencies are acceptable. The JVM implementation and/or operating system may not respond well to the construction of too many threads. For example, they may run out of system resources associated with threads. Also, as the number of threads increases, thread scheduling and context switching overhead can overwhelm processing times.

4.1.3.1 Executors

The coding style seen in class `ThreadPerMessage` can become a problem because of its direct reliance on class `Thread`. Such usages can make it more difficult to adjust thread initialization parameters, as well as thread-specific data (see §2.3.2) used across an application. This can be avoided by creating an interface, say:

```
interface Executor {
  void execute(Runnable r);
}
```

This interface can be implemented with classes such as:

```
class PlainThreadExecutor implements Executor {
  public void execute(Runnable r) {
    new Thread(r).start();
  }
}
```

These implementations may be used in classes such as:

```
class HostWithExecutor {                        // Generic code sketch
  protected long localState;
  protected final Helper helper = new Helper();
  protected final Executor executor;

  public HostWithExecutor(Executor e) { executor = e; }

  protected synchronized void updateState(...) {
    localState = ...;
  }

  public void req(...) {
    updateState(...);
    executor.execute(new Runnable() {
      public void run() {
        helper.handle(...);
      }
    });
  }
}
```

The use of such interfaces also permits replacement of threads with lightweight executable frameworks.

4.1.4 Worker Threads

Lightweight executable frameworks fill the gap between open calls and thread-per-message designs. They apply when you need to introduce limited concurrency, at the expense of some usage restrictions, in order to maximize (or at least improve) throughput and minimize average latencies.

Lightweight executable frameworks can be constructed in many ways, but all stem from the basic idea of using one thread to execute many unrelated tasks (here, in succession). These threads are known as *worker* threads, *background* threads, and as *thread pools* when more than one thread is used.

Each worker continually accepts new `Runnable` commands from hosts and holds them in some kind of `Channel` (a queue, buffer, etc. — see §3.4.1) until they can be run. This design has the classic form of a producer-consumer relationship: the host produces tasks and workers consume them by running them.

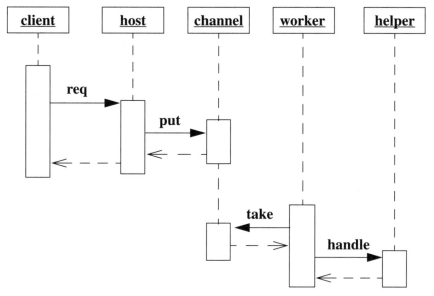

Lightweight executable frameworks can improve the structure of some task-based concurrent programs, by allowing you to package many smaller, logically asynchronous units of execution as tasks without having to worry much about performance consequences: Entering a `Runnable` into a queue is likely to be faster than creating a new `Thread` object. And because you can control the number of worker threads, you can minimize chances of resource exhaustion and reduce context-switching overhead. Explicit queuing also permits greater flexibility in tuning execution semantics. For example, you can implement `Channels` as priority queues that order tasks with more deterministic control than is guaranteed by `Thread.setPriority`. (See §4.3.4 for an example.)

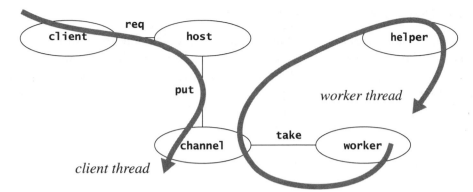

To interoperate with pure thread-based versions, worker threads can be packaged as Executors. Here is a generic implementation that could be used in the HostWithExecutor class instead of the thread-per-message version:

```
class PlainWorkerPool implements Executor {
  protected final Channel workQueue;

  public void execute(Runnable r) {
    try {
      workQueue.put(r);
    }
    catch (InterruptedException ie) { // postpone response
      Thread.currentThread().interrupt();
    }
  }

  public PlainWorkerPool(Channel ch, int nworkers) {
    workQueue = ch;
    for (int i = 0; i < nworkers; ++i) activate();
  }

  protected void activate() {
    Runnable runLoop = new Runnable() {
      public void run() {
        try {
          for (;;) {
            Runnable r = (Runnable)(workQueue.take());
            r.run();
          }
        }
        catch (InterruptedException ie) {} // die
      }
    };
    new Thread(runLoop).start();
  }
}
```

4.1.4.1   Design choices

The first decision to make surrounding lightweight executable frameworks based on worker threads is whether to create or use them at all. The main question is whether there is some property of ordinary `Thread`s that you do not need or are willing to give up. If not, it is unlikely that you will arrive at a solution that outperforms the built-in thread support on production JVM implementations.

The trade-offs that obtain the performance advantages of worker threads have several additional tunable parameters, usage consequences, and programming obligations that can impact the design and use of worker thread classes (including those contained in the `util.concurrent` package available from the online supplement).

Identity. Most worker threads must be treated "anonymously". Because the same worker thread is reused for multiple tasks, the use of `ThreadLocal` and other thread-specific contextual control techniques (see §2.3.2) becomes more awkward. To cope with this, you need to know about all such contextual data, and somehow reset it if necessary upon executing each task. (This includes information about security contexts maintained by run-time support classes.) However, most lightweight executable frameworks avoid any reliance on thread-specific techniques.

If identity is the only property of threads you are willing to give up, then the only potential performance value of worker threads is minimization of start-up overhead by reusing existing threads to execute multiple `Runnable` tasks, while still possibly bounding resource consumption.

Queuing. Runnable tasks that are sitting in queues do not run. This is one source of performance benefits in most worker-thread designs — if each action were associated with a thread, it would need to be independently scheduled by the JVM. But as a consequence, queued execution cannot in general be used when there are any dependencies among tasks. If a currently running task blocks waiting for a condition produced by a task still waiting in the queue, the system may freeze up. Options here include:

- Use as many worker threads as there are simultaneously executing tasks. In this case, the `Channel` need not perform any queuing, so you can use `Syn-chronousChannel`s (see §3.4.1.4), queueless channels that require each put to wait for a take and vice versa. Here, the host objects merely hand off tasks to worker threads, which immediately start executing them. For this to work well, worker thread pools should be dynamically expandable.

- Restrict usage to contexts in which task dependencies are impossible, for example in HTTP servers where each message is issued by an unrelated external client requesting a file. Require the helper objects to create actual `Threads` when they cannot ensure independence.

- Create custom queues that understand the dependencies among the particular kinds of tasks being processed by the worker threads. For example, most pools used for processing tasks representing transactions (see §3.6) must keep track of transaction dependencies. And the lightweight parallel framework described in §4.4.1 relies on special queuing policies that apply only to subtasks created in divide-and-conquer algorithms.

Saturation. As the request rate increases, a worker pool will eventually become saturated. All worker threads will be processing tasks and the Host object(s) using the pool will be unable to hand off work. Possible responses include:

- Increase the pool size. In many applications, bounds are heuristic estimates. If a bound is just a guess based on values shown to work well on a particular platform under test workloads, it can be increased. At some point, though, one of the other options must be taken unless you can tolerate failure if the JVM runs out of enough resources to construct a new `Thread`.

- If the nature of the service allows it, use an unbounded buffered channel and let requests pile up. This risks potential system failure due to exhaustion of memory, but this takes longer to happen than does resource exhaustion surrounding `Thread` construction.

- Establish a *back-pressure* notification scheme to ask clients to stop sending so many requests. If the ultimate clients are part of a distributed system, they may be able to use another server instead.

- *Drop* (discard) new requests upon saturation. This can be a good option if you know that clients will retry anyway. However, unless retries are automatic, you need to add callbacks, events, or notifications back to clients to alert them of the drops so that they will know enough to retry (see §4.3.1).

- Make room for the new request by dropping *old* requests that have been queued but not yet run, or even cancelling one or more executing tasks. This preference for new requests over old ones upon saturation sometimes meshes well with usage patterns. For example, in some telecommunications systems, old unserviced tasks are usually requests by clients that have already given up and disconnected.

- Block until some thread is available. This can be a good option when handlers are of predictable, short-lived duration, so you can be confident that the wait will unblock without unacceptable delays.

◆ The Host can run the task directly itself, in its current thread. This is often the best default choice. In essence, the Host momentarily becomes single-threaded. The act of servicing the request limits the rate at which it can accept new requests, thus preventing further local breakdowns.

Thread management. The `PlainWorkerPool` class is somewhat wasteful because it creates all worker threads upon start-up, whether they are needed or not, and lets them all live on indefinitely, even when the service is not being used. These problems can be alleviated by using a management class that supports:

◆ *Lazy construction*: Activate a new thread only when a request cannot be serviced immediately by an existing idle thread. Lazy construction allows users to provide large enough pool size limits to avoid underutilization problems occurring when fewer threads are running than a given computer can handle. This comes at the minor expense of occasionally higher latencies when a new request causes a new thread to be created. The start-up effects of lazy construction can be tempered by creating a small number of "warm" threads upon construction of the pool.

◆ *Idle time-outs*: Allow threads to time out waiting for work and to terminate upon time-out. This eventually causes all workers to exit if the pool is not used for prolonged periods. When coupled with lazy construction, these dead threads will be replaced with new ones if the request rate later increases.

In heavily resource-conscious applications, you may also associate other resources (such as sets of reusable graphical objects) with each worker thread, thus combining resource pools (see §3.4.1.2) with thread pools.

Cancellation. You may need to distinguish cancellation (see §3.1.2) of a task from cancellation of the worker thread performing that task. One approach is:

◆ Upon interruption, allow the current worker thread to die, but replace it if necessary with a fresh worker thread if the work queue is not empty or when a new incoming task arrives.

◆ Provide a `shutdown` method in the worker thread class that causes existing workers to die and no additional workers to be created.

Additionally, you may need to trigger some kind of error handling if a Host thread is cancelled during a task hand-off. While the silent swallowing of `InterruptedException` without queuing a task seen in `PlainWorkerPool` conforms to the minimal requirements of oneway message-passing frameworks, most applications need to take other remedial actions.

4.1.4.2 Event queues

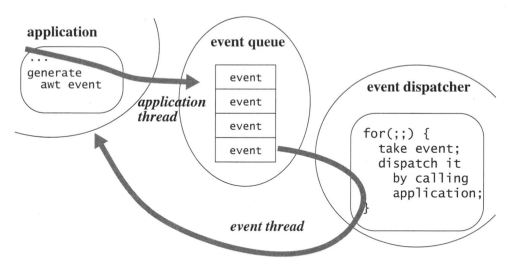

Many event-based frameworks (including the ones supported in the java.awt and javax.swing packages) rely on designs in which exactly one worker thread operates on an unbounded queue. The queue holds instances of EventObject that must be dispatched (as opposed to Runnable objects that self-dispatch), normally to *listener* objects defined by the application. Often the listeners are the same objects as those that initially generate events.

The use of a single thread operating on a single event queue simplifies usage compared to general worker-thread designs, but also imposes some limitations that are characteristic of event frameworks:

- The ordering properties of a queue can be exploited to optimize handling. For example, automatic event-filtering techniques can be used to remove or combine duplicate repaint events for the same screen area before they hit the front of the queue and are taken by the worker thread.

- You can require that all methods operating on certain objects be invoked only by issuing events onto the queue, and are thus ultimately performed by the single worker thread. This results in a form of thread confinement (see §2.3.2) of these objects. If flawlessly adhered to, this eliminates the need for dynamic locking within operations on these objects, thus improving performance. This can also reduce complexity for applications that do not otherwise need to construct threads.

This is the basis for the Swing *single-thread rule*: With only a few exceptions, all manipulation of Swing objects must be performed by the event handler thread. While not stated in AWT, it is good idea to observe this rule there as well.

- Events should not be enabled until their handlers are fully constructed and are thus ready to handle events. This holds as well for other thread-based designs (see §2.2.7), but is a more common source of error here because registering an event handler or listener *inside* its constructor is not as obvious a way to prematurely enable concurrent execution as is constructing a thread.

- Users of the event framework must never dispatch actions that block in ways that can unblock only as a result of handling a future event. This problem is encountered when implementing modal dialogs in most event frameworks, and requires an ad-hoc solution. However, more localized solutions can be obtained merely by setting a *disabled* state for interactive components that should not be used until a certain re-enabling event is received. This avoids blocking the event queue without allowing undesired actions to be triggered.

- Further, to maintain responsiveness of the event framework, actions should not block at all, and should not perform time-consuming operations.

This set of design choices causes event frameworks to have much better performance than would thread-per-event designs, and makes them simpler to program by developers who do not otherwise use threads. However, the usage restrictions have more impact in programs that do construct other threads. For example, because of the single-thread rule, even the smallest manipulations of GUI components (such as changing the text in a label) must be performed by issuing runnable event objects that encapsulate an action to be performed by the event handler thread.

In Swing and AWT applications, the methods `javax.swing.SwingUtilities.invokeLater` and `java.awt.EventQueue.invokeLater` can be used to execute display-related commands in the event handler thread. These methods create runnable event objects that are executed when taken from the queue. The online supplement contains links to a `SwingWorker` utility class that partially automates conformance to these rules for threads that produce results leading to screen updates.

4.1.4.3 Timers

The fact that Runnable tasks in worker thread designs may sit queued without running is a problem to be worked around in some applications. But it sometimes becomes a feature when actions are intended to be delayed.

The use of worker threads can both improve efficiency and simplify usage of delayed and periodic actions — those triggered at certain times, after certain delays, or at regular intervals (for example, every day at noon). A standardized timer facility can both automate messy timing calculations and avoid excess thread construction by reusing worker threads. The main trade-off is that if a worker blocks or takes a long time processing one task, the triggering of others may become delayed longer than they would be if separate Threads are created and scheduled by the underlying JVM.

Time-based daemons can be constructed as variants of the basic worker thread design described in §4.1.4.1. For example, here are the highlights of a version that relies on an unshown priority queue class (that might take a form similar to the scheduling queue illustrated in §4.3.4) and is set up to support only one worker thread:

```
class TimerDaemon {                                    // Fragments

  static class TimerTask implements Comparable { // ...
    final Runnable command;
    final long execTime;         // time to run at
    public int compareTo(Object x) {
      long otherExecTime = ((TimerTask)(x)).execTime;
      return (execTime < otherExecTime) ? -1 :
              (execTime == otherExecTime)? 0 : 1;
    }
  }

  // a heap or list with methods that preserve
  // ordering with respect to TimerTask.compareTo

  static class PriorityQueue {
    void put(TimerTask t);
    TimerTask least();
    void removeLeast();
    boolean isEmpty();
  }

  protected final PriorityQueue pq = new PriorityQueue();

  public synchronized void executeAfterDelay(Runnable r,long t){
    pq.put(new TimerTask(r, t + System.currentTimeMillis()));
    notifyAll();
  }
```

```
public synchronized void executeAt(Runnable r, Date time) {
  pq.put(new TimerTask(r, time.getTime()));
  notifyAll();
}

// wait for and then return next task to run
protected synchronized Runnable take()
 throws InterruptedException {
  for (;;) {
    while (pq.isEmpty())
      wait();
    TimerTask t = pq.least();
    long now = System.currentTimeMillis();
    long waitTime = now - t.execTime;
    if (waitTime <= 0) {
      pq.removeLeast();
      return t.command;
    }
    else
      wait(waitTime);
  }
}

public TimerDaemon() { activate(); } // only one

void activate() {
  // same as PlainWorkerThread except using above take method
}
}
```

The techniques discussed in §3.7 can be used here to improve efficiency of the waiting and notification operations.

This class can be extended to deal with periodic tasks by including additional bookkeeping to requeue them before running them. However, this also requires dealing with the fact that periodically scheduled actions are almost never exactly periodic, in part because timed waits do not necessarily wake up exactly upon the given delays. The main options are either to ignore lags and reschedule by clock time, or to ignore the clock and reschedule the next execution at a fixed delay after starting the current one. Fancier schemes are typically needed for multimedia synchronization — see the Further Readings in §1.3.5.

Timer daemons[1] can additionally support methods that cancel delayed or periodic actions. One approach is to have executeAt and other scheduling methods accept or return suitably a reworked TimerTask supporting a cancel method that sets a status flag honored by the worker thread.

---

[1]. As of this writing, a similar class is scheduled to be supported in an upcoming SDK release.

4.1.5 Polling and Event-Driven IO

Most worker thread designs rely on blocking channels in which the worker thread waits for incoming commands to run. However, there are a few contexts in which optimistic-style retry loops provide a better solution. Most involve the execution of commands stemming from messages received across IO streams.

It can be a challenge to achieve low latencies and high throughputs in heavily loaded IO-bound systems. The time taken to create a thread that performs an IO-based task adds latency, but most run-time systems are tuned such that, once threads are created, they are very responsive to new inputs arriving on IO streams. On input, they unblock with shorter latencies than you are likely to achieve via other techniques. Especially in the case of socket-based IO, these forces generally favor thread-per-IO-session designs, where a different thread is used (or reused) for each session relying on input from a different connection.

However, as the number of simultaneously active connections climbs, other approaches are (only) sometimes more attractive. Consider for example, a multiplayer game server, or a transaction server, with:

clients   **helpers**

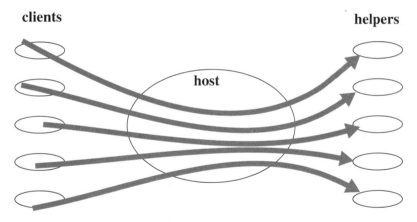

host

- Thousands of simultaneous socket connections that join and leave at a steady rate, for example, as people start and finish playing a game.

- Relatively low input rates on any given socket at any given time. However, summing across all connections, the aggregate IO rates may be very high.

- Non-trivial computation associated with at least some inputs, for example those that cause global state changes in games.

On large mainframe systems, this kind of problem is sometimes dealt with by creating a special-purpose front-end machine that multiplexes all of the inputs into a single stream that is then dealt with by the main service. The main service is often multithreaded, but its structure is simplified and made more efficient because it does not need to deal with so many apparent clients at a time.

A family of polling and event-driven designs approach such problems without requiring special front ends. While they are not (as of this writing) explicitly supported by the `java.io` and `java.net` classes, enough of the ingredients are provided to allow construction of designs that can attain good performance in these kinds of situations. (The designs are analogous to those using socket `select` and `poll` operations in other systems and languages.) We'll illustrate with inputs on sockets, but the approach also applies to outputs, to files, and to IO using more exotic devices such as sensors.

4.1.5.1 Event-driven tasks

Many IO-based tasks are initially written in a session-based style (see §2.3.1), continuously pulling commands from sockets and processing them. For example:

```
class SessionTask implements Runnable {  // Generic code sketch
  protected final Socket socket;
  protected final InputStream input;
  SessionTask(Socket s) throws IOException {
    socket = s; input = socket.getInputStream();
  }

  public void run() {                   // Normally run in a new thread
    byte[] commandBuffer = new byte[BUFFSIZE];
    try {
      for (;;) {
        int bytes = input.read(commandBuffer, 0, BUFFSIZE);
        if (bytes != BUFFSIZE) break;
        processCommand(commandBuffer, bytes);
      }
    }
    catch (IOException ex) {
      cleanup();
    }
    finally {
      try { input.close(); socket.close(); }
      catch(IOException ignore) {}
    }
  }
}
```

To enable many sessions to be handled without using many threads, the tasks first must be refactored into an event-driven style, where an event here signifies IO availability. In this style, a session consists of possibly many executions of its event-triggered task(s), each of which is invoked when input becomes available.

Event-driven IO tasks are similar in form to GUI event handlers. A session-based design can be converted into an event-driven form by:

- Isolating the basic per-command functionality in a reworked task run method that reads *one* command and performs the associated action.

- Defining the run method so that it can be *repeatedly* triggered whenever input is available to be read (or an IO exception occurs).

- Manually maintaining completion status so that the per-event action is no longer triggered when the session finishes, normally because the input has been exhausted or the connection has been closed.

For example:

```java
class IOEventTask implements Runnable {  // Generic code sketch
  protected final Socket socket;
  protected final InputStream input;
  protected volatile boolean done = false; // latches true

  IOEventTask(Socket s) throws IOException {
    socket = s; input = socket.getInputStream();
  }

  public void run() { // trigger only when input available
    if (done) return;

    byte[] commandBuffer = new byte[BUFFSIZE];
    try {
      int bytes = input.read(commandBuffer, 0, BUFFSIZE);
      if (bytes != BUFFSIZE) done = true;
      else processCommand(commandBuffer, bytes);
    }
    catch (IOException ex) {
      cleanup();
      done = true;
    }
    finally {
      if (!done) return;
      try { input.close(); socket.close(); }
      catch(IOException ignore) {}
    }
  }

  // Accessor methods needed by triggering agent:
  boolean done()      { return done; }
  InputStream input() { return input; }
}
```

4.1.5.2 Triggering

When the events driving each event-driven task are relatively infrequent, a large number of tasks can be processed by a small number of worker threads. The simplest case occurs when the number of worker threads is exactly one. Here, the worker thread repeatedly polls a list of open sockets to see if they have any input available (via `InputStream.available`) or have encountered other IO-related status changes. If so, the worker executes the associated run method.

This style of worker thread differs from the ones in §4.1.4.1 in that, rather than pulling tasks from a blocking queue and blindly running them, the worker must repeatedly check a list of registered tasks to see if any can be run. It removes each task from the list only when it claims to have completed.

One generic form is:

```
class PollingWorker implements Runnable {          // Incomplete
  private List tasks = ...;
  private long sleepTime = ...;

  void register(IOEventTask t)    { tasks.add(t); }
  void deregister(IOEventTask t) { tasks.remove(t); }

  public void run() {
    try {
      for (;;) {
        for (Iterator it = tasks.iterator(); it.hasNext();) {
          IOEventTask t = (IOEventTask)(it.next());
          if (t.done())
            deregister(t);
          else {
            boolean trigger;
            try {
              trigger = t.input().available() > 0;
            }
            catch (IOException ex) {
              trigger = true; // trigger if exception on check
            }
            if (trigger)
              t.run();
          }
        }
        Thread.sleep(sleepTime); // pause between sweeps
      }
    }
    catch (InterruptedException ie) {}
  }
}
```

Several design concerns arise here:

- Polling intrinsically relies on busy-wait loops (see §3.2.6), which are intrinsically wasteful (but still sometimes less so than context-switching). Coping with this requires empirically guided decisions about how to insert sleeps, yields, or alternative actions to strike a balance between conserving CPU time and maintaining acceptable average response latencies.

- Performance is very sensitive to the characteristics of the underlying data structure maintaining the list of registered tasks. If new tasks come and go regularly, the list of tasks can change fairly frequently. In this case, schemes such as copy-on-write (see §2.4.4) usually do not work well. But there is every reason to make traversal of the list as cheap as possible. One approach is to maintain a cached list for traversal and to update it (if necessary) only at the end of each sweep.

- Event-driven tasks should be triggered only when they have enough data to perform their associated actions. However, in many applications (for example those using free-form string-based commands), the minimal amount of data needed for triggering is not known in advance. In practice (as illustrated here), it usually suffices just to check that at least one byte is available. This exploits the fact that socket-based clients send packets — normally each packet contains an entire command. However, when commands do not arrive as units, the worker thread can stall, thus increasing latencies of other tasks unless buffering schemes are added.

- A single worker thread is not likely to be acceptable if some inputs lead to time-consuming computations or blocking IO. One solution is to require that such computations be performed in new threads or by separate worker thread pools. However, it is sometimes more efficient instead to employ multiple polling worker threads; enough so that on average there will always be a thread polling for inputs.

- The use of multiple polling worker threads requires additional coordination to make sure that two workers are not both trying to run the same task at the same time, without otherwise impeding each other's sweeps through the list of tasks. One approach is to have task classes set and honor *busy* status, for example, via `testAndSet` (see §3.5.1.4).

Given these concerns and the context dependence of the associated design decisions, it is not surprising that most frameworks are custom-built to suit the demands of particular applications. However, the `util.concurrent` package available from the online supplement includes some utilities that can be used to help build standardized solutions.

4.1.6   Further Readings

Most details about messages, formats, transports, etc., used in practice are specific to particular packages and systems, so the best sources are their accompanying manuals and documentation.

Discussions of message passing in distributed systems can be found in the sources listed in §1.2.5. Any of several packages and frameworks can be used to extend the techniques discussed here to apply in distributed contexts. For example, most of these designs (as well as most in §4.2 and elsewhere in this book) can be adapted for use in JavaSpaces. Conversely, many distributed message passing techniques can be scaled down to apply in concurrent, non-distributed settings.

Design and implementation using JavaSpaces is discussed in:

Freeman, Eric, Susan Hupfer, and Ken Arnold. *JavaSpaces™: Principles, Patterns, and Practice*, Addison-Wesley, 1999.

For different approaches, see for example the Aleph, JMS, and Ninja packages, accessible via links from the online supplement. Many commercial distributed systems are based on CORBA and related frameworks, which also include some support for oneway message passing. See:

Henning, Michi, and Steve Vinoski. *Advanced CORBA Programming with C++*, Addison-Wesley, 1999.

Pope, Alan. *The CORBA Reference Guide*, Addison-Wesley, 1998.

Some systems-level oneway messaging strategies otherwise similar to those presented here are described in:

Langendoen, Koen, Raoul Bhoedjang, and Henri Bal. "Models for Asynchronous Message Handling", *IEEE Concurrency*, April-June 1997.

An argument that single-queue, single-thread event frameworks are a better basis for application programming than thread-based frameworks may be found in:

Ousterhout, John. "Why Threads Are a Bad Idea (For Most Purposes)", *USENIX Technical Conference*, 1996.

4.2 Composing Oneway Messages

Many interprocess and distributed designs involve groups of objects exchanging oneway messages (see §1.2 and §4.5). Similar techniques may be applied within individual concurrent programs. In fact, as discussed in §4.1, a larger range of design options is available in concurrent programs than in distributed systems. Messages need not be restricted to, say, socket-based commands. Concurrent programs may also employ lighter alternatives including direct invocations and event-based communication.

However, this wide range of options also introduces opportunities for creating chaotic, difficult-to-understand designs. This section describes some simple program-level (or subsystem-level) structuring techniques that tend to produce well-behaved, readily understandable, and readily extensible designs.

A *flow network* is a collection of objects that all pass oneway messages transferring information and/or objects to each other along paths from *sources* to *sinks*. Flow patterns may occur in any kind of system or subsystem supporting one or more series of connected steps or *stages*, in which each stage plays the role of a *producer* and/or *consumer*. Broad categories include:

Control systems. External sensor inputs ultimately cause control systems to generate particular effector outputs. Applications such as avionics control systems contain dozens of kinds of inputs and outputs. For a plainer example, consider a skeletal thermostatic heater control:

Assembly systems. Newly created objects undergo a series of changes and/or become integrated with other new objects before finally being used for some purpose; for example, an assembly line for Cartons:

Dataflow systems. Each stage transforms or otherwise processes data. For example, in pipelined multimedia systems, audio and/or video data is processed across multiple stages. In *publish-subscribe* systems, possibly many data sources send information to possibly many consumers. In Unix pipes-and-filters shell programs, stages send character data, as in a simple spell checker:

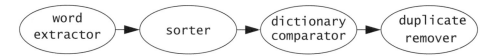

Workflow systems. Each stage represents an action that needs to be performed according to some set of business policies or other requirements; for example, a simple payment system:

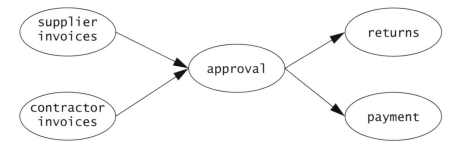

Event systems. Stages pass around and ultimately execute code associated with objects representing messages, user inputs, or simulated physical phenomena. The beginnings of many event systems take the form:

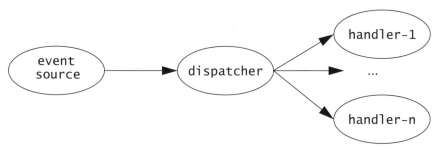

306

4.2.1 Composition

The development of flow networks entails two main sets of concerns: design of the data being passed around, and design of the stages that do the passing.

4.2.1.1 Representations

Flow networks pass around representational components — families of values or objects representing the things the flow is all about. In the introductory examples, temperatures, cardboard sheets, words, invoices, and events are the basic kinds of values and objects passed across connected stages. Often these components are interesting objects in their own rights that can perform services, communicate with other objects, and so on. But when viewed as the raw material for a flow, they are treated as mere passive representations, providing data or information rather than behavior.

While they play similar roles in the overall design of a flow system, different categories of representation types affect the details of the rest of the system:

- Information types representing the state of the world (for example values such as temperature readings, maintained as scalars or immutable ADT objects) differ from most others in that it is often acceptable to reuse old or current best-estimate values if necessary. In essence, producers have an inexhaustible supply of such values.

- Event indicators normally can be used at most once, although they may be passed around many times before being used.

- Mutable resource types (such as cartons) may be *transferred* (see §2.3.4) from each stage to the next, ensuring that each object is being operated upon by at most one stage at any given time.

- Alternatively, if the identities of mutable representation objects do not matter, they can be copied across stages as needed. Copy-based approaches are more often used in distributed flow networks in which ownership cannot be transferred across stages simply by assigning reference fields.

- Artificial data types can be used for control purposes. For example, a special *null* token may be used as a terminator that triggers cancellation and shutdown. Similarly, a special *keepalive* can be sent to inform one stage that another still exists. Alternatively, a distinct set of *sideband* control methods can be employed across stages. Sideband controls are methods used to set stages into different modes that influence their main processing. For example, a thermostat `Comparator` may have a separate control to change its threshold.

4.2.1.2 Stages

Stages in well-behaved flow networks all obey sets of constraints that are reminiscent of those seen in electrical circuit design. Here is one conservative set of composition rules that generate a small number of basic kinds of stages:

Directionality. Flow maintains a single directionality, from sources to sinks. There are no loops or back-branches from consumers to producers. This results in a directed acyclic graph (DAG) of information or object flow.

Interoperability. Methods and message formats are standardized across components, normally through conformance to a small set of interfaces.

Connectivity. Stages maintain fixed connectivity: consumers may receive messages only from known producers, and vice versa. So, for example, while a web service may have any number of anonymous clients, a given `TemperatureComparator` object may be designed to receive temperature update messages only from a designated `TemperatureSensor` object.

Connectivity is usually arranged by maintaining direct references from producers to consumers or vice versa, or by having them share access to a `Channel`. Alternatively, a network may be based on constrained use of blackboards, multicast channels, or JavaSpaces (see §4.1.6) in which producers specially tag messages destined for particular consumers.

Transfer protocols. Every message transfers information or objects. Once a stage has transferred a mutable object, it never again manipulates that object. When necessary, special buffer stages may be interposed to hold elements transferred out from one stage that cannot yet be accepted by other stages.

Transfer protocols typically rely on the basic `put` and `take` operations described in §2.3.4. When all messages involve `put`-based transfers, networks are normally labeled as *push* flow; when they involve `take`-based transfers, they are normally labeled as *pull* flow; when they involve channels supporting both `put` and `take` (and possibly `exchange`), they can take various mixed forms.

Threads. Stages may implement oneway message passing using any of the patterns described in §4.1, as long as every (potentially) simultaneously live connection from a given producer to a given consumer employs a different thread or thread-based message-sending construction.

It is rarely necessary to satisfy this requirement by issuing every message, or every stream of messages from a producer to a consumer, in a different thread. You can instead exploit connectivity rules to use threads only as needed. Most sources in push-based systems intrinsically employ threads. Additionally, any

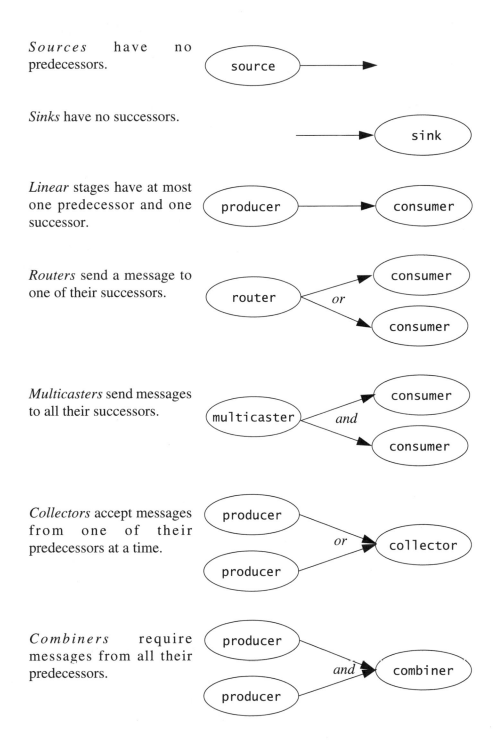

Sources have no predecessors.

Sinks have no successors.

Linear stages have at most one predecessor and one successor.

Routers send a message to one of their successors.

Multicasters send messages to all their successors.

Collectors accept messages from one of their predecessors at a time.

Combiners require messages from all their predecessors.

push stage with multiple successors that may ultimately hit a Combiner stage must issue the messages independently. Otherwise, if a thread is blocked at the combine point, there may be a possibility that the Combiner will never see the other inputs necessary to unblock it.

Conversely, most sinks in pull-based systems intrinsically employ thread-based message constructions, as do stages involved in split/join connections proceeding from the opposite direction pictured above.

These rules can be liberalized in various ways. In fact, you can adopt any set of composition rules you like. But the listed constraints serve to eliminate large classes of safety and liveness problems while also satisfying common reusability and performance goals: unidirectional flow avoids deadlock, connectivity management avoids unwanted interleavings across different flows, transfer protocols avoid safety problems due to inadvertent sharing without the need for extensive dynamic synchronization, and interface conformance assures type safety while still permitting interoperability among components.

4.2.1.3 Scripting

Adoption of standard set of composition rules makes possible the construction of higher-level tools that arrange for stages to operate *cooperatively*, without otherwise imposing centralized dynamic synchronization control. Composition of flow networks can be treated as a form of *scripting* in the usual sense of the word — semi-automated programming of the code that glues together instances of existing object types. This is the kind of programming associated with languages such as JavaScript, Visual Basic, Unix shells, and FlowMark (a workflow tool). Development of a scripting tool, or integration with an existing one, is an optional step in building systems based around flows.

This architecture is analogous to that of GUI builders consisting of a base set of widgets, packers and layout managers, code to instantiate a particular GUI, and a visual scripter that helps set it all up. Alternatively, it may be possible to script flows through direct manipulation tools by which, for example, components communicate instantly once dragged-and-dropped to connect with others.

4.2.2 Assembly Line

The remainder of this section illustrates the design and implementation of flow systems via an example assembly line applet that builds series of "paintings" in a style vaguely reminiscent of the artists Piet Mondrian and Mark Rothko. Only the principal classes are given here. Some include unimplemented method declarations. The full code may be found in the online supplement, which also includes other application-level examples of flow-based systems.

4.2.2.1 Representations

To start out, we need some base representation types. In this system, all elements can be defined as subclasses of abstract class Box, where every Box has a color and a size, can display itself when asked, and can be made to deeply clone (duplicate) itself. The color mechanics are default-implemented. Others are left abstract, to be defined differently in different subclasses:

```
abstract class Box {
  protected Color color = Color.white;

  public synchronized Color getColor()       { return color; }
  public synchronized void  setColor(Color c) { color = c; }
  public abstract java.awt.Dimension size();
  public abstract Box duplicate();                // clone
  public abstract void show(Graphics g, Point origin);// display
}
```

The overall theme of this example is to start off with sources that produce simple basic boxes, and then push them through stages that paint, join, flip, and embed them to form the paintings. `BasicBoxes` are the raw material:

```java
class BasicBox extends Box {
  protected final Dimension size;

  public BasicBox(int xdim, int ydim) {
    size = new Dimension(xdim, ydim);
  }

  public synchronized Dimension size() { return size; }

  public void show(Graphics g, Point origin) {
    g.setColor(getColor());
    g.fillRect(origin.x, origin.y, size.width, size.height);
  }

  public synchronized Box duplicate() {
    Box p =  new BasicBox(size.width, size.height);
    p.setColor(getColor());
    return p;
  }
}
```

Two fancier kinds of boxes can be made by joining two existing boxes side by side and adding a line-based border surrounding them. Joined boxes can also flip themselves. All this can be done either horizontally or vertically. The two resulting classes can be made subclasses of `JoinedPair` to allow sharing of some common code:

```java
abstract class JoinedPair extends Box {
  protected Box fst; // one of the boxes
  protected Box snd; // the other one

  protected JoinedPair(Box a, Box b) {
    fst = a;
    snd = b;
  }

  public synchronized void flip() { // swap fst/snd
    Box tmp = fst; fst = snd; snd = tmp;
  }

  //  other internal helper methods
}
```

```
class HorizontallyJoinedPair extends JoinedPair {

  public HorizontallyJoinedPair(Box l, Box r) {
    super(l, r);
  }

  public synchronized Box duplicate() {
    HorizontallyJoinedPair p =
      new HorizontallyJoinedPair(fst.duplicate(),
                                 snd.duplicate());
    p.setColor(getColor());
    return p;
  }

  // ... other implementations of abstract Box methods
}

class VerticallyJoinedPair extends JoinedPair {
  // similar
}
```

The final kind of fancy box wraps one Box within a border:

```
class WrappedBox extends Box {
  protected Dimension wrapperSize;
  protected Box inner;

  public WrappedBox(Box innerBox, Dimension size) {
    inner = innerBox;
    wrapperSize = size;
  }

  // ... other implementations of abstract Box methods
}
```

4.2.2.2 Interfaces

Looking ahead to how we might want to string stages together, it is worthwhile to standardize interfaces. We'd like to be able to connect any stage to any other stage for which it could make sense, so we want bland, noncommittal names for the principal methods.

Since we are doing oneway push-based flow, these interfaces mainly describe put-style methods. In fact, we could just call them all put, except that this doesn't work very well for two-input stages. For example, a VerticalJoiner needs two put methods, one supplying the top Box and one the bottom Box. We could avoid this by designing Joiners to take alternate inputs as the tops and bottoms, but this would make them harder to control. Instead, we'll use the somewhat ugly but easily extensible names putA, putB, and so on:

```
interface PushSource {
  void produce();
}
```

```
interface PushStage {
  void putA(Box p);
}
```

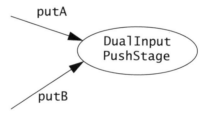

```
interface DualInputPushStage extends PushStage {
  void putB(Box p);
}
```

4.2.2.3 Adapters

We can make the "B" channels of DualInputPushStages completely transparent to other stages by defining a simple Adapter class that accepts a putA but relays it to the intended recipient's putB. In this way, most stages can be built to invoke putA without knowing or caring that the box is being fed into some successor's B channel:

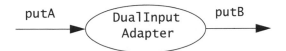

```
class DualInputAdapter implements PushStage {
  protected final DualInputPushStage stage;

  public DualInputAdapter(DualInputPushStage s) { stage = s; }

  public void putA(Box p) { stage.putB(p); }

}
```

4.2.2.4 Sinks

Sinks have no successors. The simplest kind of sink doesn't even process its input, and thus serves as a way to throw away elements. In the spirit of Unix pipes and filters, we can call it:

```
class DevNull implements PushStage {
  public void putA(Box p) { }
}
```

More interesting sinks require more interesting code. For example, in the applet used to produce the image shown at the beginning of this section, the Applet subclass itself was defined to implement PushStage. It served as the ultimate sink by displaying the assembled objects.

4.2.2.5 Connections

Interfaces standardize on the method names for stages but do nothing about the linkages to successors, which must be maintained using some kind of instance variables in each stage object. Except for sinks such as DevNull, each stage has at least one successor. There are several implementation options, including:

- Have each object maintain a collection object holding all its successors.

- Use a master connection registry that each stage interacts with to find out its successor(s).

- Create the minimal representation: define a base class for stages with exactly one successor and one for those with exactly two successors.

The third option is simplest and works fine here. (In fact, it is always a valid option. Stages with three or more outputs can be built by cascading those for only two. Of course, you wouldn't want to do this if most stages had large and/or variable numbers of successors.)

This leads to base classes that support either one or two links and have one or two corresponding attachment methods, named using a similar ugly suffix convention (attach1, attach2). Because connections are dynamically assignable, they are accessed only under synchronization:

```
class SingleOutputPushStage {
  private PushStage next1 = null;
  protected synchronized PushStage next1() { return next1; }
  public synchronized void attach1(PushStage s) { next1 = s; }
}
```

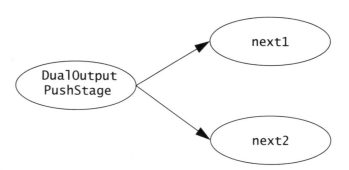

```
class DualOutputPushStage extends SingleOutputPushStage {
  private PushStage next2 = null;
  protected synchronized PushStage next2() { return next2; }
  public synchronized void attach2(PushStage s) { next2 = s; }
}
```

4.2.2.6 Linear stages

Now we can build all sorts of classes that extend either of the base classes, simultaneously implementing any of the standard interfaces. The simplest transformational stages are linear, single-input/single-output stages. Painters, Wrappers, and Flippers are merely:

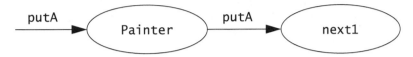

```
class Painter extends SingleOutputPushStage
            implements PushStage {
  protected final Color color; // the color to paint boxes

  public Painter(Color c) { color = c; }

  public void putA(Box p) {
    p.setColor(color);
    next1().putA(p);
  }
}
```

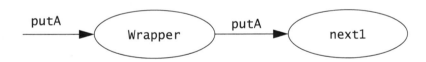

```
class Wrapper extends SingleOutputPushStage
            implements PushStage {
  protected final int thickness;

  public Wrapper(int t) { thickness = t; }

  public void putA(Box p) {
    Dimension d = new Dimension(thickness, thickness);
    next1().putA(new WrappedBox(p, d));
  }
}
```

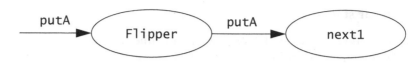

```
class Flipper extends SingleOutputPushStage
               implements PushStage {
  public void putA(Box p) {
    if (p instanceof JoinedPair)
      ((JoinedPair) p).flip();
    next1().putA(p);
  }
}
```

Painter and Wrapper stages apply to any kind of Box. But Flippers only make sense for JoinedPairs: if a Flipper receives something other than a JoinedPair, it just passes it through. In a more "strongly typed" version, we might instead choose to drop boxes other than JoinedPairs, perhaps by sending them to DevNull.

4.2.2.7 Combiners

We have two kinds of Combiners, horizontal and vertical Joiners. Like the representation classes, these classes have enough in common to factor out a superclass. Joiner stages block further inputs until they can combine one item each from putA and putB. This can be implemented via guard mechanics that hold up acceptance of additional items from putA until existing ones have been paired up with those from putB, and vice versa:

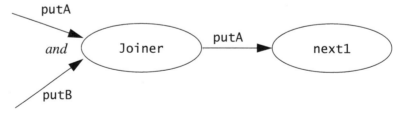

```
abstract class Joiner extends SingleOutputPushStage
                      implements DualInputPushStage {
  protected Box a = null;  // incoming from putA
  protected Box b = null;  // incoming from putB

  protected abstract Box join(Box p, Box q);

  protected synchronized Box joinFromA(Box p) {
    while (a != null)              // wait until last consumed
      try { wait(); }
      catch (InterruptedException e) { return null; }
    a = p;
    return tryJoin();
  }
  protected synchronized Box joinFromB(Box p) { // symmetrical
    while (b != null)
      try { wait(); }
      catch (InterruptedException ie) { return null; }
    b = p;
    return tryJoin();
  }

  protected synchronized Box tryJoin() {
    if (a == null || b == null) return null; // cannot join
    Box joined = join(a, b);                 // make combined box
    a = b = null;                            // forget old boxes
    notifyAll();                             // allow new puts
    return joined;
  }

  public void putA(Box p) {
    Box j = joinFromA(p);
    if (j != null) next1().putA(j);
  }

  public void putB(Box p) {
    Box j = joinFromB(p);
    if (j != null) next1().putA(j);
  }
}
class HorizontalJoiner extends Joiner {
  protected Box join(Box p, Box q) {
    return new HorizontallyJoinedPair(p, q);
  }
}
class VerticalJoiner extends Joiner {
  protected Box join(Box p, Box q) {
    return new VerticallyJoinedPair(p, q);
  }
}
```

4.2.2.8 Collectors

A Collector accepts messages on either channel and relays them to a single successor:

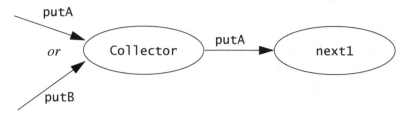

```
class Collector extends SingleOutputPushStage
                implements DualInputPushStage {
  public void putA(Box p) { next1().putA(p);}
  public void putB(Box p) { next1().putA(p); }
}
```

If for some reason we needed to impose a bottleneck here, we could define an alternative form of collector in which these methods are declared as synchronized. This could also be used to guarantee that at most one activity is progressing through a given collector at any given time.

4.2.2.9 Dual output stages

Our multiple-output stages should generate threads or use one of the other options discussed in §4.1 to drive at least one of their outputs (it doesn't matter which). This maintains liveness when elements are ultimately passed to Combiner stages (here, the Joiners). For simplicity of illustration, the following classes create new Threads. Alternatively, we could set up a simple worker thread pool to process these messages.

Alternators output alternate inputs to alternate successors:

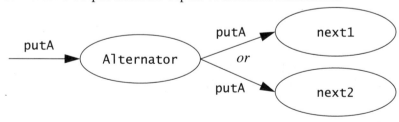

```
class Alternator extends DualOutputPushStage
                      implements PushStage {
  protected boolean outTo2 = false; // control alternation

  protected synchronized boolean testAndInvert() {
    boolean b = outTo2;
    outTo2 = !outTo2;
    return b;
  }

  public  void putA(final Box p) {
    if (testAndInvert())
      next1().putA(p);
    else {
      new Thread(new Runnable() {
        public void run() { next2().putA(p); }
      }).start();
    }
  }
}
```

Cloners multicast the same element to both successors:

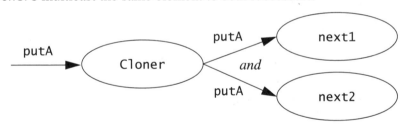

```
class Cloner extends DualOutputPushStage
               implements PushStage {

  public void putA(Box p) {
    final Box p2 = p.duplicate();
    next1().putA(p);
    new Thread(new Runnable() {
      public void run() { next2().putA(p2); }
    }).start();
  }

}
```

A Screener is a stage that directs all inputs obeying some predicate to one channel, and all others to the other:

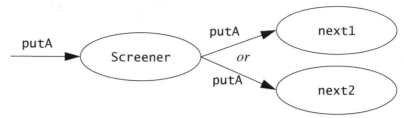

We can build a generic Screener by encapsulating the BoxPredicate to check in an interface and implementing it, for example, with a class that makes sure that a Box fits within a given (symmetric, in this case) bound. The Screener itself accepts a BoxPredicate and uses it to direct outputs:

```
interface BoxPredicate {
  boolean test(Box p);
}

class MaxSizePredicate implements BoxPredicate {

  protected final int max; // max size to let through

  public MaxSizePredicate(int maximum) { max = maximum; }

  public boolean test(Box p) {
    return p.size().height <= max && p.size().width <= max;
  }
}

class Screener extends DualOutputPushStage
               implements PushStage {

  protected final BoxPredicate predicate;
  public Screener(BoxPredicate p) { predicate = p; }

  public void putA(final Box p) {
    if (predicate.test(p)) {
      new Thread(new Runnable() {
        public void run() { next1().putA(p); }
      }).start();
    }
    else
      next2().putA(p);
  }
}
```

4.2.2.10 Sources

Here is a sample source, one that produces `BasicBoxes` of random sizes. For convenience, it is also equipped with an autonomous loop `run` method repeatedly invoking `produce`, interspersed with random production delays:

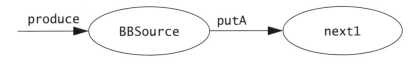

```
class BasicBoxSource extends SingleOutputPushStage
                     implements PushSource, Runnable {

  protected final Dimension size;     // maximum sizes
  protected final int productionTime; // simulated delay

  public BasicBoxSource(Dimension s, int delay) {
    size = s;
    productionTime = delay;
  }

  protected Box makeBox() {
    return new BasicBox((int)(Math.random() * size.width) + 1,
                        (int)(Math.random() * size.height) + 1);
  }

  public void produce() {
    next1().putA(makeBox());
  }

  public void run() {
    try {
      for (;;) {
        produce();
        Thread.sleep((int)(Math.random() * 2* productionTime));
      }
    }
    catch (InterruptedException ie) { } // die
  }

}
```

4.2.2.11   Coordination

Without a scripting tool based on these classes, we have to program assembly lines by manually creating instances of desired stages and linking them together. This is easy in principle, but tedious and error-prone in practice because of the lack of visual guidance about what stages are connected to what.

Here's a fragment of the flow used in the applet that produced the image displayed at the beginning of this section:

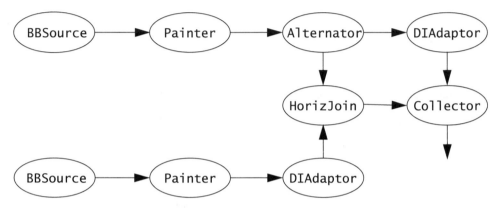

The code setting this up may be found in the online supplement. The main constructor mostly consists of many lines of the form:

```
Stage aStage = new Stage();
aStage.attach(anotherStage);
```

This is followed by invoking `start` on threads running all the sources.

4.2.3   Further Readings

Flow patterns often serve as the computational versions of use cases, scenarios, scripts, and related concepts from high-level object-oriented analysis. Most of the books on OO design and on design patterns listed in §1.3.5 and §1.4.5 describe issues relevant to the analysis, design and implementation of flow-based systems. Domain-specific issues surrounding packet networking, telecommunications, and multimedia systems often requiring more elaborate flow-based designs are discussed in the texts on concurrent and distributed systems in §1.2.5.

4.3 Services in Threads

Many tasks compute results or provide services that are not immediately used by their clients, but are eventually required by them. In these situations, unlike those involving oneway messages, a client's actions at some point become dependent on completion of the task.

This section describes some of the available design alternatives: adding callbacks to oneway messages, relying on `Thread.join`, building utilities based on *Futures*, and creating worker threads. Section §4.4 revisits and extends these techniques in the context of improving the performance of computationally intensive tasks on parallel processors.

4.3.1 Completion Callbacks

From the perspective of pure oneway message passing, the most natural way to deal with completion is for a client to activate a task via a oneway message to a server, and for the server later to indicate completion by sending a oneway *callback* message to the caller. This efficient, asynchronous, notification-based style applies best in loosely-coupled designs in which completion of the service triggers some independent action in the client. Completion callback designs are sometimes structurally identical to Observer designs (see §3.5.2).

For example, consider an application that offers several features, of which one or more require that a certain file be read in first. Because IO is relatively slow, you don't want to disable other features while the file is being read in — this would decrease responsiveness. One solution is to create a `FileReader` service that asynchronously reads in the file, and then issues a message back to the application when it has completed, so that the application can proceed with the feature(s) that require it.

4.3.1.1   Interfaces

To set up such a `FileReader`, or any other service using completion callbacks, you must first define a *client* interface for callback messages. The methods in this interface are substitutes of sorts for the kinds of return types and exceptions that would be associated with procedural versions of the service. This usually requires two kinds of methods, one associated with normal completion, and one associated with failure that is invoked upon any exception.

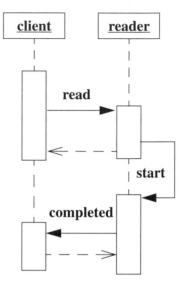

Additionally, callback methods often require an argument indicating *which* action completed, so that the client can sort them out when there are multiple calls. In many cases this can be accomplished simply by sending back some of the call arguments. In more general schemes, the service hands back a unique identifier (usually known as a *cookie*) both as the return value for the initial request and as an argument in any callback method. Variants of this technique are used behind the scenes in remote invocation frameworks that implement procedural calls via asynchronous messages across networks.

In the case of `FileReader`, we could use interfaces such as:

```
interface FileReader {
  void read(String filename, FileReaderClient client);
}

interface FileReaderClient {
  void readCompleted(String filename, byte[] data);
  void readFailed(String filename, IOException ex);
}
```

4.3.1.2   Implementations

There are two styles for implementing these interfaces, depending on whether you'd like the client or the server to create the thread that performs the service. Generally, if the service can be useful without running in its own thread, then control should be assigned to clients.

In the more typical case in which the use of threads is intrinsic to completion callback designs, control is assigned to the service method. Note that this causes callback methods to be executed in the thread constructed by the service, not one directly constructed by the client. This can lead to surprising results if any code relies on thread-specific properties such as `ThreadLocal` and `java.security.AccessControlContext` (see §2.3.2) that are not known by the service.

Here we could implement a client and server using a service-creates-thread approach as:

```
class FileReaderApp implements FileReaderClient {  // Fragments
  protected FileReader reader = new AFileReader();

  public void readCompleted(String filename, byte[] data) {
    // ... use data ...
  }

  public void readFailed(String filename, IOException ex){
    // ... deal with failure ...
  }

  public void actionRequiringFile() {
    reader.read("AppFile", this);
  }

  public void actionNotRequiringFile() { ... }
}

class AFileReader implements FileReader {

  public void read(final String fn, final FileReaderClient c) {
    new Thread(new Runnable() {
      public void run() { doRead(fn, c); }
    }).start();
  }

  protected void doRead(String fn, FileReaderClient client) {
    byte[] buffer = new byte[1024]; // just for illustration
    try {
      FileInputStream s = new FileInputStream(fn);
      s.read(buffer);
      if (client != null) client.readCompleted(fn, buffer);
    }
    catch (IOException ex) {
      if (client != null) client.readFailed(fn, ex);
    }
  }
}
```

The service class here is written to deal with a null `client` argument, thus accommodating clients that do not need callbacks. While this is not particularly likely here, callbacks in many services can be treated as optional. As an alternative, you could define and use a `NullFileReaderClient` class that contains no-op versions of the callback methods (see Further Readings). Also, as far as the service is concerned, the callback target might as well be any object at all, for example some helper of the object that requests the service. You can also replace callbacks with event notifications using the techniques illustrated in §3.1.1.6.

4.3.1.3 Guarding callback methods

In some applications, clients can process completion callbacks only when they are in particular states. Here, the callback methods themselves should contain guards that suspend processing of each incoming callback until the client can deal with it.

For example, suppose we have a `FileReaderClient` that initiates a set of asynchronous file reads and needs to process them in the order issued. This construction mimics how remote invocations are usually handled: Typically each request is assigned a sequence number, and replies are processed in sequence order. This can be a risky strategy, since it will cause indefinite suspension of ready callbacks if one or more of them never completes. This drawback could be addressed by associating time-outs with the waits.

```
class FileApplication implements FileReaderClient { // Fragments
  private String[] filenames;
  private int currentCompletion; // index of ready file

  public synchronized void readCompleted(String fn, byte[] d) {
    // wait until ready to process this callback
    while (!fn.equals(filenames[currentCompletion])) {
      try { wait(); }
      catch(InterruptedException ex) { return; }
    }
    // ... process data...
    // wake up any other thread waiting on this condition:
    ++currentCompletion;
    notifyAll();
  }

  public synchronized void readFailed(String fn, IOException e){
    // similar...
  }

  public synchronized void readfiles() {
    currentCompletion = 0;
    for (int i = 0; i < filenames.length; ++i)
      reader.read(filenames[i],this);
  }
}
```

4.3.2 Joining Threads

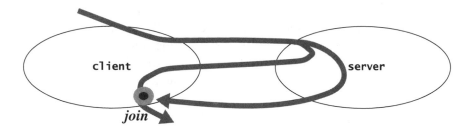

While completion callbacks are very flexible, they are at best awkward to use when a caller just needs to wait out a particular task that it started.

If an operation occurring in some thread A cannot continue until some thread B completes, you can block thread A via any of the waiting and notification techniques discussed in Chapter 3. For example, assuming the existence of a `Latch` (see §3.4.2) named `terminated` accessible from both threads A and B, thread A may wait via `terminated.acquire()`, and thread B may execute `terminated.release()` upon otherwise completing its task.

However, there is usually no reason to set up your own waiting and notification constructions, since this functionality is already provided by `Thread.join`: The `join` method blocks the caller while the target `isAlive`. Terminating threads automatically perform notifications. The monitor object used internally for this waiting and notification is arbitrary and may vary across JVM implementations. In most, the target `Thread` object itself is used as the monitor object. (This is one reason for not extending class `Thread` to add `run` methods that invoke waiting or notification methods.) In cases where these details of `Thread.join` don't fit the needs of a particular application, you can always fall back to the manual approach.

Either `Thread.join` or explicitly coded variants can be used in designs where a client needs a service to be performed but does not immediately rely on its results or effects. (This is sometimes known as *deferred-synchronous* invocation.) This is often the case when the service task is time-consuming and can benefit from CPU and/or IO parallelism, so that running it in a separate thread can improve overall throughput.

One common application is image processing. Obtaining the raw data for an image from a file or socket and then converting it into a form that can be displayed are time-consuming operations that involve both CPU and IO processing. Often, this processing can be overlapped with other display-related operations.

A version of this strategy is used by `java.awt.MediaTracker` and related classes, which should be used when they apply. Here, we'll illustrate a more generic version that can be extended and refined in various ways to support specialized applications.

To set this up, suppose there is a generic `Pic` interface for images, and a `Renderer` interface describing services that accept a URL pointing to image data and ultimately return a `Pic`. (In a more realistic setting, the `render` method would surely also throw various failure exceptions. Here, we will assume that it simply returns `null` on any failure.) Also, assume existence of a `StandardRenderer` class implementing interface `Renderer`.

`Thread.join` can be used to write clients such as the following `PictureApp` class (which invokes several made-up methods just for the sake of illustration). It creates a `Runnable` `waiter` object that both initiates the rendering thread and keeps track of the returned result.

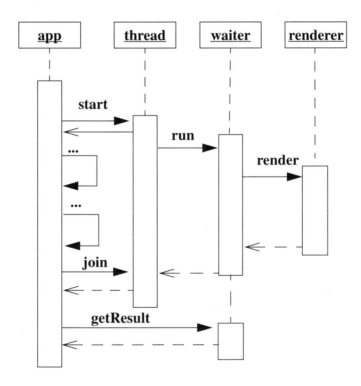

While it is common practice, the use of unsynchronized (or direct) access of internal `result` fields as seen in the `waiter` object is a bit delicate. Since access is not synchronized, correctness relies on the fact that both thread termination and the `join` method intrinsically employ `synchronized` methods or blocks (see §2.2.7).

```
interface Pic {
  byte[] getImage();
}

interface Renderer {
  Pic render(URL src);
}

class PictureApp {                              // Code sketch
  // ...
  private final Renderer renderer = new StandardRenderer();

  public void show(final URL imageSource) {

    class Waiter implements Runnable {
      private Pic result = null;
      Pic getResult() { return result; }
      public void run() {
        result = renderer.render(imageSource);
      }
    };

    Waiter waiter = new Waiter();
    Thread t = new Thread(waiter);
    t.start();

    displayBorders();  // do other things
    displayCaption();  //  while rendering

    try {
      t.join();
    }
    catch(InterruptedException e) {
      cleanup();
      return;
    }

    Pic pic = waiter.getResult();
    if (pic != null)
      displayImage(pic.getImage());
    else
      // ... deal with assumed rendering failure
  }
}
```

Thread.join returns control to the caller whether the thread completed successfully or abnormally. For simplicity of illustration, nullness of the result field is used here to indicate any kind of failure, including cancellation of the renderer. The version in §4.3.3.1 illustrates a more responsible approach.

4.3.3 Futures

The operations underlying join-based constructions can be packaged in a more convenient and structured fashion by:

- Creating *Futures* — "virtual" data objects that automatically block when clients try to invoke their field accessors before their computation is complete. A Future acts as an "IOU" for a given data object.

- Creating versions of service methods that start up one or more threads and then return Future objects that are unblocked when computations complete.

Because the mechanics surrounding futures are built into data access and service methods, they can be applied in a general fashion only if both the data objects and the service methods are defined using interfaces, not classes. However, if the associated interfaces are defined, Futures are easy to set up. For example, a Future-based `AsynchRenderer` can employ proxies around concrete implementation classes (see §1.4.2):

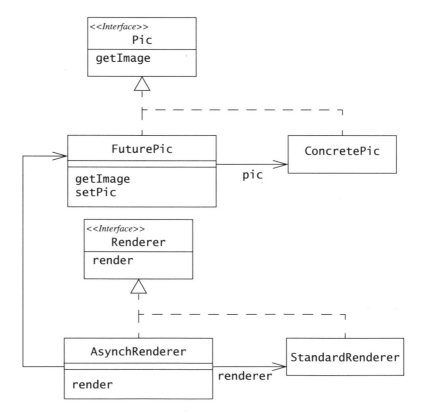

```
class AsynchRenderer implements Renderer {
  private final Renderer renderer = new StandardRenderer();

  static class FuturePic implements Pic { // inner class
    private Pic pic = null;
    private boolean ready = false;
    synchronized void setPic(Pic p) {
      pic = p;
      ready = true;
      notifyAll();
    }

    public synchronized byte[] getImage() {
      while (!ready)
        try { wait(); }
        catch (InterruptedException e) { return null; }
      return pic.getImage();
    }
  }

  public Pic render(final URL src) {
    final FuturePic p = new FuturePic();
    new Thread(new Runnable() {
      public void run() { p.setPic(renderer.render(src)); }
    }).start();
    return p;
  }
}
```

For illustration, `AsynchRenderer` uses explicit waiting and notification operations based on a `ready` flag rather than relying on `Thread.join`.

Applications relying on this class can be written in a simple fashion:

```
class PicturAppWithFuture {                            // Code sketch
  private final Renderer renderer = new AsynchRenderer();

  public void show(final URL imageSource) {
    Pic pic = renderer.render(imageSource);

    displayBorders();  // do other things ...
    displayCaption();

    byte[] im = pic.getImage();
    if (im != null)
      displayImage(im);
    else  // deal with assumed rendering failure
  }
}
```

4.3.3.1 Callables

Most designs based on Futures take exactly the form illustrated in class Asyn-chRenderer. The construction and use of such classes can be further standardized and automated by stepping up to a blander interface.

In the same way that interface Runnable describes any pure action, a Callable interface can be used to describe any service method that accepts an Object argument, returns an Object result, and may throw an Exception:

```
interface Callable {
  Object call(Object arg) throws Exception;
}
```

The use of Object here (awkwardly) accommodates, for example, adaptation of methods accepting multiple arguments by stuffing them into array objects.

While there are other options, it is most convenient to package up support mechanics via a single class that coordinates usage. The following FutureResult class shows one set of choices. (It is a streamlined version of one in the util.concurrent package available from the online supplement.)

The FutureResult class maintains methods to get the result Object that is returned, or the Exception that is thrown by a Callable. Unlike our Pic versions where all failures were just indicated via null values, it deals with interruptions more honestly by throwing exceptions back to clients attempting to obtain results.

To differentiate properly between exceptions encountered in the service versus those encountered trying to execute the service, exceptions thrown by the Callable are repackaged using java.lang.reflect.InvocationTargetException, a general-purpose class for wrapping one exception inside another.

Also, for the sake of generality, the FutureResult does not itself create threads. Instead, it supports method setter that returns a Runnable that users can then execute within a thread or any other code Executor (see §4.1.4). This makes Callables usable within lightweight executable frameworks that are otherwise set up to handle tasks initiated via oneway messages. As an alternative strategy, you could set up a Caller framework that is otherwise similar to Executor, but is more specialized to the needs of service-style tasks, for example supporting methods to schedule execution, check status, and control responses to exceptions.

```
class FutureResult {                                        // Fragments
  protected Object value = null;
  protected boolean ready = false;
  protected InvocationTargetException exception = null;

  public synchronized Object get()
   throws InterruptedException, InvocationTargetException {

    while (!ready) wait();

    if (exception != null)
      throw exception;
    else
      return value;
  }

  public Runnable setter(final Callable function) {
    return new Runnable() {
      public void run() {
        try {
          set(function.call());
        }
        catch(Throwable e) {
          setException(e);
        }
      }
    };
  }

  synchronized void set(Object result) {
    value = result;
    ready = true;
    notifyAll();
  }

  synchronized void setException(Throwable e) {
    exception = new InvocationTargetException(e);
    ready = true;
    notifyAll();
  }

  // ... other auxiliary and convenience methods ...

}
```

The FutureResult class can be used directly to support generic Futures or as a utility in constructing more specialized versions. As an example of direct use:

```
class PictureDisplayWithFutureResult {                 // Code sketch

  private final Renderer renderer = new StandardRenderer();
  // ...

  public void show(final URL imageSource) {

    try {
      FutureResult futurePic = new FutureResult();
      Runnable command = futurePic.setter(new Callable() {
        public Object call() {
          return renderer.render(imageSource);
        }
      });
      new Thread(command).start();

      displayBorders();
      displayCaption();

      displayImage(((Pic)(futurePic.get())).getImage());
    }

    catch (InterruptedException ex) {
      cleanup();
      return;
    }
    catch (InvocationTargetException ex) {
      cleanup();
      return;
    }
  }
}
```

This example demonstrates some of the minor awkwardnesses introduced by reliance on generic utilities that help standardize usage protocols. This is one reason that you might want to use FutureResult in turn to construct a more specialized and easier-to-use version with the same methods and structure as the AsynchRenderer class.

4.3.4 Scheduling Services

As discussed in §4.1.4, worker thread designs can sometimes improve performance compared to thread-per-task designs. They can also be used to schedule and optimize execution of service requests made by different clients.

As a famous example, consider a class controlling read and write access for a disk containing many cylinders but only one read/write head. The interface for the service contains just `read` and `write` methods. In practice, it would surely use file block indicators instead of raw cylinder numbers and would deal with or throw various IO exceptions, here abbreviated as a single `Failure` exception.

```
interface Disk {
  void read(int cylinderNumber, byte[] buffer) throws Failure;
  void write(int cylinderNumber, byte[] buffer) throws Failure;
}
```

Rather than servicing access requests in the order they are made, it is faster on average to sweep the head across the cylinders, accessing cylinders in ascending order and then resetting the head position back to the beginning after each sweep. (Depending in part on the type of disk, it may be even better to arrange requests in both ascending and descending sweeps, but we will stick to this version.)

This policy would be tricky to implement without some kind of auxiliary data structure. The enabling condition for a request to execute is:

> Wait until the current request cylinder number is the least greater cylinder number relative to that of the current disk head of all of those currently waiting, or is the least numbered cylinder if the head cylinder number is greater than that of all requests.

This condition is too awkward, inefficient, and possibly even deadlock-prone to try to coordinate across a set of otherwise independent clients. But it can be implemented fairly easily with the help of an ordered queue employed by a single worker thread. Tasks can be added to the queue in cylinder-based order, then executed when their turns arrive. This "elevator algorithm" is easiest to arrange by using a two-part queue, one for the current sweep and one for the next sweep.

The resulting framework combines Future-like constructs with the worker thread designs from §4.1.4. To set this up, we can define a `Runnable` class to include the extra bookkeeping associated with `DiskTasks`. The queue class uses the semaphore-based approach discussed in §3.4.1, but here applied to ordered linked lists. The server class constructs a worker thread that runs tasks from the queue. The public service methods create tasks, place them on the queue, and then wait them out before returning to clients.

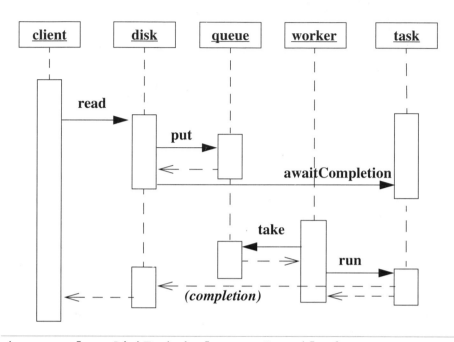

```
abstract class DiskTask implements Runnable {
  protected final int cylinder;         // read/write parameters
  protected final byte[] buffer;
  protected Failure exception = null;     // to relay out
  protected DiskTask next = null;         // for use in queue
  protected final Latch done = new Latch(); // status indicator

  DiskTask(int c, byte[] b) { cylinder = c; buffer = b; }

  abstract void access() throws Failure; // read or write

  public void run() {
    try  { access(); }
    catch (Failure ex) { setException(ex); }
    finally { done.release(); }
  }

  void awaitCompletion() throws InterruptedException {
    done.acquire();
  }

  synchronized Failure getException() { return exception; }
  synchronized void setException(Failure f) { exception = f; }
}
```

```
class DiskReadTask extends DiskTask {
  DiskReadTask(int c, byte[] b) { super(c, b); }
  void access() throws Failure { /* ... raw read ... */ }
}

class DiskWriteTask extends DiskTask {
  DiskWriteTask(int c, byte[] b) { super(c, b); }
  void access() throws Failure { /* ... raw write ... */ }
}
```

```
class ScheduledDisk implements Disk {
  protected final DiskTaskQueue tasks = new DiskTaskQueue();

  public void read(int c, byte[] b) throws Failure {
    readOrWrite(new DiskReadTask(c, b));
  }

  public void write(int c, byte[] b) throws Failure {
    readOrWrite(new DiskWriteTask(c, b));
  }

  protected void readOrWrite(DiskTask t) throws Failure {
    tasks.put(t);
    try {
      t.awaitCompletion();
    }
    catch (InterruptedException ex) {
      Thread.currentThread().interrupt(); // propagate
      throw new Failure(); // convert to failure exception
    }
    Failure f = t.getException();
    if (f != null) throw f;
  }

  public ScheduledDisk() {      // construct worker thread
    new Thread(new Runnable() {
      public void run() {
        try {
          for (;;) {
            tasks.take().run();
          }
        }
        catch (InterruptedException ie) {} // die
      }
    }).start();
  }
}
```

```
class DiskTaskQueue {
  protected DiskTask thisSweep = null;
  protected DiskTask nextSweep = null;
  protected int currentCylinder = 0;

  protected final Semaphore available = new Semaphore(0);

  void put(DiskTask t) {
    insert(t);
    available.release();
  }

  DiskTask take() throws InterruptedException {
    available.acquire();
    return extract();
  }

  synchronized void insert(DiskTask t) {
    DiskTask q;
    if (t.cylinder >= currentCylinder) {    // determine queue
      q = thisSweep;
      if (q == null) { thisSweep = t; return; }
    }
    else {
      q = nextSweep;
      if (q == null) { nextSweep = t; return; }
    }
    DiskTask trail = q;                     // ordered linked list insert
    q = trail.next;
    for (;;) {
      if (q == null || t.cylinder < q.cylinder) {
        trail.next = t; t.next = q;
        return;
      }
      else {
        trail = q; q = q.next;
      }
    }
  }
  synchronized DiskTask extract() { // PRE: not empty
    if (thisSweep == null) {                // possibly swap queues
      thisSweep = nextSweep;
      nextSweep = null;
    }
    DiskTask t = thisSweep;
    thisSweep = t.next;
    currentCylinder = t.cylinder;
    return t;
  }
}
```

4.3.5   Further Readings

ABCL was among the first concurrent object-oriented languages to offer Futures as a language construct. See:

Yonezawa, Akinori, and Mario Tokoro. *Object-Oriented Concurrent Programming*, MIT Press, 1988.

Futures are known as *wait-by-necessity* constructions in Eiffel// (a parallel extension to Eiffel). See:

Caromel, Denis, and Yves Roudier. "Reactive Programming in Eiffel//", in Jean-Pierre Briot, Jean-Marc Geib and Akinori Yonezawa (eds.) *Object Based Parallel and Distributed Computing*, LNCS 1107, Springer Verlag, 1996.

Futures and related constructs in the Scheme and Multilisp programming languages are described in:

Dybvig, R. Kent and Robert Hieb. "Engines from Continuations", *Computer Languages*, 14(2):109-123, 1989.

Feeley, Marc. *An Efficient and General Implementation of Futures on Large Scale Shared-Memory Multiprocessors*, PhD Thesis, Brandeis University, 1993.

Additional techniques associated with completion callbacks in networking applications are described in:

Pyarali, Irfan, Tim Harrison, and Douglas C. Schmidt. "Asynchronous Completion Token", in Robert Martin, Dirk Riehle, and Frank Buschmann (eds.), *Pattern Languages of Program Design, Volume 3*, Addison-Wesley, 1999.

The Null Object pattern is often useful for simplifying callback designs in which clients do not always require callback messages. See:

Woolf, Bobby. "Null Object", in Robert Martin, Dirk Riehle, and Frank Buschmann (eds.), *Pattern Languages of Program Design, Volume 3*, Addison-Wesley, 1999.

4.4 Parallel Decomposition

Parallel programs are specifically designed to take advantage of multiple CPUs for solving computation-intensive problems. The main performance goals are normally throughput and scalability — the number of computations that can be performed per unit time, and the potential for improvement when additional computational resources are available. However, these are often intertwined with other performance goals. For example, parallelism may also improve response latencies for a service that hands off work to a parallel execution facility.

Among the main challenges of parallelism in the Java programming language is to construct *portable* programs that can exploit multiple CPUs when they are present, while at the same time working well on single processors, as well as on time-shared multiprocessors that are often processing unrelated programs.

Some classic approaches to parallelism don't mesh well with these goals. Approaches that assume particular architectures, topologies, processor capabilities, or other fixed environmental constraints are ill suited to commonly available JVM implementations. While it is not a crime to build run-time systems with extensions specifically geared to particular parallel computers, and to write parallel programs specifically targeted to them, the associated programming techniques necessarily fall outside the scope of this book. Also, RMI and other distributed frameworks can be used to obtain parallelism across remote machines. In fact, most of the designs discussed here can be adapted to use serialization and remote invocation to achieve parallelism over local networks. This is becoming a common and efficient means of coarse-grained parallel processing. However, these mechanics also lie outside the scope of this book.

We instead focus on three families of task-based designs, fork/join parallelism, computation trees, and barriers. These techniques can yield very efficient programs that exploit multiple CPUs when present, yet still maintain portability and sequential efficiency. Empirically, they are known to scale well, at least up through dozens of CPUs. Moreover, even when these kinds of task-based parallel programs are tuned to maximally exploit a given hardware platform, they require only minor retunings to maximally exploit other platforms.

As of this writing, probably the most common targets for these techniques are applications servers and compute servers that are often, but by no means always, multiprocessors. In either case, we assume that CPU cycles are usually available, so the main goal is to exploit them to speed up the solution of computational problems. In other words, these techniques are unlikely to be very helpful when programs are run on computers that are already nearly saturated.

4.4.1   Fork/Join

Fork/join decomposition relies on parallel versions of divide-and-conquer techniques familiar in sequential algorithm design. Solutions take the form:

```
pseudoclass Solver {                                          // Pseudocode
  // ...
  Result solve(Param problem) {
    if (problem.size <= BASE_CASE_SIZE)
      return directlySolve(problem);
    else {
      Result l, r;
      IN-PARALLEL {
        l = solve(lefthalf(problem));
        r = solve(rightHalf(problem));
      }
      return combine(l, r);
    }
  }
}
```

It takes some hard work and inspiration to invent a divide-and-conquer algorithm. But many common computationally intensive problems have known solutions of approximately this form. Of course, there may be more than two recursive calls, multiple base cases, and arbitrary pre- and post-processing surrounding any of the cases.

Familiar sequential examples include quicksort, mergesort, and many data structure, matrix, and image processing algorithms. Sequential recursive divide-and-conquer designs are easy to parallelize when the recursive tasks are completely independent; that is, when they operate on different parts of a data set (for example different sections of an array) or solve different sub-problems, and need not otherwise communicate or coordinate actions. This often holds in recursive algorithms, even those not originally intended for parallel implementation.

Additionally, there are recursive versions of algorithms (for example, matrix multiplication) that are not used much in sequential contexts, but are more widely used on multiprocessors because of their readily parallelizable form. And other parallel algorithms perform extensive transformations and preprocessing to convert problems into a form that can be solved using fork/join techniques. (See Further Readings in §4.4.4.)

The *IN-PARALLEL* pseudocode is implemented by *forking* and later *joining* tasks performing the recursive calls. However, before discussing how to do this, we first examine issues and frameworks that permit efficient parallel execution of recursively generated tasks.

4.4.1.1 Task granularity and structure

Many of the design forces encountered when implementing fork/join designs surround task granularity:

Maximizing parallelism. In general, the smaller the tasks, the more opportunities for parallelism. All other things being equal, using many fine-grained tasks rather than only a few coarse-grained tasks keeps more CPUs busy, improves load balancing, locality and scalability, decreases the percentage of time that CPUs must idly wait for one another, and leads to greater throughput.

Minimizing overhead. Constructing and managing an object to process a task in parallel, rather than just invoking a method to process it serially, is the main unavoidable overhead associated with task-based programming compared with sequential solutions. It is intrinsically more costly to create and use task objects than to create and use stack-frames. Additionally, the use of task objects can add to the amount of argument and result data that must be transmitted and can impact garbage collection. All other things being equal, total overhead is minimized when there are only a few coarse-grained tasks.

Minimizing contention. A parallel decomposition is not going to lead to much speed-up if each task frequently communicates with others or must block waiting for resources held by others. Tasks should be of a size and structure that maintain as much independence as possible. They should minimize (in most cases, eliminate) use of shared resources, global (static) variables, locks, and other dependencies. Ideally, each task would contain simple straight-line code that runs to completion and then terminates. However, fork/join designs require at least some minimal synchronization. The main object that commences processing normally waits for all subtasks to finish before proceeding.

Maximizing locality. Each subtask should be the only one operating on some small piece of a problem, not only conceptually but also at the level of lower-level resources and memory access patterns. Refactorings that achieve good locality of reference can significantly improve performance on modern heavily cached processors. When dealing with large data sets, it is not uncommon to partition computations into subtasks with good locality even when parallelism is not the main goal. Recursive decomposition is often a productive way to achieve this. Parallelism accentuates the effects of locality. When parallel tasks all access different parts of a data set (for example, different regions of a common matrix), partitioning strategies that reduce the need to transmit updates across caches often achieve much better performance.

4.4.1.2 Frameworks

There is no general optimal solution to granularity and related task structuring issues. Any choice represents a compromise that best resolves the competing forces for the problem at hand. However, it is possible to build lightweight execution frameworks that support a wide range of choices along the continuum.

Thread objects are unnecessarily heavy vehicles for supporting purely computational fork/join tasks. For example, these tasks never need to block on IO, and never need to sleep. They require only an operation to synchronize across subtasks. Worker thread techniques discussed in §4.1.4 can be extended to construct frameworks efficiently supporting only the necessary constructs. While there are several approaches, for concreteness we'll limit discussion to a framework in util.concurrent that restricts all tasks to be subclasses of class FJTask. Here is a brief sketch of principal methods. More details are discussed along with examples in §4.4.1.4 through §4.4.1.7.

```
abstract class FJTask implements Runnable {
  boolean isDone();                   // True after task is run
  void cancel();                      // Prematurely set as done
  void fork();                        // Start a dependent task
  void start();                       // Start an arbitrary task
  static void yield();                // Allow another task to run
  void join();                        // Yield caller until done
  static void invoke(FJTask t);       // Directly run t
  static void coInvoke(FJTask t,
                  FJTask u);     // Fork and join t and u
  static void coInvoke(FJTask[] tasks); // coInvoke all
  void reset();                       // Clear to allow reuse
}
```

An associated FJTaskRunnerGroup class provides control and entry points into this framework. A FJTaskRunnerGroup is constructed with a given number of worker threads that should ordinarily be equal to the number of CPUs on a system. The class supports method invoke that starts up a main task, which will in turn normally create many others.

FJTasks must employ only these task control methods, not arbitrary Thread or monitor methods. While the names of these operations are the same or similar to those in class Thread, their implementations are very different. In particular, there are no general suspension facilities. For example, the join operation is implemented simply by having the underlying worker thread run other tasks to completion until the target task is noticed to have completed (via isDone). This wouldn't work at all with ordinary threads, but is effective and efficient when all tasks are structured as fork/join methods.

These kinds of trade-offs make `FJTask` construction and invocation substantially cheaper than would be possible for any class supporting the full `Thread` interface. As of this writing, on at least some platforms, the overhead of creating, running, and otherwise managing a `FJTask` for the kinds of examples illustrated below is only between four and ten times that of performing equivalent sequential method calls.

The main effect is to lessen the impact of overhead factors when making choices about task partitioning and granularity. The granularity threshold for using tasks can be fairly small — on the order of a few thousand instructions even in the most conservative cases — without noticeably degrading performance on uniprocessors. Programs can exploit as many CPUs as are available on even the largest platforms without the need for special tools to extract or manage parallelism. However, success also depends on construction of task classes and methods that themselves minimize overhead, avoid contention, and preserve locality.

4.4.1.3 Defining tasks

Sequential divide-and-conquer algorithms can be expressed as fork/join-based classes via the following steps:

1. Create a task class with:

   - Fields to hold arguments and results. Most should be strictly local to a task, never accessed from any other task. This eliminates the need for synchronization surrounding their use. However, in the typical case where result variables are accessed by other tasks, they should either be declared as `volatile` or be accessed only via `synchronized` methods.

   - A constructor that initializes argument variables.

   - A `run` method that executes the reworked method code.

2. Replace the original recursive case with code that:

   - Creates subtask objects.

   - Forks each one to run in parallel.

   - Joins each of them.

   - Combines results by accessing result variables in the subtask objects.

3. Replace (or extend) the original base case check with a *threshold* check. Problem sizes less than the threshold should use the original sequential code. This generalization of base case checks maintains efficiency when problem sizes are so small that task overhead overshadows potential gains from parallel exe-

cution. Tune performance by determining a good threshold size for the problem at hand.

4. Replace the original method with one that creates the associated task, waits it out, and returns any results. (In the FJTask framework, the outermost call is performed via FJTaskRunnerGroup.invoke.)

4.4.1.4 Fibonacci

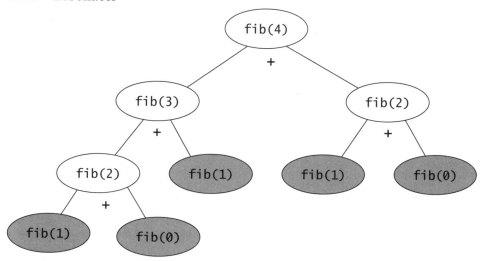

We'll illustrate the basic steps with a very boring and unrealistic, but very simple classic example: recursively computing *fib*, the Fibonacci function. This function can be programmed sequentially as:

```
int seqFib(int n) {
   if (n <= 1)
      return n;
   else
      return seqFib(n-1) + seqFib(n-2);
}
```

This example is unrealistic because there is a much faster non-recursive solution for this particular problem, but it is a favorite for demonstrating both recursion and parallelism. Because it does so little other computation, it makes the basic structure of fork/join designs easier to see, yet it generates many recursive calls — at least *fib(n)* calls to compute *fib(n)*. The first few values of the sequence are 0, 1, 1, 2, 3, 5, 8; *fib(10)* is 55; *fib(20)* is 6,765; *fib(30)* is 832,040; *fib(40)* is 102,334,155.

Function seqFib can be transformed into a task class such as the following:

```
class Fib extends FJTask {
  static final int sequentialThreshold = 13; // for tuning
  volatile int number;                        // argument/result

  Fib(int n) { number = n; }

  int getAnswer() {
    if (!isDone())
      throw new IllegalStateException("Not yet computed");
    return number;
  }

  public void run() {
    int n = number;

    if (n <= sequentialThreshold)       // base case
      number = seqFib(n);
    else {
      Fib f1 = new Fib(n - 1);          // create subtasks
      Fib f2 = new Fib(n - 2);

      coInvoke(f1, f2);                 // fork then join both

      number = f1.number + f2.number;   // combine results
    }
  }


  public static void main(String[] args) { // sample driver
    try {
      int groupSize = 2;      // 2 worker threads
      int num = 35;           // compute fib(35)
      FJTaskRunnerGroup group = new FJTaskRunnerGroup(groupSize);
      Fib f = new Fib(num);
      group.invoke(f);
      int result = f.getAnswer();
      System.out.println("Answer: " + result);
    }
    catch (InterruptedException ex) {} // die
  }
}
```

Notes:

- The class maintains a field holding the argument for which to compute the
  Fibonacci function. Also, we need a variable to hold the result. However, as is
  fairly typical in such classes, there is no need to keep two variables. For economy (bearing in mind that many millions of Fib objects might be constructed
  in the course of a computation), we can micro-optimize to use one variable,

and overwrite the argument with its result after it is computed. (This is the first of several hand-optimizations that are uncomfortably petty, but are shown here in order to demonstrate minor tweaks that can be pragmatically important in constructing efficient parallel programs.)

- The `number` field is declared as `volatile` to ensure visibility from other tasks/threads after it is computed (see §2.2.7). Here and in subsequent examples, `volatile` fields are read and/or written only once per task execution, and otherwise held in local variables. This avoids interfering with potential compiler optimizations that are otherwise disabled when using `volatile`.

- Alternatively, we could have synchronized access to the `number` field. But there is no good reason to do so. The use of `volatile` fields is much more common in lightweight parallel task frameworks than in general-purpose concurrent programming. Tasks usually do not require other synchronization and control mechanics, yet often need to communicate results via field access. The most common reason for using `synchronized` instead of `volatile` is to deal with arrays. Individual array elements cannot be declared as `volatile`. Processing arrays within `synchronized` methods or blocks is the simplest way to ensure visibility of array updates, even in the typical case in which locking is not otherwise required. An occasionally attractive alternative is instead to create arrays each of whose elements is a forwarding object with `volatile` fields.

- The method `isDone` returns true after the completion of a `run` method that has been executed via `invoke` or `coInvoke`. It is used as a guard in `getAnswer` to help detect programming errors that could occur if the ultimate consumer of an answer tries to access it prematurely. (There is no chance of this happening here, but this safeguard helps avoid unintended usages.)

- The `sequentialThreshold` constant establishes granularity. It represents the balance point at which it is not worth the overhead to create tasks, also reflecting the goal of maintaining good sequential performance. For example, on one set of runs on a four-CPU system, setting `sequentialThreshold` to 13 resulted in a 4% performance degradation versus `seqFib` for large argument values when using a single worker thread. But it sped up by a factor of at least 3.8 with four worker threads, processing several million `Fib` tasks per second.

- Rather than wiring in a compile-time constant, we could have defined the threshold as a run-time variable and set it to a value based on the number of CPUs available or other platform characteristics. This is useful in task-based programs that do not scale linearly, as is likely to be true even here. As the number of CPUs increase, so do communication and resource management costs, which could be balanced by increasing the threshold.

- The parallel analog of recursion is performed via a convenient method, `coInvoke(FJTask t, FJTask u)`, which in turn acts as:
      `t.fork(); invoke(u); t.join();`

- The `fork` method is a specialized analog of `Thread.start`. A forked task is always processed in stack-based LIFO order when it is run by the same underlying worker thread that spawned it, but in queue-based FIFO order with respect to other tasks if run by another worker thread running in parallel. This represents a cross of sorts between normal stack-based sequential calls, and normal queue-based thread scheduling. This policy (implemented via double-ended scheduling queues) is ideal for recursive task-based parallelism (see Further Readings), and more generally whenever dealing with strictly dependent tasks — those that are spawned either by the tasks that ultimately join them or by their subtasks.

- In contrast, `FJTask.start` behaves more like `Thread.start`. It employs queue-based FIFO scheduling with respect to all worker threads. It is used, for example, by `FJTaskRunnerGroup.invoke` to start up execution of a new main task.

- The `join` method should be used only for tasks initiated via `fork`. It exploits termination dependency patterns of fork/join subtasks to optimize execution.

- The `FJTask.invoke` method runs the body of one task within another task, and waits out completion. Seen differently, it is the one-task version of `coInvoke`, an optimization of `u.fork(); u.join()`.

Effective use of any lightweight executable framework requires the same understanding of support methods and their semantics as does programming with ordinary `Thread`s. The `FJTask` framework exploits the symbiosis between recursion and parallel decomposition, and so encourages the divide-and-conquer programming style seen in `Fib`. However, the range of programming idioms and design patterns conforming to this general style is fairly broad, as illustrated by the following examples.

4.4.1.5   Linking subtasks

Fork/join techniques may be applied even when the number of forked subtasks varies dynamically. Among several related tactics for carrying this out, you can add link fields so that subtasks can be maintained in lists. After spawning all tasks, an accumulate (also known as *reduction*) operation can traverse the list sequentially, joining and using the results of each subtask.

Stretching the Fib example a bit, the `FibVL` class illustrates one way to set this up. This style of solution is not especially useful here, but is applicable in contexts in which a dynamic number of subtasks are created, possibly across different methods. Notice that the subtasks here are joined in the opposite order in which they were created. Since the processing order of results does not matter here, we use the simplest possible linking algorithm (prepending), which happens to reverse the order of tasks during traversal. This strategy applies whenever the accumulation step is commutative and associative with respect to results, so tasks can be processed in any order. If the order did matter, we would need to adjust list construction or traversal accordingly.

```
class FibVL extends FJTask {
  volatile int number; // as before
  final FibVL next;      // embedded linked list of sibling tasks

  FibVL(int n, FibVL list) { number = n; next = list; }

  public void run() {
    int n = number;
    if (n <= sequentialThreshold)
      number = seqFib(n);
    else {
      FibVL forked = null;                      // list of subtasks

      forked = new FibVL(n - 1, forked); // prepends to list
      forked.fork();

      forked = new FibVL(n - 2, forked);
      forked.fork();

      number = accumulate(forked);
    }
  }

  // Traverse list, joining each subtask and adding to result
  int accumulate(FibVL list) {
    int sum = 0;
    for (FibVL f = list; f != null; f = f.next) {
      f.join();
      sum += f.number;
    }
    return sum;
  }
}
```

4.4.1.6 Callbacks

Recursive task-based fork/join parallelism may be extended to apply when other local synchronization conditions are used instead of join. In the FJTask framework, t.join() is implemented as an optimized version of:

```
while (!t.isDone()) yield();
```

Method yield here allows the underlying worker thread to process other tasks. (More specifically, in the FJTask framework, the thread *will* process at least one other task if one exists.)

Any other condition may be used in this construction rather than isDone, as long as you are certain that the predicate being waited for will eventually become true due to the actions of a subtask (or one of its subtasks, and so on). For example, rather than relying on join, task control can rely on counters that keep track of task creation and completion. A counter can be incremented on each fork and decremented when the forked task has produced a result. This and related counter-based schemes can be attractive choices when subtasks communicate back results via callbacks rather than via access to result fields. Counters of this form are small-scale, localized versions of the barriers discussed in §4.4.3.

Callback-based fork/join designs are seen, for example, in problem-solving algorithms, games, searching, and logic programming. In many such applications, the number of subtasks that are forked can vary dynamically, and subtask results are better captured by method calls than by field extraction.

Callback-based approaches also permit greater asynchrony than techniques such as the linked tasks in §4.4.1.5. This can lead to better performance when subtasks differ in expected duration, since the result processing of quickly completing subtasks can sometimes overlap with continued processing of longer ones. However, this design gives up all result ordering guarantees, and thus is applicable only when subtask result processing is completely independent of the order in which results are produced.

Callback counters are used in the following class FibVCB, which is not at all well-suited for the problem at hand but serves to exemplify techniques. This code illustrates a typical but delicate combination of task-local variables, volatiles, and locking in an effort to keep task control overhead to a minimum:

```
class FibVCB extends FJTask {
  // ...
  volatile int number = 0;        // as before
  final FibVCB parent;            // is null for outermost call
  int callbacksExpected = 0;
  volatile int callbacksReceived = 0;

  FibVCB(int n, FibVCB p) { number = n; parent = p; }

  // Callback method invoked by subtasks upon completion
  synchronized void addToResult(int n) {
    number += n;
    ++callbacksReceived;
  }

  public void run() {  // same structure as join-based version
    int n = number;
    if (n <= sequentialThreshold)
      number = seqFib(n);
    else {
      // Clear number so subtasks can fill in
      number = 0;
      // Establish number of callbacks expected
      callbacksExpected = 2;

      new FibVCB(n - 1, this).fork();
      new FibVCB(n - 2, this).fork();

      // Wait for callbacks from children
      while (callbacksReceived < callbacksExpected) yield();
    }

    // Call back parent
    if (parent != null) parent.addToResult(number);
  }
}
```

Notes:

- All mutual exclusion locking is restricted to small code segments protecting field accesses, as must be true for any class in a lightweight task framework. Tasks are not allowed to block unless they are sure they will be able to continue soon. In particular, this framework unenforceably requires that synchronized blocks *not* span forks and subsequent joins or yields.

- To help eliminate some synchronization, the callback count is split into two counters, callbacksExpected and callbacksReceived. The task is done when they are equal.

- The `callbacksExpected` counter is used only by the current task, so access need not be `synchronized`, and it need not be `volatile`. In fact, since exactly two callbacks are always expected in the recursive case and the value is never needed outside the run method, this class could easily be reworked in a way that eliminates all need for this variable. However, such a variable is needed in more typical callback-based designs where the number of forks may vary dynamically and may be generated across multiple methods.

- The `addToResult` callback method must be `synchronized` to avoid interference problems when subtasks call back at about the same time.

- So long as both `number` and `callbacksReceived` are declared as `volatile`, and `callbacksReceived` is updated as the last statement of `addToResult`, the `yield` loop test need not involve synchronization because it is waiting for a latching threshold that, once reached, will never change (see §3.4.2.1).

- We could also define a reworked `getAnswer` method that uses these mechanics so that it returns an answer if all callbacks have been received. However, since this method is designed to be called by external (non-task) clients upon completion of the overall computation, there is no compelling reason to do this. The version from the original `Fib` class suffices.

- Despite these measures, the overhead associated with task control in this version is greater than that of the original version using `coInvoke`. If you were to use it anyway, you would probably choose a slightly larger sequential threshold, and thus exploit slightly less parallelism.

4.4.1.7 Cancellation

In some designs, there is no need for keeping counts of callbacks or exhaustively traversing through subtask lists. Instead, tasks complete when any subtask (or one of its subtasks, and so on) arrives at a suitable result. In these cases, you can avoid wasting computation by cancelling any subtasks in the midst of producing results that will not be needed.

The options here are similar to those seen in other situations involving cancellation (see §3.1.2). For example, subtasks can regularly invoke a method (perhaps `isDone`) in their parents that indicates that an answer has already been found, and if so to return early. They must also set their own status, so any of their subtasks can do the same. This can be implemented here using `FJTask.cancel` that just prematurely sets `isDone` status. This suppresses execution of tasks that have not yet been started, but has no effect on tasks in the midst of execution unless the tasks' run methods themselves detect updated status and deal with it.

When an entire set of tasks are all trying to compute a single result, an even simpler strategy suffices: Tasks may regularly check a global (`static`) variable that indicates completion. However, when there are many tasks, and many CPUs, more localized strategies may still be preferable to one that places so much pressure on the underlying system by generating many accesses to the same memory location, especially if it must be accessed under synchronization. Additionally, bear in mind that the total overhead associated with cancellation should be less than the cost of just letting small tasks run even if their results are not needed.

For example, here is a class that solves the classic N-Queens problem, searching for the placement of N queens that do not attack each other on a chessboard of size NxN. For simplicity of illustration, it relies on a static `Result` variable. Here tasks check for cancellation only upon entry into the method. They will continue looping through possible extensions even if a result has already been found. However, the generated tasks will immediately exit. This can be slightly wasteful, but may obtain a solution more quickly than a version that checks for completion upon every iteration of every task.

Note also here that the tasks do not bother joining their subtasks since there is no reason to do so. Only the ultimate external caller (in `main`) needs to wait for a solution; this is supported here by adding standard waiting and notification methods to the `Result` class. (Also, for compactness, this version does not employ any kind of granularity threshold. It is easy to add one, for example by directly exploring moves rather than forking subtasks when the number of rows is close to the board size.)

```
class NQueens extends FJTask {
  static int boardSize; // fixed after initialization in main
  // Boards are arrays where each cell represents a row,
  // and holds the column number of the queen in that row

  static class Result {            // holder for ultimate result
    private int[] board = null;    // non-null when solved

    synchronized boolean solved() { return board != null; }

    synchronized void set(int[] b) { // Support use by non-Tasks
      if (board == null) { board = b; notifyAll(); }
    }

    synchronized int[] await() throws InterruptedException {
      while (board == null) wait();
      return board;
    }
  }
  static final Result result = new Result();
```

```
public static void main(String[] args) {
  boardSize = ...;
  FJTaskRunnerGroup tasks = new FJTaskRunnerGroup(...);
  int[] initialBoard = new int[0]; // start with empty board
  tasks.execute(new NQueens(initialBoard));
  int[] board = result.await();
  // ...
}

final int[] sofar;                  // initial configuration

NQueens(int[] board) { this.sofar = board;  }

public void run() {
  if (!result.solved()) {         // skip if already solved
    int row = sofar.length;

    if (row >= boardSize)         // done
      result.set(sofar);

    else {                        // try all expansions

      for (int q = 0; q < boardSize; ++q) {

        // Check if queen can be placed in column q of next row
        boolean attacked = false;
        for (int i = 0; i < row; ++i) {
          int p = sofar[i];
          if (q == p || q == p - (row-i) || q == p + (row-i)) {
            attacked = true;
            break;
          }
        }

        // If so, fork to explore moves from new configuration
        if (!attacked) {
          // build extended board representation
          int[] next = new int[row+1];
          for (int k = 0; k < row; ++k) next[k] = sofar[k];
          next[row] = q;
          new NQueens(next).fork();
        }
      }
    }
  }
}
```

4.4.2   Computation Trees

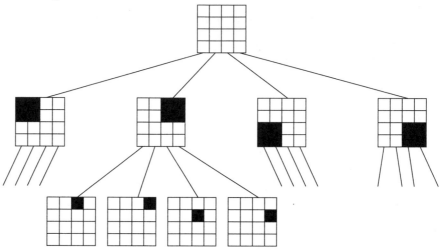

A number of computationally intensive algorithms involve tasks of the form:

```
For a fixed number of steps, or until convergence, do {
  Update one section of a problem;
  Wait for other tasks to finish updating their sections;
}
```

Most often, such algorithms perform update operations on partitioned arrays, matrices, or image representations. For example, many physical dynamics problems involve repeated local updates to the cells of a matrix. *Jacobi* algorithms and related relaxation techniques repeatedly recalculate estimated values across neighboring cells, typically using an averaging formula such as:

```
void oneStep(double[][] oldMatrix,
             double[][] newMatrix, int i, int j) {
  newMatrix[i][j] = 0.25 * (oldMatrix[i-1][j] +
                            oldMatrix[i][j-1] +
                            oldMatrix[i+1][j] +
                            oldMatrix[i][j+1]);
}
```

Normally, to save space, two different matrices are swapped as `newMatrix` and `oldMatrix` across successive steps.

Algorithms requiring that *all* tasks periodically wait for *all* others to complete do not always scale quite as well as more loosely coupled fork/join designs. Even so, these algorithms are common, efficient, and amenable to significant parallel speedups.

4.4.2.1 Building and using trees

It would be inefficient to repeatedly apply fork/join decomposition in iterative designs in order to update sections in parallel. Because the sections are the same across iterations, they can be constructed just once and then repeatedly invoked so that on each iteration, the corresponding updates execute in the same order as would be produced by a recursive solution.

Computation trees are explicit representations of the tree-structured computations implicitly arising in fork/join recursion. These trees have two kinds of nodes, internal nodes and leaf nodes, corresponding to the recursive and base cases of a recursive solution. They can be constructed and used for iterative update problems via the following steps:

1. Create a tree of task objects representing the recursive partitions, where:

   - Each internal node contains references to subpartitions, and has an update method that performs fork/join processing of each of them.

   - Each leaf node represents a finest-granularity partition, and has an update method that operates directly on it.

2. For a fixed number of steps, or until convergence, do:

   - Execute the task performing the root partition's update method.

For example, the following code illustrates the highlights of a set of classes that perform Jacobi iteration using the averaging formula shown above. In addition to updating, this version also keeps track of the differences among computed cell values across iterations, and stops when the maximum difference is within a constant EPSILON. Also, like many programs of this form, this code assumes that the matrices have been set up with extra edge cells that are never updated, so boundary conditions never need to be checked. (Alternatives include recomputing edge values using special edge formulas after each pass, and treating edges as toroidally wrapping around the mesh.)

The recursive decomposition strategy used here is to divide the mesh into quadrants, stopping when the number of cells is at most leafCells, which serves as the granularity threshold. This strategy works well so long as the numbers of rows and columns in the matrix are approximately equal. If they are not, additional classes and methods could be defined to divide across only one dimension at a time. The approach here assumes that the matrix as a whole already exists, so rather than actually dividing up cells, task nodes just keep track of the row and column offsets of this matrix that each partition is working on.

The subclass-based design used here reflects the different structure and behavior of internal versus leaf nodes. Both are subclasses of abstract base JTree:

```java
abstract class JTree extends FJTask {
  volatile double maxDiff; // for convergence check
}

class Interior extends JTree {
  private final JTree[] quads;

  Interior(JTree q1, JTree q2, JTree q3, JTree q4) {
    quads = new JTree[] { q1, q2, q3, q4 };
  }

  public void run() {
    coInvoke(quads);
    double md = 0.0;
    for (int i = 0; i < quads.length; ++i) {
      md = Math.max(md,quads[i].maxDiff);
      quads[i].reset();
    }
    maxDiff = md;
  }
}

class Leaf extends JTree {
  private final double[][] A; private final double[][] B;
  private final int loRow;      private final int hiRow;
  private final int loCol;      private final int hiCol;
  private int steps = 0;

  Leaf(double[][] A, double[][] B,
       int loRow, int hiRow, int loCol, int hiCol) {
    this.A = A;      this.B = B;
    this.loRow = loRow; this.hiRow = hiRow;
    this.loCol = loCol; this.hiCol = hiCol;
  }

  public synchronized void run() {
    boolean AtoB = (steps++ % 2) == 0;
    double[][] a = (AtoB)? A : B;
    double[][] b = (AtoB)? B : A;
    double md = 0.0;
    for (int i = loRow; i <= hiRow; ++i) {
      for (int j = loCol; j <= hiCol; ++j) {
        b[i][j] = 0.25 * (a[i-1][j] + a[i][j-1] +
                          a[i+1][j] + a[i][j+1]);
        md = Math.max(md, Math.abs(b[i][j] - a[i][j]));
      }
    }
    maxDiff = md;
  }
}
```

The driver class first builds a tree that represents the partitioning of its argument matrix. The build method could itself be parallelized. But because the base actions are just node constructions, the granularity threshold would be so high that parallelization would be worthwhile only for huge problem sizes.

The run method repeatedly sets the root task in motion and waits out completion. For simplicity of illustration, it continues until convergence. Among other changes necessary to turn this into a realistic program, you would need to initialize the matrices and deal with possible lack of convergence within a bounded number of iterations. Because each iteration entails a full synchronization point waiting for the root task to finish, it is relatively simple to insert additional operations that maintain or report global status between iterations.

```java
class Jacobi extends FJTask {
  static final double EPSILON = 0.001; // convergence criterion
  final JTree root;
  final int maxSteps;
  Jacobi(double[][] A, double[][] B,
         int firstRow, int lastRow, int firstCol, int lastCol,
         int maxSteps, int leafCells) {
    this.maxSteps = maxSteps;
    root = build(A, B, firstRow, lastRow, firstCol, lastCol,
                 leafCells);
  }

  public void run() {
    for (int i = 0; i < maxSteps; ++i) {
      invoke(root);
      if (root.maxDiff < EPSILON) {
        System.out.println("Converged");
        return;
      }
      else root.reset();
    }
  }

  static JTree build(double[][] a, double[][] b,
                     int lr, int hr, int lc, int hc, int size) {
    if ((hr - lr + 1) * (hc - lc + 1) <= size)
      return new Leaf(a, b, lr, hr, lc, hc);
    int mr = (lr + hr) / 2; // midpoints
    int mc = (lc + hc) / 2;
    return new Interior(build(a, b, lr,   mr, lc,   mc, size),
                        build(a, b, lr,   mr, mc+1, hc, size),
                        build(a, b, mr+1, hr, lc,   mc, size),
                        build(a, b, mr+1, hr, mc+1, hc, size));
  }
}
```

4.4.3   Barriers

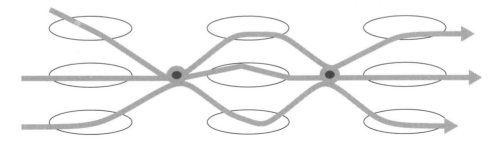

Recursive decomposition is a powerful and flexible technique, but does not always fit well with the structure of iterative problems, and usually requires adoption of a lightweight execution framework for efficient implementation. A more direct path to a solution of many iterative problems is first to divide the problem into *segments*, each with an associated task performing a loop that must periodically wait for other segments to complete. From the perspective of tree-based approaches, these designs flatten out all the internal nodes and just deal with the leaves.

As with recursive tasks, there are opportunities to specialize `Threads` to make them more attuned to the demands of parallel iteration (see Further Readings). However, there is usually less to be gained by doing so, in part because all thread construction overhead is restricted to the start-up phase. Here we illustrate the basic mechanics using regular `Threads` each executing a single `Runnable`. When using `Threads`, granularity thresholds must in general be substantially higher than when using lightweight executable classes (although still substantially lower than those needed in distributed parallel designs). But the basic logic of iterative algorithms is otherwise identical, regardless of granularity. In many iterative problems, little potential parallelism is wasted by using coarse granularities. When all threads perform approximately the same actions for approximately the same durations, creating only as many tasks as CPUs, or perhaps a small multiple of the number of CPUs, can work well.

While it is always possible to hand-craft the necessary control mechanics using waiting and notification constructs, it is both more convenient and less error-prone instead to rely on standardized synchronization aids that encapsulate these mechanics. The synchronization device of choice in iterative designs is a *cyclic barrier*. A cyclic barrier is initialized with a fixed number of parties that will be repeatedly synchronizing. It supports only one method, `barrier`, that forces each caller to wait until all parties have invoked the method, and then resets for the next iteration. A basic `CyclicBarrier` class can be defined as follows:

```
class CyclicBarrier {

  protected final int parties;
  protected int count;      // parties currently being waited for
  protected int resets = 0;  // times barrier has been tripped

  CyclicBarrier(int c) { count = parties = c; }

  synchronized int barrier() throws InterruptedException {
    int index = --count;
    if (index > 0) {          // not yet tripped
      int r = resets;         // wait until next reset

      do { wait(); } while (resets == r);

    }
    else {                    // trip
      count = parties;        // reset count for next time
      ++resets;
      notifyAll();            // cause all other parties to resume
    }

    return index;
  }
}
```

(The `util.concurrent` version of this class available from the online supplement deals more responsibly with interruptions and time-outs. Fancier versions that reduce memory contention on the lock and on the fields may be worth constructing on systems with very large numbers of processors.)

The `CyclicBarrier.barrier` method defined here returns the number of other threads that were still waiting when the barrier was entered, which can be useful in some algorithms. As another by-product, the `barrier` method is intrinsically `synchronized`, so it also serves as a memory barrier to ensure flushes and loads of array element values in its most typical usage contexts (see §2.2.7).

A barrier may also be construed as a simple consensus operator (see §3.6). It gathers "votes" among several threads about whether they should all continue to the next iteration. Release occurs when all votes have been collected and agreement has thus been reached. (However, unlike transaction frameworks, threads using this `CyclicBarrier` class are not allowed to vote "no".)

With barriers, many parallel iterative algorithms become easy to express. In the simplest cases, these programs might take the form (eliding all problem-specific details):

```
class Segment implements Runnable  {                // Code sketch
  final CyclicBarrier bar; // shared by all segments
  Segment(CyclicBarrier b, ...) { bar = b; ...; }

  void update() { ... }

  public void run() {
    // ...
    for (int i = 0; i < iterations; ++i) {
      update();
      bar.barrier();
    }
    // ...
  }
}

class Driver {
  // ...
  void compute(Problem problem) throws ... {
    int n = problem.size / granularity;
    CyclicBarrier barrier = new CyclicBarrier(n);
    Thread[] threads = new Thread[n];

    // create
    for (int i = 0; i < n; ++i)
      threads[i] = new Thread(new Segment(barrier, ...));

    // trigger
    for (int i = 0; i < n; ++i) threads[i].start();

    // await termination
    for (int i = 0; i < n; ++i) threads[i].join();
  }
}
```

This structure suffices for problems requiring known numbers of iterations. However, many problems require checks for convergence or some other global property between iterations. (Conversely, in a few *chaotic* relaxation algorithms you don't even need a barrier after each iteration, but can instead let segments free-run for a while between barriers and/or checks.)

One way to provide convergence checks is to rework the CyclicBarrier class to optionally run a supplied Runnable command whenever a barrier is about to be reset. A more classic approach, which illustrates a technique useful in other contexts as well, is to rely on the index returned by barrier. The caller obtaining index zero (as an arbitrary, but always legal choice) can perform the check while all others are quietly waiting for a *second* barrier.

For example, here a a barrier-based version of a segment class for the Jacobi problem described in §4.4.2. Collections of JacobiSegment objects can be initialized and run by a driver of the generic form given above.

```java
class JacobiSegment implements Runnable {          // Incomplete
  // These are same as in Leaf class version:
  double[][] A;        double[][] B;
  final int firstRow;  final int lastRow;
  final int firstCol;  final int lastCol;
  volatile double maxDiff;
  int steps = 0;
  void update() { /* Nearly same as Leaf.run */ }

  final CyclicBarrier bar;
  final JacobiSegment[] allSegments; // for convergence check
  volatile boolean converged = false;

  JacobiSegment(double[][] A, double[][] B,
                int firstRow, int lastRow,
                int firstCol, int lastCol,
                CyclicBarrier b, JacobiSegment[] allSegments) {
    this.A = A;    this.B = B;
    this.firstRow = firstRow; this.lastRow = lastRow;
    this.firstCol = firstCol; this.lastCol = lastCol;
    this.bar = b;
    this.allSegments = allSegments;
  }

  public void run() {
    try {
      while (!converged) {
        update();
        int myIndex = bar.barrier(); // wait for all to update
        if (myIndex == 0) convergenceCheck();
        bar.barrier();               // wait for convergence check
      }
    }
    catch(Exception ex) {
      // clean up ...
    }
  }

  void convergenceCheck() {
    for (int i = 0; i < allSegments.length; ++i)
      if (allSegments[i].maxDiff > EPSILON) return;
    for (int i = 0; i < allSegments.length; ++i)
      allSegments[i].converged = true;
  }
}
```

4.4.4 Further Readings

For a survey of approaches to high-performance parallel processing, see

Skillicorn, David, and Domenico Talia, "Models and Languages for Parallel Computation", *Computing Surveys*, June 1998.

Most texts on parallel programming concentrate on algorithms designed for use on fine-grained parallel machine architectures, but also cover design techniques and algorithms that can be implemented using the kinds of stock multiprocessors most amenable to supporting a JVM. See, for example:

Foster, Ian. *Designing and Building Parallel Programs*, Addison Wesley, 1995.

Roosta, Seyed. *Parallel Processing and Parallel Algorithms*, Springer-Verlag, 1999.

Wilson, Gregory. *Practical Parallel Programming*, MIT Press, 1995.

Zomaya, Albert (ed.). *Parallel and Distributed Computing Handbook*, McGraw-Hill, 1996.

Pattern-based accounts of parallel programming include:

Massingill, Berna, Timothy Mattson, and Beverly Sanders. *A Pattern Language for Parallel Application Programming*, Technical report, University of Florida, 1999.

MacDonald, Steve, Duane Szafron, and Jonathan Schaeffer. "Object-Oriented Pattern-Based Parallel Programming with Automatically Generated Frameworks", in *Proceedings of the 5th USENIX Conference on Object-Oriented Tools and Systems (COOTS)*, 1999.

The FJTask framework internally relies on a *work-stealing* task scheduler based on the one in Cilk, a C-based parallel programming framework. In work-stealing schedulers, each worker thread normally runs (in LIFO order) tasks that it constructs, but when idle steals (in FIFO order) those constructed by other worker threads. More details, including explanations of the senses in which this scheme is optimal for recursive fork/join programs, may be found in:

Frigo, Matteo, Charles Leiserson, and Keith Randall. "The Implementation of the Cilk-5 Multithreaded Language", *Proceedings of 998 ACM SIGPLAN Conference on Programming Language Design and Implementation (PLDI)*, 1998.

The online supplement includes more realistic examples of the techniques discussed in this section. It also provides links to the Cilk package and related frameworks, including Hood (a C++ follow-on to Cilk) and Filaments (a C package that includes a specialized framework supporting barrier-based iterative computation).

4.5 Active Objects

In the task-based frameworks illustrated throughout most of this chapter, threads are used to propel conceptually active messages sent among conceptually passive objects. However, it can be productive to approach some design problems from the opposite perspective — active objects sending each other passive messages.

To illustrate, consider an active object that conforms to the WaterTank description in Chapter 1:

```
pseudoclass ActiveWaterTank extends Thread {        // Pseudocode
  // ...
  public void run() {
    for (;;) {
      accept message;
      if (message is of form addWater(float amount)) {
        if (currentVolume >= capacity) {
          if (overflow != null) {
            send overflow.addWater(amount);
            accept response;
            if (response is of form OverflowException)
              reply response;
            else ...
          else ...
        else ...
      }
      else if (message is of form removeWater(float amount)) {
        ...
      }
    }
  }
}
```

Pseudocode is used here because there is no built-in syntax for passing messages from one active object to another, only for direct invocation among passive objects. However, as discussed in §4.1.1, similar issues may be encountered even when using passive objects. Any of the solutions described there apply equally well here: adopting message formats of various kinds, transported across streams, channels, event queues, pipes, sockets, and so on. In fact, as shown in the WebService example leading off this chapter, it is easy to add task-based constructions to designs otherwise based on active

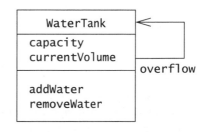

objects. Conversely, most task-based designs discussed in this chapter work equally well when some objects are active rather than passive.

Further, the use of Runnables as messages leads to a boring but universal (at least in some senses) form of active object: a minor variant of a common worker thread design that also conforms to the initial abstract characterization of active objects as interpreters in §1.2.4:

```
class ActiveRunnableExecutor extends Thread {
  Channel me = ... //  used for all incoming messages

  public void run() {
    try {
      for (;;) {
        ((Runnable)(me.take())).run();
      }
    }
    catch (InterruptedException ie) {} // die
  }
}
```

Of course, such classes are not very useful unless they also include internal methods that manufacture Runnables to execute and/or send to other active objects. It is possible, but unnatural, to write entire programs in this fashion.

However, many components in reactive systems can be usefully construed as active objects that operate under more constrained rules and message-passing disciplines. This includes especially those objects that interact with other computers or devices, often the main externally visible objects in a program.

In distributed frameworks such as CORBA and RMI, externally visible active objects are themselves ascribed interfaces listing the messages that they accept. Internally, they usually have a more uniform structure than does ActiveWater-Tank. Typically, they contain a main run loop that repeatedly accepts external requests, dispatches to internal passive objects providing the corresponding service, and then constructs reply messages that are sent back to clients. (The internal passive objects are the ones explicitly programmed when using CORBA and RMI. The active objects, sometimes known as *skeletons*, are usually generated automatically by tools.)

It is very possible to take an active, actor-style approach to the design of other components as well. One reason for designing entire systems from this point of view is to take advantage of well-developed theory and design techniques associated with particular sets of rules surrounding active entities and their messages. The remainder of this section gives a brief overview of the most well-known and influential such framework, CSP.

4.5.1 CSP

C.A.R. Hoare's theory of Communicating Sequential Processes (CSP) provides both a formal approach to concurrency and an associated set of design techniques. As discussed in the Further Readings in §4.5.2, there are a number of closely related approaches, but CSP has had the largest impact on concurrent design and programming. CSP has served as the basis of programming languages (including occam), was influential in the design of others (including Ada), and can be supported in the Java programming language through the use of library classes.

The following account illustrates the JCSP package developed by Peter Welch and colleagues. The package is available via links from the online supplement. This section provides only a brief synopsis. Interested readers will want to obtain copies of the package, its documentation, and related texts.

4.5.1.1 Processes and channels

A CSP *process* can be construed as a special kind of actor-style object, in which:

- Processes have no method interface and no externally invocable methods. Because there are no invocable methods, it is impossible for methods to be invoked by different threads. Thus there is no need for explicit locking.

- Processes communicate only by reading and writing data across *channels*.

- Processes have no identity, and so cannot be explicitly referenced. However, channels serve as analogs of references (see §1.2.4), allowing communication with whichever process is at the other end of a channel.

- Processes need not spin forever in a loop accepting messages (although many do). They may read and write messages on various channels as desired.

A CSP *channel* can be construed as a special kind of Channel, in which:

- All channels are synchronous (see §3.4.1.4), and so contain no internal buffering. (However, you can construct *processes* that perform buffering.)

- Channels support only read ("?") and write ("!") operations carrying data values. The operations behave in the same way as take and put.

- The most fundamental channels are one-to-one. They may be connected only to a single pair of processes, a writer and a reader. Multiple-reader and multiple-writer channels may also be defined.

4.5.1.2   Composition

Much of the elegance of CSP stems from its simple and analytically tractable composition rules. The "S" in CSP stands for *Sequential*, so basic processes perform serial computations on internal data (for example adding numbers, conditional tests, assignment, looping). Higher-level processes are built by composition; for a channel c, variable x, and processes P and Q:

c?x -> P	Reading from c enables P
c!x -> P	Writing to c enables P
P ; Q	P followed by Q
P || Q	P and Q in parallel
P [] Q	P or Q (but not both)

The choice operator P [] Q requires that P and Q both be communication-enabled processes (of form d?y -> R or d!y -> R). The choice of which process runs depends on which communication is ready: Nothing happens until one or both communications are ready. If one is (or becomes) ready, that branch is taken. If both are (or become) ready, either choice may be taken (nondeterministically).

4.5.1.3   JCSP

The JCSP package supports CSP-based design in a straightforward way. It consists of an execution framework that efficiently supports CSP constructs represented via interfaces, classes, and methods, including:

- Interfaces ChannelInput (supporting read), ChannelOutput (supporting write) and Channel (supporting both) operate on Object arguments, but special versions for int arguments are also provided. The principal implementation class is One2OneChannel that supports use only by a single reader and a single writer. But various multiway channels are also provided.

- Interface CSProcess describes processes supporting only method run. Implementation classes Parallel and Sequence (and others) have constructors that accept arrays of other CSProcess objects and create composites.

- The choice operator [] is supported via the Alternative class. Its constructor accepts arrays with elements of type Guard. Alternative supports a select method that returns an index denoting which of them can (and then must) be chosen. A fairSelect method works in the same way but provides additional fairness guarantees — over the course of multiple selects, it will choose fairly among all ready alternatives rather than always selecting one of them. The only usages of `Alternative` demonstrated below use guard type `AltingChannelInput`, which is implemented by `One2OneChannel`.

- Additional utilities include `CSProcess` implementations such as `Timer` (which does delayed writes and can also be used for time-outs in `Alternative`), `Generate` (which generates number sequences), `Skip` (which does nothing at all — one of the CSP primitives), and classes that permit interaction and display via AWT.

4.5.1.4 Dining philosophers

As a classic demonstration, consider the famous Dining Philosophers problem. A table holds five forks (arranged as pictured) and a bowl of spaghetti. It seats five philosophers, each of whom eat for a while, then think for a while, then eat, and so on. Each philosopher requires two forks — the ones on the left and right — to eat (no one knows why; it is just part of the story) but releases them when thinking.

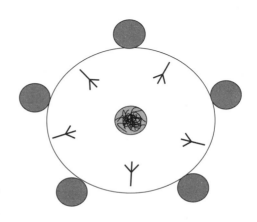

The main problem to be solved here is that, without some kind of coordination, the philosophers could starve when they pick up their left forks and then block forever trying to pick up their right forks which are being held by other philosophers.

There are many paths to a solution (and yet more paths to non-solution). We'll demonstrate one described by Hoare that adds a requirement (enforced by a Butler) that at any given time, at most four philosophers are allowed to be seated. This requirement suffices to ensure that at all times at least one philosopher can eat — if there are only four philosophers, at least one of them can get both forks. This solution does not by itself ensure that all five philosophers eventually eat. But this guarantee can be obtained via use of `Alternative.fairSelect` in the `Butler` class to ensure fair processing of seating messages.

We'll use a simple, pure CSP style where all channels are one-to-one and messages have no content (using `null` for messages). This puts a stronger focus on the synchronization and process construction issues. The system is composed of a `College` with five `Philosophers`, five `Forks`, and one `Butler` (standing in the bowl of spaghetti!), connected using `One2OneChannels`.

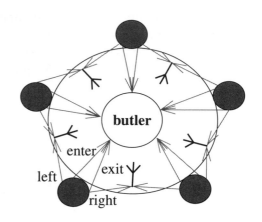

Since everything must be either a process or a channel, forks must be processes. A `Fork` continuously loops waiting for a message from one of its users (either its left-hand or right-hand philosopher). When it gets a message from one indicating a fork pick-up, it waits for another indicating a fork put-down. (While it might be more tasteful to indicate pick-ups versus put-downs via different kinds of messages or message contents, this protocol using null messages suffices.)

In JCSP, this can be written as:

```
class Fork implements CSProcess {

  private final AltingChannelInput[] fromPhil;

  Fork(AltingChannelInput l, AltingChannelInput r) {
    fromPhil = new AltingChannelInput[] { l, r };
  }

  public void run() {
    Alternative alt = new Alternative(fromPhil);

    for (;;) {
      int i = alt.select();    // await message from either
      fromPhil[i].read();      // pick up
      fromPhil[i].read();      // put down
    }

  }
}
```

The Butler process makes sure that at most N-1 (i.e., four here) philosophers are seated at any given time. It does this by enabling both enter and exit messages if there are enough seats, but only exit messages otherwise. Because Alternative operates on arrays of alternatives, this requires a bit of manipulation to set up. (Some other utilities in JCSP could be used to simplify this.) The exit channels are placed before the enter channels in the chans array so that the proper channel will be read no matter which Alternative is used. The fairSelect is employed here to ensure that the same four philosophers are not always chosen if a fifth is also trying to enter.

```
class Butler implements CSProcess {

  private final AltingChannelInput[] enters;
  private final AltingChannelInput[] exits;

  Butler(AltingChannelInput[] e, AltingChannelInput[] x) {
    enters = e;
    exits = x;
  }

  public void run() {
    int seats = enters.length;
    int nseated = 0;

    // set up arrays for select
    AltingChannelInput[] chans = new AltingChannelInput[2*seats];
    for (int i = 0; i < seats; ++i) {
      chans[i] = exits[i];
      chans[seats + i] = enters[i];
    }

    Alternative either = new Alternative(chans);
    Alternative exit = new Alternative(exits);

    for (;;) {
      // if max number are seated, only allow exits
      Alternative alt = (nseated <  seats-1)? either : exit;

      int i = alt.fairSelect();
      chans[i].read();

      // if i is in first half of array, it is an exit message
      if (i < seats) --nseated; else ++nseated;
    }
  }
}
```

The Philosopher processes run forever in a loop, alternating between thinking and eating. Before eating, philosophers must first enter their seats, then get both forks. After eating, they do the opposite. The eat and think methods are just no-ops here, but could be fleshed out to (for example) help animate a demonstration version by reporting status to JCSP channels and processes that interface into AWT.

```
class Philosopher implements CSProcess {

    private final ChannelOutput leftFork;
    private final ChannelOutput rightFork;
    private final ChannelOutput enter;
    private final ChannelOutput exit;

    Philosopher(ChannelOutput l, ChannelOutput r,
                ChannelOutput e, ChannelOutput x) {
        leftFork = l;
        rightFork = r;
        enter = e;
        exit = x;
    }

    public void run() {

        for (;;) {

            think();

            enter.write(null);          // get seat
            leftFork.write(null);       // pick up left
            rightFork.write(null);      // pick up right

            eat();

            leftFork.write(null);       // put down left
            rightFork.write(null);      // put down right
            exit.write(null);           // leave seat

        }

    }

    private void eat() {}
    private void think() {}
}
```

Finally, we can create a College class to represent the parallel composition of the Forks, Philosophers, and Butler. The channels are constructed using a JCSP convenience function create that creates arrays of channels. The Parallel constructor accepts an array of CSProcess, which is first loaded with all of the participants.

```
class College implements CSProcess {
  final static int N = 5;

  private final CSProcess action;

  College() {
    One2OneChannel[] lefts = One2OneChannel.create(N);
    One2OneChannel[] rights = One2OneChannel.create(N);
    One2OneChannel[] enters = One2OneChannel.create(N);
    One2OneChannel[] exits = One2OneChannel.create(N);

    Butler butler = new Butler(enters, exits);

    Philosopher[] phils = new Philosopher[N];
    for (int i = 0; i < N; ++i)
      phils[i] = new Philosopher(lefts[i], rights[i],
                                 enters[i], exits[i]);

    Fork[] forks = new Fork[N];
    for (int i = 0; i < N; ++i)
      forks[i] = new Fork(rights[(i + 1) % N], lefts[i]);

    action = new Parallel(
      new CSProcess[] {
        butler,
        new Parallel(phils),
        new Parallel(forks)
      });
  }

  public void run() { action.run(); }

  public static void main(String[] args) {
    new College().run();
  }
}
```

4.5.2   Further Readings

CSP has proven to be a successful approach to the design and analysis of systems that can be usefully expressed as bounded sets of identityless, interfaceless processes communicating via synchronous channels. CSP was introduced in:

Hoare, C. A. R. *Communicating Sequential Processes*, Prentice Hall, 1985.

An updated account appears in:

Roscoe, A. William. *The Theory and Practice of Concurrency*, Prentice Hall, 1997.

Several of the texts listed in Chapter 1 (including the book by Burns and Welling in §1.2.5.4) discuss CSP in the course of describing constructs in occam and Ada.

Other related formalisms, design techniques, languages, and frameworks have adopted different base assumptions that adhere more closely to the characteristics of other concurrent systems and/or to different styles of analysis. These include Milner's CCS and π-calculus, and Berry's Esterel. See:

Milner, Robin. *Communication and Concurrency*, Prentice Hall, 1989.

Berry, Gerard. "The Foundations of Esterel", in Gordon Plotkin, Colin Stirling, and Mads Tofte (eds.), *Proof, Language and Interaction*, MIT Press, 1998.

As package support becomes available for these and related approaches to concurrent system design, they become attractive alternatives to the direct use of thread-based constructs in the development of systems that are best viewed conceptually as collections of active objects. For example, *Triveni* is an approach based in part on Esterel, and is described in:

Colby, Christopher, Lalita Jategaonkar Jagadeesan, Radha Jagadeesan, Konstantin Läufer, and Carlos Puchol. "Objects and Concurrency in Triveni: A Telecommunication Case Study in Java", *USENIX Conference on Object-Oriented Technologies and Systems (COOTS)*, 1998.

Triveni is supported by a Java programming language package (see the online supplement). Among its main differences from CSP is that active objects in Triveni communicate by issuing events. Triveni also includes computation and composition rules surrounding the interruption and suspension of activities upon reception of events, which adds to expressiveness especially in real-time design contexts.

Index

Note: Entries of the form DP(nnn) are references to Gamma, Erich, Richard Helm, Ralph Johnson, and John Vlissides. *Design Patterns: Elements of Reusable Object-Oriented Software.* Addison-Wesley, 1995.

A

ABCL
bibliographic reference; 341
abrupt termination
See Also cancellation; exceptions; failure
as interruption response, issues; 170
as failure response; 162
Abstract Data Type (ADT)
term description; 72
AbstractTank class (code); 63
acceptance
Ada concurrency constructs; 182
of messages, state-based; 181-182
access
See Also visibility
control
confinement use of; 99
lack, as problem; 147
security vs. multithreaded practices; 39
using thread groups; 17
accessors
chained node traversal use; 84
lock, java.awt use; 144
synchronization reduction; 118-119
term description; 8
AccountHolder class (code); 134
AccountRecorder class (code); 134
AccountUser class (code); 250, 259-260
acquire-release protocols
See Also synchronization; Sync interface
implementation of; 265-267
latches use; 229
locks; 77

acquire-release protocols (*continued*)
mutex; 148
semaphore use; 220
actions
delegating; 268-274
joint; 237-248, *See Also* state; transactions
delegation techniques using; 268
splitting classes with; 265
provisional, as rollback technique; 163
state dependent; 273-274
activation(s)
constraints; 161
oneway message examples; 285
remote activation protocols; 286
active
ActiveRunnableExecutor class, (code); 368
activity-centric vs. object-centric views; 37
objects; 30, 367-376
bibliographic references; 376;
remote message passing use; 31
actors
active object design and use; 367-376
CSP processes as; 369
models; 30
compared with tasks; 281-282
Ada
bibliographic references; 33
concurrency constructs; 182
CSP impact on; 369
tasking; 286
Adapter pattern; 59-60, DP(139)
See Also before/after patterns; Composite pattern; containment; delegation; Proxy pattern
AdaptedPerformer class, (code); 59
AdaptedTank class, (code); 60
as before/after pattern; 58
confinement use; 108

Adapter pattern *(continued)*
in flow networks; 314-315
method adapters; 64-65
interface use; 64
mutex use; 150-151
as naming incompatibility solution; 59
read-only adapters; 132-135
implementation steps; 132
subclassing compared with; 61
synchronization layering; 109
Address class (code); 110
AdjustableDim class (code); 126
AdjustableLoc class (code); 126
administrative control
of concurrent execution; 21
ADT (Abstract Data Type)
as immutability application; 72-73
agent(s)
mobile agent frameworks, runnable event
message format use; 286
aggregation
fixed containment as implementation of; 108
inheritance anomaly issues applicable to;
214
operations, synchronization of; 80-81
synchronization weakening impact; 119
Aleph
bibliographic reference; 304
algorithms
See Also patterns
computation tree; 358
concurrent, bibliographic references; 33
concurrent programming, bibliographic
references; 33
deadlock detection, (footnote); 194
divide-and-conquer
custom queue use; 293
Fork/Join pattern; 344
Dekker's; 280
elevator, scheduling service use; 337
Jacobi; 358
wait-free, bibliographic references; 145
alias
detection, as liveness protection; 88, 152
Alternator class (code); 321
ambiguity
avoiding, with final keyword; 12
animation
AnimationApplet class, (code); 120
ParticleApplet illustration of; 9
anomalies
See inheritance anomalies

anonymous
identity of worker threads; 292
inner classes
implementing Runnable as; 9
Method Adapters pattern use; 64
read-only adapter classes; 135
synchronized Adapter classes, creating; 109
API documentation
See http://java.sun.com
apparent-self argument
delegation alternative to this; 62
applet(s)
Applet class
ParticleApplet use (code); 11
start method; 9
stop method; 9
conventions; 9
java.applet package; 286
applications
component-based software; 20
embedded systems; 20
GUI-based applications; 20
I/O processing; 20
mobile code; 20
number crunching; 20
simulation; 20
web services; 19
architectures (computer)
bibliographic references; 98
array(s)
bounded buffer use; 200, 223
Copy-on-Write pattern; 138
locking restrictions; 74
volatile; 97
as-if-serial semantics
term description; 91
aspect-oriented programming
bibliographic reference; 67
assembly
systems, as oneway message structure; 305
AssertionError class (code); 58
assignment
See Also atomic(ity); commit; state
atomic commitment use in place of; 140
asynchronous
activities, event-based system use; 23
AsynchRenderer class, (code); 333
cancellation; 169
termination; 174-175
ATCheckingAccount class (code); 243
Atomic Commitment pattern
as optimistic update technique; 140-141

atomic(ity)
  See Also confinement; exclusion
  Atomic Commitment pattern; 140-141
  of fields; 129
  of guarded waits; 188
  Java memory model guarantees and rules;
      93-94
  joint actions; 237-248
  objects
      requirements for; 78-79
      See Also synchronization
  `synchronized` block use; 7
  `synchronized` method and block
      relationship to; 77
  term description; 6, 40
  transactions; 249
  `volatile` keyword impact on; 74
ATSavingsAccount class (code); 244
attributes
  representation; 26
  safety; 41
  term description; 2
authors
  See bibliography, authors
autonomy
  in concurrency control; 21
AWT
  See `java.awt` package

B

Back-Offs
  See Also recovery
  exponential; 165
  in joint actions; 242
  mutex use; 151-152
  timed; 197
back-pressure notification
  as saturation response; 293
balancing
  design forces; 117
balking
  `BoundedBufferWithSemaphores` support
      of; 224
  as guarded method strategy; 179
  layering guards technique as alternative to;
      211
  as time-out backup strategy; 181
`BankAccount` class
  (code); 241
  `AccountUser` class; 250
`BarePoint` class (code); 109

barriers; 362-365
  cyclic, term description; 362
  in Fork/Join pattern, callbacks; 353
  as task-based parallel programming design;
      343
`BasicBox` class (code); 312
`BasicBoxSource` class (code); 323
batons
  group confinement protocols; 111
before/after patterns; 57-67
  See Also Adapter pattern; layering;
      subclassing
  Adapter pattern; 58
  bibliographic references; 66
  Command Object pattern; 64
  Conflict Sets pattern; 204
  error handler use; 166
  in Readers and Writers pattern; 208
  Method Adapters pattern
      interface use; 150
      mutex use; 58
  in Readers and Writers pattern; 207-210
  self-checking code use; 58
  subclass-based; 58, 61-63
begin
  term description; 251
bibliography
  active objects; 376
  authors
      *Note: A star indicates first author in a
          listed bibliographic reference.*
      *Abelson, Harold; 66
      *Adve, Sarita; 98
      *Agha, Bul; 35
      *Agha, Gul; 35
      Agrawala, Ashok; 36
      Anderson, Bruce; 217
      *Andrews, Gregory; 33
      *Apt, Krzysztof; 54
      *Arnold, Ken; 18, 36
      Arnold, Ken; 304
      *Atkinson, Colin; 54
      Bacon, David; 115
      *Bacon, Jean; 264
      Bal, Henri; 304
      *Barbosa, Valmir; 35
      *Beck, Kent; 55, 67
      *Ben-Ari, M.; 33
      Berg, Daniel; 34
      *Bernstein, Arthur; 33

bibliography, authors *(continued)*
*Berry, Gerard; 376
Bhoedjang, Raoul; 304
*Birman, Kenneth; 35
*Birtwistle, Graham; 33
Blaha, Michael; 54
Bobrow, Daniel; 66
Booch, Grady; 18
*Booch, Grady; 54
*Briot, Jean-Pierre; 35
*Buhr, Peter; 33
*Buhr, R.J.A.; 54
*Burns, Alan; 33, 36
*Buschmann, Frank; 66
*Bustard, David; 33
*Butenhof, David; 34
Campbell, Roy; 235
*Campione, Mary; 18
*Cardelli, Luca; 115
*Cargill, Thomas; 280
*Caromel, Denis; 341
*Carriero, Nicholas; 54
Casselman, R.S.; 54
Cattell, Rick; 264
*Cellary, Wojciech; 264
*Chandy, K. Mani; 54
Coffin, Michael; 33
*Colby, Christopher; 376
*Cook, Steve; 54
*Coplien, James; 66
*Coulouris, George; 35
Crowston, Kevin; 248
*Czajkowski, Grzegorz; 177
*D'Souza, Desmond; 54
*Dahl, Ole-Johan; 33
Dahl, Ole-Johan; 33
Danforth, Scott; 66
Daniels, John; 54
Davis, Geoff; 33
*de Champeaux, Dennis; 54
de Champeaux, Dennis; 115
des Rivieres, Jim; 66
Dijkstra, Edsger; 33
Dispasquale, Mark; 34
Dollimore, Jean; 35
*Dybvig, R. Kent; 341
*Dyson, Paul; 217
Eddy, Frederick; 54
Elder, John; 33
*Epema, Dick H.J.; 235
*Fagin, Ronald; 248
Faure, Penelope; 54
Feeley, Marc; 341

bibliography, authors *(continued)*
Fekete, Alan; 264
Feldman, Jerry; 177
*Filman, Robert; 35
Fisher, Maydene; 264
*Fishwick, Paul; 55
*Fleiner, Claudio; 177
*Forman, Ira; 66
Forman, Ira; 248
Fortier, Michel; 33
*Foster, Ian; 366
*Fowler, Martin; 18, 66, 145
*Francez, Nissim; 248
*Freeman, Eric; 304
Friedman, Daniel; 35
*Frigo, Matteo; 366
Galvin, Peter; 34
*Gamma, Erich; 66, 217
Gamma, Erich; 67
Garlan, David; 66
*Gehani, Narain; 33
Geib, Jean-Marc; 35
Gelenbe, E.; 264
Gelernter, David; 54
Gharachorloo, K.; 98
*Gibbs, Simon; 55
Goldberg, Arthur; 115
*Gomaa, Hassan; 36
Gordon, Andrew; 115
*Gosling, James; 18
Gosling, James; 18
*Gray, Jim; 264
Guerraoui, Rachid; 35
*Guerraoui, Rachid; 35
Gullekson, Garth; 36
Halpern, Joseph; 248
Hamilton, Graham; 264
Hansen, Per Brinch; 33
*Hanson, David; 34
Hapner, Mark; 264
Harrison, Tim; 341
*Hartley, Stephen; 34
Helm, Richard; 66
Hennessy, John; 98
*Henning, Michi; 304
*Herlihy, Maurice; 145
Hieb, Robert; 341
Hoare, C.A.R.; 33
*Hoare, C.A.R.; 376
*Hogg, John; 115
*Holmes, David; 66
*Holt, R.C.; 34
Holt, R.C.; 115

bibliography, authors *(continued)*
  *Holub, Allen; 34
  *Humphrey, Watts; 55
  Hupfer, Susan; 304
  Irwin, John; 67
  *Jackson, Michael; 54
  Jacobson, Ivar; 18
  Jagadeesan, Lalita Jategaonkar; 376
  Jagadeesan, Radha; 376
  *Jain, Raj; 55
  *Jarvinen, Hannu-Matti; 248
  *Jensen, Kurt; 54
  Johnson, Ralph; 66
  Joy, Bill; 18
  *Khoshafian, Setrag; 264
  *Kiczales, Gregor; 66, 67
  Kindberg, Tim; 35
  Kramer, Jeff; 34
  Kurki-Suonio, Reino; 248
  Lamping, John; 67
  *Lamport, Leslie; 54
  *Langendoen, Koen; 304
  Laufer, Konstantin; 376
  Lea, Doug; 54, 115
  Leiserson, Charles; 366
  *Leveson, Nancy; 54
  *Levi, Shem-Tov; 36
  *Lewis, Bil; 34
  Lewis, Philip; 33
  *Li, Gong; 177
  Lohr, Klaus-Peter; 35
  Loingtier, Jean-Marc; 67
  Lopes, Cristina Videira; 67
  Lorensen, William; 54
  Lowry, Andy; 115
  *Lynch, Nancy; 35, 264
  *MacDonald, Steve; 366
  Maeda, Chris; 67
  *Magee, Jeff; 34
  *Malone, Thomas; 248
  *Manna, Zohar; 54
  Marques, Jose Alves; 66
  *Massingill, Berna; 366
  Mattson, Timothy; 366
  McGettrick, Andrew; 33
  *McHale, Ciaran; 217
  *McKenney, Paul; 158
  Mendhekar, Anurag; 67
  Merritt, Michael; 264
  Meunier, Regine; 66
  *Michael, Maged; 145
  *Milner, Robin; 376
  Misra, Jayedev; 54

bibliography, authors *(continued)*
  *Mizuno, Masaaki; 280
  Morzy, Tadeusz; 264
  Moses, Yoram; 248
  *Mullender, Sape; 35
  Myhrtag, Bjorn; 33
  *Nelson, Greg; 34
  Nierstrasz, Oscar; 35
  *Nierstrasz, Oscar; 35
  *Norton, Scott; 34
  Nygaard, Kristen; 33
  O'Sullivan, Bryan; 36
  Olderog, Ernst-Rudiger; 54
  Omohundro, Stephen; 34
  *Ousterhout, John; 304
  *Patterson, David; 98
  Pereira, Joao; 66
  Pneuli, Amir; 54
  *Pope, Alan; 304
  Premerlani, William; 54
  Puchol, Carlos; 376
  *Pyarali, Irfan; 341
  Randall, Keith; 366
  *Raynal, Michel; 36
  Reenskaug, Trygve; 54
  *Renzel, Klaus; 177
  Reuter, Andreas; 264
  *Rising, Linda; 66
  *Rito Silva, Antonio; 66
  Riveill, Michel; 35
  Rohnert, Hans; 66
  *Roosta, Seyed; 366
  *Roscoe, A. William; 376
  *Rosenschein, Jeffrey; 248
  Roudier, Yves; 341
  Rozenberg, Grzegorz; 54
  *Rumbaugh, James; 18, 54
  Sakkinnen, Markku; 248
  Sanders, Beverly; 366
  *Sane, Aamod; 235
  Schaeffer, Jonathan; 366
  Scheifler, Robert; 36
  *Schimmel, Curt; 98
  Schmidt, Douglas C.; 341
  *Schneider, Fred; 33
  Scott, Kendal; 18
  Scott, Michael; 145
  *Selic, Bran; 36
  *Shaw, Mary; 66
  *Silberschatz, Avi; 34
  *Skillicorn, David; 366
  Sommerlad, Peter; 66
  *Sommerlad, Peter; 235

bibliography, authors *(continued)*
Stal, Michael; 66
Steele, Guy; 18
*Stoutamire, David; 34
Stoutamire, David; 177
*Strom, Robert; 115
*Stroud, Robert; 248
Sussman, Gerald; 66
Systa, Kari; 248
Szafron, Duane; 366
Talia, Domenico; 366
*Tanenbaum, Andrew; 34
Tokoro, Mario; 341
Tsichritzis, Dennis; 55, 35
*Ungar, David; 66
*van Leeuwen, Jan; 35
Vardi, Moshe; 248
Vinoski, Steve; 304
Vlissides, John; 66
von Eicken, Thorsten; 177
von Renesse, Robert; 35
Waldo, Jim; 36
Walrath, Kathy; 18
Ward, Paul; 36
*Watkins, Kevin; 55
*Wegner, Peter; 55
Wegner, Peter; 35
Weihl, William; 264
Wellings, Andrew; 33
Wellings, Andy; 36
Welsh, Jim; 33
*White, Seth; 264
Wills, Alan; 54, 115
*Wilson, Gregory; 366
Wollrath, Ann; 36
*Woolf, Bobby; 341
Yellin, Daniel; 115
Yemini, Shaula; 115
Yonezawa, Aki; 35
Yonezawa, Akinori; 35
*Yonezawa, Akinori; 341
Zlotkin, Gilad; 248
*Zomaya, Albert; 366
Zorzo, Avelino; 248
before/after patterns; 66-67
concurrency control; 235
concurrent algorithms; 33
concurrent programming; 33-34
confinement; 115
exclusion; 98, 115
failure; 177
forces; 54-55
JLS (Java Language Specification); 18

bibliography *(continued)*
joint actions; 248
objects; 33-36
oneway messages; 304, 324
parallel decomposition; 366
refactoring
exclusion-based; 145
state-based; 217
synchronization; 98
thread services; 341
threads, introduction; 18
transactions; 264
UML diagrams; 18
utilities
implementation; 280
lock; 158
binary
latch, *See* latches
semaphore, term description; 220
blocking
event queue issues; 296
as policy domain; 50
as saturation response; 293
in single-threaded processes; 22
threads, `join` use for; 329
blocks
synchronization of; 76
bottom-up design
liveness as priority for; 49
`BoundedBuffer` (code); 200
`BoundedBufferWithDelegates` (code); 271-272
`BoundedBufferWithMonitorObjects` (code); 273-274
`BoundedBufferWithSemaphores` (code); 224
`BoundedBufferWithStateTracking` (code); 201
`BoundedCounter` compared with; 200
`BoundedCounter` interface (code); 180
`BoundedCounterWithAccept` (pseudocode); 182
`BoundedCounterWithStateVariable` (code); 202
`BoundedCounterWithWhen` (pseudocode); 181
`Box` abstract class (code); 311
`BoxPredicate` class (code); 322
buffers
bounded
as channel; 200
delegated action version; 270-272
semaphores use with; 223-225
`BufferArray` class, (code); 223
exchanger use with; 231

buffers *(continued)*
  polling design use; 303
  unbounded; 130, 293
busy waits; 196-198
  latching application; 230
  layered guard alternative; 211
  in polling; 303
`Butler` class (code); 373

C

`C` class (code); 174
callables
  `Callable` interface, (code); 334
  Futures pattern use; 334-336
callbacks
  completion
    bibliographic reference; 341
    implementation issues; 326
    joining threads comparison with; 329
    as thread service strategy; 325-328
  error handler use; 166, 167
  in Fork/Join pattern; 353-355
caller copy
  as confinement protocol; 102
calls (open)
  See open calls
`CancellableReader` class (code); 172
cancellation 169-176
  See Also exceptions
  bibliographic reference; 177
  in Fork/Join pattern; 355-357
  in mutexes; 150
  interrupted waits; 188
  `InterruptedException` handling; 170-171
  multiphase; 175-176
  retry termination upon; 165
  timed wait triggering of; 194
  in worker threads; 294
`Canvas` class
  `ParticleCanvas` use, (code); 8
capabilities
  group confinement protocols; 111
capacity
  as performance measure; 46
  term description; 46
cascading
  algorithms, retry use by; 165
  failures, `InvocationTargetException`
    indication of; 167
catch clause
  error handling relationship to; 167
  handling, in mutexes; 150
  `notify` strategies; 191

CCS
  bibliographic reference; 376
`Cell` class (code); 87
`CellUsingBackoff` class (code); 152
`CellUsingReorderedBackoff` (code); 153
changes
  state
    as triggers; 182
    Copy-on-Write pattern handling; 136
    immutable object analog to; 73
    `notifyAll` indication of; 189
    in Readers and Writers pattern; 207
    vetoable; 261-263
channels
  `Channel` interface
    (code); 199, 225
  CSP, term description; 369
  message passing use; 286
  synchronous
    exchanger relationship to; 231
    semaphores use to implement; 225-226
    term description; 225, 292
    Worker Thread pattern use; 292
  term description; 28
  Worker-Threads pattern use; 290
check-out/check-in protocol
  in resource pool management; 221
checking
  check-and-act strategies
    as conservative state-dependent strategy;
      160
    as guarded wait policy; 188
  of conditions, `while` loop use; 187
  Double Check pattern, as synchronization
    reduction tool; 120-121
  failure, escalation rule issues; 198
checkpointing
  as rollback technique; 163
Cilk package
  bibliographic reference; 366
`Class` **class**
  field protection by; 77
classes
  See Also code listings
  collapsing; 273-274
  inner; 9, 12, 64
  locking; 77
  as message format; 286
  refactoring
    exclusion strategies; 117-145
    state-dependent strategies; 199-217
  splitting 124-126
  term description; 2

cleanup
  during cancellation; 169
clean-fail
  term description; 163
clearing
  interruption status, of threads; 16
client
  ClientUsingSocket class, (code); 165
  side locking
    transactions and; 249
    traversal and; 81-82
  term description; 2
Cloner class (code); 321
CLOS (Common Lisp Object System)
  bibliographic references; 66
closed systems
  client-side locking in; 82
  notify use; 192
  reference confinement checking; 100
  reusability issues; 49-50
  wait use; 192
closures
  See Method Adapters
code
  conventions; 2
code listings
  AbstractTank; 63
  AccountHolder; 134
  AccountRecorder; 134
  AccountUser; 259-260
  AccountUser class; 250
  ActiveRunnableExecutor; 368
  ActiveWaterTank; 367
  AdaptedPerformer; 59
  AdaptedTank; 60
  Address; 110
  AdjustableDim; 126
  AdjustableLoc; 126
  Alternator; 321
  AnimationApplet; 120
  AssertionError; 58
  AsynchRenderer; 333
  ATCheckingAccount; 243
  ATSavingsAccount; 244
  BankAccount; 241
  BarePoint; 109
  BasicBox; 312
  BasicBoxSource; 323
  BoundedBuffer; 200
  BoundedBufferWithStateTracking; 201
  BoundedBufferWithDelegates; 271-272
  BoundedBufferWithMonitorObjects;
    273-274

code listings *(continued)*
  BoundedBufferWithSemaphores; 224
  BoundedCounter; 180
  BoundedCounterWithAccept; 182
  BoundedCounterWithStateVariable; 202
  BoundedCounterWithWhen; 181
  Box; 311
  BoxPredicate; 322
  BufferArray; 223
  Butler; 373
  C; 174
  Callable; 334
  CancellableReader; 172
  Cell; 87
  CellUsingReorderedBackoff; 153
  Channel; 199, 225
  ClientUsingSocket; 165
  Cloner; 321
  Collector; 320
  College; 375
  ColoredThing; 262-263
  CondVar class; 233
  CopyOnWriteArrayList; 138
  CyclicBarrier; 363
  DataRepository; 158
  DevNull; 315
  Disk; 337
  DiskReadTask; 339
  DiskTask; 338
  DiskTaskQueue; 340
  DiskWriteTask; 339
  doSwapValue; 89
  Dot; 137
  DualInputAdapter; 315
  DualInputPushStage; 314
  DualOutputPushStage; 316
  EagerSingletonCounter; 86
  EmptyingLoop; 232
  Even; 75
  EvilAccountRecorder; 135
  ExceptionEvent; 168
  ExceptionEventListener; 168
  Executor interface; 289
  ExpandableArray; 79
  ExpandableArrayWithIterator; 83
  FailedTransferException; 259
  Failure; 253
  Fib; 349
  FibVCB; 354
  FibVL class; 352
  FIFOSemaphore class; 278-280
  FileApplication; 328
  FileReader; 326

code listings *(continued)*
 FileReaderApp; 327
 FillAndEmpty; 231
 FillingLoop; 232
 FJTask; 346
 Flipper; 318
 Fork; 372
 Fraction; 72
 FutureResult; 335
 GamePlayer; 193
 GuardedClassUsingNotify; 192
 GuardedWait; 187
 HandledService; 166
 Handler; 283
 HorizontallyJoinedPair; 313
 HostWithExecutor class; 289
 ImmutableAdder; 71
 ImmutablePoint; 136
 InsufficientFunds; 133
 Interior; 360
 Inventory; 204-205
 IOEventTask; 301
 Jacobi; 361
 JacobiSegment; 365
 JoinedPair; 312
 Joiner; 319
 JTree; 360
 LatchingThermometer class; 230
 LazySingletonCounter; 85
 Leaf; 360
 LinkedCell; 123
 LinkedQueue; 131
 ListUsingMutex; 154
 LockManager; 156
 LockSplitShape; 128
 MaxSizePredicate; 322
 Mutex; 148, 220
 NQueens; 356-357
 Observer; 247
 OpenCallHost; 287
 Optimistic; 140
 OptimisticDot; 141
 OwnedPartWithGuard; 216
 Painter; 317
 Part; 143
 Particle; 7
 ParticleApplet; 11
 ParticleCanvas; 8
 ParticleUsingMutex; 149
 ParticleUsingWrapper; 151
 PartWithGuard; 215
 PassThroughShape; 125
 Person; 129

code listings *(continued)*
 Philosopher; 374
 Pic; 331
 PictureApp; 331
 PictureAppWithFuture; 333
 PictureDisplayWithFutureResult; 336
 PlainThreadExecutor class; 289
 PlainWorkerPool; 291
 Player; 229
 Plotter; 100
  showNextPointV2 method; 102
 PollingWorker class; 302
 Pool class; 222
 Printer; 114
 PrintService; 114
 PriorityQueue class; 297
 Procedure; 80
 ProxyAccount; 258
 PThreadsStyleBuffer class; 234
 PushSource; 314
 PushStage; 314
 ReaderWithTimeout; 173
 ReadWrite; 208-209
 ReadWriteLock; 157
 Relay; 73
 Renderer; 331
 RetryableTransferException; 259
 RWLock class; 210
 ScheduledDisk; 339
 Screener class, (code); 322
 Segment; 364
 Semaphore; 266-267
 ServerUsingCallback; 167
 ServerWithAssignableHelper; 122
 ServerWithException; 166
 ServerWithOpenCall; 122
 ServerWithStateUpdate; 121
 ServiceIssuingExceptionEvent; 168
 ServiceUsingThreadLocal; 105
 ServiceUsingThreadWithOutputStream;
  104
 SessionBasedService; 101
 SessionTask class; 300
 SetCheck; 90
 Shape; 124
 SimpleBoundedCounter; 189
 SimpleTransBankAccount; 257
 SingleOutputPushStage; 316
 Solver; 344
 SpinLock; 198
 StackEmptyException; 211
 StatelessAdder; 71
 StaticCounter; 86

385

code listings *(continued)*
  Subject; 247
  swapValue; 89
  Sync; 265
  SynchedPoint; 109
    getPoint method; 132
  SynchronizedAddress; 110
  SynchronizedInt; 129
  SynchronousChannel; 226
  Tank; 58
  TankOp; 64
  TankWithMethodAdapter; 65
  Terminator; 176
  ThreadPerMessageHost class; 288
  ThreadPerSessionBasedService; 103
  ThreadWithOutputStream; 104
  TimeOutBoundedCounter; 195
  TimerDaemon class; 297
  Transactor; 253
  TransBankAccount; 254
  TSBoolean; 242
  VerticallyJoinedPair; 313
  VFloat; 97
  Waiter; 331
  WaitingStack class; 212
  WaterTank; 26
  WebService; 283
  WithMutex; 150
  WrappedBox; 313
  Wrapper; 317
  X; 186
collapsing
  classes, delegated action use of; 273-274
collection(s)
  See Also java.util package
  classes, ThreadGroup use by; 17
  Collection framework, Adapter pattern
      use for layered synchronization; 109
  operations, synchronization of; 80-81
  read-write lock use; 158
  stable, Copy-on-Write pattern use; 137
  of synchronized objects, traversal of; 80
collectors
  Collector class, (code); 320
  term description; 309
  College class (code); 375
  ColoredThing class (code); 262-263
combiners
  in flow networks
      assembly line example; 318-319
      term description; 309
Command Object pattern DP(233)
  as before/after pattern; 64

commands
  message format; 286
  oneway message examples; 285
commit
  atomic, as optimistic update technique; 140-
      141
  conservative and optimistic techniques,
      (table); 256
  failure, transaction frameworks, handling;
      259
  term description; 251
communication
  object, term description; 28
  as thread autonomy vs. overhead tradeoff; 23
  among threads, methods for; 16
compare and swap
  as optimistic update technique; 140
compilation
  dynamic, extensibility impact; 51
  static type safety; 70
compiler
  optimization, impact on program execution;
      91
completion
  callbacks, bibliographic reference; 341
completion *(continued)*
  Completion Callbacks pattern
      implementation; 326
      joining threads comparison with; 329
      as thread service strategy; 325
  flags, volatile keyword use; 97
  indicators, latches use for; 230
component
  See Also java.beans package
  based software, as concurrent programming
      application; 20
  frameworks, command message format use;
      286
Composite pattern; DP(163)
  as Adapter pattern variation; 59
composition
  See Also layering
  Composition-Filters system, bibliographic
      references; 217
  context-dependence; 52
  CSP; 370
  delegation-based; 59
  of flow networks; 307-310
  inheritance anomaly issues; 214
  layering concurrency control with,
      bibliographic reference; 66
  of oneway messages; 305-324

computation
objects, types of; 28
safety representation constraints; 42
trees; 358-361
building and using; 359
as task-based parallel programming
design; 343
computer systems
as concurrent execution construct; 21
ConcreteTank class (code); 63
concurrency
algorithms for, bibliographic references; 33
ConcurrentModificationException; 138
constructs
bibliographic references; 18
execution; 21-23
using; 5-18
control; 219-235
bibliographic references; 235
functionality separation from, Template
Method pattern use; 212
concurrent programming
bibliographic references; 33-34
concurrent programming compared with; 19
constraint, term description; 182
distributed programming vs.; 19-20
event-based; 24-25
languages; 25
object-oriented; 1-68
vs. sequential programming OO; 24
systems; 25
term description; 19
condition(s)
checking, while loop use; 187
postconditions
before/after pattern relationship to; 58
optimistic strategy check of; 161
rules use for representation of; 27
term description; 159
preconditions
before/after pattern relationship to; 58
representation of, rules use for; 27
term description; 159
testing, as guarded method strategy; 179
queues; 275
race, term description; 40
slipped; 190
variables 233
bibliographic references; 235
concurrency control utility use; 233-234
as mutex application; 155
CondVar class, (code); 233

confinement
See Also exclusion; immutability
Adapter pattern use; 108
as exclusion strategy; 69, 99-115
Factory Method pattern use; 101
formalisms, bibliographic references; 115
within groups; 111-115
impact on lock releasing strategies; 7
across methods; 100-102
nested monitors and; 215-216
within objects; 107-110
read-only adapters as alternative to; 132
within threads; 103-106, 295
conflict(s)
Conflict Sets pattern; 203-206
transaction use; 258
read-write; 40
resolution; 206, 240
write-write; 40
connections
in flow networks; 315
OO, term description; 28
connectivity
as flow network composition rule; 308
consensus
barrier use; 363
in transactions; 251
conservative
state-dependent strategies; 160
transactions; 251, 255
consistent
term description; 40
constraints
invariant; 27
properties, JavaBeans; 261
representational; 42-43
safety; 41
constructors
of immutable objects; 74
lazy thread; 294
in event frameworks; 296
synchronized keyword not part of; 76
thread; 13-14
containment
fixed, term description; 108
hierarchical
lock ordering manager use; 156
as nested monitor handling tool; 216
layered, open container use; 142
multilevel, lock utility use; 145
as node locking technique, during traversal;
84
open containers; 142-145

contention
contention-based failures, retry overhead issues; 165
factors than hinder performance; 47
lock; 44
context
in transaction frameworks; 106
dependence; 49
switching
vs. busy waits; 303
minimizing; 225
performance; 47
term description; 32
in Thread-Per-Message pattern; 288
variables, inner class capture of; 12
continuation
See Also interrupts, ignoring
continuation *(continued)*
as interruption response; 170
as failure response; 163, 162
control
logical control state, defining; 182-183
mechanisms, message acceptance, locks as form of; 78
methods, for threads; 16
systems, as oneway message structure; 305
cookie
term description; 326
cooperation
in delegation; 162
coordination
in flow networks; 324
task, bibliographic reference; 248
copying
by caller, as confinement protocol; 102
Copy-on-Write pattern; 136-141
atomic commitment; 140-141
internal copy-on-write; 137-138
optimistic updates; 139
in multicasting; 261
CopyOnWriteArrayList class (code); 138
error handler use; 167
joint action design use; 246
by receiver, as confinement protocol; 102
as reference access technique; 132
CORBA
active object use; 368
bibliographic references; 304
org.omg.corba, request message format use; 286
coroutines
term description; 24

correctness
as safety and liveness; 38
vs. quality of service; 20
countdowns
term description; 229
counting semaphore
See semaphore
coupling
lock, *See* hand-over-hand locking
participant, as joint action design issue; 238
CSP (Communicating Sequential Processes); 369-375
bibliographic references; 376
as concurrent programming style; 25
thread confinement requirements; 103
currentThread method
Thread class; 16
cyclic barriers
CyclicBarrier class, (code); 363
term description; 362

D

daemons
actor-based threads use with; 282
status attribute, in threads; 14
term description; 14
timers; 297-298
databases
bibliographic references; 264
dataflow
systems, as oneway message structure; 306
DataRepository class (code); 158
deadlock; 87
avoidance
back-off as technique for; 151
in flow networks; 310
in helper method design; 269
in joint action design; 240
with open container techniques; 142
as resource management technique; 113
resource ordering strategy; 88
shuffle; 153
detection algorithms, (footnote); 194
as joint action design issue; 238
term description; 45
time-out use to handle; 194
decision tables
as logical state analysis tool; 202
decomposition
of classes, as delegation design strategy; 268
Fork/Join pattern; 344-457
parallel; 343-366
bibliographic references; 366

decoupling
observers; 245-247
deferred-synchronous invocation
term description; 329
degradation
as performance measure; 46
term description; 46
Dekker's algorithm; 280
delegation
Adapter pattern as a form of; 59
as composition style; 59
to exception handlers; 162, 166-168
vs. inheritance; 61-62, 214
joint action use; 237
of state-dependent actions; 268-274
in object-based confinement,; 108
Self language bibliographic reference; 66
denial
resource, term description; 175
of service; 150
dependencies
state; 159-280
design
of action delegation; 268-270
bibliographic references; 54
bottom-up; 49
decisions, encapsulation rule; 214
encapsulation of, in versioned iterator; 84
forces; 37-55
of guarded waits; 187
inheritance anomalies; 212-214
of joint action; 238-244
liveness issues, in wait-based strategies; 189
notification strategies; 189
patterns, bibliographic references; 66
policy-driven 50-51
refactoring; 117
rewriting as tool; 214
rules 70
state-based; 181
top-down; 49
Worker Threads pattern tradeoffs; 292-294
"Design Patterns" reference
bibliographic reference; 66
destroy method
`Thread` class; 16
device
control, busy wait use; 196
`DevNull` class (code); 315
diagrams
notation; 3
Dining Philosophers problem
CSP solution; 371-375

directionality
as conflict resolution strategy; 240
as flow network composition rule; 308
DisCo
bibliographic reference; 248
`Disk` interface (code); 337
`DiskReadTask` class (code); 339
`DiskTask` abstract class (code); 338
`DiskTaskQueue` class (code); 340
`DiskWriteTask` class (code); 339
dispatching
event queues; 296
distributed systems
active object use; 30, 368
bibliographic references; 35, 237, 248
failure; 45
message formats; 286
programming; 19, 21
divide-and-conquer algorithms
in Fork/Join; 344-348
documentation
of policies; 70, 123, 162, 216
and reusability; 52-53
`doSwapValue` method (code); 89
`Dot` class (code); 137
`OptimisticDot` (code); 141
Double Check pattern
as synchronization reduction tool; 120-121
double dispatching
in joint action design; 238
dual output states
in flow networks; 320-322
`DualInputAdapter` class (code); 315
`DualInputPushStage` interface (code); 314
`DualOutputPushStage` class (code); 316
dynamic
compilation; 51
exclusion control; 143

E

`EagerSingletonCounter` class (code); 86
efficiency
of buffers; 225
as busy wait issue; 196
delegation techniques use; 268
vs. extensibility, in joint action design; 238
as performance measure; 46
of resource management; 290
term description; 46
Eiffel
bibliographic reference; 341
elevator algorithm
scheduling service use; 337

embedded systems
client-side locking in; 82
closure use with; 49
as concurrent programming application; 20
EmptyingLoop class (code); 232
encapsulation
See Also confinement
of closed systems; 49
of design decision rule; 214
of guards; 187, 214
of locking; 82
of notifications; 214
object, term description; 28
of states; 254
engineering methods
bibliographic references; 55
entry
term description; 286
enumeration
enumerate method, ThreadGroup class; 17
logical state variable use; 202
equality
equals method, overriding; 73
tests, in Adapters; 62
errors
See Also exceptions
Error class
abrupt termination for; 162
error handling; 167
thread termination by; 14
handlers; 163, 294
indicators, latches use for; 230
visibility-based; 95
Esterel
bibliographic reference; 376
Euclid
bibliographic references; 33
Even class, (code); 75
event(s)
change, vetoable; 261
channels, term description; 28
error handling use; 166
event-based programming; 24-25
Event-Driven I/O pattern; 299-303
EventDispatchThread class (java.awt),
    ParticleApplet use; 12
EventQueue class (java.awt),
    ParticleApplet use; 12
frameworks
Copy-on-Write pattern use; 137
as oneway message structure; 306
error handler use; 163, 167
runnable event message format use; 286

event(s) *(continued)*
indicators, latches use for; 230
message format; 286
notifications, callback replacement by; 328
oneway message examples; 285
queues, in Worker Threads; 295-296
runnable, term description; 286
EvilAccountRecorder class (code); 135
evolution
of class design; 117
as open system characteristic; 50
exceptions; 161-178
See Also cancellation; errors; failure
bibliographic references; 177
ConcurrentModificationException; 138
ExceptionEvent (code); 168
ExceptionEventListener (code); 168
exchanger requirements; 231
FailedTransferException (code); 259
IllegalMonitorStateException; 184
InterruptedIOException; 173
InterruptedException
    cancellation use; 12, 16, 169-171
    as interrupted wait response; 188
    mutex methods use; 148
    retry handling; 165
    in signature of guarded method; 188
    time-out use; 194-195
InvalidThreadStateException; 14
InvocationTargetException; 167
NullPointerException; 18, 162
in optimistic designs; 160
RuntimeException class 14, 162
ServerWithException; 166
ServiceIssuingExceptionEvent; 168
StackEmptyException; 211
try-and-see strategy use; 162-168
uncaughtException method; 18
UnsupportedOperationException; 135
exchangers
See Also latches; semaphores
bibliographic reference; 235
buffer-based; 270
concurrency control utility use; 231-232
exchange protocol; 112
exclusion; 69-158
See Also confinement; conflict sets;
        immutability; synchronization
bibliographic references; 98, 115
confinement use; 99-115
as consistency maintenance mechanism; 40
in guarded methods; 180
mutex; 148-156

exclusion *(continued)*
    resource ordering; 88-89
    semaphore use; 220-221
    strategies for; 69
    synchronization use; 75-98

execution
    concurrent execution constructs; 21-23
    state; 42, 203, 208, 275

executors
    `Executor` interface, (code); 289
    Futures pattern use; 334
    `HostWithExecutor` class, (code); 289
    `PlainThreadExecutor` class, (code); 289
    in worker threads; 291

exhaustion
    resource; 45

`ExpandableArray` (code); 79

`ExpandableArrayWithIterator` (code); 82

`ExpandableArrayWithIterator` (code); 83

exponential back-off
    retry use of; 165

extensibility
    See Also reusability
    as advantage of OO programming
        languages; 25
    protected qualifier use for; 3
    Conflict Sets pattern issues; 206
    Futures pattern, callables use; 334
    mutex design considerations; 150
    `notify` design issues; 192
    in oneway messages; 305-324
    as open system advantage; 50
    optimization for; 51

Extension Object pattern
    bibliographic reference; 217

extreme programming
    bibliographic references; 55

F

Factory Method pattern; DP(107)
    hand-off protocol use; 101
    transaction framework use; 253

failure
    See Also cancellation; exceptions
    bibliographic references; 177
    dealing with; 161-178
    distributed; 45
    escalation; 198
    `FailedTransferException` (code); 259
    `Failure` class, (code); 253
    in joint actions, bibliographic reference; 248
    as optimistic update issue; 139
    in versioned iterators; 84

fairness
    See Also performance; scheduling
    bibliographic references; 235, 248
    lock release, not guaranteed; 77
    priority methods as aid to; 14
    semaphores use to enhance; 227-228
    term description; 197
    in Thread-Per-Message pattern; 288

fast-fail iterators
    See Also traversal
    term description; 82

fault-tolerance
    in concurrency control; 21

Fibonacci example
    `Fib` class, (code); 349
    `FibVCB` class, (code); 354
    `FibVL` class, (code); 352
    Fork/Join pattern; 348-351

fields
    accessors; 118-119
    as attribute representations; 26
    initial values; 94
    isolating; 128-129
    static, `Class` use to protect; 77
    term description; 2
    thread-specific; 104
    visibility; 95
    `volatile`; 97

FIFO (First-In-First-Out)
    `FIFOSemaphore` (code); 278-280
    fairness; 227
    in Fork/Join pattern; 351
    queue; 130

Filaments package
    bibliographic reference; 366
    `FileApplication` class (code); 328
    `FileReader` interface (code); 326
    `FileReaderApp` class (code); 327
    `FillAndEmpty` class (code); 231
    `FillingLoop` class (code); 232

filters
    `Screener` class, (code); 322

`final` keyword
    See Also immutability
    buffer-based exchanger use; 270
    design strategies use of; 7
    immutability use; 74
    and inner classes; 12
    joint action design use; 238

`finally` clauses
    as cleanup location choice; 101
    in failure handling; 163-164

finite state machine (FSM)
bibliographic references; 217
as logical state analysis tool; 202
fixed containment
term description; 108
FJTask abstract class (code); 346
flexibility
See Also reusability
as delegation advantage; 61
as transaction advantage; 250
as worker thread advantage; 290
Flipper class (code); 318
Flow Networks patterns; 305-324
assembly line example; 311-324
bibliographic references; 324
development issues; 307-310
Flyweight pattern; DP(195)
immutability in; 73
forces; 37-55
balancing; 38, 49, 117
bibliographic references; 54-55
foreign code
cancellation issues; 175
forget protocol
in object confinement; 112
Fork class, (code); 372
Fork/Join pattern; 344-357
computation tree relationship to; 359
Fibonacci example; 348-351
formats
of messages, oneway; 286
Fraction class (code); 72
frameworks
component; 286
distributed; 368
event; 24
JavaSpaces, message passing use; 286
lightweight executable .
mapping to threads; 23
Worker Threads pattern as; 290
Fork/Join pattern as; 346-347
mobile agent; 286
FSM (finite state machine)
bibliographic references; 217
as logical state analysis tool; 202
function pointers
Method Adapters pattern; 64
Futures pattern
bibliographic references; 341
as concurrent programming style; 25
FutureResult class, (code); 335
join-based thread construction use; 332-336
thread service use; 325

G

GamePlayer class
(code); 193
actor-based threads use; 282
Player (code); 229
get methods
See accessors
getThreadGroup method; 17
give protocol
in object confinement; 112
GOF (Gang of Four)
bibliographic reference; 66
granularity
of concurrency; 21
in Fork/Join pattern; 345
of locks; 117
in Conflict Sets pattern; 206
splitting classes to obtain; 124
hand-over-hand traversal; 154
of notifications
improving; 199-217
of timed wait; 185
graphs
Visitor pattern support of iteration over; 84
ground objects
in Adapters; 108
groups
confinement within; 111-115
guarded methods; 179-198
See Also state
GuardedClassUsingNotify class, (code); 192
GuardedWait class, (code); 187
busy waits compared with; 196
callback use; 328
as conservative strategy; 160
fairness; 197
joint actions as; 237-248
layering; 211-212
See Also monitors
GUI-based applications
as concurrent programming application; 20
message formats; 286

H

hand-off protocol
term description; 101
hand-over-hand locking
mutex use for; 154
HandledService class (code); 166
Handler class (code); 283
handlers
error, as failure response; 166-168

hashcodes
hashCode method, overriding; 73
System.identityHashCode method; 88
helper(s)
See Also refactoring; splitting; utilities
delegation to, as efficiency technique; 268
lock splitting use; 273
splitting; 270
state-dependent action splitting use; 273
term description; 2
transaction framework use; 259
Hermes
bibliographic references; 115
hierarchical
containment
lock ordering manager use; 156
as nested monitor handling tool; 216
ordered locking, open container use; 142
history
log
as conflict documentation; 206
term description; 42
variables; 42
Hood package
bibliographic reference; 366
HorizontallyJoinedPair class (code); 313
host
term description; 2
hostile denial of service
resisting, mutex design; 150
HTTP servers
Worker Thread pattern use; 292

I

IO
See Also event(s)
channels use for; 28
as concurrent programming application; 20
event-driven; 299-303
interrupt handling precautions; 171
IOEventTask class (code); 301
liveness of; 44
retrying; 165
revocation; 171-173
rollback inapplicable for; 164
identity
ADT-style class masking of; 73
cookie use for, in completion callback
services; 326
equality testing; 222
object, term description; 28
transaction, key use for; 252
worker threads; 292

ignoring interrupts
See Also continuation; interrupt(s)
reasons for; 176
IllegalMonitorStateException
wait set violation causes; 184
image processing
deferred-synchronous invocation use; 329
immutability
See Also confinement; copy-on-write;
exclusion; synchronization
applications; 71-74
abstract data types; 72-73
sharing; 73
value containers; 73
construction of immutable objects; 74
as exclusion strategy; 69, 71-73
ImmutableAdder class, (code); 71
ImmutablePoint class
(code); 136
confinement use; 102
partial, term description; 73
incompatibilities
naming, Adapter pattern as solution for; 59
independence
as distributed computing advantage; 21
indexed
traversal, client-side locking and; 81-82
inheritance
See Also subclassing
anomalies; 51, 212-214
bibliographic references; 217
term description; 213
compared with delegation; 62
synchronized keyword not part of; 76
initialization
of immutable objects, constructor rules; 74
latches use for; 229
lazy, disadvantages and alternatives; 121, 86
inner classes
advantages and disadvantages of; 12
implementing Runnable as; 9
Method Adapters pattern use; 64
synchronization, outer class relationship; 76
instances
term description; 2
InsufficientFunds class (code); 133
intention locks
term description; 207
interaction diagrams
notation for; 3
interception
See layering

interfaces
of completion callback; 326
in flow networks; 313
in before/after patterns; 58
interfaces *(continued)*
`synchronized` keyword not part of; 76
term description; 9
of transaction participants; 253
interference
as concurrency problem; 6, 24
`Interior` class (code); 360
internal
disciplines, for open containers; 143-144
Internet
as open system example; 50
interoperability
as flow network composition rule; 308
interrupt(s)
See Also cancellation; exceptions; failure; recovery
ignoring; 176
`interrupt` method; 17
interrupted waits; 185, 188
`InterruptedException` class
cancellation use; 169
`interrupt` reasons for issuing; 16
as interrupted wait response; 188
mutex methods use; 148
retry handling; 165
as signature of guarded method; 188
stopping threads with; 12
as interruption response; 170-171
time-out use; 194
`InterruptedIOException`; 173
thread; 169-171
invalidation relations
term description; 206
`InvalidThreadStateException` class
triggering condition for; 14
invariants
as consistent state safety mechanism; 39
preserving, copy-on-write use; 136
self-checking code preservation of; 58
state constraints; 27
tests for, bibliographic reference; 67
weakening; 118
`Inventory` class (code); 204
inversions
priority, term description; 228
invocation
deferred-synchronous, term description; 329
`InvocationTargetException`
cascading failure indication; 167

IP (Interacting Processes)
bibliographic reference; 248
`isAlive` method; 14, 176
isolating fields
as synchronization splitting; 128-129
iteration
fast-fail, term description; 82
in Jacobi algorithm example; 361
open call in linked list use; 123
performance advantages, in Copy-on-Write pattern use; 138
vs. recursion, as barrier design consideration; 362
synchronization weakening impact; 119
versioned; 82-84
Visitor pattern extension of; 84
Iterator pattern; DP(257)
See iteration; traversal

J

Jacobi algorithm
as computation tree algorithm; 358
`Jacobi` class, (code); 361
`JacobiSegment` class, (code); 365
java.awt package
event handling in; 24
`EventDispatchThread` class; 10, 295
`ParticleApplet` use; 12
`EventQueue` class; 12
`Graphics` class; 6
message format use; 286
lock accessor use; 144
`MediaTracker` class; 329
java.beans package
vetoable changes in; 261-263
java.lang package
`Object`, as lock; 127
`Runnable` interface, *See* `Runnable` interface
`Thread` class; *See* thread(s)
`ThreadGroup` class; 17
`ThreadLocal` class; 105
Java Language Specification (JLS)
bibliographic reference; 18
memory model; 90-97
java.net package
`Socket`, time-out interrupts; 171
java.rmi package
request message format use; 286
java.util package
`Collection` framework
Adapter pattern use; 109
read-only adapter use; 135
`Iterator` class, fail-fast iterator use; 82

JavaSpaces
    bibliographic reference; 304
    message passing use; 286
javax.swing package
    event handling in; 24
    single-thread rule; 295
JCSP package; 370-371
    CSP support; 369
    Dining Philosophers solution using; 372
JDBC
    bibliographic references; 264
    as standardized transaction framework; 250
JMS
    bibliographic reference; 304
join(ing)
    join method; 16
    JoinedPair class, (code); 312
    Joiner abstract class, (code); 319
    term description; 251
    threads; 329-331
    transactions; 255
joint actions; 237-248
    See Also transactions
    bibliographic references; 248
    delegation techniques using; 268
    splitting classes with; 265
    transactions, relationship to; 249
JTree abstract class (code); 360
JTS
    as standardized transaction framework; 250
JVM (Java Virtual Machine)
    term description; 19

K

keepalive
    term description; 307
key
    as transaction identification; 252

L

latches
    busy wait use; 197
    concurrency control utility use; 229-230
    Double Check pattern use in; 120
    joint action design use; 240
    LatchingThermometer class, (code); 230
    term description; 229
    variables; 230
latency
    See Also forces; performance
    in I/O bound systems; 299
    as oneway message force; 287
    term description; 46

layering
    See Also before/after patterns; composition
    control policy, subclassing use for; 207-214
    guards;,211-212
    policy control; 57-58
    synchronization; 109
lazy
    initialization; 85, 121
    LazySingletonCounter class, (code); 85
    thread construction; 294
Leaf class (code); 360
leaks
    confinement guarantees; 99
legacy code
    Adapter pattern use; 108
    condition variable use; 233
lightweight
    executable frameworks
        as concurrent execution construct; 23
        Fork/Join pattern use; 346-347
        mapping to threads; 23
        volatile keyword use with; 97
        Worker Threads pattern as; 290
    transaction protocols; 261-263
linear
    objects; 111
    stages in flow networks; 309, 317
linked
    data structures, lock splitting techniques;
        130-131
    LinkedCell class, (code); 123
    LinkedQueue class, (code); 131
    lists
        as bounded buffer data structures; 223
        open call use; 123
        ordered, scheduling service use; 337
        traversal, hand-over-hand locking; 154
    tasks
        callback-based approaches compared
            with; 353
        in Fork/Join pattern; 351-352
LISP
    bibliographic references; 66
listeners
    collections of; 137
lists
    See Also linked, lists
    ListUsingMutex class, (code); 154
livelock
    as liveness failure; 45, 139
    as retry strategy danger; 151
    term description; 45

liveness; 44-45
  See Also blocking; deadlock; fairness;
       forces; lockouts
  as bottom-up design strategy priority; 49
  as correctness concern; 38
  CPU contention; 44
  difficulties in proving; 227
  failures; 44
  of flow networks; 310
  granularity impact on; 124
  guarded method issues; 181
  of joint actions; 238, 240
  method and block synchronization; 147
  missed signals; 190
  resource ordering; 88-89
  vs. safety; 87
    balancing; 38
    in lock granularity design; 117
    reusability impact; 49
  term description; 6
  time-out use to preserve; 194
  waiting design issues; 189
locality
  See Also forces; performance
  as force in Fork/Join pattern; 345
  performance aspects; 47
lock(ing)
  See Also synchronization
  accessors, `java.awt` use; 144
  acquiring; 77
  array restrictions; 74
  client-side
    transactions using; 249
    traversal using; 81-82
  coupling; 154
  explicit acquisition of; 89
  granularity; 117
  hand-over-hand, mutex use; 154
  hierarchical containment; 216
  intention; 207
  joint action design use; 240
  layering; 110
  liveness of; 44
  `LockManager` class, (code); 156
  lockouts, as nested monitor issue; 215
  `LockSplitShape` class, (code); 128
  methods and block, limitations of; 147
  mutex, lock utility use; 148-156
  non-block-structured
    chained node traversal use; 84
    condvar use; 154-155
  `Object` instance as; 127
  objects as; 76

lock(ing) *(continued)*
  ordered
    hierarchical, open container use; 142
    mutex use; 153
    managers; 156
  patterns for, bibliographic references; 158
  performance of; 47
  read-write locks; 157-158, 209-210
  `ReadWriteLock` interface
    (code); 157
    `ReadWrite` support of; 209
    `RWLock` extension of; 210
  recursive, term description; 77
  reentrant, term description; 77
  release; 77
  rules for interference avoidance; 6
  `RWLock` class, (code); 210
  scope, slipped condition issues; 190
  semaphores as; 220-221
  serialization of synchronized methods by; 75
  Singleton pattern implementation using; 85
  splitting
    class splitting compared with; 127
    implementation steps; 127
    as synchronization splitting method; 127-
       128
  in state-dependent action splitting; 273
  synchronization; 75-98
  term description; 6
  as thread-aware mechanism; 31
  utilities; 147-158
    interrupt handling by; 171
    multilevel containment use; 145
  wait invocation impact on; 184
  as wait set component; 184
lockouts (nested monitor)
  as liveness failure; 215
  term description; 45
log (history)
  term description; 42
logical state
  analysis; 199
  defining; 182-183
  variables; 42, 202

M

managers
  of multiple lock ordering; 156
mapping
  object models; 26-32
  `MaxSizePredicate` class (code); 322
measurement
  of performance; 46

mechanics
monitor; 184-186
synchronization; 76-78
threads; 13-18
Mediator pattern; DP(273)
joint action design use; 238
Memento pattern; DP(283)
checkpointing use of; 163
memory model; 90-97
bibliographic references; 98
mergesort
as divide-and-conquer algorithm; 344
Mesa
bibliographic references; 33
message(s)
acceptance using locks; 78
bibliographic references; 304
conversion protocol, error handler use; 167
as object communication mechanism; 28
oneway; 285-304
composing; 305-324
ordering, in Readers and Writers; 207
state-based acceptance of; 181-182
Thread-Per-Message pattern; 288-289
metaclass
bibliographic reference; 66
metaobject protocol
bibliographic references; 66
Method Adapters pattern; 64-65
mutex use; 150-151
method(s)
confinement,
across; 100-102
group confinement relationship; 111
protocols for; 102
control, for threads; 16
guarded; 179-198
busy waits compared with; 196
callback use; 328
implementation steps; 184
joint actions as; 237-248
monitor mechanics; 184-186
for joint action solutions; 239-240
notification, properties of; 184
static, for threads; 16-17
synchronization of; 76
term description; 2
wait, properties of; 184
missed signals
avoiding, in helper method design; 269
as liveness failure; 45, 221
term description; 45, 190

mobile
agents; 286
code; 20
modal dialogs
event queue issues; 296
models
attributes; 26
behavior; 27
bibliographic references; 34
Java memory model; 90-97
object; 26-32
active; 30, 367-376
mixed; 31-32
passive; 29
Modula-3
bibliographic references; 33
monitors
See Also guarded methods
mechanics of; 184-186
nested
confinement and; 215-216
lockouts, term description; 45
performance; 47
Specific Notification pattern use; 275
in state-dependent action splitting; 273
term description; 184
multicast
in flow networks; 309, 321
frameworks, Copy-on-Write pattern use; 137
JavaBeans; 261
open call use; 287
multilevel
containment, lock utility use; 145
Multiphase Cancellation pattern; 175-176
utility for; 176
multiple
code inheritance; 62
participants, in joint actions; 237-248
multiplexing
as I/O bound system solution; 299
multithreaded systems
bibliographic references; 33
mutex (mutual exclusion lock)
condition variable use with; 233
lock utility use; 148-156
Mutex class, (code); 148, 220
semaphore use to implement; 220-221

N

naming
incompatibilities; 59
nested monitors; 215-216
avoiding; 221, 275, 277

networks (flow)
   development issues; 307-310
   term description; 305
Ninja
   bibliographic reference; 304
non-block-structured locking
   chained node traversal use; 84
nondeterminism
   as concurrent program characteristic; 24
nonlinearity
   of performance degradation; 47
notation
   diagrams; 3
notifications; 189-193
   Copy-on-Write pattern use; 137
   error handling use; 166
   event, callback replacement by; 328
   improving efficiency of; 268-280
   in different programming languages; 25
   lock splitting use; 127
   logical state analysis impact on; 199-200
   methods, properties of; 184
   `notify`
      actions upon invocation; 185
      conditions for use of; 191
      fairness; 227
      `notifyAll` compared with; 191
   `notifyAll`
      actions upon invocation; 185
      `notify` compared with; 191
   oneway message examples; 285
   as policy domain; 50
   priority; 228
   refinement; 199-217
   using semaphores; 225
   single; 191-193
   Specific Notification pattern; 275-280
NQueens chess problem
   Fork/Join pattern example; 356
   `NQueens` class, (code); 356-357
Null Object pattern
   bibliographic reference; 341

O

object(s)
   See Also `java.lang` package
   active; 30, 367-376
   atomic, requirements for; 78-79
   bibliographic references; 33-36
   communication, term description; 28
   concurrency and, perspectives on; 19-36
   confinement within; 107-110
   construction; 74

object(s) *(continued)*
   encapsulation, term description; 28
   identity; 28, 62
   mappings, sequential; 29
   as modeling tool; 28
   models; 26-32
   object-centric vs. activity-centric views; 37
   stateless, term description; 71
   structure; 28
   synchronization of; 76
Observer pattern; DP(293)
   `CopyOnWriteArrayList` use for; 138
   decoupling; 245-247
   `Observer` class, (code); 247
   completion callback relationship to; 325
   JavaBeans listener use; 261
occam programming language
   CSP as basis of; 369
one-shot
   See latches
oneway messages; 285-304
   bibliographic reference; 304
   composing messages; 305-324
      bibliographic reference; 324
   failure strategies; 163
   thread services compared with; 325
online supplement
   See http://java.sun.com/Series
Open Calls pattern; 121, 287
   notification use; 192
   `OpenCallHost` class, (code); 287
   as synchronization reduction tool; 121-123
   term description; 122
   Worker-Threads pattern relationship; 290
Open Containers pattern; 142-145
   external locking; 144-145
   internal locking; 143-144
open systems; 50-51
   bibliographic references; 55
   deadlock in; 89
   `notify` design issues; 192
   reference confinement checking issues; 100
operating systems
   bibliographic references; 34
   processes; 21
operations
   as behavior representation tool; 27
   term description; 2
optimistic
   `Optimistic` class, (code); 140
   `OptimisticDot` class, (code); 141
   state-dependent strategies; 160
      Conflict Sets pattern variant; 206

optimistic *(continued)*
transactions; 251, 255
update
as copy-on-write technique; 139
retry use by; 165, 299
rollback use; 163
optimization
closure advantages for; 49
impact on program execution; 91
for extensibility, vs. for performance; 51
premature, avoidance rule; 214
Orca
bibliographic references; 33
ordering
hierarchical locking, open container use; 142
Java Memory Model rules; 93, 96
lock, mutex use; 153
of multiple locks, lock manager use; 156
resource; 88-89
`volatile` keyword impact on; 74, 97
overhead
of concurrency control; 21, 47, 165, 290
`OwnedPartWithGuard` class (code); 216

P

`Painter` class (code); 317
parallel
decomposition; 343-366
programming
bibliographic references; 366
vs. concurrent programming; 32
`Part` class (code); 143
participants
multiple, in joint actions; 237-248
transaction; 252-258
particle applet; 6-12
`Particle` class (code); 7
`ImmutablePoint` compared with; 136
as invariant example; 136
`ParticleUsingMutex` (code); 149
`ParticleUsingWrapper` (code); 151
`ParticleApplet` class (code); 11
`makeThread` method; 101
`ParticleCanvas` class (code); 8
`PartWithGuard` class (code); 215
Pass-Through Host pattern; 125
latency of; 287
`PassThroughShape` class, (code); 125
passive objects
models; 29

patterns
bibliographic references; 66
conferences, bibliographic reference; 66
vs. components and frameworks; 57
exception handling, bibliographic
references; 177
lock, bibliographic references; 158
parallel programming; 366
structural, for concurrency control; 199-217
term description; 57
types; *See* Adapter, Atomic Commitment,
Back-Offs, before/after patterns,
Command Object, Composite,
Conflict Sets, Copy-on-Write, Double
Check, Event-Driven I/O, Extension
Object, Factory Method, Flow
Networks, Flyweight, Fork/Join,
Futures, Mediator, Method Adapters,
Null Object, Observer, Open Calls,
Open Containers, Pass-Through Host,
Proxy, Readers and Writers, Rings,
Roll-Forward Rollback, Sessions,
Singleton, Specific Notification,
State, Strategy, Template Methods,
Vetoable Changes, Visitor, Worker
Threads
peer
term description; 2
performance; 46-48
See Also contention; efficiency; granularity;
latency; overhead; scalability;
throughput; locality
analysis, bibliographic references; 55
of buffers; 225
granularity; 117
of lightweight executable frameworks; 23
latency; 287
lazy thread construction; 294
measurement; 46
of notifications; 189, 191, 199-217
of optimistic updates; 139
of parallel designs; 345
of polling; 303
thread confinement advantages 295
of Thread-Per-Message pattern; 288
of `volatile`; 119
of waiting; 199-217
of Worker Threads; 290-292
permanent variables
term description; 230
permits
count, semaphore use; 266
term description; 220

persistence
    objects, term description; 32
    transaction frameworks; 250
`Person` class (code); 129
Petri Nets
    bibliographic references; 54
`Philosopher` class (code); 374
`Pic` interface (code); 331
`PictureApp` class (code); 331
`PictureAppWithFuture` class (code); 333
`PictureDisplayWithFutureResult` class
        (code); 336
pipes
    command message format use; 286
    and filter systems,; 306
    term description; 21
`PlainWorkerPool` class (code); 291
PLoP conferences
    bibliographic reference; 66
`Plotter` class (code); 100, 102
point-of-no-return
    rollback use; 164
    synchronous channel use; 226
    term description; 164
policies
    control layering, as structuring principle; 57
    domains; 50
    failure; 162
    fairness; 227
    vs. mechanisms; 212
    in open systems; 50
    in Readers and Writers pattern; 207
    safety; 70
    security; 17
polling
    `PollingWorker` class, (code); 302
    retry use by; 165
    for task triggering; 302-303
pools
    `Pool` class, (code); 222
    bibliographic reference; 235
    implementation; 221-222
    per-thread; 106
    thread pools; 292-294
portability
    See Also reusability
    of concurrent programming vs. parallel
        programming; 32, 343
    impact on real-time support; 20
    priority scheduling impact on; 228
POSA
    bibliographic reference; 66

POSIX threads (pthreads)
    concurrency constructs; 25
    condition variable use; 233
    spurious wakeup potential, (footnote); 188
    `synchronized` lock differences from; 77
postconditions
    before/after pattern relationship to; 58
    optimistic strategy check of; 161
    representation of, rules use for; 27
    term description; 159
postings
    oneway message examples; 285
precedence
    forcing, resource ordering use for; 88
preconditions
    before/after pattern relationship to; 58
    checking; 161
    representation of, rules use for; 27
    term description; 159
    testing, as guarded method strategy; 179
predicates
    latching; 230
preemptive time-slicing
    term description; 22
printing
    collection elements, as traversal example; 81
    `Printer` class, (code); 114
    `PrintService` class, (code); 114
priority(s)
    inversions, term description; 228
    `PriorityQueue` class, (code); 297
    thread; 14-15, 228
`Procedure` interface (code); 80
process(es)
    actor models of; 30
    as concurrent execution construct; 21-22,
        103
    CSP, term description; 369
producer-consumer relationship
    in oneway message composition; 305
    `ParticleApplet`, (thread diagram); 10
    Worker-Threads pattern use; 290
programming
    aspect-oriented, bibliographic reference; 67
    concurrent
        bibliographic references; 33-34
        term description; 19
    OO; 24
    parallel; 32
properties
    in JavaBeans; 261
protected keyword
    in concurrency control policies; 213

protocols
  acquire-release; 77
    implementation of; 265-267
    mutex as example of; 148
    semaphore as example of; 220
  for confinement across methods; 102
  check-out/check-in; 221
  distributed; 237, 248
  hand-off; 101
  failure; 163
  in open systems; 50
  remote activation; 286
  transaction; 251-252
  transfer; 111, 308
  two-phase, in transaction frameworks; 251
provisional action
  as rollback technique; 163
Proxy pattern; DP(207)
  See Also Adapter pattern
  as Adapter pattern variation; 59
  Adapter relationship to; 61
  in Futures pattern; 332
  `ProxyAccount` class, (code); 258
  in transaction frameworks; 258
pthreads
  See POSIX threads
publish-subscribe
  systems, as dataflow system example; 306
pull-based flow
  in flow networks; 308
push-based flow
  in flow networks; 308, 313
  `PushSource` interface (code); 314
  `PushStage` interface (code); 314
put protocol
  See Also buffer(s); channel(s)
  as object confinement protocol; 112

Q

quality of service (QOS)
  vs. correctness; 20
queues
  condition; 275
  event; 295-296
  FIFO; 130
  `PriorityQueue` class, (code); 297
  scheduling service use; 337
  in Worker Threads; 292
quicksort
  as divide-and-conquer example; 344

R

race conditions
  term description; 40
reactive systems
  active object use; 368
read(ing)
  of code by humans; 24
  `read`, `Channel.take` compared with; 199
  read-only adapters; 132-135
    implementation steps; 132
  read-write conflicts
    immutable objects free from; 71
    race conditions resulting from; 40
  Readers and Writers pattern
    before/after version; 207-210
    read-write locks; 157-158
  `ReaderWithTimeout` class, (code); 173
  `ReadWrite` abstract class, (code); 208-209
  `ReadWriteLock` interface
    (code); 157
    `ReadWrite` support of; 209
    `RWLock` extension of; 210
  `RWLock` class, (code); 210
real-time
  soft, hard real-time control compared; 20
  systems, bibliographic references; 36
receive
  as use of `Channel.take`; 199
receiver copy
  as confinement protocol; 102
recovery
  See Also Back-Offs; cancellation; failure;
      retry; Roll-Forward; Rollback
  in transaction frameworks; 259
recursion
  in computation trees; 359
  in divide-and-conquer algorithms; 344
  in Fork/Join pattern; 351-353
  vs. iteration; 362
  as locality tool; 345
  in open calls; 123
  recursive locking, term description; 77
reduction
  parallel, term description; 351
  of synchronization; 118-123
reentrancy
  non-reentrant, simple mutex locking; 149
  reentrant locking, term description; 77
refactoring
  bibliographic reference; 145, 217
  exclusion strategies; 117-145
  state-dependent strategies; 199-217
  tasks into event-driven form; 300

references
accessing, read-only adapters use; 132
to acquaintances; 43
confinement of; 99, 107
in Double Check pattern; 120
to representation objects; 43
unique, bibliographic references; 115
reflection
bibliographic references; 66
Method Adapters pattern use; 65
term description; 29
transaction framework use; 252
relaxation
algorithms; 358, 364
relays
Relay class (code); 73
oneway message examples; 285
release
acquire-release protocols
mutex as example of; 148
release semaphore use; 220
consistency models, bibliographic
references; 98
of locks; 7, 77, 198
remote activation protocols
class message format use; 286
Renderer interface (code); 331
rendezvous
exchangers use; 231
reorderings
mutex use; 153
representation
of attributes; 26, 42-43
of behaviors; 27
of connections; 27
in flow networks; 307
granularity, in Conflict Sets pattern; 206
state; 217
requests
dropping, as saturation response; 293
message format; 286
resource(s)
denial; 175
bibliographic references; 177
exchange; 231
exhaustion; 45
failure; 162
confinement; 111
management efficiency; 290
ordering; 88-89, 240, 143, 156
pools; 221-222, 106, 294
bibliographic reference; 235
revocation; 171-173

responsiveness
See Also liveness
priority relationship to; 15
to thread interrupts; 170
resume method
deprecation; 16
retry
See Also recovery
as failure response; 162, 165
RetryableTransferException class,
(code); 259
timed, blocked I/O handling use; 173
reusability; 48-53
See Also composition; documentation;
extensibility; forces; packaging;
portability
in closed subsystems; 49-50
of concurrency control utilities; 219
of notification techniques; 199-217
as object-centric quality concern; 38
in open systems; 50-51
of patterns, components and frameworks; 57
term description; 48
in transaction frameworks; 249
of waiting techniques; 199-217
reversion
rollback use for; 164
revocation
resource, as cancellation technique; 171-173
strategies, foreign code handling use of; 175
rings
as group confinement structure; 113-115
synchronization, bibliographic reference; 66
token ring networks; 111
RMI (remote method invocation)
active object use; 368
role
term description; 9
variables, term description; 183
Roll-Forward pattern; 164
See Also recovery
FIFO semaphore use; 277
synchronous channel; 226
as interruption response, issues; 170
in transaction protocols; 252
as failure response; 164
Rollback pattern; 163-164
See Also recovery
conditions that preclude use of; 164
retry compared with; 165
as interruption response, issues; 170
in transaction protocols; 251
as failure response; 163

routers
  in flow networks, term description; 309
rules
  composition, for flow networks; 308-310
  CSP composition; 370
  construction of objects; 74
  design; 50
  inheritance anomaly avoidance; 214
  Java Memory Model; 93
  locking, for interference avoidance; 6
  ordering, Java memory model; 96
  scheduling; 277
  single thread (swing); 295-296
runnable
  See Also `java.lang` package
  events, term description; 286
  objects, message format; 286
  run method; 9
  `Runnable` interface; 13, 290
    active object use; 368
    threads required to implement; 9
    in threads, strategies for use; 13
    Worker Threads pattern use; 290
  threads, priority impact on schedulers; 15
`RuntimeException` class
  abrupt termination for; 14, 162
  error handling; 167

S

safe-point
  interrupt checking at; 170
  term description; 164
safety; 39-43
  See Also exclusion; forces; invariants
  attributes; 41
  compilation insufficient to ensure; 70
  constraints; 41-43
  exclusion techniques use; 69
  in flow networks; 310
  vs. liveness; 38, 49, 87
  of native code; 108
  as correctness concern; 38
  vs. performance; 117
  representation constraints; 42
  in top-down design; 49
  type; 39
Sather
  bibliographic references; 33
saturation
  in Worker Threads; 293-294
scalability
  as performance goal; 343
  as performance measure; 46

scalar data types
  locking; 76
scenarios
  flow network relationship to; 324
  `ScheduledDisk` class (code); 339
scheduling
  busy wait impact on; 196-197
  explicit, as conflict resolution strategy; 240
  fairness, bibliographic reference; 235
  FIFO; 227
  in Fork/Join frameworks; 351
  performance; 47
  priority; 14
  of processes; 21
  of semaphores; 227-228
  services; 337-340
  Specific Notification pattern support; 275
  as Thread-Per-Message pattern issue; 288
  timer issues; 298
  `yield` impact on; 17
Scheme
  bibliographic references; 66
  Futures in, bibliographic reference; 341
scoping
  confinement use of; 99
  lock, slipped condition issues; 190
  as method confinement technique; 100
  in `ThreadLocal` applications; 105
  `Screener` class (code); 322
scripting
  in flow network; 310, 324
security
  in OO programming languages; 25
  confinement relationship to; 99
  foreign code, cancellation issues; 175
  management, bibliographic reference; 177
  multithreaded safety impact on; 39
  policies, thread groups use; 17
  `SecurityManager` use; 175
segmentation
  barriers use of; 362
  `JacobiSegment` class, (code); 365
  `Segment` class, (code); 364
Self language
  bibliographic reference; 66
self-checking code
  before/after pattern use; 58
semantics
  as-if-serial; 91
  channel; 225
  Conflict Sets pattern documentation of; 203
  execution; 290
  Java memory model; 91

semantics *(continued)*
method locking impact on; 117
now-or-never; 179
`Sync` interface implementation issues; 265
weakening of; 240
semaphores; 220-228
binary, term description; 220
bounded buffer use of; 223-225
concurrency control utility use; 220
fairness of; 227-228
FIFO; 277-280
mutex implementation using; 220-221
resource pool use of; 221-222
scheduling service use; 337
`Semaphore` class, (code); 266-267
synchronous channels use of; 225-226
thread priority issues; 228
send
as use of `Channel.put`; 199
sequence numbers
Singleton pattern use for assigning; 88
serialization
request message format use; 286
runnable objects; 286
of synchronized methods; 75
servers
term description; 2
`ServerUsingCallback` interface, (code); 167
`ServerWithAssignableHelper` class, (code); 122
`ServerWithException` interface, (code); 166
`ServerWithOpenCall` class, (code); 122
`ServerWithStateUpdate` class, (code); 121
services in threads
bibliographic references; 341
scheduling; 337-340
design alternatives for; 325-341
`ServiceIssuingExceptionEvent` class, (code); 168
`ServiceUsingThreadLocal` class, (code); 105
`ServiceUsingThreadWithOutputStream` class, (code); 104
Session pattern; 101
vs. event-driven tasks; 301
`SessionBasedService` class, (code); 101
`SessionTask` class, (code); 300
Thread-Per-Message pattern use; 288
set(s)
conflict, as exclusion refinement; 203-206
set methods; 8, 261
`SetCheck` class, (code); 90
wait set, term description; 184
`Shape` class (code); 124

sharing
of immutable objects; 73
shared memory multiprocessors; 32
as thread autonomy vs. overhead tradeoff; 22
side-effects
undoing, as optimistic update issue; 139
sideband controls
term description; 307
signals
See notifications
missed; 45, 190
signatures
guarded method indication in; 188
`synchronized` keyword not part of; 76
term description; 9
`SimpleTransBankAccount` class (code); 257
Simula
bibliographic references; 33
as first OO language; 24
simulation
bibliographic references; 54
as concurrent programming application; 20
single
notifications; 191-193
single-check idiom; 121
`SingleOutputPushStage` class, (code); 316
threaded event frameworks; 296
bibliographic reference; 304
threading, as saturation response; 294
Singleton pattern; DP(127)
lazy initialization; 121
statics and; 85-86
`ThreadLocal` use; 105
sinks
in flow networks; 309, 315
skeletons
term description; 368
`sleep` method
Thread class; 17, 185
slipped conditions
term description; 190
SMP (shared-memory multiprocessor)
Java Memory Model rules; 92
object model mapping to; 32
sockets
command message format use; 286
event-driven IO; 299
as message passing tool; 30
time-out handling; 173
software analysis
bibliographic references; 54
`Solver` class (pseudocode); 344

source code
See code listings
sources in flow networks
assembly line example; 323
term description; 309
Specific Notification pattern; 275-280
bibliographic reference; 280
spin locks
See Also busy waits
bounded, runtime system use; 196
Double Check pattern use in; 120
SpinLock class, (code); 198
splitting
classes
with state-dependent actions; 268, 273
for synchronization; 124-126
locks; 127-128
synchronization; 124-131
Spring
bibliographic references; 115
spurious wakeups
potential for, (footnote); 188
stable collections
Copy-on-Write pattern use; 137
stacks
StackEmptyException class, (code); 211
stages
of flow networks; 308-310
staleness
See Also visibility; memory model
synchronization weakening; 118-119
start(ing)
applets; 9
threads; 14
starvation
as fairness issue; 197
term description; 45
state
See Also conditions; confinement; event(s);
guarded methods; immutability; joint
actions; synchronization; transactions
changes
as action triggers; 182
Copy-on-Write pattern handling; 136
vs. immutable objects; 73
notifyAll indication of; 189
consistency; 39, 188
dependence; 159-280
encapsulation of, in transactions; 254
execution state tracking
Conflict Sets pattern use; 203
Readers and Writers pattern use of; 208
notify use; 191

state *(continued)*
invariants; 27, 39
logical state; 42, 183-183
logical state tracking; 199-202
reference objects as part of; 43
representation, bibliographic references; 217
StateCharts; 183
State pattern; DP(305)
logical control state use; 183
state-dependent actions use; 268
state-based message acceptance; 181-182
stateless
objects, term description; 71
tasks, Worker Thread pattern use; 292
term description; 121
StatelessAdder class, (code); 71
tracking; 199-202
updating, as object computation; 28
variables; 42
static
analysis; 50
methods, for threads; 16-17
Singleton pattern and; 85-86
static, in ThreadLocal applications; 105
StaticCounter class, (code); 86
synchronization; 77-78
term description; 28
status
interruption; 16, 170-171
stop method
Applet class; 9
Thread class, deprecation of; 16, 174-175
Strategy pattern; DP(315)
error handler use; 166
streams
Worker Thread pattern use; 299-303
structure(ing)
classes
exclusion strategies; 117-145
state-dependent strategies; 199-217
lightweight executable frameworks; 23, 345
oneway messages; 305-324
synchronization, confinement techniques; 99
subclassing
Adapters compared with; 61
avoidance of, in defining threads; 14
in before/after patterns; 61-63
control policy layering; 207-214
implementation policies; 157
inheritance anomalies; 212-214
term description; 213
synchronization; 207
vs. ThreadLocal; 105

Subject class (code); 247
suspend method
  deprecation; 16
suspension
  guarded; 180-183
  of threads, sleep use for; 17
swapValue method (code); 89
Swing
  See javax.swing package
symmetry
  breaking, resource ordering use for; 88
Sync interface
  (code); 265
  Channel compared with; 199
  Mutex implementation of; 148, 220
  ReadWriteLock comparison with; 157
  Semaphore implementation of; 266-267
  semaphore utility support; 220
SynchedPoint class (code); 109
  getPoint method, (code); 132
synchronization; 75-98
  See Also exclusion; lock(ing)
  of aggregate operations; 80-81
  bibliographic references; 98
  block and method synchronization; 76
  of busy waits; 197
  in cyclic barriers; 363
  full; 78-79
  of guarded waits; 188
  immutable field initialization use; 74
  of indexed traversal 81-82
  Java Memory Model semantics; 93
  layered; 109
  locks, thread interrupt handling; 171
  mechanics of; 76-78
  of methods and blocks; 76, 147
  modifying; 117
  using mutex; 148
  nested, alias detection use; 88
  nested monitor problem; 215
  non-block-structured; 84
  of notifications; 192
  object-based containment use; 108
  ordering; 88
  read-only adapter use; 132
  reducing; 118-123
  splitting; 124-131
  statics; 77-78
  in transactions; 249
  traversal of collections; 80-84
  vs. volatile; 118, 350
  wait set interaction; 184
SynchronizedAddress class (code); 110

SynchronizedInt class (code); 129
synchronous channels
  SynchronousChannel class (code); 226
  exchanger relationship to; 231
  semaphores use to implement; 225-226
  term description; 225, 292
  Worker Thread pattern use; 292
syntropy
  bibliographic reference; 54
system
  closed; 49
  open; 50
  programming
    concurrent; 25
    bibliographic references; 34

T

tail calls
  term description; 100
take protocol
  See Also buffer(s); channel(s)
  as object confinement protocol; 112
TankOp interface (code); 64
TankWithMethodAdapter class (code); 65
target
  term description; 2
tasks
  task-based threads; 281-282
  in Fork/Join pattern; 347-348
Tcl/Tk
  event handling in; 24
Template Method pattern; 62-63, DP(325)
  before/after control using; 62, 212
  Readers and Writers pattern use; 207
temporal logic
  bibliographic references; 54
term descriptions
  anomalies - inheritance; 213
  as-if-serial semantics, (footnote); 91
  atomic; 6, 40
  attributes; 2
  barriers, cyclic; 362
  begin; 251
  binary, semaphore; 220
  calls, open; 122
  capacity; 46
  channels; 28
    CSP; 369
    synchronous; 225, 292
  classes; 2
  clean-fail; 163
  client; 2
  collectors in flow networks; 309

term descriptions (*continued*)

combiners in flow networks; 309
commit; 251
communication, object; 28
concurrency; 19
    constraint programming; 182
conditions
    postconditions; 159
    preconditions; 159
    race; 40
    slipped; 190
connections, OO; 28
conservative, transactions; 251
consistent; 40
constraints, concurrent constraint
        programming; 182
containment, fixed; 108
context switch; 32
cookie; 326
coroutines; 24
countdowns; 229
CSP (Communicating Sequential Processes)
    channels; 369
    process; 369
cyclic barriers; 362
daemons; 14
deadlock; 45
deferred-synchronous invocation; 329
degradation; 46
denial, resource; 175
distributed failure; 45
efficiency; 46
encapsulation, object; 28
entry; 286
events
    channels; 28
    runnable; 286
exclusion; 1
exhaustion, resource; 45
failure, distributed; 45
fairness; 197
fast-fail iterators; 82
fields; 2
fixed containment; 108
flow network; 305
hand-off protocol; 101
helper(s); 2
history log; 42
host; 2
identity, object; 28
immutability, partial; 73
inheritance anomalies; 213
instances; 2

term descriptions (*continued*)

interfaces; 9
invalidation relations; 206
inversions, priority; 228
invocation, deferred-synchronous; 329
iteration, fast-fail; 82
join(ing); 251
keepalive; 307
latches; 229
latency; 46
livelock; 45
liveness; 6
lock(ing); 6
    recursive; 77
    reentrant; 77
lockouts, nested monitor; 45
log, history; 42
method(s); 2
missed signals; 45, 190
monitors; 184
    nested lockouts; 45
multicast in flow networks; 309
nested monitor lockouts; 45
networks, flow; 305
objects
    communication; 28
    encapsulation; 28
    identity; 28
    stateless; 71
OO programming, connections; 28
Open Calls pattern, open calls; 122
operations; 2
optimistic transactions; 251
parallel programming; 32
partial immutability; 73
patterns; 57
peer; 2
permanent variables; 230
permits; 220
persistence, objects; 32
pipes; 21
point-of-no-return; 164
postconditions; 159
preconditions; 159
preemptive time-slicing; 22
priority inversions; 228
processes; 21
    CSP; 369
programming
    concurrent; 19
    parallel; 32
protocols, hand-off; 101
race conditions; 40

term descriptions *(continued)*
  recursion, recursive locking; 77
  reduction; 351
  reentrant locking; 77
  references to
    acquaintances; 43
    representation objects; 43
  reflection; 29
  relations, invalidation; 206
  resource
    denial; 175
    exhaustion; 45
  reusability; 48
  role; 9
    variables; 183
  routers in flow networks; 309
  runnable events; 286
  safe-point; 164
  scalability; 46
  semantics, as-if-serial, (footnote); 91
  semaphores, binary; 220
  servers; 2
  sessions; 101
  sets, wait set; 184
  sideband controls; 307
  signals, missed; 45, 190
  signatures; 9
  sinks in flow networks; 309
  skeletons; 368
  slipped conditions; 190
  sources in flow networks; 309
  starvation; 45
  stateless; 121
    objects; 71
  static; 28
  subclassing, inheritance anomalies; 213
  synchronous channels; 225, 292
  tail calls; 100
  target; 2
  threads; 13
    background; 290
    pools; 290
    worker; 290
  throughput; 46
  transactions; 249
    conservative; 251
    optimistic; 251
  traversal; 80
  variables
    permanent; 230
    role; 183
  wait set; 184

termination
  See Also cancellation; error; interrupt
  abrupt, as failure response; 162
  asynchronous; 174-175
  detection, bibliographic references; 177
  Java memory model guarantees; 95
  Terminator class (code); 176
test-and-test-and-set
  See Double Check pattern
this keyword
  as callback argument; 107
  constructor precautions; 74
  in delegation designs; 62
thread(s)
  background, term description; 290
  bibliographic references; 18
  blocking, join use for; 329
  cancellation; 169-176
  communication among, methods for; 16
  concurrency control alternatives to; 21
  as concurrent execution construct; 22-23
  confinement; 103-106, 295
  constructor; 13-14
    restrictions; 95
  control methods; 16
  diagrams; 3
  fields specific to; 104
  flow network composition rules; 308
  interruption; 169-171
  lightweight executable frameworks; 23
  Java Memory Model rules; 92, 95
  joining; 95, 329-336,
  lazy construction; 294
  lock interaction with; 77
  management of; 294
  performance; 47
  pools; 290
  priorities; 14-15, 228
  relationship to Runnable; 9
  restricting access to; 17
  runnable, priority impact on schedulers; 15
  service threads; 325-341
  starting; 14
  static methods; 16-17
  stopping; 14
  task-based vs. actor-based; 281-282
  term description; 13
  Thread class; 13-18
  Thread-Per-Message pattern; 288-289
  thread-per-session design; 103
  thread-specific data; 103-106
  ThreadGroup class; 17-18
    thread constructor use; 13

thread(s) *(continued)*
ThreadLocal class; 105
ThreadPerMessageHost class, (code); 288
ThreadPerSessionBasedService class, (code); 103
ThreadWithOutputStream class, (code); 104
worker threads; 290
throughput
See Also forces; performance
in I/O bound systems; 299
as parallel programming performance goal; 343
as performance measure; 46
term description; 46
time
See Also overhead; latency
busy wait impact on; 196
sharing; 32
slicing; 22
temporal logic, bibliographic references; 54
time-out
See Also cancellation
balking as backup strategy to; 181
as blocked read handling strategy; 171
as guarded method strategy; 179
I/O handling; 173
in Worker Thread pattern; 294
timed waits; 194-195
back-off use; 151
compared with untimed waits; 185
Mutex.attempt operation use; 148
TimeOutBoundedCounter class, (code); 195
TimerDaemon class, (code); 297
timers; 297-298
timing thresholds, latches use for; 230
token
group confinement protocols; 111
passing, as conflict resolution strategy; 240
tracking state; 199-202
Conflict Sets pattern use; 203
Readers and Writers pattern use of; 208
transaction(s); 249-264
bibliographic references; 264
conservative, term description; 251
creating; 258-260
custom queue use; 293
optimistic, term description; 251
participants; 252-258
protocols; 251-252
term description; 249
Transactor interface, (code); 253

TransBankAccount interface (code); 254
SimpleTransBankAccount class, (code); 257
transfer protocols
in flow networks; 308
in group object management; 111
traversal
Copy-on-Write pattern use; 137
hand-over-hand locking, mutex use for; 154
indexed, client-side locking and; 81-82
as polling design issue; 303
synchronization weakening issues; 119
of synchronized object collections; 80
term description; 80
trees
computation; 358-361
building and using; 359
iteration over; 84
triggering
busy wait contrast with; 197
IO tasks; 303
Triveni
bibliographic reference; 376
trust
as confinement protocol; 102
try-and-see strategies
as optimistic strategy; 160-161
try/finally
in before/after locking; 150
TSBoolean class (code); 242
Turing
Universal Turing Machine, JVM as; 29
two-phase protocols
in transaction frameworks; 251
type safety;
multithreaded safety compared with; 39

U

UML diagrams
bibliographic references; 18
notation for; 3
uncaughtException method
ThreadGroup class; 18
undo
rollback use for; 164
uniqueness
as confinement access guarantee; 99
Universal Turing Machine
JVM as; 29
Unix
shutdown; 176
UnsupportedOperationException class
read-only adapter use; 135

updates
    atomic commitment use; 140
    vs. immutable representations; 73
    optimistic
        as copy-on-write technique; 139
        retry use by; 165
        rollback use; 163
    state variable requirements; 183
use cases
    flow network relationship to; 324
    Use Case Maps, bibliographic references; 54
`util.concurrent`
    See `http://java.sun.com/Series`
utilities
    bibliographic references; 158, 280
    concurrency control
        implementation of; 265-280
        using; 219-235
    lock; 147-158

V

value
    containers, as immutability application; 73
variables
    See Also state
    condition; 233-234
        bibliographic references; 235
    history; 42
    latching; 230
    permanent, term description; 230
    role, term description; 183
    state; 42, 202
version(ing)
    of iterators; 82-84
    tracking; 43
`VerticallyJoinedPair` class (code); 313
Vetoable Changes pattern
    implementation steps; 262
    transaction handling of; 261-263
`VFloat` class (code); 97
visibility
    memory model rules; 93-96
    `volatile` keyword impact on; 74, 93, 97
Visitor pattern; 84, DP(331)
    in joint action design; 238
Visual Basic
    event handling in; 24
`volatile fields`; 97
    use in Fork/Join pattern; 350, 352, 355
    in latching thresholds; 230
    performance; 119
    vs. synchronization; 128
    visibility; 74, 93, 94

W

wait-by-necessity
    bibliographic reference; 341
waits
    busy; 196-198
    conditional; 181
    guarded; 187-188
    I/O, thread interrupt handling; 171
    interrupted; 188
    liveness of; 44
    lock splitting use; 127
    methods, properties of; 184
    in Specific Notifications; 275
    sets; 184, 233
    interrupt handling; 171
    refinement; 199-217
    timed; 194-195
        actions compared with untimed waits;
            185
        back-off use; 151
        `Mutex.attempt` operation use; 148
    `wait` method; 184, 191
    wait-free algorithms
        bibliographic references; 145
        optimistic update use; 139
    `Waiter` class, (code); 331
    `WaitingStack` class, (code); 212
WaterTank class
    (code); 26
    `AbstractTank` class, (code); 63
    `ActiveWaterTank` class (pseudocode); 367
    `AdaptedTank` class, (code); 60
    `Tank` interface, (code); 58
`WebService` class (code); 283
WHEN construct
    as conditional wait expression; 181
`WithMutex` class (code); 150
Worker Threads pattern; 290-298
    encapsulation of `Runnable`; 14
    in Event-Driven I/O; 299-303
    Fork/Join pattern use; 346
    scheduling service use; 337
    vs. threads; 292
    with thread-based confinement; 106
workflow
    systems, as oneway message structure; 306
working memory
    Java Memory Model use; 92
`WrappedBox` class (code); 313
`Wrapper` class (code); 317
wrapping
    See Adapter pattern

write(ing)
    Copy-on-Write pattern; 136-141
        atomic commitment; 140-141
        internal copy-on-write; 137-138
        optimistic updates; 139
    `CopyOnWriteArrayList` class
        (code); 138
        error handler use; 167
        Observer use; 246
    Readers and Writers pattern
        before/after version; 207-210
        read-write locks; 157-158
    `ReadWriteLock` interface
        (code); 157
        `ReadWrite` support of; 209
        `RWLock` extension of; 210
    `RWLock` class, (code); 210
    `write`, `Channel.put` compared with; 199
    write-write conflicts; 40, 71

X

X class (code); 186

Y

`yield` method
    in spinloops; 196
    `Thread` class; 17

The Addison-Wesley Java™ Series

Ken Arnold · James Gosling

The Java™ Programming Language
Second Edition

ISBN 0-201-31006-6

Mary Campione · Kathy Walrath

The Java™ Tutorial
Second Edition

Object-Oriented Programming for the Internet

ISBN 0-201-31007-4

Campione · Walrath · Huml · Tutorial Team

The Java™ Tutorial
Continued

The Rest of the JDK™

ISBN 0-201-48558-3

Patrick Chan

The Java™ Developers
ALMANAC
1999

ISBN 0-201-43298-6

Patrick Chan · Rosanna Lee

The Java™ Class Libraries
Second Edition, Volume 2

java.applet java.awt java.beans

ISBN 0-201-31003-1

Patrick Chan · Rosanna Lee · Douglas Kramer

The Java™ Class Libraries
Second Edition, Volume 1

java.io java.lang java.math
java.net java.text java.util

ISBN 0-201-31002-3

Patrick Chan · Rosanna Lee · Douglas Kramer

The Java™ Class Libraries
Second Edition, Volume 1
Supplement for the Java™ 2 Platform
Standard Edition, v1.2

ISBN 0-201-48552-4

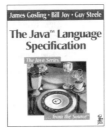

James Gosling · Bill Joy · Guy Steele

The Java™ Language
Specification

ISBN 0-201-63451-1

James Gosling · Frank Yellin · The Java Team

The Java™ Application
Programming
Interface, Volume 1
Core Packages

ISBN 0-201-63453-8

James Gosling · Frank Yellin · The Java Team

The Java™ Application
Programming
Interface, Volume 2
Window Toolkit and Applets

ISBN 0-201-63459-7

Li Gong

Inside Java™ 2
Platform Security

Architecture, API Design,
and Implementation

ISBN 0-201-31000-7

Jonni Kanerva

The Java™
FAQ

ISBN 0-201-63456-2

Doug Lea

Concurrent
Programming in Java™
Second Edition

Design Principles and Patterns

ISBN 0-201-31009-0

Sheng Liang

The Java™
Native Interface

Programmer's Guide
and Specification

ISBN 0-201-32577-2

Tim Lindholm · Frank Yellin

The Java™ Virtual
Machine Specification
Second Edition

ISBN 0-201-43294-3

Shannon · Hapner · Matena · Pelegri-Llopart · Cable · Davidson

Java™ 2
Enterprise Edition
Specifications

ISBN 0-201-70456-0

Henry Sowizral · Kevin Rushforth · Michael Deering

The Java™ 3D
API Specification

ISBN 0-201-32576-4

Kathy Walrath · Mary Campione

The JFC
Swing Tutorial

A Guide to Constructing GUIs

ISBN 0-201-43321-4

White · Fisher · Cattell · Hamilton · Hapner

JDBC™ API Tutorial and
Reference, Second Edition

Universal Data Access for
the Java™ 2 Platform

ISBN 0-201-43328-1

Please see our web site (http://www.awl.com/cseng/javaseries)
for more information on these titles.

Addison-Wesley Computer and Engineering Publishing Group

How to *Interact* with Us

1. Visit our Web site

http://www.awl.com/cseng

When you think you've read enough, there's always more content for you at Addison-Wesley's web site. Our web site contains a directory of complete product information including:

- Chapters
- Exclusive author interviews
- Links to authors' pages
- Tables of contents
- Source code

You can also discover what tradeshows and conferences Addison-Wesley will be attending, read what others are saying about our titles, and find out where and when you can meet our authors and have them sign your book.

2. Subscribe to Our Email Mailing Lists

Subscribe to our electronic mailing lists and be the first to know when new books are publishing. Here's how it works: Sign up for our electronic mailing at **http://www.awl.com/cseng/mailinglists.html**. Just select the subject areas that interest you and you will receive notification via email when we publish a book in that area.

3. Contact Us via Email

cepubprof@awl.com
Ask general questions about our books.
Sign up for our electronic mailing lists.
Submit corrections for our web site.

bexpress@awl.com
Request an Addison-Wesley catalog.
Get answers to questions regarding your order or our products.

innovations@awl.com
Request a current Innovations Newsletter.

webmaster@awl.com
Send comments about our web site.

mikeh@awl.com
Submit a book proposal.
Send errata for an Addison-Wesley book.

cepubpublicity@awl.com
Request a review copy for a member of the media interested in reviewing new Addison-Wesley titles.

We encourage you to patronize the many fine retailers who stock Addison-Wesley titles. Visit our online directory to find stores near you or visit our online store: **http://store.awl.com/** or call **800-824-7799**.

Addison Wesley Longman
Computer and Engineering Publishing Group
One Jacob Way, Reading, Massachusetts 01867 USA
TEL 781-944-3700 • FAX 781-942-3076